Managing Mexico

Managing Mexico

ECONOMISTS FROM
NATIONALISM TO
NEOLIBERALISM

Sarah Babb

PRINCETON UNIVERSITY PRESS
PRINCETON AND OXFORD

Second printing, and first paperback printing, 2004
Paperback ISBN 0-691-11793-4

The Library of Congress has cataloged the cloth edition of this book as follows

Babb, Sarah, 1966–
Managing Mexico : Economists from Nationalism to Neoliberalism / Sarah Babb.
p. cm.
Includes bibliographical references and index.
ISBN 0-691-07483-6 (alk. paper)
1. Mexico—Economic policy. 2. Economists—Mexico.
3. Economics—Mexico—History—20th century. 4. Globalization.

HC135.B214 2002
338.972—dc21   2001036270

British Library Cataloging-in-Publication Data is available

This book has been composed in Sabon

Printed on acid-free paper. ∞

www.pupress.princeton.edu

Printed in the United States of America

3   5   7   9   10   8   6   4   2

CONTENTS

ABBREVIATIONS

CIDE   Centro de Investigación y Docencia Económica (Center for Economics Education and Research)

CONACYT   Consejo Nacional de Ciencia y Tecnología (National Council on Science and Technology)

ITAM   Instituto Tecnológico Autónomo de México (Autonomous Technological Institute of Mexico)

UNAM   Universidad Nacional Autónoma de México (Autonomous National University of Mexico)

TABLES AND FIGURES

Figures

PREFACE

THIS BOOK was inspired during my first year in Mexico City—a year that coincided with the end of the presidential administration of Carlos Salinas and the glory days of a set of free-market policies known locally as *neoliberalismo*, or neoliberalism. Salinas was a technocrat educated at Harvard University, and his administration was packed with the "best and the brightest" U.S.-trained economists in the country. At the time I arrived, Salinas was putting the finishing touches on a package of radical policy reforms that were designed to set Mexico on the road to free-market-based prosperity, reforms that included the privatization of state-owned firms and Mexico's entry into the North American Free Trade Agreement.

One thing that I noticed during that first year in Mexico was how difficult it was to evaluate Salinas and his policies from a critical point of view. After years of economic stagnation following the outbreak of the debt crisis in 1982, economic growth was picking up. True, inequality and poverty had increased, but it was easy to dismiss these as side effects of the debt crisis rather than an outcome of economic liberalization per se. Criticisms of neoliberalism seemed to be coming mostly from left-wing government officials (made suspect by their role in creating the debt crisis) and more radical leftists (made marginal by the collapse of communism in 1989). Even more important, the policies of the government in power were solidly backed by the advice of experts—mainstream economists in Mexico and around the world who devoutly believed that only liberated markets would pull Mexico up to the economic level of the developed countries.

However, as I learned more about Mexican economic history and met older generations of Mexican economists, I began to acquire a historical perspective on Mexican neoliberalism. I learned that only a few decades earlier, Mexico had been experiencing an extraordinary period of economic expansion and industrialization, lasting roughly from the middle of the 1930s until the beginning of the 1970s. At that time, the creed of government economists—including the foreign-trained ones—was that economic development required substantial government intervention. I discovered that some Mexican economists of the older generation thought that current government policy was relying excessively on markets. One of these economists assured me that Mexico's apparent prosperity rested on a weak foundation, namely, volatile foreign portfolio investment.

This latter analysis turned out to be correct. Shortly after my return to the United States in 1994, a series of grave political, social, and economic crises climaxed in the form of the Mexican peso crisis. The presidential succession of Carlos Salinas by Ernesto Zedillo set off a crisis of confidence in the overvalued Mexican peso, a tidal wave of capital flight, and a currency devaluation. Salinas fled to Ireland, and Mexico suffered its worst economic downturn since the Great Depression. Significantly, this enormous debacle led to no reevaluation of either neoliberal policies or the U.S.-trained technocrats who promoted them. Rather, a Yale-trained finance minister was replaced by a Stanford-trained finance minister, an International Monetary Fund structural adjustment package was signed, and economic policy continued essentially as before.

This book tells the story of how economic expertise has been constructed in Mexico over the course of most of the twentieth century. During an approximately seventy-year period beginning in the 1930s, the Mexican economics profession evolved from being a nationalist, leftist discipline to becoming a bastion of U.S.-style neoclassical models and free-market-promoting technocrats. The history of the Mexican economics profession provides broader insights into the ways that economic policies—and the ideas that inform them—are shaped by domestic and international forces.

The following chapters represent the culmination of an intense, even torturous five-year process during which I learned a great deal. They were made possible by the support of a number of institutions and countless individuals. For my first wonderful year of study in Mexico, I am indebted to the Pre-dissertation Fellowship Program of the Social Science Research Council. The research upon which this book is based was conducted in 1995–96 with a Fulbright–García Robles fellowship. The Colegio de México served as my institutional home during both years, giving me access to an excellent library and a stimulating social milieu. Many thanks to the Sociedad de Ex-Alumnos of the ITAM for giving me access to a database that helped me answer many important questions for my research. I am also indebted to Francisco Zapata of the Centro de Estudios Sociológicos at the Colegio de México for hosting me at the Colegio, and for his many helpful suggestions during my stay in Mexico. I would also like to thank the dozens of individuals who agreed to be interviewed during the course of my research.

The individual who contributed the most to this book was Víctor Urquidi, who recommended readings, helped schedule interviews, took me out to lunch, and read through all my chapters—all the while serving as an invaluable source of encyclopedic information on the history of economic policy in Mexico. Without Víctor, this book would not have been possible. Among the innumerable other individuals in Mexico whose help went into realizing this project were Eduardo Turrent at the Banco de México, Guillermo Maldonado at the Monterrey Tec (ITESM), and Blanca Heredia at the CIDE. Gustavo Del Angel is an intellectual kindred spirit who has clarified my thinking on a number of issues. Thanks also to Alicia Salmerón, Luis Anaya, Carlos Salas, and Antonio Ibarra for helping clear up a number of doubts and misconceptions.

For their help in framing and interpretation while I was living in Mexico, struggling to make sense of it all, I am enormously grateful to Frank Safford, Arthur Stinchcombe, and Mark Granovetter, who diligently maintained e-mail (and snail mail) lines of communication. I am indebted to Bruce Carruthers for also keeping in touch, for helping me keep my eye on the ball, and for keeping the faith. Bryant Garth gave me useful feedback and an institutional enclave at the American Bar Foundation at the time when I most needed one. A fellowship from the College of Arts and Sciences at Northwestern University provided support for writing up the dissertation that served as a basis for this manuscript. For their assistance during later stages of this manuscript, I thank Robert Zussman, whose support enabled me to restart my engines after a year's hiatus, and Marion Fourcade-Gourinchas, who provided helpful suggestions, creative ideas, and a refreshingly Continental perspective. I am also grateful to Mauro Guillén and Roderic A. Camp, who both plowed through my manuscript in record time, and whose comments helped me immensely in whipping it into shape. Thanks also to Ken Shadlen for his comments on chapter 6.

Nonacademic forms of support were also critical to the realization of this book. I thank Arnaldo Moya for many home-cooked meals and witty conversations, and Fanni Muñoz for being there when I needed her. I am grateful to Alicia Salmerón for the loan of her apartment in Tlalpan, where I lived as I was finishing the final manuscript revisions. Most of all, I want to thank my parents, Nancy and Alan Babb, whose love, pride, and support enabled me to survive the researching, writing, and rewriting of this book, and who kept the home fires burning during my many travels.

Managing Mexico

Chapter 1

NEOLIBERALISM AND THE GLOBALIZATION

OF ECONOMIC EXPERTISE

Toward the end of the 1960s, one of the founding fathers of Mexico's first economics program published a slim volume titled *To a Young Mexican Economist*. Jesús Silva Herzog's message was particularly directed toward the growing numbers of Mexican economists receiving graduate degrees from foreign universities. As a former government official, self-taught economist, and self-described "socialist," Silva Herzog warned against the facile application of alien theories to complex local realities. "[T]heories created in the great centers of capitalism should not be submissively applied [to less developed countries]," he wrote. "Each theoretical adaptation should be made after careful analysis, with our feet planted on our own soil and with a clear vision of the primary needs and the legitimate aspirations of the people" (Silva Herzog 1967: 36).[1]

Several decades later, the young economists to whom Silva Herzog had directed his advice had matured into an extraordinarily powerful technocracy. Dominated by economists trained at Harvard, Yale, MIT, and the University of Chicago, three consecutive presidential administrations transformed the Mexican economy with a series of neoliberal reforms. These reforms included the widespread privatization of state industries, the revision of the Mexican Constitution to help ensure the property rights of foreign investors, and the lifting of protectionist trade barriers under the North American Free Trade Agreement.

These policies met with the widespread approval of the international community, including foreign investors, multilateral institutions such as the International Monetary Fund (IMF), and a number of prestigious foreign economists. In a 1992 interview with *Forbes* magazine (titled "We Don't Tax Capital Gains"), Mexico's finance minister, MIT Ph.D. Pedro Aspe, expounded on the role of current account deficits in developing countries and subsequently apologized to his interviewer for sounding "professorial." Impressed with Dr. Aspe's expertise, the *Forbes* interviewer replied, "Don't apologize. It's a pleasure to meet someone running an economy who understands economics" (Michaels 1992: 67).

This book examines the history of the Mexican economics profession to explore the interaction between economic ideas and material conditions. Sixty years ago, Mexico's first economics program (at the Autonomous National University, or UNAM) was known for its nationalist, populist, and even socialist bias, and trained its students for careers in a burgeoning government bureaucracy. Since the 1980s, however, neoliberal reforms have been overseen by a large cohort of U.S.-trained economists, and an elite group of internationally renowned undergraduate economics programs have been training their students in U.S.-style, neoclassical economics. The story of the journey of Mexican economics from nationalism to neoliberalism provides key insights into how policy paradigm shifts (Hall 1993) occur in developing countries—and the relative roles of domestic and international factors in the construction of economic expertise.

THE SOCIAL CONSTRUCTION OF ECONOMIC KNOWLEDGE

This book builds on a substantial body of academic work demonstrating how systems of social-scientific knowledge are socially and historically constructed (Rueschemeyer and Skocpol, eds., 1996; Wittrock and Wagner 1996; Fourcade-Gourinchas 2000; Rueschemeyer and Van Roseem 1996; Schweber 1996; Kuhnle 1996; Weir 1989; Weir and Skocpol 1985; Furner and Supple 1990). Social-scientific knowledge in different national contexts is shaped by "... historically changing and cross-nationally varying institutional configurations—interrelations among states and social structures" (Skocpol and Rueschemeyer 1996: 4). Distinct national economic, cultural, and institutional contexts generate different "organizational ideologies" within the private sector (Guillén 1994) and distinct approaches to government intervention in the economy and social policy (Dobbin 1994; Campbell and Lindberg 1990; Weir and Skocpol 1985). Economics professions in different nations reflect these particular sets of conditions.

Given this diversity of national contexts, the recent trend toward neoliberal convergence seems surprising. After all, neoliberal transitions have occurred almost everywhere—irrespective of level of development (France vs. Mexico), regime type (England under Thatcher vs. Chile under Pinochet), or cultural context (India vs. Argentina). One possible explanation for such convergence is that policymakers in diverse national contexts have arrived at common technical solutions, based on a common set of problems: neoliberalism "works."

In keeping with this idea, Hall (1993) contends that Britain's "policy paradigm" shift under Thatcher occurred through a process of "social learning"—a process of empirical disconfirmation that roughly parallels Kuhn's (1962) observations about scientific paradigms. The disconfirmation of "policy paradigms" is naturally more complex, involving multiple social actors, political parties, and groups of economic experts—all working in and around the state to collectively "puzzle out" which policies work best. Moreover, policy paradigms are overturned through explicitly political processes: "the movement from one paradigm to another . . . is likely to involve the accumulation of anomalies, experimentation with new forms of policy, and policy failures that precipitate a shift in the locus of authority over policy and initiate a wider contest between competing paradigms. This contest may well spill beyond the boundaries of the state itself into the broader political arena" (Hall 1993: 280).

Hall's analogy to Kuhnian scientific paradigms has been widely cited, since it usefully captures the enormity and depth of the changes involved. It also provides a means of supplementing Marxist notions (economic ideas as ideological superstructure of the dominant classes) with a more cognitive approach. However, it leaves an important question unanswered—namely, if neoliberalism "works" so well, why was it not implemented forty years before?

One compelling answer to this question is that the world in which economic policy is made today is markedly different from that of the postwar period. Salient changes that occurred after 1950 included the rise of a liberal trade regime, the emergence of "post-Fordist" systems of flexible production, and the rise of a highly integrated system of global financial markets (McKeown 1999; Piore and Sabel 1984; Helleiner 1994). These developments reveal an important difference between paradigms of the sort Kuhn looked at (i.e., in physics) and the sort that determine national economic policies. Economies are thoroughly human constructions—social structures that evolve and change over time, and thereby require new sets of analytical and ideological tools to make sense of them. Whereas Kuhn's physicists accumulated knowledge about an unchanging external world until paradigmatic transformation was unavoidable, economic policy paradigms sometimes reflect changes in the external environment (Babb and Fourcade-Gourinchas 2000).

During the postwar period, economics professions in diverse national contexts were shaped by the Keynesian paradigm, which presumed an active government role in creating desirable levels of growth and employment by managing aggregate demand (Hall, ed., 1986). The term "Keynesianism" notwithstanding, by the time that Keynes's writings became well known, policymakers around the world had *already* been experimenting with countercyclical policies, as a way of ameliorating the effects of the Great Depression (Weir and Skocpol 1985). Keynesianism was a broad set of policy prescriptions that were suited for the circumstances of national economies during the decades following the collapse of international capital markets in the 1930s. The Bretton Woods system was set up in 1945 for the purpose of maintaining international monetary stability, which Keynes saw as a fundamental precondition for conducting effective national macroeconomic policies (Simmons 1999: 37–38). Under Bretton Woods, a strong system of capital controls was instituted and maintained, exchange rates were fixed, and international monetary equilibrium was maintained by judicious injections of cash by the IMF. With such restrictions in place, it was possible for governments to develop relatively independent national economic policies designed to maximize employment without triggering unacceptable levels of inflation.

One of the characteristics of the postwar economic context seems to have been its ability to foster a relative diversity of economic and social policy models. In other words, Keyensianism was a sort of umbrella paradigm that could incorporate a great deal of cross-national variety. Thus, while some capitalist-bloc nations promoted a great deal of government intervention in the economy (i.e., in Scandinavia), others maintained more classically "liberal" arrangements (i.e., in the United States). Welfare states also varied greatly, in terms of both coverage and institutional structure (cf. Esping-Anderson 1990; Weir and Skocpol 1985). This ecumenical proliferation of policy models was also reflected at the level of national economics professions: during the postwar period, a number of different regions specialized in different "schools" of economic thought, such as Stockholm School in Sweden, the French regulationist school, and the United Nations Economic Commission for Latin America (ECLA).

Over time, however, the Keynesian paradigm was put under increasing pressure by a number of changes in the world economy. One change of vital importance is what Helleiner (1994) has dubbed "the re-emergence of global finance"—so called because it mirrored an earlier historical epoch of financial-market globalization, definitively ended by the collapse of financial markets in the early 1930s. Beginning in the 1960s, the growth of offshore capital markets capable of evading national regulations made it increasingly difficult to insulate national currencies from speculation and devaluation. These were the circumstances leading up to the collapse of the Bretton Woods system in 1971 and the abandonment of fixed exchange rates.

These developments (along with other transformations within the global economy, such as the rise of a liberal trade regime) placed economic policymakers around the world within a new set of constraints and opportunities. Independent national economic policies became more difficult to maintain, since attempts to induce economic expansion could lead to capital flight, devaluation, and inflation (McNamara 1998; Simmons 1999; Goodman 1992). Under the old economic order, national policies had been determined by the interplay of domestic political parties, local interest groups, and national institutions—giving rise to a diversity of different social contracts within different national contexts (Weir and Skocpol 1985). Under the globalized system that was emerging, however, governments needed increasingly to appeal to *international* as well as national constituencies. Whereas during the postwar period policymakers needed primarily to cater to the interests of domestic constituencies (such as business, labor, and the middle class), today they must attend to the interests of foreign investors and international financial institutions (Maxfield 1997).

Although the rules governing economic policy had changed, comprehension of how the new rules worked occurred through prolonged national processes of social learning, involving political parties, think tanks, state structures, and national economics professions (Babb and Fourcade-Gourinchas 2000). Often, national governments (particularly governments of the left) attempted to play by the "old rules"—as with Mitterand's attempts to stimulate the French economy in the early 1980s—and failed miserably, as France's subsequent devaluations and inflationary episodes suggest (Loriaux 1991; Goodman 1992). Over the long term, the result was a widespread retreat from interventionist policies and a convergence toward more liberal ones, which included independent central banks, monetary union (in Europe), and privatization (Keohane and Milner, eds., 1996; Maxfield 1997; Visser and Hemerijck 1997; McNamara 1998; Kitschelt et al., eds., 1999). Significantly, these policies no longer appeared as the agenda of particular interests and political parties; rather, the neoliberal model became a sort of "common sense"—a conventional wisdom endorsed by parties of the left and right alike.

Paralleling these changes in policy models have been transformations in national systems of economic expertise. Since at least the 1970s, economics professions around the world have become noticeably Americanized (Johnson [Harry] 1973; Coats, ed., 1996). In the words of one observer, "the use of the English language and American ideas, techniques, and research styles in textbooks, economic journals, and academic dissertations has become almost overwhelming" (Coats 1996: 4). American graduate programs export economists to diverse parts of the globe,[2] and American economists are cited with disproportionate frequency (Aslanbeigui and Montecinos 1998; Frey and Eichenberger 1993: 185; Coats 1996: 3–11). This change is significant, since economics in the United States has historically been known to be less statist, more mathematical, and more prone to value abstract generalizations over local knowledge than in Western Europe (Johnson [Harry] 1977; Frey et al. 1984; Frey and Eichenberger 1993). Thus, the Americanization of economics around the world can be viewed as one aspect of the policy paradigm shift—one piece in the larger puzzle of neoliberal convergence.

From this very brief historical overview, a general picture emerges. The collapse of international financial markets in the early 1930s created the conditions for a variety of experimentations with state intervention in economic and social policy, the rise of Keynesianism, and a general flourishing of a variety of national schools of economic thought. Since the 1960s, the reglobalization of finance and related transformations in the world economy have had the opposite effects: a convergence at the practical level toward policies aimed at minimizing inflation and satisfying investors, and at the ideological level in the form of the Americanization of national economics professions. Whereas during the earlier period, the influence of national institutional structures and social groups predominated, during the later period, policy paradigms and economic expertise increasingly reflected the influence of international constituencies. The following section discusses some particularities of how these global historical processes played out in Latin America.

CHANGING POLICY PARADIGMS IN LATIN AMERICA

In general, historical transformations in the policy paradigms of developing countries over the course of the twentieth century have paralleled the global trends outlined above. However, there have also been some notable differences. First, the particular problems of developing countries stimulated somewhat different forms of government intervention than those prevailing in the industrialized world. Developing nations have adopted a variety of interventionist policy models, ranging from state socialism (China) to a variety of state promotions of capitalist development (e.g., Mexico, South Korea). Since a satisfactory account of all these models could occupy several volumes, the following sections focus on the Latin American experience. Second, international pressures have played a more salient and obvious role in the economic policies of poor countries than they have in the policies of wealthy ones—particularly since the early 1980s.

From Laissez-Faire to Developmentalism

During the first decades of the twentieth century, Latin American nations' economic policies were generally conducted according to the dictates of economic liberalism—the nineteenth-century version of today's "neoliberalism." According to classical economic theory, economically backward nations were best off specializing in producing the goods in which they had a "comparative advantage" and trading freely with other nations for industrial goods. Latin American countries toward the beginning of the twentieth century were open to international trade, tended to specialize in the export of minerals and agricultural commodities, and received enormous quantities of foreign investment (Díaz Alejandro 1984). During this period, "money doctors"—foreign financial-reform "experts" such as Edwin W. Kemmerer of Princeton University—helped financially strapped governments gain (or regain) the confidence of foreign investors. In keeping with the conventional wisdom of their day, money doctors would advise their clients to set up independent central banks, to practice fiscal and monetary rectitude, and to adhere to the gold standard (Drake, ed., 1994).

After 1929, however, everything changed. The global economic crisis caused the prices of Latin American exports to plummet, and many governments to default on their foreign debts. The Depression also slowed the flow of foreign investment to a trickle, and thereby brought the era of the "money doctors" to a close. The laissez-faire, export-oriented model of the nineteenth century was abandoned throughout Latin America, since the following of "sage foreign advice" was no longer rewarded with large flows of foreign investment. The result was a generalized closing toward international trade and finance, and a growing involvement of the state in promoting economic development (Díaz Alejandro 1984: 17–22).

Thus, when the United Nations Economic Commission for Latin America (ECLA) was organized in 1948 with its seat in Santiago, Chile, its role was to provide a theoretical rationale for policies that had already been implemented as pragmatic responses to a common set of circumstances. The policy strategy elaborated by ECLA theorists (most notably Raúl Prebisch) postulated basic differences between the developed countries of the "core" and the developing ones of the "periphery." The ECLA challenged the central premises of classical economic theory, which asserted that through "comparative advantage" rich and poor countries alike could specialize in different kinds of exports and thereby both benefit from free international trade. Rather than continuing to rely on exports of primary materials and foodstuffs, the ECLA argued that peripheral countries needed at all costs to industrialize through active government policies aimed at protecting "infant industries" from foreign competition and at protecting salaries to maintain demand for domestically produced industrial products (Villarreal 1984: 165).

Latin American developmentalism was not identical to the Keynesian paradigm of industrialized countries, since the latter focused on the securing of the "aggregate volume of output corresponding to full employment," rather than the promotion of activity within particular economic sectors (Skidelsky 1977: 34). However, developmentalism paralleled and complemented Keynesianism in a number of important ways. First, the two shared a common rejection of the minimalist government role endorsed at the turn of the century: Keynesianism and developmentalism both advocated a strong government role in the economy.

Second, Keynesianism provided a new theoretical justification for developing countries to pursue policies that were fundamentally different from those of the industrialized world. As Hirschman (1981) observed, Keynesianism broke the "ice" of neoclassical "monoeconomics"—the idea that there is a single set of economic laws applicable at all times and in all places. Keynesian thinking established that there were (at least) two different kinds of economics: the orthodox or classical variety, which held true for economies at full employment, and another for economies where human and material resources were not being fully employed (Hirschman 1981: 3–6). This lent legitimacy to ECLA's claim that Latin America needed to implement policies that differed substantially from those prevailing in the industrialized world (where, for example, trade barriers were being lifted under the auspices of the General Agreement on Tariffs and Trade). Although neoclassical economists in the United States and elsewhere disagreed with the ECLA's prescriptions, there were also a number of core economists who concurred with Latin America's postwar economic model. In 1961, Hirschman observed on the basis of firsthand experience that "a substantial and perhaps dominant group of Western economists share some of the ECLA's most characteristic points of view" (Hirschman 1961: 37). Among the most prominent economists of this postwar "development" school of economics were Arthur Lewis, Gunnar Myrdal, and Ragnar Nurkse. The development economists believed "that traditional economic analysis, which has concentrated on the industrial countries, must . . . be recast in significant respects when dealing with underdeveloped countries" (Hirschman 1981: 3).

The "Breakdown" of Developmentalism and the Rise of Neoliberalism

By the 1970s, developmentalist policies in Latin America began to draw significant criticism from both radical and conservative directions (cf. Hirschman 1981: 14–19). Two factors appear to have been responsible for the abandonment of the developmentalist paradigm. One was the widespread impression that the "easy phase" of the import substitution model had ended. Protectionism had successfully created domestic industries that were producing simple goods but was apparently less successful in promoting the domestic production of intermediate and capital goods; in the meantime, it had created a permanent class of inefficient industries with profits guaranteed by government protection. Among the symptoms of the "exhaustion" of import substitution were chronic unemployment in many countries, as well as chronic inflation, currency overvaluations, and balance-of-payments problems. Moreover, developmentalism had not solved long-standing problems of social inequality in Latin America (Solís 1973: 8; Love 1990, 1996; Franko 1999: 65–67). A new school of thought known as "dependency theory," which combined some theories associated with the ECLA and with Marxism, arose as a self-conscious alternative to developmentalism in Latin America (Love 1990).

The second factor was a shift in the global economy that began to create a new set of incentives for Latin American governments. During the post-war period, a new set of multilateral institutions (including the World Bank, International Monetary Fund, and Inter-American Development Bank) provided loans, but only for specific and circumscribed purposes. Beginning in the late 1960s, however, the "rebirth of global finance" was making it possible for Latin American governments to borrow from private foreign sources at variable interest rates. Briefly, international borrowing seemed to offer a potential solution to the "exhaustion" of the developmentalist model, by providing resources to address long-standing economic and social problems. Driven by anti-inflationary monetary policy in the United States, global interest rates began to rise after 1979, and heavily indebted governments suddenly found it difficult or impossible to meet their debt service payments. In 1982, Mexico had the honor of inaugurating the Third World debt crisis when the Mexican finance minister declared that Mexico would be unable to continue servicing its external debt.

The tremendous levels of external borrowing that led up to the debt crisis are often blamed on the irresponsibility of corrupt—or at least self-serving—politicians. While there may be some truth to this interpretation, it must also be admitted that the disastrous outcome of the lending boom of the 1970s was not widely foreseen—least of all, it seems, by the lenders who stood to lose in the case of default. Indeed, what appears to have occurred is an unusually harsh process of social learning. The new world of global finance presented Latin American policymakers with a whole new framework of opportunities and constraints. The opportunities seemed at first to be unlimited: foreign funds helped satisfy political constituencies without accruing the political costs associated with redistributive policies. But when global interest rates rose, the high cost of past decisions quickly became apparent: tremendous macroeconomic problems, accompanied by a significant loss of national policy autonomy.

Social learning in a new and not-yet-understood context takes time. Just as some European governments attempted vainly to continue expansionary Keynesian policies in the context of a worldwide recession and rapid capital mobility, some Latin American governments attempted to implement an array of "heterodox" policies (Kahler 1990). In the context of expanding external debts and declining import revenues, however, these policies contributed to hyperinflation and the electoral defeat of the parties that supported them (Edwards 1995: 17–40).

In addition to the "market discipline" of capital flight, Latin American governments also faced more overt, political pressures. The beginning of the debt crisis coincided with the first years of the Reagan administration and the inauguration of a new era of "policy-based lending." Simply put, multilateral and U.S. government agencies, such as the World Bank, IMF, and U.S. Treasury, were committed to using debt relief as a lever to win market-oriented policy reforms from the governments of developing countries (Kahler 1990; Stallings 1992; George and Sabelli 1994). If the governments of developing countries wanted loans to continue servicing their debts, they would have to reduce budget deficits, cut government spending, and open their economies to foreign competition.

This new policy agenda was clearly linked to an ideological shift within the U.S government. Although at home the Reagan administration practiced "military Keynesianism," its agenda abroad was much more doctrinaire. Unfortunately, the origins and nature of the neoliberal revolution in the United States have been subject to little serious scholarly study. In general, the new market-oriented paradigm was "neither as elegant nor as coherently focused as Keynesianism" (Biersteker 1992: 107). Although it was clearly related to trends within the American economics profession, it could not be traced to any particular school of thought: it was neither precisely "monetarist" nor exactly "Chicago School," but more vaguely "promarket."

Its ambiguous origins notwithstanding, this policy agenda was endorsed not only by U.S. policymakers and the officials of multilateral organizations but also by many economists, both in the United States and abroad. Founded in 1981 for the study of international economic policy, the Institute for International Economics became a forum for like-minded economists from around the world to come together with U.S. policymakers to agree on a new set of guidelines for policymaking in developing countries. These guidelines came to be called "the Washington Consensus" (Williamson, ed., 1990: xiii). The Washington Consensus was essentially a new set of taken-for-granted assumptions, which constituted "the common core of wisdom *embraced by all serious economists*, whose implementation provides the minimum conditions that will give a developing country the chance to start down the road to the sort of prosperity enjoyed by the industrialized countries" (Williamson 1994: 18, my emphasis). Among these points of consensus were trade liberalization, the encouragement of direct foreign investment, the privatization of state enterprises, and the adoption of private property rights.

One of the defining characteristics of this new consensus was that developed and developing countries shared a common set of universal economic laws. As one of the Institute's recent publications put it:

> The evidence that macroeconomic stability, a market economy, and outward orientation are beneficial to economic growth and (with slight qualifications) a relatively equitable distribution of income is by now reasonably compelling. What is new is the conviction that they are not just policies that are good for the "First World," but that they are also needed to make the transition from the "Second World" and that they are equally desirable for the "Third World" as well. At least in intellectual terms, we today live in one world rather than three. (Williamson and Haggard 1994: 530)

The significance of this point of view cannot be overstated. In direct contrast to the point of view that prevailed among ECLA and development economists during the postwar period, the new view prescribes the same economic medicine for all nations, regardless of level of development. This idea—an item of faith among neoliberal reformers and their supporters around the world—has brought an end to the multiple models of the Keynesian era and a return to "monoeconomics."

In the context of the debt crisis, this paradigm shift had tremendous consequences for economic policies in developing countries. During the 1980s and '90s, there were a number of fundamental and mutually related changes in economic policymaking in Latin America, including an impressive array of neoliberal reforms, the "technocratization" of policymakers, and the Americanization of national economics professions (Markoff and Montecinos 1993; Domínguez, ed. 1997; Williamson, ed. 1994). In 1992, *Business Week* magazine noted that in Latin America free-market reforms were being implemented by ". . . a new generation of leaders, many of them educated in the U.S. A continental network of Harvard, Chicago and Stanford grads are back home atop business and government ministries spreading a new market mind-set" (Baker and Weiner 1992: 51). As Markoff and Montecinos (1993) pointed out, there was a "ubiquitous rise of economists" in top policymaking positions. These economists replaced Latin America's postwar developmentalist model with a new, more "market friendly" variety, which was essentially the model endorsed by the Washington Consensus.

At the same time, there was a noticeable Americanization of Latin American economics professions. Consequently, today aspiring young economists in Brazil, Argentina, Mexico, Chile, and elsewhere are drawn to prestigious undergraduate programs specializing in U.S.-style economics, which provide an ideal launching pad for subsequent graduate train-

ing in the United States (cf. Loureiro 1996; Silva 1991; Babb 1998). Thus,
Latin America's policy paradigm shift has occurred not only at the level
of practice but also at the level of ideas. Not only have policies changed,
but the institutionalized means of *thinking* about these policies have
changed as well.

MEXICAN ECONOMICS IN SOCIOLOGICAL PERSPECTIVE

This book looks at how national and international contexts shaped Mexican economic expertise over time. From the founding of Mexico's first
economics program in 1929 and throughout the postwar period, the Mexican economics profession was most profoundly influenced by domestic
constituencies, organizations, and institutions. These included: a state initially constructing a stable corporatist base among peasants and workers,
and later playing an active role in promoting economic development; a
private sector initially in opposition to government-sponsored populism
and later placated by the state's probusiness policies; and a growing cadre
of internationally oriented state bureaucrats (particularly within the central bank) eager to import foreign models of expertise. During this earlier
period, Mexican economics encompassed a broad spectrum of tendencies,
from Marxist to populist to developmentalist—but was always and everywhere a fundamentally nationalist and statist discipline.

In contrast, as Mexico became increasingly immersed in global financial markets, the Mexican economics profession was transformed into a
highly internationalized discipline, dominated and defined by an emerging
class of "global experts." These professionals are the recipients of highly
internationalized training (usually American) and claim to possess a uni-
versally applicable variety of expertise. Most important, they have actively promoted Mexico's insertion within the global economy through
liberalizing Mexico's system of economic governance. These global experts are likely to play an ongoing role in defining Mexican economic
policy, no matter what electoral transformations occur in the future.

The Mexican case is likely to be of more general interest for two reasons. First, Mexico has an economic and institutional history similar to
that of many developing countries, particularly those of Latin America.
Relative backwardness, import substitution in the postwar period, credit-
financed populism in the 1970s, and the debt crisis of the 1980s—these
are all historical factors that Mexico shares in common with other Latin
American nations. Second, Mexico presents a rather extreme example of
phenomena that today can be witnessed throughout the developing
world: the protagonistic role of U.S.-trained technocracy in governing
economic policy and the Americanization of national economics profes-

sions. Both as a prototype (i.e., a typical example) and as an ideal-type (i.e., an extreme or "pure" example), the Mexican case holds important implications for other nations.

Data and Methods

Like the development economists of the postwar era, I was fundamentally interested in institutional change over time. For economists, this sort of diachronic analysis is facilitated by the existence of (reasonably) reliable national economic data over long periods of time. However, I was interested not in the Mexican *economy*, but rather Mexican *economics*—a subject about which very little systematic data has been collected. Fortunately for my research project, the peso devaluation of 1994–95 made it possible for me to stay in Mexico for an extended period (by stretching the dollars I received from my grant), enabling me to gather a large and eclectic body of information from various sources. These sources include, but are not limited to, archival documents, newspaper articles, Mexican economics publications, secondary sources (such as the works of Mexican and Mexicanist scholars), a database of biographical information from the ITAM Alumni Association, and numerous interviews with Mexican economists and government officials.

My most consistent source of information over time was a selection of more than 250 undergraduate theses from the two most historically important Mexican economics programs: those of the public National University (UNAM) and the private Autonomous Technological Institute of Mexico (ITAM). Few Mexican economists of any theoretical stripe would dispute the historical significance of these two programs. The UNAM was home to Mexico's first economics program, established in 1929 within the School of Law and expanded in 1934 to become a full-fledged School of Economics. Set up by private business groups in 1946 as a deliberate challenge to this UNAM monopoly, the ITM (which became known as the ITAM after becoming officially autonomous in 1962) was a little-noticed "night school" of marginal importance until it was Americanized from the mid 1960s through the early 1970s. Today, the ITAM is widely recognized as both a bastion of neoliberal ideas and one of the most important sources of government technocrats.

My decision to look at undergraduate theses was originally motivated by the scarcity of archival records from Mexican economics programs. At first, I hoped to base my study on course syllabi from different years to determine the specific works that economics undergraduates were required to read in the different programs and at different times. Unfortunately, I was unable to find any such syllabi collections. In contrast, the undergraduate theses of Mexican economics programs are freely available to the public in university libraries. Although doubtless a less valid reflection of the content of the courses taken by economics undergraduates (this discrepancy is particularly notable in UNAM theses from the 1970s), the theses do have the advantage of reflecting, however imperfectly, what the students "got out" of their economics education.

To analyze these theses, my method was to thoroughly read the introduction and conclusion, where main theoretical points and citations were made, and review the body of the text for methodological approaches. I coded each thesis for theoretical citations, methodology, application (to private or public sector), and various rhetorical features (most important, position on government intervention in the economy). A more detailed account of how I analyzed and coded the theses can be found in appendix A.

Because this book takes the form of "telling a story," it is organized chronologically. Chapters 2 and 3 discuss the predevelopmentalist decades of the 1920s and '30s, crucial years during which the Mexican state established its base of political support and the institutional bases for government intervention in the economy; these were also the years when UNAM economics was founded, and when the idea of a private alternative to the UNAM was conceived. Chapter 4 discusses Mexican developmentalism and evidence of this ideology in undergraduate theses from the UNAM and the ITM. Chapter 5 similarly utilizes evidence from these undergraduate theses to document the breakdown of Mexican developmentalism and the splitting of Mexican economics into radically different subprofessions. Chapters 6 and 7 discuss the rise of neoliberalism in Mexico along with the role of privately educated, foreign-trained Mexican economists in the implementation of free-market policies. Finally, chapter 8 considers the issue of the globalization of economic expertise, and what is distinctive about processes of "social learning" in developing countries.

Sociological Perspectives

There are a number of theoretical issues in sociology addressed throughout the course of this book. These issues fall broadly into three categories of sociological "literatures" or subfields: the literature on professions, the literature on organizations and institutions, and the literature on "multiple capitalisms" and local institutional logics.

PROFESSIONS AND THEIR CONSTITUENCIES

Although this book is indebted to the sociology of knowledge in spirit (and, to a certain extent, in method), I chose to frame my study within the sociology of professions[3] literature. While sociologists of knowledge tend to focus on the struggles that occur within certain fields of knowledge (cf. Latour 1987; Yonay 1998), the sociology of professions looks at how expert knowledge is constructed and applied within a broader societal framework of institutions and clients. My research in Mexico gave me a taste of how enormously the profession of economics could vary from country to country—how social science professions reflect national systems of institutions and relations between state and society (Rueschemeyer and Skocpol, eds., 1996). This experience also left me with the question of *how* sociologists should theoretically account for this apparent relationship between social scientific expertise, on the one hand, and national institutional context, on the other. The sociology of professions, which deals explicitly with the relationship between groups of experts and the societies in which they are embedded, seemed best suited for this theoretical task.

Professions are "occupational groups controlling the acquisition and application of various kinds of knowledge" (Abbott 1988: 1). Early studies of professions focused on the issue of what characteristics distinguish a "profession" from other occupations (cf. Caplow 1954; Wilensky 1964). A later tradition focused on professional "powers" and the ways that professions use the state to secure monopolies over certain kinds of work and other privileges (cf. Freidson 1970; Larson 1977). This book follows a relatively recent trend in the sociology of professions, which looks at how professions vary in different national contexts (cf. Abbott 1988; Krause 1996).

Within any given society, many ideas coexist and compete with one another. What makes professions special is that they make rules about which ideas are to be considered knowledge and who is allowed to call themselves an expert. The power of professions is derived from their legitimacy, "founded on the achievement of socially recognized expertise" (Larson 1977: xvii). In the United States, doctors were once seen as prototypical examples of professions, since doctors were (until recently) extremely successful at maintaining a monopoly on legitimate medical advice (cf. Larson 1977: 37). In part, this monopoly reflected the medical profession's success in securing the protection of the state: uncertified individuals caught practicing medicine were subject to legal prosecution. At a more fundamental level, however, the success of medicine can be traced to its legitimacy: most Americans believed in the expert knowledge of doctors and were reluctant to question their diagnoses and prescriptions—unless they got a second opinion from another doctor.

Legitimacy, buttressed by belief in professional expertise, insulates professional diagnoses and prescriptions from outside challenges. But to whom, precisely, must professionals legitimate their claims? Drawing on the work of Abbott (1988) and more recent work documenting cross-national patterns in professions, I claim that professions fundamentally require legitimation from organizations or actors with *resources*, to whom I refer as professional *constituencies*. This is because professionals are, by definition, experts who *get paid to exercise their expertise*. Characteristic differences among professions in different countries can be traced to differing national constituencies. Whereas in the United States professionals have historically tended to receive payment from private individuals and organizations, in Continental Europe states generally took a more direct role in professionalization, through such means as designing and funding professional programs and hiring their graduates to work as public servants (Burrage and Torstendahl 1990; Abbott 1988; Cocks and Jarausch, eds., 1990; Heidenheimer 1989; Torstendahl and Burrage 1990).

Chapters 2 and 3 show that since the Mexican revolution of 1910–17, Mexican professions have tended to resemble the state-centered, Continental model. Mexico's first economics program was established in 1929 at the Autonomous National University by government officials, for the purpose of training state bureaucrats. However, chapter 3 also shows that Mexican economics had more than one potential constituency. In 1946, disgruntled business groups in disagreement with government policy established an alternative to the state-centered, left-leaning UNAM economics program: the ITM (later called the ITAM). Chapters 3 through 6 outline the historical trajectories of the UNAM and ITM/ITAM economics programs through the present and discuss how graduates of the two programs fared in the job market over time. While radical leftist influence within the UNAM program eventually caused it to separate from its most crucial constituency—the Mexican state—the ITAM program became increasingly Americanized and, beginning in the 1970s, increasingly prominent within the Mexican government. The fate of the ITAM, along with a number of Mexican economics programs that came to emulate it, shows how economic globalization *decreased the importance of national constituencies* and *increased the importance of international constituencies* for the Mexican economics profession. This process of Americanization and internationalization is outlined in chapters 5 through 7.

CHANGING INSTITUTIONS

Institutions are the rules governing social behavior, from customs and other informal-cultural rules to laws and other formal-legal forms of social regulation (North 1990). The impacts of different institutional arrangements on societies, as well as how institutions are constructed in the first place, have been studied from a variety of disciplinary perspectives, including economics (e.g., Coase 1983; North 1990), political science (e.g., March and Olsen 1984; Hall, ed., 1986), and sociology (for an excellent review of this literature, see Scott 1995).

This book looks in detail at how a number of institutions changed over time and interacted with one another, including systems of economic governance and systems of professional knowledge. It therefore falls generally into a cross-disciplinary tradition known as "historical institutionalism" (see Steinmo, Thelen, and Longstreth 1992). The rise of neoliberalism can be viewed as institutional transformation on a global scale, including the passage of laws giving autonomy to central banks and property rights to foreign investors, and the elimination of tariffs on foreign imports. The result has been what neoinstitutionalist sociologists call "institutional isomorphism": a convergence of institutional patterns (i.e., national policies) such that diverse organizations (i.e., national governments) come to look more similar (cf. DiMaggio and Powell 1983; Scott and Meyer, eds., 1994; Boli and Thomas 1997; Boli and Thomas, eds., 1999).

From a neoinstitutionalist point of view, what forces might be responsible for this global convergence? One possible answer is that states imitated other states that they perceived as successful, which made different states look more similar over time. This notion is compatible with a neoinstitutionalist school of thought to which I will refer as "world-cultural" theory. The central premise of this theory is that contemporary nation-states share a common culture of rationality: a "rationalized world-culture." This common culture leads to shared values, forming the basis for an ongoing process of imitation and the international spread of organizational and institutional models (Scott and Meyer, eds., 1994; Boli and Thomas 1997; Boli and Thomas, eds., 1999).

A world-cultural explanation for the adoption of the neoliberal paradigm around the world would begin with the observation that nation-states have *always* imitated one another as part of their search for solutions to common problems. For example, during the nineteenth century, the Japanese government systematically set out to imitate British models of organization (such as the postal service) in the hopes of achieving Britain's rapid economic growth and military prowess (Westney 1987). Thus, institutional isomorphism among nation-states predates neoliberal convergence by a matter of centuries.

There is much in this study that confirms the theoretical propositions of world-cultural theory. Chapter 2 shows that following the revolution of 1910–17, Mexican state-builders explicitly looked to foreign models in their construction of a central bank, development bank, the Finance Ministry, and a host of other institutions. Indeed, the founding of Mexico's first economics program in 1929 was conceived as a project for training students in the latest economics knowledge and techniques developed abroad, to the end of developing a corps of competent administrators to work within the government bureaucracy. Moreover, chapters 4 and 5 clearly demonstrate that actors from the central bank played an ongoing and critical role in bringing both the Mexican government and the Mexican economics profession up to date with international standards.

However, to understand the very recent development of neoliberal reforms, I believe it is useful to draw on a somewhat different neoinstitutionalist account, namely, DiMaggio and Powell's (1991) discussion of institutional isomorphism within organizational fields. Organizational fields are networks of structurally equivalent organizations in ongoing communication, such as universities or nation-states. It is often observed that such organizations tend to become more alike over time. To explain why this occurs, DiMaggio and Powell (1983) identify three sorts of institutional isomorphism: mimetic, coercive, and normative. Mimetic isomorphism essentially corresponds to the processes identified by world-cultural theorists: organizations in the same "line of business" (i.e., nation-states) share common values and organizational structures, and therefore often imitate one another as a way of minimizing uncertainty.

Unlike world-cultural isomorphism, which is founded on legitimation and shared values, coercive and normative isomorphism are fundamentally about power: the power of external organizations with resources, in the former, and the power of certified experts, in the latter. Coercive isomorphism[4] occurs when organizations conform to the standards of powerful external actors, under the pressures of resource dependence. Thus, universities ostensibly in the business of higher education will support expensive athletics programs because donation-paying alumni are interested in winning football games. Normative isomorphism occurs among organizations (such as universities) that are staffed by professionals (such as university administrators). Often such organizations will converge because of pressures from the professions that staff them. An example is the widespread trend in the United States toward university-business partnerships, led by academic administrators with management degrees. I have chosen to refer to normative isomorphism as "expert isomorphism" throughout this book, since I believe this latter term is more recognizable as related to the power of professionals.

For the purposes of examining liberalizing reforms in Mexico and other developing countries, these latter two categories have great potential utility. Unlike mimetic isomorphism, the categories of coercive and normative/expert isomorphism have the potential to incorporate power and resource inequalities between core and periphery. Such inequalities have become particularly salient since the outbreak of the debt crisis in 1982. During the 1980s and '90s, "policy-based lending" by the U.S. government, the IMF, and other multilateral organizations, along with the growing need to foster investor confidence, had a tremendous impact on national policies of developing countries (cf. Stallings 1992; Kahler 1990 and 1992; Williamson and Haggard 1994). As Williamson and Haggard

(1994) candidly remark, "belief in the benefits of economic reform is much less widely held among politicians than among economists, and is even less widely endorsed by the general public, let alone by the specific interests that stand to lose" (p. 531). Thus, even among those who support neoliberal reforms, it is recognized that the debt crisis provided a critical impetus for change in the face of vested interests that could have prevented it.

Therefore, "coercive isomorphism" in DiMaggio and Powell's sense has clearly played an important part in the recent paradigm shift in Mexico and the rest of the developing world. Since 1982, Third World governments adopted liberalizing reforms in part to gain access to the resources of powerful external actors—most important, multilateral institutions and foreign investors. However, coercive isomorphism is perhaps the least interesting theoretical observation to be made about Mexico's neoliberal transformation. What is more striking is the extent to which the neoliberal paradigm shift has been brought about through expert or normative isomorphism—pressures exerted on the state not by external actors (i.e., foreign investors, the IMF), but by a group of professionals *within* the state.

The presence of U.S.-trained economists in the governments of developing countries today is astoundingly strong. These foreign-trained technocrats tend to share a common cognitive framework and set of guiding assumptions—in short, a common ideology—with foreign policymakers and international financiers. They also have social ties with U.S. policymakers and the officials of multilateral organizations—not only from their grad school days but also from prior appointments within international organizations (often the IMF). A growing body of evidence suggests that these technocrats have been instrumental in pushing forward liberalizing reforms in a number of Third World governments. In a cross-national study, Williamson and Haggard (1994) found that economists trained in U.S. universities played a prominent role in promoting reforms in eight of the fifteen nations studied (in Chile, Colombia, Indonesia, Korea, Mexico, Turkey, Brazil and Peru). More recent cases of U.S.-trained technocrats promoting neoliberal reforms include Costa Rica (Nuñez 1998), Vietnam (Kolko 1997) Pakistan (Holloway et al. 1996), and the Philippines. Moreover, even after neoliberal reforms are implemented, U.S.-trained economists play an important role in the ongoing management of market-oriented economies (Silva 1991; Puryear 1994).

Mexico presents an ideal-typical example of this trend. Since the middle of the 1980s, Mexico's shift to freer markets has been accompanied by "the rise within the Mexican economic policy bureaucracy of a group of young foreign-educated professional economists who worked in tandem and used their technical expertise as well as their positions of responsibil-

ity to lead Mexico in a new direction" (Golob 1997: 98). In the 1980s and
'90s, U.S.-trained economists rose to prominence in every single branch of
Mexican economic policymaking, in some ostensibly noneconomic
branches (such as education), and, most recently, to the presidency itself.

The role of U.S.-trained technocrats in promoting liberalizing reforms
in Mexico constitutes a clear example of expert isomorphism—convergence based on the power of professionals to reshape the organizations
and institutions within which they are embedded. But what is the source
of these professional powers? I claim that the success of a profession fundamentally rests upon its support by a constituency—in other words, a
group with the resources to support the practice of expert knowledge.
Professions need not generate widespread belief in their expertise; it is
sufficient to find a group that is willing to pay for it.

This perspective helps tremendously in explaining the extraordinary
proliferation of opportunities for U.S.-trained economists in the finance
ministries, central banks, and even presidencies of developing countries.
After all, this trend has occurred in societies where a significant proportion of the population is illiterate (13% in Mexico). If one were to carry
out a survey on the Mexican economics profession, it is unlikely that a
majority of Mexicans would have much notion of what economists do—
and even fewer would be able to evaluate the technocrats' economic policy (although many might be critical of the government). The power of
Mexican technocracy most assuredly does *not* derive from popular belief
in the expertise of foreign-trained economists.

Instead, the success of economists in the Mexican government must
fundamentally be traced to their legitimation by resource-bearing constituencies. Chapters 6 and 7 show that since the 1970s, but most particularly
since the outbreak of the debt crisis in 1982, the rise of neoliberal technocrats in Mexico has tended to be fostered by the legitimation of international and foreign, rather than national and domestic, constituencies. Foreign investors, multilateral institutions, and U.S. government officials are
the gatekeepers controlling access to vital resources, without which the
Mexican government would face grave macroeconomic difficulties. To
negotiate with these powerful external actors and organizations, the Mexican government has pushed to the top of the policymaking hierarchy a
group of individuals who inspire international trust and confidence—both
because of their formal credentials and because of their international social ties (for a more general argument, see Markoff and Montecinos
1993).

This means that although expert isomorphism (i.e., economists in government pushing neoliberal reforms) has been a key factor in Mexico's
neoliberal transition, coercive isomorphism has been behind this expert
isomorphism. In other words, the rise of the U.S.-trained technocrats is a

phenomenon that can be attributed largely to resource dependence. The pervasive and multifaceted role of external pressures in Mexico's neoliberal transition is almost certainly generalizable to other developing countries (but not to developed ones). The implications this has for processes of "social learning" in the developing world is discussed in chapter 8.

Local Institutional Logics

For many foreign investors, the administration of President Carlos Salinas de Gortari (1988–94) seemed to be a dream come true: it was friendly to international capital, apparently "democratizing" (while at the same time maintaining order), and surrounded by a team of English-fluent technocrats to whom foreign investors could relate. At the same time, internationally renowned economists who visited Mexico were impressed—not only with the government technocrats but with Mexican economics more generally, populated as it was with English-fluent Ph.D.'s from American universities.

This book shows that the twin phenomena of the internationalization of Mexican economics and the internationalization of Mexican technocracy are directly related. For reasons outlined above, during the 1980s and '90s there was a tremendous proliferation of opportunities for foreign-trained economists to work within the Mexican government, since top-level technocrats preferred to work with subordinates like themselves (often their former students). This high-profile trend swelled the enrollments of internationalized economics programs such as those of the ITAM and the Colegio de México; the success of these programs, in turn, led other programs to emulate them. At the same time, Mexico's technocratic government was willing to provide ample financial support for the most elite, Americanized sector of Mexican economics.

As a result of the trends mentioned above, Mexican economists with graduate degrees from Harvard, MIT, or the University of Chicago were increasingly able to find work as *academic* economists. This has meant that an elite sector of the Mexican economics profession has come strongly to resemble its counterpart in the United States. Not only do these economists have graduate degrees from American universities, but they work within academic institutions—in contrast to earlier generations of Mexican economists who had to work as full-time public officials.

One of the fundamental lessons of this book, however, is that appearances can be misleading. Recent literature suggests that we should be skeptical of the idea that neoliberal convergence will create a homogeneous whole—"one world," based on a single set of institutional patterns. Even though markets and capitalism are the order of the day, there continue to exist a number of "capitalisms" based on very different institutional arrangements (cf. Evans 1995; Hollingsworth and Boyer, eds., 1997; Hamilton and Biggart 1988; Soskice 1999; Hollingsworth, Schmitter, and Streeck, eds., 1994). Similarly, although national systems of economic expertise have come to resemble one another in many respects, we should expect important national variations to remain.

Thus, although American visitors may still be impressed by the apparent familiarity of Mexico's most elite economics departments, the "institutional logic" (cf. Biggart and Guillén 1999) undergirding Mexican economics remains radically different from that of its disciplinary counterpart in the United States. Most important, Mexican economics is still fundamentally guided by the logic and the resources of the Mexican state—a very different base from that of American economics, which is fundamentally an academic profession.

Conclusion

National systems of social-scientific expertise reflect local institutional and material conditions. As national economies have become more global, there has been a corresponding globalization of economic expertise, paralleling the transnational adoption of the neoliberal paradigm. Nevertheless, national context still matters. The following chapter shows how the Latin American and peculiarly Mexican context shaped the Mexican economics profession during the first several decades of the twentieth century.

Chapter 2

THE ORIGINS OF MEXICAN ECONOMICS

In 1929, Mexico's first economics program was inaugurated at the public Autonomous National University of Mexico (UNAM). From the outset, this program bore little resemblance to economics departments in the United States. Its founders were mostly public officials rather than academics, and their scholarly credentials in the field of economics were mostly scant or nonexistent. Its salaries were prohibitively low, which effectively restricted the teaching of economics to full-time government bureaucrats, who offered classes in the mornings or evenings. Students were not expected to pursue careers in business, or to enter graduate programs in economics (which did not exist in Mexico), but rather were overwhelmingly destined for government jobs.

This chapter examines the origins of Mexican economics in cross-national and comparative perspective. Unlike economics in the United States, which evolved in the context of a decentralized state and a network of privately endowed universities, Mexican economics was indelibly marked by the increasingly strong and activist postrevolutionary state. As a result, Mexican economics would bear little resemblance to the private and university-centered profession in the United States. Rather, it was a state-centered profession in the Continental mold—albeit one with a particularly Mexican flavor.

COMPARATIVE PERSPECTIVES ON EXPERT KNOWLEDGE

During the Great Depression, a British economist named W. H. Hutt published a book lamenting economists' lack of public prestige. He wrote:

> It has often been pointed out that the economist in the university is in a different position from most of his scientific colleagues in other branches of study. They are generally believed to be experts in their subject. The man in the street will not usually want to question the teachings of the mathematician, the chemist or biologist. Where the layman does not understand, he will usually take as gospel what the scientist tells him. But whilst there are few intelligent members of the public who would dare to argue with a professor of mathematics about his subject, there are few who would *not* be prepared to question the validity of an economist's teachings. (Hutt 1936: 36)

Like the members of all professions, economists have had to resolve their own dilemmas of professional legitimation by staking out what Abbott (1988) calls their professional jurisdiction. Economists of all nations have had to face the recurring problem of public skepticism regarding their expertise in the face of economic crisis and decline.

Nevertheless, professional legitimation is *not* principally made, in Hutt's terminology, to "the man in the street." Although professionals may wish for greater public recognition and approval, their status as professionals does not necessarily depend in any direct way on such recognition. Rather, as individuals who invest years of their life in expensive (at least in terms of opportunity cost) training, and who consequently get paid to practice their expertise, the principal dilemma of any profession is to find a group or entity with resources to sustain it. The distinction used in ordinary language between "amateur" and "professional" implicitly captures this notion extremely well: whereas a professional makes a living from providing his or her services, a mere amateur does not.

The seemingly obvious fact that professionals need to find someone to pay them has generally been overlooked in the professions literature, which has focused by tradition on the distinction between "professional" and "worker" rather than "professional" and "amateur" (cf. Caplow 1954; Wilensky 1964). The question addressed by highlighting the professional/worker distinction is how it is that a group of self-styled experts come to achieve the sort of autonomy and prestige that are awarded to, say, doctors, and not to automobile mechanics. In contrast, the professional/amateur dichotomy implicitly poses such questions as how doctors are able to pay for their medical training and support themselves and their families (without having to take second jobs as automobile mechanics, for example). Whereas the former question is about status, the latter is about livelihood.

Once we begin to study professions in developing countries, it becomes clear that the question of livelihood is analytically prior to the question of status in professions. In countries where resources are scarce, autonomy and prestige seem to be rather remote problems compared with the more immediate dilemma of making a living. In Mexico, for example, there is the persistent problem of unemployment and underemployment among physicians, who often must search for second jobs in order to make ends meet. This dilemma does not reflect Mexicans' lack of faith in the expertise of doctors. Rather, it is a reflection of the fact that most Mexicans cannot afford to pay for the private medical insurance that would give them access to well-paid doctors in private practices.

The notion that professions need resources provides a new take on the observations of Abbott (1988), Larson (1977), and others who have used the Weberian concept of legitimation to illuminate the processes whereby some professions succeed and others fail at certain times and places. Usually used within the context of politics rather than occupations, "legitimation" implies "inner justifications" or *belief* on the part of a critical mass of individuals (Weber 1946: 78). If political legitimacy is founded on widespread belief in the rightness of the political order, it seems natural to assume that professional legitimacy would be based on widespread belief in expertise.

However, this concept of legitimacy requires significant reframing in the context of professions. It is true that widespread belief in expertise may, under many circumstances, help professions flourish (particularly in societies with large middle classes able to pay for professional services). But widespread belief in expertise is neither necessary nor sufficient for the success of a given profession. For economics to be a sucessful profession in Mexico, most Mexicans do not need to believe in the expertise of economists (or even know what economists are); rather, it is sufficient that *some* organizations in Mexico be willing to pay economists. Conversely, occasionally professions may be materially supported by actors or organizations with no belief in their expertise. For example, Halliday and Carruthers (1996) discuss how the enactment of insolvency legislation in the 1980s in England led to the creation of a new sort of lawyer empowered to oversee certain procedures; English corporations may not have wanted to hire these lawyers, but the government required it of them.

This suggests that in the context of professions, the cognitive content of the notion of legitimacy must be set aside. Rather, it is more useful to think of professional legitimation in terms of the transfer of resources. An individual or group legitimates a profession by helping to sustain it materially. Borrowing from resource mobilization literature, I use the term "constituency" to refer to a group providing material resources that help sustain a profession (McCarthy and Zald 1977: 1221). Professional constituencies provide resources either by financing professional training (as when states or private groups fund universities) or by paying for professional services. Examples of constituencies are national public organizations (such as the state, or smaller organizations within the state, such as a central bank or publicly funded hospitals), international organizations (like the IMF), private for-profit organizations (such as corporations), private nonprofit organizations (such as universities), or private individuals.

The identification of different professional constituencies is particularly useful for explaining cross-national patterns of professionalization because it provides a causal bridge between expert knowledge and social structure. Different kinds of societies provide different sorts of economic, political, and cultural contexts, thereby giving rise to different professional constituencies. These constituencies, in turn, help create broad cross-national patterns in professionalization—most outstandingly, the difference between state-centered and private-centered professional systems. Whereas Anglo-American professions have tended to develop independently of the state (which they utilize to secure legal monopolies over particular kinds of work), in Continental Europe states have generally taken a more direct role in professionalization, through such means as designing and funding professional programs, and playing a leading role in hiring their graduates (Burrage and Torstendahl 1990; Abbott 1988; Cocks and Jarausch 1990; Heidenheimer 1989; Torstendahl and Burrage 1990; Krause 1996).[1] Since the Mexican revolution, professions in Mexico have tended to resemble the Continental rather than the Anglo-American model.

THE REVOLUTIONARY ROOTS OF MEXICAN ECONOMICS

At the outset of the Mexican revolution in 1910, the nation's professions were as underdeveloped as its economy. Under the dictatorship of Porfirio Díaz (1876–1910), Mexico was a highly stratified society, governed by a tiny elite and overwhelmingly populated by an impoverished and sometimes even indentured class of peasants. Of the three professions (not counting the military) surviving from the colonial era—the clergy, law, and medicine—only the clergy probably had a significant proportion of nonelite clients (Cleaves 1987: 7). The vast majority of Mexicans lacked the resources to support the services of professionals: as much as they may have needed doctors, agronomists, and engineers, they could not serve as an effective constituency for these professionals. The Mexican revolution—and the strong, centralized state that it created—made it possible for older professions to expand and new ones to be established. Cleaves (1987) notes that in Mexico, as in Continental Europe, delayed capitalist development meant that professionals were less powerful in relation to the state and generally more dependent on the state for employment (pp. 2–3). The consolidation of the postrevolutionary Mexican state after 1917 would prove an important stimulus to both professionalization and middle-class formation.

From Díaz Dictatorship to Sonoran Dynasty

During the Díaz dictatorship, the closest thing to a group of professional economists was a famous clique of wealthy government officials known as the "*científicos*" (scientists), the most famous of whom was José Limantour—Porfirio Díaz's minister of finance from 1893 to 1911. The científicos were devotees of the philosophers Comte and Spencer and believers in social Darwinism and "gradual" transition to democratic rule when the population was sufficiently educated; the party they formed in 1892 adopted the positivist motto "Order and Progress." The científicos were not true economists but rather lawyers (along with the occasional engineer) who had learned economics through reading and practical experience (Nieto 1986: 39–40; Camp 1991). Like the neoliberal technocrats that came to power nearly a century later, the científicos were believers in free trade and openness to foreign investment.

Under the guidance of the científicos, the Díaz dictatorship promoted a form of progress that Knight (1986: 513) likens to the "conservative modernization" observed by Barrington Moore, in that it attempted to push forward rapid economic development and political centralization without social and political reform. Commercialized agriculture was expanded, and thousands of peasants lost their land to large haciendas (Haber 1989: 18). Díaz maintained social hierarchies and protected the interests of landlords, monopolies, and foreign companies. The economic result of Porfirian policy was a productive structure dependent on the export of primary products (agriculture, minerals, and later petroleum), with inefficient monopolistic and oligopolistic industries, and an economy that was extremely vulnerable to fluctuations in international markets. The Porfirian Mexican economy was particularly dependent on the United States, with which it realized 74% of its exports and 58% of its imports (Ayala Espino 1988: 68–71).

The most important historical consequence of the Porfirian modernization program was arguably the Mexican revolution (1910–17), which brought into power a regime with a new social, political, and economic agenda. Private industrial investment under the Díaz regime had been carried out mostly in railroads and extractive industries, and mostly by foreign companies, who by 1910 accounted for between 67 and 73% of the total invested capital recorded (Haber 1989: 12). The Porfirian domestic entrepreneurial class was weak, undercapitalized, protected from external competition, and entirely dependent on an extremely limited internal market, since the Mexican middle class was extremely small. Therefore, Mexican industry was, according to one economic historian, "almost entirely dependent upon producing for the working class, whose incomes did not permit them to consume much beyond inexpensive consumer nondurables like coarse cotton cloth, cigarettes, soap, beer, and other low-cost items" (Haber 1989: 29).

Thus, Mexican revolutionaries confronted an economy that could not be relied on to grow and prosper on its own. In 1917 a group of revolutionary generals known popularly as the "Sonoran dynasty" came to power. The Sonorans recognized that market forces could not be relied on to guarantee a functioning economy any more than political liberties could be relied on for order. In order to survive, the Mexican state had to assume an active role in both promoting economic development and fostering political stability, whether through co-optation or repression. As a result, the Sonorans promoted a peculiar form of capitalism with populist and nationalist overtones and interventionist implications. The Constitution of 1917 promised a more active state role in the economy than that envisioned by Madero. Article 27 gave the government ultimate ownership of land and mineral rights, and along with Article 73 "expressed clearly the possibility of the intervention of the State in almost any area of the economy" (Ayala Espino 1988: 93). Article 123—a sweeping piece of labor legislation covering such issues as the eight-hour day and child labor legislation—gave the government power to regulate relations between capital and labor.

In the words of Knight (1986), "the genius of the revolutionary leadership [was] its capacity to harness the energy and grievances of the popular movement to antithetical ends—state-building and capitalist development" (p. 527). Gradually, the emerging Mexican state created the institutional bases for state intervention in the economy. In 1917, the Ministry of Industry, Commerce, and Labor was established. The power and scope of fiscal policy was increased from 1924 to 1927, with the establishment of an income tax, the broadening of the tax base, and the endowment of the Finance Ministry with jurisdiction over budgetary decisions. In 1925 a central bank (Banco de México) was established, along with the Agricultural Credit Bank; in the same year, the National Highway Commission was formed, and the construction of much-needed roads soon commenced. Moreover, as in many countries, the Depression had the effect in Mexico of stimulating increased state involvement in promoting economic growth and stability.

The Founding of Mexican Economics

Of all Mexican professions, it was economics that owed the greatest debt to the revolution. Unlike, law, medicine, engineering, architecture, and agronomy—all of which had been established as university programs before 1917—Mexican economics was essentially "invented" by a group of postrevolutionary state-builders. From the very beginning, Mexican economics was a statist profession in the Continental model, and was able to thrive and expand because of the state's growing involvement in the Mexican economy.

The first economics program in Mexico was formed within the Law School of the Autonomous National University of Mexico (UNAM) in 1929 and was later expanded to become a School of Economics in 1935. The program's origins can be traced directly to a meeting of intellectuals and state institution-builders at the beginning of 1929. These individuals belonged to a new generation reaching political maturity during the *maximato,* who were disillusioned with Calles's policies and believed in more vigorous state intervention than Calles had been willing to undertake (Knight 1991: 248). Too young to have fought in the revolution, many of these individuals supported it as students and became *cardenistas,* Marxists, or Marxist sympathizers. Although ideologically heterogeneous, the most important common feature shared by the founders of the UNAM economics program was the commitment to building national state institutions in the service of economic development. The founding of an economics program was conceived as part of this project.

The founders of economics at the UNAM shared the common project of creating a cadre of state bureaucrats who could take charge of economic policymaking. Since the reign of Porfirio Díaz and his científicos, Mexican economic policy had been entrusted to lawyers. Law in Mexico was not the specialized profession that it is today in the United States, but was rather a more general humanistic training that included the study of history, philosophy, and other disciplines. Like liberal arts education in the United States, a law education in Mexico was supposed to work in a variety of areas, and economic policymaking was one of them. In the words of UNAM rector Castro Leal in 1929, lawyers had been making economic policy "as dilettantes" (Pallares Ramírez 1952: 50).

One of the reasons that the need for economists seemed so pressing was undoubtedly that international standards for economic policymaking had been upgraded since the years of the *porfiriato.* During the first decades of the twentieth century, economic policymaking in capitalist nations became more homogeneous, with a much more internationally agreed-upon set of standards and methods. For example, in 1920, the League of Nations sponsored an international financial conference in Brussels, at which central bankers and finance ministers from around the world met to lay out what they considered to be the universal truths of government monetary, financial, trade, and fiscal policy; its recommendations were unanimously approved by those in attendance (League of Nations 1920: 7). Internationally recognized standards for economic policymaking techniques—such as the calculation of balances of payments and national accounts—provided a set of guidelines for what any government economist should know, irrespective of national origin.

The original idea for creating an economics program is commonly attributed to Narciso Bassols, who was director of the UNAM Law School from 1928 to 1929. Bassols was part of a generation of Mexican intellectual contemporaries who attended the National Law School and participated in the organized prorevolutionary student movement in the mid-teens; he was described by one contemporary as "a revolutionary in disagreement with the social organization of his times, with clear and definite socialist leanings" (Mabry 1982: 43; Silva Herzog 1970: 149). A supporter of "socialist education" and fervent *cardenista*, Bassols served first as secretary of the interior and later as secretary of finance under the Cárdenas administration.

Bassols's claim to original founding fatherhood of economics at the UNAM, however, was contested by Daniel Cosío Villegas, who claimed in his autobiography that Bassols was more interested in renovating the teaching of law than starting a new program in economics. According to this version, Cosío Villegas had the original idea and later managed to overcome Bassols's reluctance in order to get the project underway (Cosío Villegas 1977: 140). Cosío Villegas was the most academic of the founding fathers of Mexican economics and perhaps the one most influenced by foreign ideas. He had studied economics in the United States—at Harvard, Cornell, and the University of Wisconsin—at the London School of Economics, and at the Ecole Libre de Sciences Politiques in France with funding from the Rockefeller Foundation supplemented by income from writing as a foreign correspondent for a Mexican newspaper; what he saw abroad provided inspiration for creating an economics program in Mexico (Krauze 1980: 54). A classmate and prorevolutionary comrade of Bassols, Cosío Villegas was probably best described as a revolutionary intellectual who subscribed to no dogma in particular and who believed, in the words of his biographer, that "the State had the great opportunity to serve as a catalyst, as a bellows, as a real promoter, but not as means and end" (Krauze 1980: 64). Cosío Villegas supported Cárdenas's land reform policies and was a friend of many leftist intellectuals but was not precisely a leftist himself (Krauze 1980: 88). Cosío Villegas was the first director of the UNAM economics program within the Law School and would later go on to play an important role in shaping the Economic Research Department at the central bank.

Two other founders of UNAM economics who had been influenced by exposure to economics programs abroad were Antonio Espinosa de los Monteros and Eduardo Villaseñor. Espinosa had received a bachelor of science degree in the United States and later took graduate courses with Cosío Villegas at Harvard. Unlike Cosío Villegas, Espinosa received his master's degree, and he later became director of Nacional Financiera during the Cárdenas administration. Villaseñor had never received a formal undergraduate degree, but while working as Mexican commercial attaché in London in the late 1920s took night school classes at the London School of Economics, where he became particularly impressed by the new monetary theories of John Maynard Keynes (Villaseñor 1974: 58). Villaseñor was director of the Agricultural Credit Bank, became undersecretary of finance under Cárdenas, and director of the central bank from

1940 to 1946. Never an orthodox central banker, Villaseñor saw the Banco de México as an important institution for promoting economic development. Under his directorship, the central bank founded an Industrial Studies Department for the promotion of economic development through studies of different industries and scholarships for Mexicans to learn technical skills abroad. Villaseñor was also responsible for an important project in 1945 in which the Banco contracted the Armour Research Foundation in Chicago to conduct an extensive series of studies on Mexico's potential for industrial development (*Problemas agrícolas* . . . : 5).

Enrique González Aparicio was primarily responsible for the transformation of the economics program at the UNAM into a full-fledged School of Economics in 1935 and became the school's first director. González Aparicio was a lawyer who also studied for a year at the London School of Economics in 1934 and subsequently went to the Soviet Union to make "educational observations" (Silva Herzog 1970: 263; Pallares Ramírez 1952: 96). An intellectual with Marxist tendencies (interview, Sánchez Navarro 9/29/95), he was an enthusiastic supporter of Cárdenas's expropriation of the petroleum industry (Sousa and González Aparicio 1938: 49). His employment history included a number of economic policymaking posts, including the Finance Ministry, the Ministry of Agriculture, the Bank of Ejidal Credit, and director of the National Workers' Bank (Pallares Ramírez 1952: 96).

Among the most conservative of the founders of economics at the UNAM was Manual Gómez Morín, a member of the "Seven Sages." A lawyer by profession, Gómez Morín had also studied economics at Columbia University while spending two years (1921–22) in New York resolving disputes between Mexico and foreign banks and petroleum companies (Maxfield 1990: 40). He became respected as an expert on economic policy at a very young age, and was the author of the original legislation for the formation of the central bank in 1925 and the Agricultural Credit Bank in 1926. Although he was against the imposition of Marxism in the university, and opposed to Cárdenas's brand of land reform, he was nevertheless a dedicated supporter of the Mexican revolution since his days as a law student. His disillusion with *cardenismo* later led him to found the right-wing National Action Party (PAN) in 1939. Ideologically, Gómez Morín was quite similar in outlook to Miguel Palacios Macedo, another lawyer involved in the foundation of the UNAM economics program and one of the program's first professors (Cosío Villegas 1977: 40).

The most important founder of economics at the UNAM was Jesús Silva Herzog. Silva Herzog not only shaped the initial program but also guided its trajectory during its first twenty years of existence. He had been a prorevolutionary journalist in his youth and was a self-styled Marxist but became disillusioned with the Soviet Union while there as Mexican ambassador in the late 1920s (Silva Herzog 1970: 128). An insatiable institution-builder, Silva Herzog was put in charge of organizing the economics library of the secretary of finance in 1928, the first economics library in Mexico. He later founded the Department of Economic Studies at National Railroads of Mexico in 1931, and the Mexican Institute of Economic Studies in the same year (which lasted only fifteen months), and was undersecretary of finance from 1942 to 1945. Although Silva Herzog had no formal university degree, he served as director of the UNAM School of Economics from 1940 to 1942 and was subsequently called upon three times to be interim director. Silva Herzog was a charismatic speaker and extremely popular among his students; he was known especially for his classes in the history of economic thought.

The government-centered vision of the School's founders is evidenced by its unambiguous advertisement as a program for training public sector officials. The announcement of the new program in a financial journal read: "Licenciados[2] in economics can assume the administrative posts of greatest importance in the Federal Government and in the local governments because their knowledge qualifies them most especially for that end" ("La carrera de economista" 1929: 6). The idea that economists could also play a useful role in the private sector was mentioned but downplayed. A well-known UNAM economics professor from these early years later remarked that "it is obvious that in the first stages of the progress of a country, it is the state and the state's decentralized agencies that make the greatest demand upon the professional services of economists. It is in later stages, after certain national economic progress, when the demand for professional services in private enterprise grows" (Loyo [Gilberto] 1949: 399). Where the private sector was weak and underdeveloped, and where the state was responsible for pushing forward economic development, it was logical for economists to work in the government and not in the private sector.

To help economics graduates find government employment, and to make the program more appealing to students concerned with future career possibilities, Cosío Villegas and Espinosa approached President Portes Gil (1928–30) with the idea of establishing a legal monopoly for economists in certain areas of public administration. As a result, Article 63 of the Organic Law of the Budget Department of the Federation reserved middle-level administrative positions—such as subdirector of Customs and director of the Office of Patents—for licenciados in economics. Since at the time there were only a handful of individuals with such a degree (necessarily acquired abroad), the law stated that if economists could not be found to occupy these positions, they should be occupied by "those individuals that the Executive considers sufficiently able" (Pallares Ramírez 1952: 46–47).

The Fight for a Professional Jurisdiction

In keeping with Abbott's observations concerning fights for territory within professional "systems," the appearance of a new profession competing for public-sector jobs caused concern among members of professions with established footholds in the Mexican government bureaucracy. Opposition to the new profession was voiced in 1931, when modifications in the economics programs were proposed. Lawyers and accountants objected that the economics program contained too many courses in law and accounting; Professor José León of the Accounting School demanded that the number of classes in this discipline be reduced (Pallares Ramírez 1952: 74; Consejo Universitario 1931a). It was also objected that economics was a useless program preparing students for "an empirical-bureaucratic career, whose functions were easily carried out," and that it was not necessary "to dedicate 5 or 6 years of study to obtain a degree and with this guarantee to perform tasks of such an easy nature" (Pallares Ramírez 1952: 74). A somewhat contradictory argument was that economists were not prepared to do anything useful, and that graduates of the program would be unable to find employment; it was therefore suggested that the economics program be merged with that of a more "lucrative profession" such as business administration (Consejo Universitario 1931b).

In order to calm these fears of competition, a group of students met with Professor León to explain the differences between the functions of economists and accountants: economists were supposed to create national wealth, whereas the function of accountants was to "order, classify and expound upon the results of existing elements" (Pallares Ramírez 1952: 75). Professor Silva Herzog's eloquent defense of economics at the University Council attests to the profession's public-sector origins and purpose:

> For some years I have been in charge of offices designed to carry out economic studies.
>
> First I participated in the organization of the Ejidal Agricultural Banks, and very frequently we ran into the problem of not being able to find people trained in economics that could help us with the tasks we had to perform. Later I was in charge of the Office of Economic Statistics. My difficulties were great because I could not find anyone who could collaborate with me effectively; the employees were routine and deficiently prepared bureaucrats;

I needed neither lawyers nor accountants but economists capable of interpret-
ing the social phenomena synthesized in the statistical tables. One year later
I was put in charge of organizing the Library and Economic Archives of the
Secretary of Finance; the same problem occurred. The problem persists, I
need economists and I can't find them. (Quoted in Pallares Ramírez 1952: 77)

The objections of lawyers and accountants not withstanding, the economics program was expanded to a full-fledged School of Economics in 1935,
and the destiny of economists in the Mexican public sector was sealed.

Taxi Professors and Part-Time Students

As many Mexicanist scholars have noted, social mobility in postrevolutionary Mexico tended to run through political rather than economic
channels. In the words of Silva Herzog, "Politics is the easiest and most
profitable profession in Mexico" (quoted in Hansen 1971: 125). The recruitment of new generations of political elites through the university was
of summary importance for satisfying individual aspirations for social
betterment. During the decades following the revolution, the public and
free National University offered tremendous opportunities for social mobility, as a new generation of Mexicans made social ties that would lead to
future political success. Camp (1980) notes that the National University
historically functioned both as a space for forming social ties among students who would later form *camarillas* (political friendship networks) and
as a point of contact between the old generation of public servants and
the new generation of students aspiring to work in government. The "taxi
professor"—who works full-time in the public sector and teaches a class
in the morning or evening—identifies students with particular promise,
befriends them, and finds them jobs in public administration. The pent-
up demand for economists cited by Silva Herzog was apparently so great
that many economics students were hired while they were still completing
their studies. As a more formal supplement to personal channels, the Colegio Nacional de Economistas—the official professional society of economists—was later founded in 1951 (Cleaves 1987: 81).

The newly founded School of Economics prospered under the taxi-professor system, which rapidly channeled economics students into government jobs. With the exception of a few individuals who had received economics training as a result of extraordinary circumstances—such as
Víctor Urquidi and Josué Sáenz—the majority of the first professors at
the School of Economics were either lawyers or engineers by profession,
and full-time employees of the public sector. Salaries were simply too low
at the UNAM to live on, and full-time professors in economics were nonexistent. Many of the early students were also government employees

with degrees in law and accounting (Camp 1975: 139). The school was conveniently located at Cuba 92, a beautiful Porfirian-era building only a few blocks from the National Palace, and within walking distance of most government ministries: some so-called taxi professors were undoubtedly in reality "pedestrian" professors. In the early 1940s, there were no full-time instructors; as late as 1960, there were only two full-time professors for a total of 1,686 registered students (interview, Urquidi 9/19/95; UNAM 1981).

The taxi-professor phenomenon was advantageous for the consolidation of the Mexican economics profession within the public sector, as professors with degrees in law or engineering pulled young economists into their respective government ministries. Once economists had entered a given ministry, those who managed to move up the administrative ladder could use their position to pull in more economics students in turn. Nevertheless, the phenomenon of professors and students working as bureaucrats caused some worry about the quality of the program. In 1954, Silva Herzog expressed concern about extremely low professors' salaries, which meant that only full-time public servants could give classes: "and since in order to earn their living they occupy their time in some other activity, they can neither always prepare their courses well nor be present in class on the day that the material is supposed to be presented." Regarding the students, Silva Herzog remarked that "[t]he classes in the School of Economics are given from 8 to 9 in the morning and again starting at 5:30 in the afternoon. The bulk of the young people registered work from 6 to 7 hours daily, and logically and inevitably do not have the time necessary for fully pursuing their studies" (Silva Herzog 1954: 22–23).

These concerns notwithstanding, Silva Herzog himself was a prime example of a taxi professor who found promising students jobs in public administration. Indeed, he was probably the single most important taxi professor of the first three decades of UNAM economics (Camp 1975: 139; interviews, Alanís Patiño 8/21/95 and Urquidi 9/19/95). As undersecretary of finance in the 1940s, Silva Herzog was a key connection for finding jobs for UNAM economics students and sent many of them for training in public administration at the U.S. Bureau of Budget (interview, Urquidi 9/19/95).

In part to train economics students to be effective government functionaries, in 1940, Jesús Silva Herzog founded the Institute for Economic Research (IIE) within the UNAM. Within the institute's Department of Economic Research, third- and fourth-year economics students received training in team research and the editing of memorandums, among other skills. In the Laboratory Department, second- and third-year students learned to use calculating machines, how to calculate and interpret statistics and indexes, and how to access information on the national and international economies (Pallares Ramírez 1952: 103).

The apparent success of Mexican economists in securing employment raises the question: did the first economists emerging from the UNAM in the late 1930s and early 1940s supplant lawyers and accountants, as the latter had feared? The absence of evidence of ongoing conflict between economists and other groups of professionals within the Mexican state suggests that there were few jurisdictional struggles following the initial difficulties during the early 1930s. The absence of such inter-professional struggles probably reflects an abundance of opportunities founded in a general expansion of the Mexican state bureaucracy. Government institutions and policy tools constructed to make capitalism work in Mexico provided fertile ground upon which the seed of the economics profession could prosper without causing a major disturbance for other professions.

STATE EXPANSION AND THE EMPLOYMENT OF ECONOMISTS

The period beginning in the 1930s and continuing through the 1950s was known for substantial economic growth, industrialization, and state policymaking expansion in Mexico. During the 1930s, the Mexican economy acquired some of the basic characteristics that it would retain during the postwar period: industrialization oriented toward a domestic market, the decreasing importance of imported finished goods (many of which were now manufactured in Mexico), and the growing importance of imported raw materials (Cárdenas 1994: 61). Manufacturing rose from 11.3% of the Mexican GNP in 1932 to 18% in 1958 (Ayala Espino 1988: 130, 132). This apparently unspectacular figure seems more interesting if we consider that during this period there was substantial economic growth in *all* sectors (with an average real GNP growth[3] of 4.8% from 1930 until 1958); it therefore reflects an impressive real growth in the manufacturing sector.

Although the policies of this period were full of contradictions and discontinuities—especially in the area of redistributive policies—there were important continuing trends and long-term evolutionary patterns in the area of economic policy. The institutions and policy tools developed in the 1920s and '30s became the basis for an ongoing commitment of the government to the promotion of economic development. Cárdenas, while more concerned with politics than economics during most of his administration, stimulated industry and agriculture through infrastructural development, and laid the foundations of industrial promotion through selective tax exemption (González 1981: 266–67). Although not as friendly to organized workers and peasants as Cárdenas had been (and more friendly to foreign investors), the administrations of Avila Camacho (1940–46), Miguel Alemán (1946–52), and Ruiz Cortínez (1952–58) were committed to economic growth and industrialization, with state intervention as a means to this end. As Avila Camacho's finance minister put it, "the Administration proposes to work actively for the industrialization of the Mexican Republic, until this is attained. The State does not want to take the role of [entrepreneur], but rather to help private enterprise to take charge of transforming the country" (quoted in Mosk 1954: 61). State intervention for the promotion of economic development had the simultaneous effects of stimulating GNP growth and industrialization, on the one hand, and creating a real economic policymaking bureaucracy, on the other.

State interventionism in postrevolutionary Mexico developed in several different stages. The 1917 Constitution made provisions for government intervention in the economy, although it would be nearly two decades before the Mexican state had the ability carry it out. The fruition of Mexican *dirigisme* in the 1930s, '40s, and '50s can be attributed to two factors: first, the founding of economic policymaking institutions and the consequent introduction of new policymaking tools; and second, the impact of the Great Depression. During the 1930s, an intelligent policymaker looked around the world and saw that the only apparently successful economies—from western European fascism to Stalinism to Roosevelt's New Deal—were ones in which the state took a leading role. Consequently, Mexico began both to take full advantage of the institutions and tools it had been constructing for nearly two decades and to build new ones. For the first time since the revolution the Mexican government had both the desire to intervene and the wherewithal to do so. The result was both economic and government bureaucratic expansion; the latter provided new horizons for the employment of economists.

The Banco de México

Some of the most important advances in economic policymaking occurred within the Mexican central bank (Banco de México). Founded in 1925, the Banco was initially unable to have much effect on either inflation or growth for several reasons. First, it operated on a metallic reserve system, and its bills were mistrusted by a public that had suffered greatly from revolutionary inflation. This limited the Banco's power to effect expansionary monetary policy through printing money. Second, all Mexican banks were not initially required to affiliate with the Banco, which meant that it could not influence the economy through raising or lowering reserve requirements. And third, the Banco was committed to defending the value of the peso in relation to other currencies, since the conventional economic wisdom of the day was that one needed to adhere to metallic standards and uphold the exchange rate.

Alberto Pani assumed the position of finance minister in 1932 and became famous for defying the orthodox economic wisdom that had been followed in both monetary and fiscal policy in Mexico.[4] The Mexican central bank, like many central banks around the world in the 1930s, was remade from a mere guardian against inflation to an active agent in stimulating economic growth. Unlike his predecessor, Pani allowed the peso to devalue, which resulted in some inflation but also led to economic growth, since the demand for products produced in Mexico (now cheaper relative to those produced abroad) grew both inside and outside Mexico (Cárdenas 1994: 46). Pani's task was made easier by the fact that in 1932 Mexicans were more willing to accept Banco de México notes; by then, not only had confidence in the stability of the government and the goodness of its money been established, but deflation was such a problem that people were desperate to accept any sort of money.

Whereas the previous finance minister had maintained a budget surplus during the first years of the Depression, Pani ran a small fiscal deficit funded by the central bank (Cárdenas 1994: 36). The money supply was expanded through the coinage of silver and the use of Banco de México bills to pay public employees, which had a snowball effect as these individuals pressed others to accept their bills as money (Cárdenas 1994: 49). In 1935, silver was demonetized, and bills became the only legal money in circulation (Cárdenas 1994: 68). Increases in the circulating medium brought about by Pani's policies caused some inflation but also had positive effects on economic growth. In 1936, all banks were obliged to affiliate with the Banco, which endowed the central bank with the important policy tool of reserve requirements (Cárdenas 1994: 67). And in the same year the Finance Ministry was empowered to issue treasury bills as a means of acquiring resources from the central bank. In the 1930s, the Banco de México began to assume the characteristics of a modern central bank, which had the result of both making monetary policy possible and making fiscal policy more flexible, since for the first time since the revolution the Finance Ministry was able to draw upon funds that it did not immediately have.

Other Institutions in Mexican Development

The Finance Ministry had been evolving into a more modern, powerful institution since the mid-1920s, when debt contracted as a by-product of the revolution made it necessary to adhere to the standards of foreign creditors and public officials. As a consequence of these foreign pressures, the ministry upgraded its accounting and budgeting procedures in accordance with foreign standards, since up until this period the Finance Ministry "did not even have reliable information on salaries and the number of employees of each government office" (Zebadúa 1994: 283). In 1926 officials contacted foreign agencies such as the U.S. Institute for Government Research, the Rockefeller Foundation, and the General Accounting Office of the U.S. government for suggestions on how to become more modern and efficient (Zebadúa 1994: 283–84).

It was also during the mid-1920s that the ministry was endowed with more power over budgetary decisions and an income tax (*impuesto sobre la renta*) was established. Although this tax would have little coverage until the 1930s, it constituted a landmark in Mexican fiscal policy in that it would lead to a more stable source of revenues for the government (which had previously been dependent on import and export taxes, which were extremely vulnerable to international fluctuations) (Cárdenas 1994: 80). Exemptions from these and other taxes and tariffs would be used as a way of promoting industries that the government deemed important to national economic development. According to King (1970), tax exemptions for fostering industries existed beginning in 1926, and were operated jointly by the Ministry of Finance and the Ministry of Commerce and Industry (then called Industry and Trade).[5] In 1939 and 1941, legislation expanded these exemptions. The 1941 Law of Manufacturing Industries gave five-year tax exemptions to industries that were considered new or "necessary."

Another important foundation for Mexican state interventionism was the growth of financial intermediation through institutions designed to satisfy the need for credit. Mostly founded during the 1930s, these institutions enabled the Mexican government to put private capital to work by assuming risks in making loans to particular sectors, which consequently benefited from lower interest rates than they would have been able to obtain in the market; these institutions also lent to the government for its own projects. They were the Agricultural Credit Bank (1926), the National Urban Mortgage and Public Works Bank (1933), the industrial development bank or Nacional Financiera (1934), the Ejidal Credit Bank (1935), and the Foreign Commerce Bank (1937). Nacional Financiera was relatively insignificant until its charter was revised in 1940 but subsequently achieved an impressive profit record for itself and made a substantial contribution to industrial development (King 1970: 74, 71). Nacional Financiera and its sister institutions also became an important source of capital accumulation for the financing of public projects. From 1939 to 1945, there was 140.1% real growth in public investment, mostly in roads, ports, railroads, irrigation, the extraction of petroleum, and electricity (Cárdenas 1994: 109–10). Meanwhile, the expropriations of the

Cárdenas administration had created the parastate sector, another source of revenue and means for encouraging economic development.

The final institutional linchpin for setting the course of Mexican interventionism from the 1930s onward was the protection of domestic industries, which evolved later than other policy tools. Tariffs were increased both in terms of amounts and number of items protected in 1930, but this was a practical measure designed to increase government revenue rather than part of an overall protectionist policy (Cárdenas 1994: 51). Mexican industry was stimulated in the 1930s by the devaluation and in the early 1940s by wartime demand; in neither case was protection considered the main factor leading to domestic industrial expansion. Subsequently, however, both tariffs and import licenses came to play an increasingly important role in Mexican industrial policy. In 1947 an "ad valorem" component was added to tariffs. In practice, this was administered such that tariffs were charged according to either the actual price or the "official" price of the product—whichever was highest (King 1970: 75). Since the "official" price was decided in the Finance Ministry, this system probably enabled the ministry to have substantial discretion in discouraging some sorts of imports and encouraging others. A new system of import licenses, administered by the Commerce Ministry, was also implemented in 1947 (King 1970: 76; Izquierdo 1964: 252).

PUBLIC-SECTOR EMPLOYMENT OF ECONOMISTS: 1935–1958

Economics benefited more than other professions from these developments, since this profession had been created for the very purpose of staffing government economic bureaucracies. During its early years in the late 1920s and early 1930s, the UNAM economics program had several times run the risk of being shut down "because of the lack of professors and even of students, since in the year 1930 there was only a single student registered" (Silva Herzog 1954: 18). But by 1939 the total number of students registered within the program (for all years) had risen to 271, which reflected both a general growth in the university system and an increase in the appeal of studying economics (UNAM 1981: 255).

Part of the rise in the School of Economics's popularity had, no doubt, to do with a perception that graduates had solid employment prospects within the government. The first graduates in economics from the UNAM were confronted with a sort of virgin territory within a growing government bureaucracy so desperate for economic expertise that its officials were willing to hire students before they finished their course work. Cosío Villegas observed in his memoirs that the legislation reserving government posts for economists was quickly made redundant: "the appetite of the country for economists shortly thereafter led institutions like the Banco de México to establish an ascending salary scale for economics students, which began with those in their first year" (Cosío Villegas 1977: 141–42). Mexican economics flourished not because of an extensive and rigorously enforced legal monopoly but because officials in government ministries felt that economics graduates could be useful assistants in the rapidly multiplying functions of the government in guiding the Mexican economy.

The story of the early success of UNAM economics serves as an illustration of how Mexican professionalization differed from the Anglo-American model of professionalization through legislative sanction (i.e., through the government giving professions legal monopolies over certain forms of work paid for by private clients). As Cleaves's (1987) book illustrates for a number of Mexican professions (including law, medicine, economics, engineering, and agronomy), Mexican professionalization more closely resembled analogous processes in Continental Europe, where the state played a direct role in the training and the employment of professionals. For example, in Mexico doctors were trained at the public UNAM, and many went on to positions in the state-funded hospital system that expanded after the 1940s; many engineers (also trained at the UNAM) found employment in Mexico's state-owned petroleum industry. The petroleum industry had been nationalized during the Cárdenas administration.

Because of the youth of the profession and the individuals practicing it, Mexican economists did not at this time participate in the actual formulation of economic policies, with two notable exceptions: Antonio Espinosa de los Monteros, who had received an M.A. in economics from Harvard and was director of Nacional Financiera from 1936 to 1945, and Ramón Beteta, who interrupted his law studies at the UNAM to study economics at the University of Texas and was finance minister from 1946 to 1952. The three best-known economic policymakers of the postwar period—Finance Ministers Eduardo Suárez and Antonio Ortíz Mena, and central bank director Rodrigo Gómez—were trained in law (Suárez and Ortíz Mena) and accounting (Gómez) respectively.

During this period, while lawyers and other professionals did the policymaking, the economists working below them administrated and conducted studies. One economist hired by the Banco de México's Department of Economic Studies in 1946 recalled that almost all his fellow employees were UNAM economics students but that all the office managers but one were noneconomists, adding that his job was "to produce yards and yards of adding machine tape" (interview, Calderón 8/23/95). The division of labor between lawyers and economists at the time—with the former in charge of the intellectual labor of policymaking and the latter entrusted with technical tasks—seems to have been the source of a certain level of frustration among economists who felt that it was their responsibility to "pick up the pieces" left by incompetent lawyers' policymaking (cf. De la Peña 1942: 33).

The two most desirable places to work as an economist during this period were then (and probably are still today) the Finance Ministry and the Banco de México; the former because of its tremendous power and discretion in formulating economic policies and imposing them on other ministries, and the latter because of its somewhat autonomous position vis-à-vis the Finance Ministry, its broad, macroeconomic perspective, its organizational stability, and its impressive benefits package. Many authors have identified the Finance Ministry as the heart and brain of the Mexican economic policymaking bureaucracy (Shelton 1964: 114; Blair 1964: 198; King 1970: 99). Not only did the finance minister have a say in the policies of the Banco de México and Nacional Financiera; he also intervened in policies that technically fell under the purview of the Industry and Commerce Ministry, such as the Law of New and Necessary Industries.

A list of government agencies employing economists and the sorts of tasks they performed, drawn up by an UNAM economics graduate (Pallares Ramírez 1952), provides a broader perspective on where economists worked within the public sector, as well as a general idea of the tasks they performed. Areas in which UNAM economics graduates could work within the Finance Ministry included the Bureau of Credit, within which the first posts for economists were created in 1934, and the Bureau of Commercial Revenues, where economists worked beginning in 1938. In the former, economists participated in the formulation of monetary decrees, the modification of credit laws, and studies of investment and banking; in the latter, studies and decrees were formulated regarding commercial taxes. A notable area employing economists was the bureau in charge of the administration of the income tax, where economists audited firms' costs and profits, and calculated coefficients for taxing different kinds of businesses. In the area of trade and industrial policy, economists could work within the National Tariff Commission (a bureau of the Finance Ministry dealing with the modification of existing tariffs and the creation of new ones) or the Bureau of Financial Studies, which carried out investigations on trade policy, fiscal policies, and so forth, and identified "new" or "necessary" industries to be exempted from taxes (Pallares Ramírez 1952: 331–35).

Although not as influential as the Finance Ministry, the Banco de México attracted the finest economics students from the UNAM for a number of reasons. First, unlike other ministries, which had a nearly complete turnover of upper- and middle-level personnel every six years (since the finance minister was a member of the presidential cabinet), the Banco de México was seen as both relatively meritocratic and relatively insulated from political turnover. The Banco was one of the first economic policymaking organizations to have psychological and aptitude tests as prerequisites for entrance (interview, Ghigliazza 7/19/94). Although it was more difficult to enter than other organizations, once an individual entered the Banco he or she could count on a job for life, with a comfortable pension waiting at the end and all manner of fringe benefits (such as low-interest loans and a food ration (interview, Sáenz 10/6/95)). Finally, the Banco had the singular advantage of dealing with large-scale macroeconomic issues, which meant that a promising individual could in time be recruited to an interesting position, rather than spending the rest of his or her career overseeing the implementation of a particular policy within a circumscribed area.

More than other ministries, the Banco de México was located within a strong international "organizational field" of central banks, which had as a group become more important institutions since the experience of the 1930s had shattered the myths of economic orthodoxy and demanded a more active role for central banks. Hamilton (1982) notes that since its foundation in the 1920s, the Banco de México benefited from various visits of personnel from the U.S. Federal Reserve, with which it worked closely (p. 83). In 1937, the Banco's Economic Studies Department benefited from a visit by an expert from the New York Federal Reserve, who explained how economic studies were carried out in the United States (Pallares Ramírez 1952: 342). And in 1946, an international meeting of central bankers in Mexico City had an entire section devoted to the importance of cooperation between Departments of Economic Studies (Banco de México 1946: 311). At the meeting, Dr. Woodlief Thomas of the Board of Governors of the Dallas Federal Reserve explained that

> central banks require abundant data relating to the functioning of the banking system and developments in business, industry, agriculture, and the monetary economy, in order to more effectively administer the affairs of the central banking system. (Banco de México 1946: 327)

A speaker from the Banco de México pointed out that

> in some countries the disturbances caused by the depression of 1930–1933 and those brought on by the wartime period 1939–1945 have obliged central banks to take a series of measures, related with the control of exchange rates, with the allocation of imports, with the absorption of market funds, etc., which have demanded statistical information and contact with daily economic life that can only be obtained through creating special groups of investigators. (Banco de México 1946: 315)

Now that central banks were supposed to be concerned with more than inflation, more information was required; it was the job of the Banco's Department of Economic Studies to provide this information. Daniel Cosío Villegas, who was head of Economic Studies from 1941 to 1944, played an important role both in modernizing and expanding the department and in recruiting UNAM economics students to staff it, with the collaboration of Jesús Silva Herzog. Cosío Villegas also helped establish a new scholarship program to send promising employees to study economics abroad (Krauze 1980: 101, 109; interview, Urquidi 9/1/95). The Department of Economic Studies underwent a dramatic expansion from 1932, when it had only five employees, to 1952, when it had fifty-seven. This expansion was the logical result of the Banco de México's acquisition of true central bank status and effective policymaking tools.

The four different branches of the Banco's Economic Studies Department were (1) Banks, Money, and Credit, (2) Balance of Payments, (3) National Income, and (4) Special Studies. Banks, Money, and Credit was in charge of collecting and analyzing statistics on the balances of Mexico's credit institutions, as well as determining the amount and composition of money in circulation, the quantity of money outside the bank; it was also supposed to conduct studies that could help establish reserve requirements. Balance of Payments was supposed to determine Mexico's balance of payments through measuring the different ways that money flowed in and out of the country; the technologies for measuring these data effectively were incorporated during the 1940s with the help of officials from U.S. Federal Reserve (Pallares Ramírez 1952: 344–45; interview, Urquidi 9/1/95). National Income was in charge of calculating the Mexican national income, and Special Studies conducted investigations in order to be able to make economic policy suggestions to the Finance Ministry (Pallares Ramírez 1952: 346–7). Taken as a whole, the Economic Studies Department was responsible for generating information on all major aspects of the Mexican macroeconomy.

Another area of the Banco de México in which economists worked, albeit in smaller numbers, was the Department of Industrial Studies. This department exemplified the unorthodox vision of the proper task of central bankers that prevailed in the decades following the Great Depression. Its task was to help promote industrial development through providing scholarships for Mexicans to learn technical skills (such as engineering or industrial chemistry) abroad and through conducting and publishing studies on particular industries and natural resources (Pallares Ramírez 1952: 350–59). Its staff consisted mostly of engineers, with a small number of economists.

Nacional Financiera—the government's development bank—also hired economists, particularly to work in its Department of Financial Studies. Like the central bank (but to a somewhat lesser degree), Nacional Financiera belonged to an international organizational field of development banks. When it became necessary to negotiate with postwar multilateral institutions concerned with development, such as the World Bank and the Eximbank, Nacional Financiera upgraded its macroeconomic competence and relied on the expertise of its economists (Nacional Financiera 1994).

The Ministry of Commerce and Trade was technically in charge of policies for promoting domestic industry but in reality seems to have deferred a great deal to the demands of the Finance Ministry: the areas listed as employing economists were described as conducting studies and offering opinions, but not usually as actually formulating policies. In the ministry's Department of Economic Studies, economists were to conduct studies so that the department could "offer opinions" on which industries needed protection and exemption from taxes or in other policy areas (such as agriculture or mining). The Bureau of Prices, which also employed economists, seems to have been endowed with more responsibility and discretion, since officials in this area not only carried out studies but actually made decisions in such areas as price-fixing and the distribution of scarce products. Other areas employing economists in the Ministry of Industry and Commerce were the Bureau of Statistics, where officials put together studies of industries, indexes, and tendencies, and the Bureau of Commerce, which carried out studies on imports and exports (Pallares Ramírez 1952: 335–37).

Graduates and even students of the UNAM School of Economics in the 1940s and '50s faced a wide variety of employment possibilities, but they were almost all in the public sector. In addition to the areas listed above, economists found employment within the public financial intermediation bureaucracy (e.g., in the National Urban Mortgage and Public Works Bank, within the industrial development bank, the Agricultural Credit Bank, etc.), at the Ministry of Communication and Public Works, and in several other branches of government.[6] Pallares Ramírez's (1952) first-hand account of the first decades of the UNAM School of Economics only lists one private-sector firm—the National Bank of Mexico—as an employer of economists (pp. 361–63). And UNAM economics professor Moisés de la Peña wrote in 1932 that "there are some [graduates in economics] in the service of two Ministries, a single one in the States, a half dozen in the banks and none in private business" (De la Peña 1942: 33).

CONCLUSION

During its first decades of existence, Mexican economics was probably the single most state-centered profession within a system of state-centered professions. The founders of Mexico's first economics program were mostly government officials and were all active participants in the project of building state institutions in the aftermath of the Mexican revolution. At a time when economics in the United States was dominated by academic practitioners (cf. Yonay 1994 and 1998), the figure of the full-time, academic economist did not exist in Mexico. The reason was simple: the resources to support such academicians did not exist. Mexican economists were trained at the public UNAM, for tuitions so low as to be essentially free. The self-taught professors who instructed them received only nominal payment, and used morning and evening classes to recruit promising young economists to government ministries. Mexican economics resembled the Continental more than the Anglo-American model.

Throughout the developing world—but particularly in Latin America— there are similar examples of economics professions that were born and raised in the shelter of interventionist governments. Chile's first economics program was founded at the public University of Chile during the Depression, shortly after the Chilean government began to assume a new activist role in confronting the economic crisis; its first graduates went to work for the government (Escobar Cerda 1953: 836). Although Argentina's first economics program was founded in 1913, it was not until the 1930s—with the increasing role of economists within an activist government—that the program took off (Dagnino 1989: 195–97). In India—an Asian nation with a postwar policy framework broadly resembling that of Latin America—economists similarly rose to become the vanguard of government-sponsored economic development; after independence in 1947, there was an influx of economists into the Indian government "in the belief that this would make a significant contribution to the stimulation of economic development of the country" (Ambirajan 1981: 98). The link between developmentalist states and professional economics in these countries suggests that in developing countries with a tradition of weaker, less activist government, we would find professional economics either absent or less developed. This appears to have occurred in Peru, which lacked the strong developmentalist state of the larger Latin American countries in the 1930s and '40s. As a result, the Peruvian economics profession was not truly developed until the 1960s and '70s (Conaghan 1998).

An interesting feature of Mexico's first economics program was that the year of its founding was also the year of a global economic transformation of tremendous historical importance. The collapse of international financial markets in the early 1930s ushered in an era in which Latin American governments could be relatively unconcerned with the demands of international creditors, after the evaporation of foreign loans and a rash of defaults. This meant than many of the orthodox economic measures endorsed by foreign creditors and "money doctors" could be abandoned, as governments struggled to recover economic growth during a time of global depression. Mexican finance minister Pani's abandonment of the gold standard and promotion of countercyclical measures in the early 1930s is only one example of many such experimentations throughout Latin America (Díaz Alejandro 1984; Cárdenas 1994).

Mexican economics was founded on the cusp of these transformations. Therefore, it seems that a range of "isomorphic" processes played a role in the formation of this new profession. From the very beginning, Mexican economics was an internationally oriented discipline, designed to train future government bureaucrats in the latest and most up-to-date policymaking techniques. In part, demand for these techniques reflected the Mexican government's need to satisfy international creditors. As Zebadúa (1994) observes, the modernization of Mexico's Finance Ministry during the 1920s was directly related to these external pressures. No matter how salubrious the effects of these pressures may have been for Mexican economic policymaking, this presents a clear example of "coercive isomorphism" (DiMaggio and Powell 1983).

On the other hand, the deglobalization of financial markets after 1929 gave Mexican policymakers much more leeway in conducting economic policy. State institution-builders like Jesús Silva Herzog and Daniel Cosío Villegas remained committed to bringing international standards to Mexican economic policymaking (and Mexican economics). However, in the absence of external pressures, this affinity for international models reflected a more voluntary, "world-cultural" form of isomorphism, based on a culture common to economic policymakers around the world. Furthermore, after the 1920s, Mexican economics came to reflect the increased importance of national over international policy agendas. During the 1930s, the Mexican state's most important project was not the satisfaction of international creditors but rather the construction of a popular base among peasants and workers. As we will see in the following chapter, this environment helped incubate an economics program with strongly leftist and populist overtones.

Chapter 3

MARXISM, POPULISM, AND
PRIVATE-SECTOR REACTION: THE SPLITTING
OF MEXICAN ECONOMICS

Economic backwardness, Gerschenkron observes, is congenial to potent ideologies:

> To break through the barriers of stagnation in a backward country, to ignite the imaginations of men, and to place their energies in the service of economic development, a stronger medicine is needed than the promise of better allocation of resources or even of the lower price of bread. . . . What is needed to remove the mountains of routine and prejudice is faith—faith, in the words of Saint-Simon, that the golden age lies not behind but ahead of mankind. (1962: 24)

Thus, many of the individuals who reached positions of influence during the reign of Napoleon III in France were not Bonapartists but Saint-Simonian socialists. Saint-Simon, as Gerschenkron hastens to point out, was not a radical but did uphold such tenets of socialism as the abolition of inheritance and the establishment of a planned economy. Thus, it was worthy of note that this ideology coexisted with nineteenth-century French industrialization and not the teachings of Smith and Ricardo. In later nineteenth-century Russia, Marxism played a similar role of stoking the faith of a society in the throes of a traumatic development process (Gerschenkron 1962: 25–26).

The complexities of the ideology of the Mexican revolution from its initiation in 1910 through the revolutionary revival of Cárdenas have been the subject of many scholarly studies that cannot be discussed fully here. For the purposes of this analysis it is important to note that the institution founded in 1929 to provide an expanding policymaking bureaucracy in Mexico—the School of Economics at the UNAM—was neither classically liberal nor pragmatically developmentalist. Rather, from the very beginning a critical mass of its founders and professors were individuals with sympathies for Marxist and other socialist ideas. These ideological leanings made sense given the school's dense ties to the state, and the state's corporatist base and developmentalist commitments.

However, the Marxism of the National School of Economics was not "revolutionary socialism" in Marx's sense of the term but rather "the socialism of the Mexican revolution." The economy that emerged after the Mexican revolution was mixed: essentially capitalist but with a strong role for the government in economy and society. Important figures in the foundation of UNAM economics, such as Narciso Bassols and Jesús Silva Herzog, apparently saw little contradiction between their positions as high-level government officials in this government, on the one hand, and their Marxist rhetoric, on the other. The Mexican economics profession of the 1930s and '40s found its only constituency in the state, and the state was necessarily concerned both with its legitimacy—founded in large measure through the incorporation of peasant and worker groups—and with the task of pulling Mexico out of economic backwardness. Marxist ideology may not have been precisely tailored to meet the needs of such a country, but it provided a powerful set of ideas to inspire individuals involved in this project: in Gerschenkron's words, it was a source of faith.

Meanwhile, this ideological framework that was so appealing to Mexican state-builders was viewed with misgiving by actors from the private sector—the other potential constituency of Mexican economics. Capitalists saw little that they could use and a great deal that they did not like in the brand of economics espoused at the National School of Economics. As a result, the first split within the Mexican economics profession occured in the 1940s, with the foundation of the Mexican Technological Institute (ITM)—which would later become the autonomous ITAM, the notorious bastion of "neoliberal" ideology in the 1980s and '90s. This chapter discusses the ideas available to the UNAM School of Economics, the ways these ideas were utilized, and the origins of the foundation of the ITM.

Comparative Perspectives on Social Science

Like other professions, the social sciences are structured by national institutional contexts and the professional constituencies to which they give rise. In general, the existing literature suggests that social sciences sponsored by strong, centralized states turn out rather differently than those of the more decentralized American system. For example, in late-developing Germany, the state took on a direct role in the promotion of economic development and the reproduction of professional expertise. German universities produced social science and other professionals to staff government bureaucracies, and were subject to the regulative authority of the *Kurator*, a direct employee of the state (Wittrock and Wagner 1996: 105–6; Shils 1982: 439). As a result of such direct state intervention, the Ger-

man professoriate became a "major partner in the national power structure," and the German academy fostered interventionist and even socialist
theoretical perspectives congenial to the priorities of the state, as in the
Association for Social Policy (Rueschemeyer and Van Roseem 1996: 137).

Moreover, the evidence suggests that in countries with more statist traditions, social scientists often had more leeway to advocate not only
"from . . . the point of view of the state" (in the words of Weir and Skocpol 1985) but also on behalf of particular social groups supporting the
government in power, such as workers or peasants. For example, in Sweden and Norway during the 1930s, economists of the Stockholm and Oslo
schools advocated interventionist and redistributive policies within social
democratic parties (Berg 1981; Weir and Skocpol 1985).

In the United States, on the other hand, a different government role in
economy and society generated a less activist sort of social scientist.
Whereas in the nineteenth and twentieth centuries the French and German
states tended to intervene directly in the economy through such means as
government ownership of industry, the American state wielded its influence over economic development through institutional means such as the
development and enforcement of systems of property rights (Campbell
and Lindberg 1990). This distinctively American government role in the
economy had direct consequences for the professionalization of American
social science, which in contrast to Germany could not benefit from the
employment possibilities afforded by a large and centralized civil service.
Rather, American social sciences became university-based professions
with an arm's-length relationship with the federal government (Schweber
1996: 149).

The universities providing an institutional home for American social
science historically exhibited important differences from their Continental counterparts. For reasons that may ultimately have been political, economic, or even cultural, the Continental tradition of the "national university" never took hold in the United States.[1] American colleges and
universities were autonomous corporations subject to government charter
(Shils 1982: 446). Thus, the American government's role with respect to
universities was analogous to its role in professions: one of legal certification rather than direct intervention. Private universities funded by tuition,
fees, and private endowments traditionally dominated elite higher education in the United States (although state universities now account for a
larger proportion of graduates). Even the state universities that proliferated after the Civil War always had a strong component of private funding
(particularly through tuitions).[2] Moreover, they were governed by independent boards of trustees, overseers, or regents and were seldom subject
to direct control by state governments. Unlike German professors, the
professors of American state universities were not civil servants, since they

were generally governed by internal university policy rather than by the authority of the state (Shils 1982: 447–52).

The institutional separation between the state and social science in the United States had a profound and ongoing effect on the role of American social scientists in social and economic policy. For one thing, the "core" of the economics profession in the United States has tended to be composed of academicians rather than civil servants. In his survey of a sample of American economics articles between 1920 and 1960, Backhouse (1998) finds that the vast majority of authors were affiliated with academic institutions (except during the Second World War, when cadres of prestigious academic economists were recruited to work for the American government) (p. 95). A survey of American economics and econometrics doctorates between 1960 and 1974 shows that more than 68% intended to work in academia, as opposed to 5.6 and 7.5% in the federal and state governments, respectively (Coats, ed., 1992). Economics in the United States has been a remarkably successful social science in recent decades not because of its role in training civil servants but rather because of its role as a prebusiness degree, which makes economics an unusually popular social science major (Klamer and Colander 1990: 197).[3]

For another thing, there is evidence suggesting that the institutional logic of American social science has tended to produce more apolitical or conservative disciplines than those that developed elsewhere. The work of historian Mary Furner (1975) shows that the institutional separation between American social science and the state led to the emergence of a national economics profession that was unusually dependent on fostering an appearance of objectivity and neutrality. Appearing to be a neutral, "scientific" discipline helped economists avoid threatening the interests of the trustees of elite private universities in which they worked. After a series of highly publicized academic freedom cases in the late nineteenth century (as a result of which several prominent economists were fired), American economics became a notably quiet and scholarly discipline. It was led by economists who, "Either because partisanship violated their principles or because it was not compatible with recruitment and advancement in the profession . . . avoided letting themselves become too closely identified with any controversial program" (Furner 1975: 159). Harry Johnson (1977) similarly observes that McCarthyism during the 1950s helped make American economics into an unusually mathematical and scientistic discipline. Economists concerned with preserving their jobs learned "habits of self-censorship which directed economists toward research and toward theorizing about how the American economic system worked and could be made to work better and away from dangerous thoughts about the justice of the system and the possibility of revolutionizing it" (p. 98).

The tendency for American economists to be apolitical or conservative has been noted by a number of authors, and for different historical periods. According to Barber (1981), during the 1930s, most mainstream academic economists[4] in the United States were so unsympathetic to interventionist policies that economists played no role in the policy elite of Roosevelt's first New Deal administration (although a few young rebel economists came in the second). Stryker (1990) shows how more progressive and interventionist social scientists were systematically selected out of the New Deal bureaucracies, concluding that "the U.S. welfare state selects out scientific expertise that tends to undermine markets, market ideology, and U.S. capitalism" (p. 704). Stryker contends that the political weakness of U.S. labor made it difficult for progressive social scientists to find a permanent institutional home in government bureaucracies.

In summary, different professional constituencies at the national level historically tended to produce economics disciplines with divergent institutional bases—and even divergent ideologies—in different national contexts. With these connections between professionalization and social structure in mind, it is easy to see why professional economics in Mexico and other developing countries would tend to resemble Continental rather than the U.S.-style disciplines. In many Latin American nations during the twentieth century, the state assumed a leading role in both economic development and the financing of higher education through national universities. Mexican economics evolved within such a statist framework, and was therefore more heavily politicized—and more congenial to leftist ideology—than economics in the United States.

The Legacy of the Mexican Revolution in the 1930s

The UNAM economics program was founded and consolidated during a politically tumultuous time, as the Mexican state was formed out of the multiple forces that had contended for power during the revolution. While reactionary forces fought to reestablish the old regime, revolutionary military and political leaders struggled among themselves until 1935 as to who would control the country. Rather than overlooking the demands of peasants and workers, as Porfirio Díaz had done, the new government utilized them in the service of state formation. Government leaders used populist or even socialist-sounding rhetoric in their speeches. Diego Rivera and other artists from the Mexican school of mural painting were contracted by the government to paint public buildings with images of revolutionary peasants and workers. The revolutionary Regional Confederation of Mexican Workers (CROM in Spanish) was created, and organized labor was co-opted through government support of strikes; at the same time, the government established centralized peasant organizations and implemented limited land reforms (Hamilton 1982: 73). In 1929, the National Revolutionary Party (PNR) was established to incorporate different regional and partisan interests under the umbrella of the Sonoran regime.

Around the time of the establishment of the UNAM School of Economics, however, the Mexican revolution seemed to be in a period of stagnation and decline. Known as the *maximato*, the period between 1925 and 1934 was when the revolutionary general and strongman Plutarco Elias Calles occupied the presidency and subsequently controlled three successive presidencies from behind the scenes. In 1930, Calles declared the revolutionary land reform—especially the collectively owned *ejidos*—to be a failure, and efforts were made to end such reform, along with labor agitation (Knight 1991: 247).

In 1934, the presidency of Lázaro Cárdenas arrived to breathe new life into the revolution by taking the old Sonoran strategy of mass mobilization to new extremes. Cárdenas conducted an unprecedented and extensive presidential campaign in which he traveled around the country, even to the most remote areas, listening to the complaints of ordinary people. As president, Cárdenas took the side of workers against owners in strikes, which increased in number as a result: whereas there were only 13 recorded strikes in Mexico in 1933, in 1935 this number rose to 642 (Knight 1991: 251). Meanwhile, he renewed the revolutionary promise of land reform: more peasants got land under the Cárdenas administration than under all previous administrations combined, and more than twice as much land was distributed. Moreover, unlike his predecessors, Cárdenas's reforms touched the landholdings of large commercial owners, and stressed the collectively owned *ejidos* rather than small property-holding (Hamilton 1982: 177).

The Cárdenas presidency was better known for its political than its economic accomplishments, and economic policymaking was not at the center of President Cárdenas's agenda. The worst effects of the Depression had already been mitigated by expansionary monetary policies during the previous administration. The Cárdenas administration—like many governments around the world in the 1930s—recognized the need for government intervention in the economy and investment in infrastructure (Cárdenas 1994: 74). But Cárdenas was more concerned with the distributive issues that garnered political support. As Knight (1991) puts it, the regime "appreciated that raising wages would deepen the domestic market to the advantage of some sectors of industry. Yet this Keynesian approach cannot be seen as the raison d'être of Cardenista labor policy" (p. 273).

54   CHAPTER THREE

Perhaps Cárdenas's most important contribution to Mexican economic development was his reinforcement of Mexican political stability
and corporatism, established under Calles, which laid the groundwork
for thirty years of spectacular economic expansion. These years witnessed
the transition from personalistic government by a strongman to institutional rule. Unlike Calles, Cárdenas did not attempt to run the country
from behind the scenes after his term was over in 1940, and after that
time the predictable machinery of single-party politics (relatively) peace-
fully effected the transition from one government to another every six
years. The official party established by Calles (the PNR) was renamed the
Party of the Mexican Revolution (PRM) in 1938, and for the first time
officially incorporated labor, peasants, and "popular" sectors. From
1940 onward, the bureaucratic machinery of the government would administer and channel workers' demands, thus providing future administrations with an important tool for capitalist expansion through the control of labor.[5]

Political priorities notwithstanding, the Cárdenas regime left some important legacies for state intervention in the Mexican economy. Cárdenas's nationalization of the railroad (1937) and petroleum (1938) industries, which served the short-term goal of mobilizing labor and nationalist
support, established important forms of direct state intervention in the
economy, as did the creation of the National Electricity Commission in
1938. Like Roosevelt in the United States, Cárdenas embarked on an am-
bitious program of public works for the production of infrastructure,
which had the simultaneous effects of creating jobs and stimulating industry; these projects were financed through deficit spending supported by
the central bank (Mosk 1954: 59). During the last years of the Cárdenas
presidency, the foundations of industrial development policies through
tax and tariff exemptions were laid (González 1981: 266–67). Moreover,
Cárdenas continued the institution-building tradition of his Sonoran predecessors. In 1935 the National Agricultural and National Ejidal Banks
were established for the financing of small property-holders and collective
farmers, respectively. That same year, the central bank was strengthened,
becoming the sole emitter of banknotes and endowed with controls over
private banks (Ayala Espino 1988: 197). In 1937, the National Bank of
Foreign Commerce was established to help finance the production of ex-
portable goods, and the Banco Obrero was created for the financing of
cooperatives and small artisanal businesses.

These undoubtedly important contributions to Mexican economic
expansion, however, were not perceived as such during the Cárdenas period and went largely unappreciated by the economic elites who stood
to benefit most from growth. The Sonorans' populist rhetoric had made

business groups nervous, but Cárdenas's stronger language and willingness to support workers against their employers made them furious.

The opposition that *cardenismo* generated among capitalists was mirrored among certain groups of university students. The National University (which became the autonomous UNAM in 1929) had been, like most Latin American public universities of the period, a training ground for elites. It had first been inaugurated during the dying days of the old regime (in 1910), when many students were supporters of Porfirio Díaz (Mabry 1982: 7). More than twenty years later, conservative student groups were a powerful force within the UNAM. When labor leader and public education official Vicente Lombardo called for Marxism to be the "only ideological basis for university teaching" in 1933, the response was a strike by conservative law students (Mabry 1982: 111–20). The years 1934–40 saw numerous struggles between leftist and rightist student factions.

Where did the newly established economics program at the UNAM fall within this debate? There is no readily available historical evidence documenting the participation of economics students in the movement against socialist education; this may be due the fact that the economics program was so small that their participation caused little notice. However, there is contrasting evidence of economics students favoring the teaching of socialist ideas. During the conservative administration of Ortíz Rubio (1930–32), government spies were sent into the classroom of Professor Federico Bach, a known Marxist, who was consequently expelled from the country for being a "communist agitator." This event created a "violent, rebellious climate" among students—apparently among Marxist students, who blamed non-Marxist students and professors for Bach's expulsion—and a delegation from the university subsequently convinced President Ortíz Rubio to let Bach return from his exile in Cuba (Pallares Ramírez 1952: 82).

Although the UNAM economics program was a mere appendage of the Law School until the official foundation of the School of Economics in 1935, there seem to have been important ideological differences between economics students, on the one hand, and those merely studying law, on the other. In particular, it appears that while UNAM law students were famous for their right-wing protests against the government, at least some UNAM economics students were defenders of the left. This political difference is logical given the substantially different origins of the two schools: in contrast to the Law School, which had existed since before the revolution, the School of Economics at the UNAM was the creation of individuals committed to revolutionary ideals, as well as to their own futures within a growing state economic policymaking bureaucracy. Economics at the UNAM, in other words, was created by and for the revolutionary state.

MEXICAN POLITICAL IDEOLOGY IN THE 1930S

The populist ideological climate that prevailed in Mexico during the 1930s was partly made possible by the economic deglobalization that accompanied the Great Depression and the Second World War. Only a decade or two earlier, Latin American governments had been borrowing heavily on international financial markets. When debts needed to be refinanced, many of these countries invited internationally renowned economics experts like Princeton economist Edwin Kemmerer to help diagnose their economic ills and recommend policy reforms in keeping with the neoclassical wisdom of the day—such as cutting taxes and government spending, returning to the gold standard, and establishing independent central banks. The possibility of ongoing foreign loans made adherence to neoclassical orthodoxy a relatively acceptable price to pay, since increased access to foreign loans could be obtained by governments willing to take the harsh medicine prescribed by the "money doctors" (Eichengreen 1994).

After the global economic crisis of the late 1920s, however, developing countries could neither continue to finance their debt nor hope to regain access to international financial resources. International markets for Third World products dried up, and domestic currency devaluations and economic crises made foreign imports prohibitively expensive. Economic isolation meant that there was no longer any benefit to be gained from implementing neoclassical prescriptions: governments could no longer hope to be rewarded for orthodox policies by being given access to foreign loans. The result was a freedom to experiment with ideologies and policies that would have been unthinkable only decades earlier, an extreme example of which was Cárdenas's nationalization of British oil fields. Mexico's first economics program was institutionalized during this period, and it bore the mark of a particular historical conjuncture during which the international resource dependence of Mexico and other developing countries was extremely low.

Various factors contributed to the appeal of Marxist rhetoric and ideas in Mexico in the 1930s. The temporal overlap of the Mexican and Russian revolutions notwithstanding, there was little public discussion of Marxist ideas in Mexico before 1910, and although socialist ideas became fashionable among intellectuals during the revolution, these ideas "concealed what were essentially populist and statist positions. Use of the term [socialism] reflected the increasingly widely held view that the revolutionary state's supreme goal was to establish social peace and collective well-being by enforcing class equilibrium" (Carr 1992: 15).

Indeed, a great deal of the socialist rhetoric used in Mexico during the revolution and afterward was employed in the service of a corporatist and interventionist state attempting to galvanize support among workers and peasants. The use of such language by Mexican political leaders was a postrevolutionary tradition that reached its height during the Cárdenas presidency. The campaign for "socialist education," originally supported by President Calles as a means of breaking the power of the Church in primary and secondary education, was continued more vigorously under Cárdenas, whose Six Year Plan included a commitment to education based on "the socialist doctrine sustained by the Mexican Revolution" (Knight 1991: 265). During the Cárdenas administration, socialist realism became culturally fashionable in Mexico, and controls on leftist publications were lifted, resulting in a great boom of Marxist literature (Knight 1991: 265; Loyo [Engracia] 1991: 170).

Socialist rhetoric and ideas in Mexico were made even more fashionable by the international intellectual climate of the 1930s. The economic collapse of the early 1930s on the one hand, and the rise of fascism on the other, seemed to indicate one of two choices (in the words of Strachey in his book on economic crises): either communism or barbarism. As a Mexican economic historian of the period put it, "The fashionable prophecy among numerous intellectual groups and politicians of the western world was at the time the imminent fall of capitalism, the fatal fulfillment of the prophecy of Marx" (Krauze 1985: 312). Economic orthodoxy seemed to have been utterly disproved, and capitalist democracy seemed a contradiction in terms. This view naturally resonated among Mexican state-builders, whose article of faith was that the state needed to intervene to promote economic prosperity and social peace: much of the appeal of Marxism in Mexico in the 1930s represented "a confusion between socialism and statization of the economy that would only be cleared up much later" (Villegas 1993: 110). Thus, the Marxism of Mexican economics in the 1930s represented not a call to revolution but a recognition of the defects of capitalism and the need for poor countries like Mexico to take a more active approach to solving social and economic problems than those prescribed by laissez-faire economics. Or as one of the school's first professors recalls, Marxism prevailed "because Mexico was a very poor country, and we thought that it would be the salvation of the nation" (interview, Alanís Patiño 9/13/95).

While perhaps not the most appropriate ideology for training economists to be bureaucrats within a developmentalist state, Marxism was the only nonorthodox economic theory widely available in Mexico in the 1930s. Milder interventionist theories, such as Keynesianism, were not generally known or understood: a Mexican translation of Keynes's *Gen-*

eral Theory did not appear until 1942.[6] The United Nations Economic
Commission for Latin America (ECLA), with its prescriptions for inward-
oriented development through state intervention and import substitution,
would not be founded until 1947. Marxism, in addition to its virtue of
being internationally fashionable, was a potent theoretical framework for
critiquing the defects of free-market capitalism.

The Fondo de Cultura Económica

One of the problems facing the first economics students at the UNAM
was the lack of reading material in the field, which reflected a more general scarcity in the late 1920s and early 1930s. The economics student
necessarily had to read foreign authors, but most economics literature
was in English, which the majority of students could not read (Cosío Villegas 1977: 143). In the 1920s, the majority of the books read in Mexico
were published abroad, since like most other Latin American countries,
México had not developed a real publishing industry. Mexico had a low
population density and a rate of illiteracy commensurate with its level of
economic backwardness—61.5% of the population over the age of ten
in 1930 (Loyo [Engracia] 1988: 259; INEGI 1994: 117). Added to this
difficulty on the demand side was the high cost of paper on the supply
side, a by-product of the high level of protection of the private paper
industry (Loyo [Engracia] 1988: 251). As a result of these preceding factors, the books of interest to an economist were both few and prohibitively expensive.

By the early 1930s, growing radicalism in Mexico was having a favorable impact on the availability of left-wing literature, and the Universidad
Obrera (Workers' University) published a translation of *Capital* and other
works by Marx and Marxist authors (Loyo [Engracia] 1988: 271). But it
was not until the establishment of the Fondo de Cultura Económica in
1934 that the barriers to economics and other social science education in
Mexico truly began to disappear. The Fondo was established specifically
to help remedy the deficiency of published materials in economics; not
surprisingly, its founding members were mostly the same individuals involved in founding UNAM economics, including Jesús Silva Herzog, Eduardo Villaseñor, and Daniel Cosío Villegas. It is also not surprising to
find that different branches of the government economic policymaking
bureaucracy provided the initial financing for the Fondo: the Banco de
México donated ten thousand pesos, the Finance Ministry donated five
thousand, and the National Mortgage and Public Works Bank four thousand (Chumacero 1980: 10).[7] The Fondo also benefitted from the creation
of the Paper Production and Importation Company under Cárdenas,

which received a government subsidy and tax and tariff exemptions (Loyo [Engracia] 1988: 273).

The Fondo's most fundamental mission was not to publish original works—although it came increasingly to do so—but to publish much-needed translations of works from other languages. This the Fondo accomplished through both books and its *Trimestre Económico*, the first economics journal in Latin America. The first two editions of the *Trimestre* in 1934 contained translations of recent articles by Irving Fisher and Keynes, lists of recent books to be published in economics internationally, and reviews of several such works. The first two directors of the *Trimestre* were Daniel Cosío Villegas and Eduardo Villaseñor. Both Cosío and Villaseñor, it should be recalled, had received some economics training abroad, and both had been instrumental both in the founding of the National School of Economics and in the modernization of the Banco de México. Originally without an official editorial board, the first issue of the *Trimestre* had on its masthead a list of fifty-eight "collaborators." These included figures associated with the foundation and early years of the National School of Economics (among them the more conservative figures, Miguel Palacios Macedo and Manuel Gómez Morín), populist labor leader Vicente Lombardo Toledano, and American scholar Frank Tannenbaum.

The first two translations of books to emerge from the Fondo in 1935 were William P. Sheah's *Silver Dollars* and Harold J. Laski's tome on the life and thought of Marx. Both provide a fair representation—both in form and in content—of the sort of reading probably required of early students at the National School of Economics.[8] Both were extremely brief (around one hundred pages) and summarized a great deal of information in a short space. The first generations of economics students, as we saw in the previous chapter, tended to have full-time jobs in the government (according to Camp [1975], the majority had such jobs) and did not have much time to read extensively; such summaries suited the needs of "taxi students." Indeed, in an interview, a former student of the National School of Economics in the early 1940s recalled that students did not read original works but rather relied on summaries presented in lectures (interview, Meyer L'Epée 7/15/96).

Both Sheah and Laski were also representative of the sort of theoretical perspective current at the National School of Economics during these years. Sheah's work, in addition to summarizing useful information about the history of monetary policy and the banking system, is a work dedicated to overturning the economic orthodoxy of the gold standard—a popular cause in Mexico in the mid-1930s, which had benefited greatly from Pani's expansionary monetary policies. The ideology of Laski's work on Marx is obvious, and requires no further elaboration. Together, the two works exemplified the interventionist and Marxist-tinged nature of economics as it was taught in Mexico in the early 1930s. Among other important early translations from the Fondo were Birnie's *Economic History of Europe* (1936), Strachey's *Nature of Crises* (1939—also a Marxist work), and Scott's *Elementary Course in Economics* (1941).

THE NATIONAL SCHOOL OF ECONOMICS IN THE 1930S AND '40S

One of the defining characteristics of the National School of Economics during this period was its teaching of "social" economics. As one of the first professors at the school put it:

> This new profession of economist has . . . a high and noble social significance . . . because of the nature of the facts the economist necessarily has to think not at the level of individual problems and interests, but rather at the level of social interests and problems, attempting always to find scientific solutions and means for reaching these solutions in society. (Loyo [Gilberto] 1949: 394)

The notion that the economist needed to think in terms of solving larger social problems was similar to the ideas promoted by the institutionalist school in the United States at the time (although it contrasted with the views of neoclassical economists) (Yonay 1998). The idea of economist as social reformer was particularly characteristic of the thinking of Jesús Silva Herzog, the most influential founder of economics at the UNAM, who wrote that "the economist without social preoccupations . . . is a mutilated being who moves in a narrow space, without wings on his thought and without constructive and creative capacity" (Silva Herzog 1967: 35). "Social economics," moreover, supposed that a well-rounded economist should have some understanding of history, philosophy, and the social sciences, rather than confine himself to measurements and mathematical formulas: as Silva Herzog pointed out, "political economy is not a mathematical science, but rather a social science closely related to sociology and political science" (Silva Herzog 1967: 24–25). This philosophy would continue to characterize the school for more than half a century.

Compatible with this social philosophy at the National School of Economics were the socialist and state-interventionist ideas in vogue among Mexican intellectuals at the time. Among the required courses listed in the 1936 plan of studies for the National School of Economics were the economic and social theory of Marxism, the history of socialist doctrines, the Mexican agrarian problem, and a course called "the state in economic life"; elective courses included the history of social movements and problems of the planned economy (Pallares Ramírez 1952: 105–6). Such courses were congenial to the political and cultural environment of the Cárdenas regime (1934–40) but not so compatible with the environment of the later presidencies of Avila Camacho (1940–46) and Lucas Alemán (1946–52), both of which were friendlier to business interests and less congenial to social reforms.[9] It was probably the recognition of this change in political climate that led Jesús Silva Herzog as the school's director in 1940 to reform the plan of studies to make it more technical and less politically contentious.[10] While Silva Herzog was always known for his revolutionary rhetoric (which reportedly made his classes quite popular), he was also a pragmatist who understood that the niche that Mexican economics was destined to fill was the practical role of staffing the government bureaucracy.

This shift in emphasis notwithstanding, the leftist slant of the National School of Economics would continue throughout the coming decades. Many of its most prestigious professors, while loyal to the government and dependent on it for employment, were convinced of the efficacy of Marxism as a theoretical framework and state intervention as a practical necessity, and continued to teach in accordance with their beliefs. In a 1975 study of the graduates of the National School of Economics through 1961, Camp finds that of the fifteen most notable professors selected by interviews and published materials, eleven were leftists of some stripe; nine of these eleven "leftist" professors reached middle- to high-level government posts during their careers (Camp 1975: 140–41). During the first decade of economics at the UNAM, students with more conservative points of view had no choice but either to learn a great deal of leftist material or else to study some other discipline, since no other economics school existed in Mexico. One former student who entered the UNAM in 1946 recalled:

> Of course they taught us Marxism, but not all of us were Marxists. I remember on one exam I answered all the questions "Marx said this," and "Marx said that." The professor finally got irritated and asked, "Well, what do *you* say?" I told him I wasn't being tested on what I thought, but on what Marx thought, and he gave me a 10. (Interview, Calderón 8/23/95)[11]

My review of the seventy-five economics theses from the UNAM from the years 1934 through 1945 (see the complete results in appendix A) shows that the leftist ideology espoused within the program was essentially pragmatic and statist rather than revolutionary. Or rather, if it was revolutionary, it was the Mexican revolution and not revolutionary socialism that was extolled. The theses provide a clue as to the training and employment prospects of UNAM economists, since they represent an exercise in applied knowledge and technique. Clearly, one of the skills acquired at the

National School of Economics was the gathering and utilization of descriptive statistics: 84% of the theses utilized such statistics, and tables often occupied dozens of pages supplementing the text. Descriptive statistics could be used in different government agencies as the basis for policymaking decisions: monetary policy decisions, for example, were based on estimates of inflation constructed from price indexes. Econometric methods were apparently unknown at the School of Economics during this period, since none of the theses utilized them. Mathematical modeling as a way of expressing economic theories occurred in only seven out of seventy-five theses.

The typical thesis from 1934 to 1945 was atheoretical (only 44% of the theses had theoretical citations) and oriented toward a very specific practical problem; most made no explicit reference to normative issues, such as the efficacy of state intervention in the economy. To take a representative example, one thesis discussed the exploitation of *guayule*, a rubber-producing plant native to Mexico. The author's humble goal was "to contribute with my small effort to the knowledge of those aspects of the national economy that could be a source of wealth for my country" (Vázquez 1936: 1). After describing this product's history and geography and presenting many pages of tables concerning its production and other related statistics, the author concluded with policy recommendations for encouraging the production of guayule, through such measures as selective tax incentives. One can imagine this individual subsequently working in an administrative position in the Agricultural Credit Bank.

Theses written before the end of Cárdenas administration (1936–40) were more likely to discuss agricultural themes, whereas theses written during the subsequent Avila Camacho presidency were more oriented toward industrial themes. Several theses from the 1930s made reference to agricultural cooperatives, an important topic during the era of land redistribution to *ejidos*. An important theme appearing in the 1940s was the need for Mexico to industrialize in order to free itself from dependence on foreign imports and to become a developed country: "Industry is the motor of the contemporary economy; a country without industry is condemned to implacable imperialist exploitation" (Saavedra 1941: 11). Regardless of content, what most of the theses had in common was the same general format: an introduction, followed by descriptive statistical tables, followed by policy recommendations. The fact that policy recommendations played such an important role in the theses attests to the perceived importance of the government in solving economic problems of all sorts, from turpentine production from pines in the northern state of Durango to the film industry in Mexico City. Through such policy recommendations it is possible to gauge atheoretical theses' positions on state intervention in the economy, since some theses call for less active measures (e.g.,

TABLE 3.1
Position on State Intervention, UNAM 1934–45

	UNAM 1934–45 N (%)
Less intervention advocated	0 (0)
Existing interventions supported	30 (40)
More intervention advocated	21 (28)
No position on intervention	24 (32)
Total	75 (100)

tax incentives) and some call for more active ones (e.g., nationalization of all private industries, to take an extreme example).

More theoretically oriented theses often made explicit justifications for government intervention in the economy:

> The program of industrial development supposes . . . a necessary intervention of the state, since if it is left to the private sector to attend to it, the results will be quite unsatisfactory. (Díaz Martínez 1943: 52)

> Contemporary life poses as a categorical imperative the intervention of the State in the greater part of economic, political and social activities of nations. (Andrade Muñoz 1945: 123)

If we combine theoretical and nontheoretical positions on state interventionism (table 3.1), we find that 40% of the theses are moderately interventionist and 28% are strongly interventionist (see appendix A for category definitions), with no theses calling either implicitly or explicitly for less state intervention.

Intervention was so frequently called for because the experience of the Depression of the 1930s had made the laissez-faire prescriptions of classical economists untenable:

> Before this picture of contemporary reality, how can the orthodox economist continue to sustain his principles of stability, equilibrium, optimum use of resources, harmony of interests, self-regulation, self-adustment, etc.? If he attempts to do so, is it not at the cost of losing all contact with reality? (Botas Santos 1944: 95)

A notable theme was that capitalism was fraught with internal contradictions and defects that needed state intervention to be corrected—a rhetorical element occurring in 17% of the theses:

> In our opinion, free competition did not function effectively in the immediate past, and will be even less able to function tomorrow due, fundamentally, to the complexity of economic phenomena, to the lack of elasticity in the system, to the instability of the economic rythm, and due to multiple causes that fall outside of this study. (Salinas Lozano[12] 1944: 11)

TABLE 3.2
Most-Cited Authors, UNAM 1934–45
(Total N = 75, Theses with Theoretical Cites = 44%)

	N	%
Karl Marx	10	13.3
Adam Smith	8	10.6
Gustavo Cassel	4	5.3
David Ricardo	4	5.3
John Strachey	4	5.3
Ernst Wagemann	4	5.3
F. Antezana Paz	3	4.0
Fritz Bach	3	4.0
C. T. Eheberg	3	4.0
Gottfried Haberler	3	4.0
J. M. Keynes	3	4.0
R. Jacques Turgot	3	4.0
Alfredo Weber	3	4.0

As we will see in the following chapter, this sort of rhetoric would become even more pronounced during the 1950s, when Keynesian and developmentalist thought had a more established presence at the UNAM School of Economics.

In keeping with the spirit of the era, the writings of Marx—cited either directly or through secondary works—had a strong presence among the theses (table 3.2). Marx was the most-cited author in the theses from 1934 to 1945, and was present in over 13% of all the theses, or 30% of those with theoretical citations. However, only four (5%) of the theses used Marxist theory at the center of their analyses, and only 3 (4%) of the theses mentioned socialism approvingly, with two (about 3%) disapproving. In other words, Marxism was utilized as an analytical tool, but revolutionary socialism was very much an exception rather than a rule at the National School of Economics. In contrast, reference to the goals of the *Mexican* revolution was made in 12% of the theses.

One of the reasons why Marx was so frequently cited was most probably the lack of other available theories for explaining the problems of developing countries and prescribing active state involvement to remedy the defects of capitalism. Adam Smith was the second-most cited author, and was cited in about 11% of the theses. The explanation for the coexistence of two such seemingly unlikely companions—Marx and Smith—at the top of the list is that they were both classical authors, and therefore available to a student of economics in Mexico in the 1930s and early '40s. Keynes was cited only three times between 1939 and 1945 (the first Mexican translation of Keynes, as mentioned before, was not published until 1942). Another relatively frequently cited author was Ernst Wagemann, a heterodox Continental economist who believed in a more vigorous role for the state in the economy.

The relatively frequent citation of Marx, therefore, must be seen in historical context and not taken as an indication of convinced socialist sentiments. One indication supporting this interpretation was the combination of extravagant Marxist rhetoric with rather pedestrian prescriptions for the governments of developing countries. One thesis advocated state control of the electrical industry in dramatic language, asserting that this was "the indispensable antecedent for bringing humanity to the final stage of communism that will necessarily be the solution to the problems that periodically appear in the bourgeois structure, dragging Western culture to a disastrous fall" (Ortega Mata 1939: 4). The immediacy of the Great Depression, on the one hand, and fascism in Europe, on the other, obviously contributed to the appeal of Marxist ideas. The Fondo de Cultura Económica's translation of Strachey's Marxist work on economic crises was cited four times. Strachey interpreted the events of the 1930s as an indication that the nations of the world faced two choices:

[T]he fundamental importance of the economic discoveries of Marx lies in that only they permit us to perceive the alternatives we are confronted with. And these alternatives are, as Marx himself said, barbarism or communism. (Strachey 1939: 29)

Although this dire diagnosis of the inherent contradictions of capitalism was clearly accepted by many authors, the prescribed cure—Soviet-style communism—was clearly not. Indeed, the first thesis to be defended at the National School of Economics in 1934 discussed and compared fascist and Marxist philosophies of human welfare, and came to the conclusion that neither was applicable to the conditions of Mexico (Hornedo 1934).

The students writing theses during the first seventeen years of the economics program at the UNAM tended toward pragmatic, atheoretical approaches to specific problems. More theoretically inclined authors utilized available ideas—particularly those of Marx—to explain the problems confronted by Mexico and to prescribe solutions; the usual prescription, for both theoretical and atheoretical theses, was to call for more state involvement in the economy. Marxism, while not tailored to the immediate needs of postrevolutionary Mexico, was an available theory that took the economic and social flaws of capitalism into account. But very few authors were willing to follow Marx's and Strachey's reasoning to its logical conclusion, namely, a call for socialist revolution.

It should be emphasized that that the ideology that predominated at the National School of Economics during its first decades was neither representative of that of Mexican government officials as a whole nor imposed on the university as the "line" of the official party (as it would have been in the Soviet Union). The Mexican National University became the autonomous UNAM in 1929, which officially separated the governance of the university from the state.[13] Scholarship on the history Mexican higher education suggests that subsequently, government influence over the UNAM has been indirect rather than direct (Mabry 1982; Levy 1980). Rather, the school appears to have been a sort of institutional enclave for many of the more leftist and socially motivated government intellectuals. More conservative government officials apparently became disillusioned with the school's focus and abandoned it early on. For example, the school's abandonment by conservative professor Miguel Palacios Macedo in the early 1930s was allegedly due to an ideological dispute with Jesús Silva Herzog (interview, Sánchez Navarro 9/29/95). Manuel Gómez Morín, a decidedly nonleftist lawyer who wrote the original constitution of the Banco de México, appears to have played little part in the activities of the school after its initial foundation. Although Silva Herzog and others like him may have appeared to be in the mainstream of the ruling party during the Cárdenas years, more conservative presidencies showed that the social economists represented a single tendency within the official party of the Mexican revolution and not the party as a whole.

Thus, the National School of Economics was neither the ideological mouthpiece of the Mexican government nor even fully representative of Mexican government ideology. Nevertheless, the government constituency of Mexican economics is a key factor for explaining the leftist tone of the UNAM economics program. This was not only because leftists with ties to the government were involved in the program's foundation but, even more important, because the postrevolutionary Mexican state was a professional constituency relatively tolerant of left ideologies. Like economics in some Continental European nations, Mexican economics both argued "from the point of view of the state" and advocated on behalf of the groups that were beginning to form the corporatist base of this state. As a result, the emphasis on objectivity and neutrality familiar in American economics was replaced in Mexico by a deliberate and explicit commitment to social justice.

The structure and ideology of Mexico's first economics program reflected the underlying constituency for Mexican economics: a developmentalist government that depended on a corporatist base for its consolidation and survival. The Mexican state provided the resources supporting the nascent economics profession through two main channels. First, the Mexican government provided the university, within which economics education could take place, and the professors to teach there. Mexico's Autonomous National University has historically been institutionally bound to the state in a way that seems completely unfamiliar to contemporary American observers. In the United States, we are accustomed to an arrangement in which undergraduates pay high tuitions that are subsidized by government loans—but are essentially paid for by the future private earnings of students. Even so-called public or state universities in the United States have significant tuitions, are substantially funded through private resources, and have boards of regents in which private-sector interests are heavily represented. In contrast, tuition at the UNAM was so low as to be essentially free. The direct cost of economics education in Mexico was not paid by the students but rather by the state that provided the university infrastructure and such salaries as there were, and by the taxi professors who taught classes in the mornings or evenings for almost no pay.

A second way that the Mexican state served as a constituency for economics was through hiring and promoting the students who graduated as economists. Had the Mexican government not offered employment to economics graduates (and students), these aspiring young professionals would doubtless have studied law, engineering, or some other subject. As it was, the incentive to study economics was clear: a place in the government bureaucracy. In short, as a profession, Mexican economics owed its very existence to the Mexican government.

The Mexican private sector, on the other hand, played almost no role in financing Mexican economics during its first two decades. As one business leader who attended the UNAM Law School in the early 1930s explained, "We in the private sector, first of all, did not want Marxist elements in our administration. And second, we didn't see how an economist could help in the development of our businesses. We felt that it was natural for economists be bureaucrats, employees of the government" (interview, Sánchez Navarro 9/29/95). During the post-1940 period, Mexican businessmen were most likely to have degrees in law or engineering—not economics (Camp 1989: 67).

THE FOUNDING OF THE ITM

A recurring theme in the theses from the first decades of economics at the UNAM was the condemnation of economics as a tool for increasing private profits. One student asserted that "the knowledge of the student that comes out of the classrooms of our School to obtain the degree of Licenciado in Economics, should necessarily be directed toward the ends of the general interest rather than individual interests, as tends to occur in other professions" (Saavedra 1941: 11). Another suggested that "the economist should occupy himself exclusively with the analysis of what is rather than what ought to be. His field is theoretical argumentation, and he should not become involved in the world of business" (Botas Santos 1944: 98). In a sense, these positions made a virtue of necessity, since graduates were not trained to be of use to private-sector employers.

However, another student felt that it was important for economists to expand beyond the boundaries of the public sector:

> The economist, because of his sense of responsibility and to do honor to professional ethics, should make an effort to make his function widely known, thus directing his activities toward the resolution of economic problems, both individual and collective, through more technical application of his knowledge. (Gutiérrez 1944: 79)

Unlike the authors who glorified the dedication of the economist to the common good in government, this writer strongly criticized the absence of economists from business:

> Private businesses do not know how and why to take advantage of the knowledge of economists—which is not to be wondered at, since the economists themselves do not know for certain what they are good for; nevertheless, it is in the private economy that they can most effectively work for the progress of the country and for the cultural and social uplifting of the Mexican people, since in public life they cannot be heard due to the degenerate interests of the politicians. (Gutiérrez 1944: 9)

In a backward country such as Mexico, another author pointed out, an underdeveloped, unsophisticated private sector does not need to make use of the tools available to an economist:

> In our commercial, banking and industrial sphere, it is still considered that the degree of Licenciado in Economics has no practical application in the daily battles of business. . . . The cause of this . . . can be found in the economic conditions of the country. (Márquez Gómez 1944: 5)

Whether exalted, lamented, or simply observed, the lack of prospects for economists outside the public sector was a fact clearly perceived by students at the National School of Economics. When the private sector was mentioned in UNAM theses, it tended to be in the context of emphasizing the deficiencies of markets left unregulated. Often, the impression given by the theses was of a Mexico with little or no industry—a vast, underdeveloped wasteland, ripe for state intervention:

> Mexico is a country with a semicolonial economic structure, predominantly agricultural, with varied natural resources, but lacking in capital to exploit them. (Mekler 1942: 129)

This view of Mexico in the 1930s and early '40s was biased and not altogether true. Economic historian Steven Haber, for example, discusses the brisk growth of Mexican industry after the crisis was overcome in 1933, and points out that it was actually during the 1930s that industry became the most important contributor to the Mexican GDP: during these years, Mexico was not merely "underdeveloped" but rather "developing" in the fullest sense of the term (Haber 1989: 171).

Who were the private-sector actors at this time, and what were their relations with the government? Unfortunately, scholarly work on twentieth-century Mexico has tended to focus almost exclusively on the state rather than on the private sector, with the result that there is no complete history of the Mexican private sector available. Some partial accounts, however, can be found. Haber (1989) traces the evolution of a group of industries of Porfirian origin that were able to prosper after the revolution. Among these industries were steel and glass, both centered in the northern industrial city of Monterrey; paper, located near Mexico City; soap, in Durango; cotton textiles, mostly in Veracruz; beer, located around Mexico City, Veracruz, and Monterrey; cigarettes; and cement. Haber notes that these industries were characterized by large size and a high degree of market concentration (Haber 1989: 45–54). Another characteristic of these industries was the predominance of joint financial-industrial conglomerates, according to Haber a response to perceived risk on the part of investors (Haber 1989: 67). This phenomenon in Mexico—noted by many authors, including Maxfield (1990: 48)—makes it analytically difficult to separate the interests of these older industrialists from those of the banks, since banks and industries tended to be joined in single companies. The Porfirian capitalists were joined by newcomers in subsequent years: these included revolutionary officers who prospered in business through political connections (Hamilton 1982: 84) and firms created after the economic recovery in 1932, which were smaller and more specialized than their Porfirian counterparts (Haber 1989: 185–87).

What were the positions of Mexican capitalists with regard to the state and its economic programs? Discussions of the political positions of Mexican business groups are usually organized according to the official "chambers" that the government required all businesses with capitalization of over five hundred pesos to join beginning in 1936 (Shafer 1973: 44). For the purposes of simplification here, however (and to avoid confusing the reader with a forest of acronyms), two main groups stand out for the period discussed in this chapter: the older Porfirian industrialists, banks, and merchants, which tended to take a more conservative, antigovernment attitude; and the "new group" of smaller manufacturers formed in the 1930s and '40s, which subsequently annoyed the older industrialists with their consistently progovernment position (Shafer 1973: 59; Mosk 1954: 21–52).

The new group—which represented a small but significant force in the Mexican business community by the 1940s—stood to benefit most through expanded government protection and credit controls, and consequently came to toe the government line more generally as a way of garnering support (Vernon 1963: 167–68). Whereas the new group consequently supported the government on a wide range of issues, including land reform and labor legislation, the older, bigger industrialists were consistently wary of expanded government intervention in the economy, redistributive policies, and labor unions (Mosk 1954: 24–27). Industrialists in older industries, such as beer, were satisfied with existing arrangements and saw little to be gained through either expanded protection (since they were often dependent on foreign inputs and oriented toward exporting rather than an internal market) or credit controls (since they often had interlocking directorates with major banks), and a great deal to be lost through government support of labor agitation (Vernon 1963: 167; Mosk 1954: 25, 27).

The Cárdenas administration represented a watershed in relations between older industrialists and banks and the government. Cárdenas alienated conservative businessmen not only with his words but also with his deeds: his fiery rhetoric of "socialist education" was matched by land redistributions, the support of strikes, and expropriations of foreign property. In 1936, the policy of supporting workers against employers in strikes brought Cárdenas into conflict with Monterrey's most prominent industrial family, the Garza-Sadas; it was during this conflict that Cárdenas announced in an inflammatory speech that if employers were "tired of the social struggle," they could "turn their industries over to the workers or the government" (LaBotz 1988: 61). Meanwhile, Cárdenas's failed attempt to increase private investment through legislation led to government accusations of speculation, and bankers expressed their displeasure with the administration through large-scale capital flight (Maxfield 1990: 62).

Both older industrialists and banks subsequently participated in the foundation of institutions of higher education to provide an alternative to what they perceived as left-wing ideology at state-run universities. The Technological Institute of Monterrey (ITESM), founded by local industrialists in 1943, mainly emphasized technical fields, such as engineering and business administration. Modeled on the Massachusetts and California Institutes of Technology, the "Monterrey Tech" would not acquire an economics department until 1954 (Levy 1986: 121). Another private university, the Iberoamericana, was also founded in the 1940s, with a conservative, Catholic orientation, but the Ibero would not acquire an economics department until the 1960s.

More significant for the development of economics in Mexico was the foundation of the Mexican Cultural Association in 1946 and subsequent foundation of the Mexican Technological Institute (ITM), with economics as its centerpiece program. The association was the creation of a group of businessmen who were explicitly interested in providing an alternative to what they perceived as the leftist slant of the UNAM. The institutions listed as founding partners of the Mexican Cultural Association included seven major Mexican banks, the central bank, and several Monterrey firms, including the Moctezuma beer company and the Monterrey Iron and Steel Smelting Company. The first board of directors of the association included businessmen, bankers, and individuals with careers in both private and public finance.[14]

The president of the association, from its founding to his death in 1967, was Raúl Bailleres, a banker who founded Crédito Minero (later Banco Cremi), the first bank in Mexico to specialize in the financing of mining operations. A self-taught businessman with no formal academic training, Bailleres also presided over a financial group with controlling interests in the Monterrey-based Moctezuma beer company and the department store chain Palacio de Hierro ("Raúl Bailleres" 1988: 6). Another prominent director of the association was Aníbal de Iturbide, who became director of the Banco Nacional de México in 1945, and director of Banco Comercial Mexicano in 1955 ("Aníbal de Iturbide" 1988: 8). Aaron Sáenz, another founding member of the association, was a sugar-processing magnate who had made his fortune through political connections acquired during the revolution, and who served in various important positions during the *maximato*, including minister of education (1930) and minister of industry and commerce (1930–31). Sáenz was known for his close ties to the conservative Monterrey business groups and was also president of Banco Azucarero, a bank specializing in investment in the sugar industry, which would later become the Banco de Comercio e Industria (Hamilton 1982: 87, 89).

Luis Montes de Oca and Carlos Novoa were members of the association's first board of directors with careers in both public and private finance. Montes de Oca was an accountant who had been minister of finance from 1927 until 1932 and was well known for his role in the external debt negotiatioins in 1930. He was later director of the Banco de México from 1935 to 1940, and he subsequently retired from public life to a career as a private banker. Montes de Oca was the founding member with the most significant ties to the world of Mexican intellectuals, and it was through him that the ITM was able to recruit Miguel Palacios Macedo—who allegedly left the National School of Economics because of its leftist bias—to teach at the ITM (Negrete 1988: 10). Novoa's career was in this sense the inverse of Montes de Oca's: he began as a private banker who became president of the Mexican Bankers' Association (ABM) in 1936 and was director of the central bank (Banco de México) from 1946 until 1952.

A 1988 interview with Aníbal Iturbide leaves no doubt as to the purpose of the Mexican Cultural Association and the school it created:

> [In 1946] *cardenista* ideology, in our opinion mistaken, was still very much in effect. The ideas of the government of General Cárdenas still had an important influence in the ideological development of Mexican life and politics, which to us seemed most unfortunate for the the search for a balanced development of the country . . . we thought that to encourage the industrial development of Mexico we had to try to change people's mentality, because it was predominantly a socialist, leftist mentality, which is what predominated in the political sphere. . . . This was essentially the reason that impelled us to create the Mexican Technological Institute, having as its goal the creation of a School of Economics from which would graduate the men who would in the future manage both the private and public economies of Mexico. . . .
>
> The idea began to take shape during the government of General Lázaro Cárdenas, when we saw that his policies did not coincide with what we thought.
>
> We believed that with the *cardenista* ideology in full effect there did not exist sufficient encouragement for the investment of the capital that would initiate the process of transformation of an agricultural-mining country to an industrial one. . . . The School of Engineering was discarded because we arrived at the conclusion that we could not be efficient if we tried to include too many branches. We decided on three or four, giving preference always to the School of Economics, because in our opinion it was the base upon which the future of Mexico would turn. (Negrete 1988: 9–10).

The "*cardenista*," state interventionist ideology criticized by Iturbide and his fellow members of the Asociación was clearly associated with the UNAM School of Economics. An article in the March 15, 1946, edition of the magazine *Tiempo* quoted one of the ITM's founders (whose identity was left unspecified) as saying, "We need liberal economists, not contaminated with state interventionism and who defend our interests," and criticizing the National School of Economics: "the National University and its School of Economics, sunk in permanent disorder and . . . possessed of a statist orientation, cannot guarantee the formation of well-trained technicians, whom banks and private businesses can trust" ("Economistas" 1988: 13–14).

These plans to create a competing school of economics alarmed administrators at the UNAM, leading UNAM rector Gilberto Loyo to write a letter to the Asociación's cofounder Carlos Novoa attempting to dissuade him from the project:

[O]ur School . . . is not made up of fanatical individuals of the extreme left, but rather economists that know their science. . . .even though there exist among our students, graduates, and professors, as is obvious, some people of the extreme left, this small number of people do not give the institution a sectarian tone, and have never used their classrooms to make propaganda (Loyo [Gilberto] 1946a).

On July 3, Loyo spoke to a meeting of the Mexican Bankers' Club about why it would be unwise to start a new school of economics (Loyo [Gilberto] 1946b). These efforts notwithstanding, the ITM began classes that same year, with 22 students attending.[15] While this number of students seems rather small to have constituted a threat to the National School of Economics, it should be considered that the latter had a total of only 381 students, 122 of them in their first year in 1946 (UNAM 1981: 257). The ongoing influence of the Mexican Cultural Association in the trajectory of the ITM (later the autonomous ITAM) would be felt through its power to appoint the school's rector for an indefinite term (Levy 1986: 133).

CONCLUSION

The newly minted profession of economics in Mexico was strongly shaped by the global historical context of the Great Depression, during which the Mexican state turned its attention from the satisfaction of international creditors—an issue of great importance in the 1920s—and toward the mobilizing of domestic support. Particularly during the Cárdenas presidency, the state that emerged was one that tolerated or even endorsed leftist ideology. This trend was reflected both in the first publications of the Fondo de Cultura Económica and in the first UNAM economics theses. However, we have seen that this did not make the National School of Economics "socialist" in the strong sense of the word. What conservative businessmen found objectionable in the UNAM economics program was not an explicit program for socialist revolution but threatening-sounding rhetoric that reminded them that within the existing postrevolutionary order, political leaders could be found for whom the values of private property were not sacrosanct.

It is worth noting that Mexico's first private economics program was founded for specifically ideological rather than practical reasons. Private sectors need to reach a critical level of organizational complexity in order to demand the services of professional experts. Economics appears to require a relatively high level of complexity; for example, whereas accountants were hired extensively by Spanish businesses during the nineteenth century, economists did not work within the private sector until the 1950s (Guillén 1989: 69, 132). The Mexican private sector of the 1930s, while

certainly not as incipient and underdeveloped as the earliest UNAM economics theses implied, was nevertheless probably not sophisticated
enough to make the hiring of professionals (rather than family members,
for example) imperative. Therefore, it is doubtful that the Mexican Cultural Association would have founded its alternative program in 1940s
without the stimulus of an ideologically hostile program against which to
react.

In creating the ITM, Mexican business leaders hoped to provide a political counterweight to the ideology of the UNAM School of Economics.
Mexican economics has not been the only economics profession to undergo this sort of professional "splitting" between public- and private-
sector versions. For example, in the late nineteenth century, some German
businessmen found the discourse of German economists to be uncomfort-
ably close to socialism, and therefore founded their own more conservative, business-oriented economics programs (Lindenfeld 1990: 215–16).
A more recent example of politically motivated private economics emerging from government-business conflict can be found in Argentina. In 1977
an economics research program based in local business-group opposition
to government policies was founded in the province of Córdoba. Local
business leaders felt that the military dictatorship, while paying lip service
to laissez-faire ideology, was actually practicing a brand of interventionist
crony capitalism that favored business in and around Buenos Aires at the
expense of the provincial private sector. A key figure in this research institute was Domingo Cavallo, a Harvard-trained economics Ph.D. who later
stamped out inflation, balanced the budget, and privatized state-owned
enterprises under the Menem administration (N'haux 1993: 30–90).
Thus, even within a single nation, social sciences may have more than one
potential constituency.

Would the ITM succeed in carving out an ideologically distinct brand
of economics, thereby differentiating itself from the UNAM? In the following chapter, we will see that there were various factors that impeded
the ITM from formulating a radically different sort of economics program. One was the relative peace that generally characterized relations
between the government and the private sector during the years from the
end of the Cárdenas administration through 1970. Another was that the
dominant paradigm for economics in the postwar period, both in Mexico
and internationally, presupposed a strong role for the state in fostering
economic growth and stability. The result was a surprising degree of convergence between the two programs.

Chapter 4

THE MEXICAN MIRACLE AND ITS

POLICY PARADIGM, 1940–1970

U NLIKE the turbulent decades after the revolution, the postwar period in Mexico was characterized by relative social peace as well as the impressive economic growth popularly known as the Mexican Miracle. State intervention in the economy, along with growing economic sophistication, created demand for economists in both private and public sectors, although it was still predominantly in the latter where most Mexican economists found employment. Economics programs in private schools—notably the ITM (which became the autonomous ITAM in 1962) and the Monterrey Tech—flourished, as businessmen became more educated about the role and functions of economists in the private firm.

Of greater theoretical interest during this period, however, was the evolution of the role of the economist in the public sector, and the concomitant evolution of the most important center for the training of public sector economists: the National School of Economics at the UNAM. After the great social upheavals of the Cárdenas administration, the focus of Mexican government policy turned from social issues and redistributive politics to the task of promoting economic development. The growing need for economists as technicians within a developmentalist bureaucracy was mirrored in the growing technification of the UNAM economics program. At the same time, consensus between the government and private sector was reflected in the private-sector-sponsored ITM economics program. Thus, Mexican economics evolved along with changes in its public-sector constituency, and became more unitary as the interests of its public and private constituencies converged.

DEVELOPMENTALISM IN MEXICO AND LATIN AMERICA

The most important theoretical model for economic development in postwar Latin America was that of the United Nations Economic Commission for Latin America (ECLA), which was organized in 1948 with its seat in Santiago, Chile. ECLA's theoretical framework constituted a prime example of the sort of regionally specific school of economic thought that pro-liferated during the postwar Keynesian regime. According to the ECLA model, developing countries behaved according to a very different set of rules from those outlined by classical and neoclassical economic theorists. Classical economic theory asserted that a regime of free international trade enabled rich and poor countries alike to benefit from capitalizing on their "comparative advantages." In contrast, ECLA argued that in a regime of free international trade, core countries gained more than periph-eral countries because of the "deterioration in terms of trade": in concrete terms, a peripheral country would continually have to sell more of its primary products on the world market in order to buy the same value of finished goods. Such inequalities inevitably provoked balance-of-pay-ments problems for peripheral countries, since the real income they re-ceived for their exports fluctuated and tended to decrease, while the amount they paid for imports remained constant or increased. Raw-mate-rial-exporting peripheral countries also suffered from structural unem-ployment, which inhibited the growth of real wages and the development of internal markets (Hirschman 1961: 12–13; Villarreal 1984: 163–64; Zapata 1990: 149–54).

ECLA argued that peripheral countries could advance only if they ceased to rely on the export of primary commodities and the import of finished industrial products. Industrialization in developing countries could not be left to the vagaries of free markets but rather needed to be promoted through active government policies aimed at protecting "infant industries" from foreign competition, along with the protection of sala-ries to help maintain domestic demand (Villarreal 1984: 165). Although ECLA's theories did not fit within the dominant neoclassical tradition of postwar international economics, they had important ties to a particular strand of this tradition, namely, the school of "development" economists, such as Lewis, Rostow, and Nurkse (cf. Martinussen 1997).

The policy prescriptions of ECLA and its theorists were known to Mexi-can economists and policymakers of the postwar period. In 1944, Raúl Prebisch gave an important series of talks at the Banco de México and a lecture at the Colegio de México (Solís 1988: 35; Love 1996: 224–25). Prebisch first used the famous terms "core" and "periphery" at a meeting of Latin American central bankers convened by the Banco de México in Mexico City in 1946 (Love 1996: 225). Juan Noyola, a prominent profes-sor at the UNAM School of Economics, was a leading ECLA theorist.

Perhaps the best measure of the intellectual influence of ECLA in Mex-ico, however, was the *Trimestre Económico*, which during the 1950s took a notable *cepalino* turn. For the first half of the 1950s, for example, Víctor Urquidi (who served as director of Mexico's ECLA chapter from 1951 to 1958) served as the *Trimestre*'s director. In addition to a number of important foreign-trained government economists (including Edmundo Flores and Raúl Salinas Lozano), the journal's editorial board during the 1950s included Raúl Prebisch, ECLA's leading intellectual. Prebisch remained on the *Trimestre*'s editorial board until 1973.

The economic policies of postwar Mexico—particularly its commitment to import-substituting industrialization—were basically in keeping with ECLA prescriptions. However, ECLA was never as important in determining government policy in Mexico as it was in other Latin American countries. According to some, this was because the Mexican government was jealous of its autonomy from external influences—especially those which, unlike the World Bank or the IMF, were not able to provide resources to complement their advice (interview, Urquidi 9/26/95). This family resemblance between developmentalist policies in postwar Mexico and ECLA prescriptions resulted from common historical antecedents rather than direct influence. The export-oriented, laissez-faire model of the late nineteenth and early twentieth centuries had been widely abandoned as a response to the global economic crisis of the early 1930s. Subsequently, there was a wave of interventionist policies throughout Latin America, including import substitution (Díaz Alejandro 1984: 17). Thus, when ECLA was organized in 1948 with its seat in Santiago, Chile, its role was to provide a theoretical rationale for policies that had already been implemented.

Aside from their common emphasis on import-substituting industrialization and other forms of government involvement in economic development, the Mexican and ECLA models were similar in that they relied—often consciously—on the effective management of political demands. In many Latin American countries, postwar economic development was furthered by relatively low levels of social conflict, which could be attributed both to the shared benefits of economic growth and to the establishment of institutional frameworks (such as labor legislation) that allowed different classes to ally around the common nationalistic project of industrialization (Zapata 1990: 143). The ECLA model was based on "coexistence among social classes, an omnipresent State, nationalism, and the attempt to generate support from the population" (Zapata 1990: 154). Similarly, postwar economic development in Mexico was made possible by the management of demands from below and by consensus between the government and the private sector.

THE MEXICAN MIRACLE

The end of the Cárdenas presidency in 1940 marked the definitive incorporation of different social sectors within the ruling party, which cleared the way for the government to redirect its attention from distributive issues to the business of fostering economic development. Under the presidency of Avila Camacho (1940–46), the government limited land reform, toned down controversial government rhetoric on such issues as socialist education, and focused on improving relations with the United States and the private sector. President Alemán (1946–52) continued in this vein by pushing through policies opposed by trade unions and legislation to protect private landholdings against expropriation; at the same time he encouraged private enterprise through infrastructural development and opening to foreign investment (Maddison et al. 1989: 123–26).[1] Both administrations dramatically increased levels of industrial protection, which demonstrated the Mexican government's commitment to promoting economic development (Hansen 1971: 48).

The three presidencies following the Cárdenas administration were all characterized by substantial economic growth at the cost of inflation, the result of policies that relied on inflationary financing of government expenditures without raising taxes. Between 1940 and 1954, GDP growth in Mexico averaged over 5% per annum (Ayala Espino 1988: 288). At the same time, statistical evidence suggests that these policies lowered real wages in both agricultural and nonagricultural sectors, while raising the real incomes of entrepreneurs, thus amounting to an added stimulus to private investment (Hansen 1971: 50).[2] Although bankers, entrepreneurs, and conservative policymakers must have approved of the firm control that was exercised over labor's demand for wages during these years (cf. La Botz 1988), many did not approve of the inflationary financing of growth during these years. One notable opponent of loose monetary policy was ITM and Banco de México founder Miguel Palacios Macedo (Cárdenas 1994:103).

In the context of a fixed exchange rate, postwar inflation had the effect of provoking balance-of-payments deficits, which led to a currency adjustment in 1948 with support from the IMF and subsequent loans from the World Bank and the U.S. Eximbank. In 1954, there was a devaluation of the peso from 8.65 to 12.5 pesos per dollar, which was accompanied by loans from the World Bank and balance-of-payments assistance from the IMF (Maddison et al. 1989: 125; Cárdenas 1994: 149).

In contrast to the inflationary growth characterizing the eighteen years following the Cárdenas presidency, from 1955 through 1970 three successive presidential administrations undertook the task of maintaining high levels of economic growth while avoiding the cycle of inflation-devaluation-deficit that had characterized the previous three administrations. The policies of "stabilizing development" were conducted during the tenure of Antonio Ortíz Mena as finance minister (during two successive administrations) and of Rodrigo Gómez as director of the central bank. As a result, the Mexican government abandoned financing public spending through direct credit from the central bank, relying instead on the sale of government bonds through the commercial banking system, reserve requirements, and external debt (Ayala Espino 1988: 343). At the same time, the government was committed to a freely convertible peso and a fixed exchange rate, and restricted the prices of consumer goods, such as gasoline, electricity, sugar, and other goods and services through a system of extensive public subsidies (Izquierdo 1995: 18–28).

Taken as a whole, the period from 1940 through 1970 was one of significant economic improvement, with annual real GNP growth rates averaging over 6%. During these years, Mexico transformed a part of its backward, predominantly agricultural economy into a dynamic industrial one and became self-sufficient in the production of many goods, such as foodstuffs, steel, many consumer goods, and basic petroleum products (Hansen 1971: 48). The policy framework responsible for this success was generally characterized by a commitment to industrial protection, a high level of direct state involvement in many areas of the economy (notably in the petroleum industry and electric power), the promotion of industry through the financial intermediation of Nacional Financiera (the state industrial development bank), and extremely low levels of taxation. These policies were implemented and managed by a growing developmentalist bureaucracy in which the services of economists became increasingly important. During the latter, "stabilizing development" period of Mexican postwar economic history (1955–70), government activities were increasingly funded through borrowing on national and international financial markets. One government institution deeply involved in borrowing on international markets was the state development bank, which financed private development projects that were consistently extremely profitable (Thompson 1979: 114; Blair 1964).

The ongoing political viability of Mexican developmentalism was partly furthered by positive results: spectacular economic growth during the postwar period created benefits that trickled down to many, if not all, social groups. But the political management of the demands of different social groups was also a crucial factor in Mexican postwar economic growth. Looking at this period retrospectively, Mexican economist Leopoldo Solís (1973) commented that "the Mexican political system has known how to harmonize the different pressures and demands resulting from the effects of rapid economic growth, especially on the distribution of wealth, thanks to which the country has enjoyed a long phase of political stability, the most prolonged that Mexico has known since Independence" (p. 7).

Social and political peace was the foundation upon which the Mexican Miracle was built. This peace, and how it was achieved, had important implications for professional economics in Mexico. After 1940, relations between the government and the private sector improved steadily, and it is easy to understand why: government policy kept taxes and wages low, expanded infrastructure, and protected domestic industries from foreign competition. Whereas consensus between government and business is easy to explain, relative peace with social groups at the bottom is more complicated. This was the central puzzle addressed by Hansen (1971) in his book on the political foundations of Mexican development. Hansen observed that Mexican economic success could partly be explained as resulting from its ability to avoid costly social expenditures, which resulted in higher levels of productive investment. Compared with other Latin American countries, Mexico spent relatively less on social programs such as social security and relatively more on infrastructure. Moreover, in 1971 Mexico had the lowest tax burden in Latin America except for Guatemala, Paraguay, and Colombia: Mexico's income distribution was highly unequal, and this inequality was not lessened by government tax and expenditure policies, as it was elsewhere in Latin America. Indeed, income inequality increased steadily in Mexico from 1950 through 1968 (Hansen 1971: 71–85; Felix 1982).[3]

Whereas the predictable result of such a scenario would be large-scale social protest and instability, Mexico in the postwar period was actually *more* stable and less prone to social conflict than other Latin American countries. How did Mexico manage to accomplish this? The answer to this important question lay in the Mexican political system. The rapid circulation of Mexican political elites provided numerous opportunities for social mobility, and economic development and the expansion of the Mexican government substantially enlarged the Mexican middle class; thus, although those at the bottom may have been worse off, discontent was defused by expanded possibilities of moving up (Hansen 1971: 180–81). At the same time, the political system provided few opportunities to question and change the existing order; political demands were limited. Formal political pluralism was a mask for an actual one-party system that precluded government policies from being undermined electorally.

Meanwhile, Mexican corporatism carefully managed nonelectoral threats to the system, such as strikes and social movements. The structure of the Institutional Revolutionary Party (PRI) incorporated official labor and agricultural sectors (along with the amorphous middle-class or "popular" sector), but these official sectors were also effective tools for the control of social demands. The government controlled labor through a joint strategy of co-optation and repression: cooperative leaders were rewarded by permanency in office and even legislative seats; dissenting leaders were imprisoned, and government-approved union leaders (known as *charros*) were put in their place (Middlebrook 1995). Moreover, if the labor sector could not be viewed as independent, the official agrarian sector was even less so, with leaders consistently imposed from above and genuine spokespeople for peasants defeated in fraudulent elections, imprisoned, or even assassinated (Hansen 1971: 113–14).

THE DEVELOPMENT BUREAUCRACY

During the years of the Mexican Miracle, the extensive powers of the Mexican president with regard to economic policy were in some respects checked by the Finance Ministry, which controlled both taxation and the budgeting process. In the 1950s and early '60s, several efforts were made by the executive to limit the power of the Finance Ministry. This resulted in the endowment of the Ministry of Natural Resources with discretion over the parastate oil industry and other areas; meanwhile, the newly created Ministry of the Presidency was supposed to coordinate different economic programs and conduct economic planning (Ayala Espino 1988: 348; Centeno 1994: 77–80; Izquierdo 1995: 49). The Ministry of the Economy was transformed into the Ministry of Industry and Commerce, a move that was intended to take power away from the Finance Ministry in the area of trade policy; symbolically, this meant that tariff policy was now to be viewed as part of deliberate effort at industrial protection rather than a mere device for capturing fiscal resources (Izquierdo 1995: 44). One effect that these measures probably had was to diffuse the demand for economic expertise throughout other branches of government.

Meanwhile, "economic planning" became a fashionable phrase in the speeches of public administrators, and a growing consensus within the government regarding the need for more carefully considered and coordinated development policies made the services of economists seem indispensable. In 1960 in a speech at the award of an economics prize, Finance Minister Antonio Ortíz Mena (a lawyer with practical expertise in the public financial sector) asserted: "We need to plan our industry and resources. In Mexico we continually have more need for the work of economists; it becomes increasingly necessary for us to think about planning the development of our economic resources" (Barrosco Castro 1961: 19). Centralized economic planning was now a real possibility in Mexico because of administrative techniques that had been vastly improved since economic policymaking institutions were founded in the 1920s and '30s. For example, by 1950 statistical analyses of government finances were developed enough to be integrated with national accounts, and by the late 1950s, fully developed national accounts data were available from the central bank (Maddison et al. 1989: 127). A system of classification for public expenditure was developed within the Finance Ministry in the early 1950s so that the ministry could more accurately keep track of government spending (interview, Urquidi 9/19/95). And during the 1960s, administrative procedures were improved in the Finance Ministry such that there could be clear and accurate specification of the control of import commodities (Solís 1981: 17).

This emphasis on planning in Mexico was part of a broader trend in Latin America and developing countries more generally, which both resulted from and helped stimulate new techniques in economic policymaking. Based on his firsthand observations of the role of economists in planning in Colombia during the 1950s, Hirschman (1971) objected that economic planning in Latin America was often premised on an overly optimistic notion of the extent to which economists armed with new techniques could serve as effective micromanagers (p. 41–62).[4]

Whether or not these interventions were as efficacious as their proponents believed, one of their effects was to put economists into increasingly important positions within Latin American government bureaucracies during the 1950s and '60s. Detailed economic plans were made possible by international advances in the statistical techniques available to national governments after the 1930s and '40s. One of the most crucial of these was national accounting, which gave rise to national income accounts during the 1930s, and after World War II gave rise to more detailed calculations of money flows between different sectors. In 1953, the United Nations published a national accounting system that became an international standard; according to one of my informants, prior to that time the U.S. Commerce Department had been a sort of mecca of national accounting among Mexican officials. At about the same time, Mexican officials interested in learning the most recent techniques for the calculation of balances of payments were conducting visits to the U.S. Federal Reserve (McNeely 1995: 76–77; interview, Urquidi 9/26/95).

In contrast to UNAM economics graduates in the 1930s and '40s, economists in Mexico in the 1950s and '60s could aspire to being more than bureaucrats and implementers of previously formulated policies and instruments, and actually participated in policy design. Of particular importance in Mexico during this period was a new generation of foreign-trained economists with higher levels of technical competence than the UNAM graduates. These economists—known as "técnicos" to Raymond Vernon, who observed them firsthand in the 1960s—had become indispensable for the government because the techniques for managing a modern capitalist economy had simply become too complicated to be left to amateurs:

By general agreement, such subjects as exchange-rate policy, fiscal and monetary policy, investment and savings policy, and similar esoteric matters can
no longer be left entirely to the rough-and-ready ministrations of the politician . . . the economic techniques have grown so complex that they are beyond the easy understanding of amateurs. (Vernon 1963: 136)

Relatively few Mexicans had studied economics abroad during this period, because there existed no extensive program of scholarships to fund
such study (except for the Banco de México personnel training program,
which will be discussed in the following section). As a result, foreign-
trained economists were a scarce and valuable resource, and quickly came
to occupy important posts. Two of the earliest examples of such economists in Mexico were Víctor Urquidi and Josué Sáenz, who received B.A.'s
in economics in the 1930s from the London School of Economics and
Swarthmore College, respectively. Sáenz became director of the Department of Credit of the Finance Ministry in 1946, and Urquidi subsequently
occupied important posts in the Banco de México and the Finance Ministry. Another prominent técnico, Edmundo Flores, received a scholarship
from the University of Wisconsin to complete his doctoral degree in agricultural economics in the late 1940s and later became an important
official in the Ministry of Agriculture and the head of the National Council of Science and Technology. Raúl Ortíz Mena,[5] a graduate of the National School of Economics, took economics classes at Harvard and the
University of Chicago in the 1940s with a Banco de México scholarship
and went on to occupy important positions in the industrial development
bank, the Finance Ministry, and the Ministry of the Presidency. Rafael
Izquierdo completed his graduate studies at McGill University in the late
1940s and became the head of an important joint Finance Ministry–
Banco de México group in the 1960s. Leopoldo Solís, an UNAM graduate
who received his Ph.D. in economics from Yale in 1959 with the help of
a Banco de México scholarship, subsequently became head of the Banco's
prestigious Department of Economic Studies. Raúl Salinas Lozano (whose
son became president of Mexico in 1988) was an UNAM economics graduate who subsequently studied economics at Harvard with a scholarship
from a government ministry (Pallares Ramírez 1952: 14). Salinas was the
first foreign-trained economist—and the first UNAM economics graduate—to occupy a top policymaking post (minister of commerce), which
he assumed in 1958.

The demand for the services of such foreign-trained economists resulted
not only from the increasingly sophisticated administrative and statistical
techniques but also from a new postwar international economic order in
which Mexico was increasingly dependent on external resources. Like

other developing countries, Mexico defaulted on its large government
debt around the time of the Great Depression. As a result, Mexican access
to the resources of foreign portfolio investors was practically nonexistent
through the 1940s; until the mid-1950s or so, Mexican economic development was financed through domestic resources. However, several historical events conspired to alter this remarkably independent state of affairs.
First, motivated by the political consideration of maintaining Mexico as
an ally during World War II, the United States facilitated a settlement of
Mexico's outstanding debt that was extremely favorable to Mexico in
1942 (Bazant 1968: 214–21). Second, the end of the war witnessed the
creation of a number of multilateral and bilateral lending institutions that
would connect Mexico once again with access to international financing.
Mexico began to borrow from the World Bank in 1948; in 1954, it dealt
with devaluation and capital flight with the help of an IMF standby loan
(Thompson 1979: 114–22).

The year 1954 represented a turning point for Mexican economic policymaking in several respects. In contrast to the inflationary policies of the
preceding decade and a half, Mexican economic policymakers committed
themselves to the goal of price stability, resulting in remarkably low rates
of inflation accompanied by ongoing high levels of economic growth.
Without the inflation tax, the government resources used to finance economic development could come either from tax revenues or from domestic and international financial markets. Due to the failure of tax reform
in Mexico during this period (discussed presently), it would be the latter
rather than the former resources that would finance Mexican development. In addition to the IMF and the World Bank, resources began to
flow into Mexico from the Eximbank, the Inter-American Development
Bank (founded in 1959), and USAID. Most important, Mexico acquired
a reputation for political and monetary stability that gave it such a good
reputation abroad that it was able to draw on the resources of private
creditors decades before such resources would become available once
more for other developing countries. By 1965, Mexico had the highest
credit rating of all developing countries and was able to issue bonds at an
interest rate only 1½ percentage points above the prime rate in the United
States (Thompson 1979: 174–85).

In addition to its political and monetary stability, a little-recognized but
undoubtedly important factor in helping Mexico secure access to foreign
resources was the growing prominence of foreign-trained economists in
its government ministries. As Vernon observed,

> the increasing flow of communications between nations and with interna-
> tional agencies on [economic] subjects has demanded that every country de-
> velop a class of responsible officials which is capable of holding up its end in

the interchange. In Mexico the economic technician has become an integral element in the decision-making process on issues affecting Mexico's development. (1963: 136)

For example, in 1951, the World Bank (then known as IBRD) and the Mexican development bank (Nacional Financiera) set up a "combined working party," the purpose of which was "to assess the major long-term trends in the Mexican economy with particular reference to Mexico's capacity to absorb additional foreign investments" (Combined Mexican Working Party 1953: ix). The group consisted of two World Bank economists and two Mexican government economists: Raúl Ortíz Mena and Víctor Urquidi, both of whom had studied economics abroad and both of whom were fluent in English.

Thus, in the postwar period, access to foreign resources could be facilitated by the presence of government technicians who "spoke the same language"—both literally and figuratively—as the officials of international organizations. In addition to mostly being fluent in English and the language of economics, many of the new técnicos worked in these international organizations, and thus had the advantage of personal networks with foreign officials and inside information. For example, early in their careers Edmundo Flores worked at the United Nations Food and Agriculture Organization (FAO) and Víctor Urquidi at the World Bank; both Urquidi and Rafael Izquierdo gained policy-related experience at the ECLA during the 1950s.

An important effect of this trend was to promote the influence of a group of economists within the Mexican government bureaucracy who had more in common, in many respects, with economists in other countries than with other Mexican officials. The presence of these individuals, while helpful for the implementation of new techniques and the securing of the resources of international organizations, was also the source of some conflict within the economic policymaking bureaucracy. Despite their role as important advisers and assistants in the area of economic policymaking, economists during this period were generally not economic policymakers themselves; lawyers and other politicians still had the final say.[6] According to Vernon (1963), the técnicos of this period were nationalists favoring industrial protection and state intervention, as well as centralized planning and the redistribution of income (pp. 138–49). Rather than placing them at odds with dominant international economic ideas, such interventionist ideology was evidence that the técnicos' views were compatible with the worldwide Keynesian consensus that prevailed at the time. However, the técnicos' ideas sometimes conflicted with those of the traditional lawyer-politicians known to Vernon as "políticos." Economic policy decisions, in the view of the técnicos, needed to be made on the basis of internationally accepted standards and by experts. In contrast, the políticos believed in making policy according to more political criteria—in particular, the effect of policies on Mexico's most powerful interest groups.

A revealing example of conflict between técnicos and políticos was the battle around tax reform in the 1960s. The United States–sponsored Alliance for Progress promised external financing in exchange for structural and social reforms in the governments of Latin American countries, and gave rise to the formulation of economic plans throughout Latin America (Izquierdo 1995: 48). One of the recommendations of the alliance was tax reform, and in 1960 Nicolas Kaldor, a world-famous economist, was invited to do a report for the Finance Ministry on tax reform in Mexico. Kaldor was a Keynesian at the London School of Economics and later at Cambridge who had worked with ECLA in the 1950s (Urquidi 1987: 919–22). He concluded that the Mexican system of taxation captured too few fiscal resources in too regressive a manner and provided unwarranted privileges for a substantial portion of national income. As a solution, he recommended radically redistributive reforms, which would have the added desirable effect of broadening the base of domestic demand (Izquierdo 1995: 69–70).

In 1961, a report based on Kaldor's recommendations was presented within the Finance Ministry by a group of Mexican economists, all of whom had studied abroad.[7] However, these reforms were discarded in favor of a more limited reform package proposed by a group of Finance Ministry lawyers. The reason for discarding the economists' proposal was apparently opposition to the reforms from the private sector, which the lawyers feared would result in capital flight (Izquierdo 1995: 68; Maddison et al. 1989: 129). This failure to implement substantial tax reforms in Mexico would have far-reaching consequences, since later efforts to increase government social and infrastructural spending would need to be financed through external debt, which would contribute to the debt crisis of the 1980s.

This conflict between economists and lawyers—or between "técnicos" and "políticos"—within the Finance Ministry illustrates some of the contradictions that exist between professional and political decisionmaking. Politicians are expected to weigh policies based on their effects on different interest groups of potential supporters or detractors (although they are also well known for their rhetoric about the common good). In contrast, professional legitimacy depends on the appearance of impartial objectivity and the adherence to standards of a community of experts. Centeno (1993) observes that "technocratic legitimacy is based on the appeal to scientific knowledge. . . . While the politicians' state is an 'empty vessel' into which their constituencies pour their needs and aspirations, the technocrat sees the state as embodying a unit that is greater than the mere sum of its parts" (p. 313). Porter (1995) similarly points out that the prescriptions of professionals in government—such as economists or civil engineers—tend to present themselves as serving the "common good" to protect themselves from the objection that their policies serve particular interests.

As a result, what professionals prescribe in a policy situation may conflict with what politicians recommend.[8] Edelman et al. (1991) similarly discuss the conflicts experienced by professionals whose role within an organization is to legitimate it through their expertise but whose professional prescriptions may harm the interests of the organization. In contrast to Edelman's example, however, this conflict between políticos and técnicos suggests that organizational change through professionalization can be limited by the degree of control that professionals have within their respective organizations. Foreign-trained Mexican economists may have been willing to model Mexican fiscal policy on international Keynesian standards but were unable to impose these changes, because the reins of economic policymaking were still in the hands of lawyers—amateurs behaving as politicians—rather than professional economists. It would not be until the 1980s that the advice of economists would have a determining effect on economic policy in Mexico.

THE BANCO DE MÉXICO IN THE POSTWAR PERIOD

The contradictory logics of politics and professions are also illustrated by the institutional constraints that the Mexican political system posed for the development of professional economics. A professional's claim to privileged status and salary is based on the legitimacy of the profession, which in turn is based on the claim of expertise and certified competence in a given field. In contrast, politicians claim privileged positions on the basis of a variety of other criteria, including constituent support and personal connections. These different forms of legitimation mean that professions in government tend to thrive in environments that are relatively insulated from the influence of politics.[9] Career civil-service bureaucracies are congenial homes for professionals because their recruitment and advancement procedures are based on merit rather than on political criteria.

In postwar Mexico, such bureaucracies were the exception rather than the rule. Mexico's notorious six-year presidential rotation system led to a complete turnover of upper-level personnel within government ministries, since desirable positions within economic policymaking ministries were awarded on the basis of political loyalty toward the incoming president, and ministers chose upper-level administrators from among their own political comrades, in turn. Thus, an economist in a responsible position within the Finance Ministry had no guarantee of advancing or even continuing in his current job during the next administration; rather than striving toward professional excellence, his energies were best directed toward cultivating the connections necessary for securing his next job.

Economists in Mexico certainly could—and indeed did—choose to "play the game" of politics, but this game was not congenial to the cultivation of the legitimacy of Mexican economists as professionals; rather, economists' reputation for expertise depended on the belief that their positions and privileges were due to their qualifications, rather than their political connections. Therefore, professional economics in Mexico needed a more stable institutional home than the highly politicized government ministries were able to provide. Not surprisingly, the areas within Mexican public administration that were most insulated from the Mexican presidential cycle gained reputations for being important centers of economic expertise. These areas—the central bank (Banco de México), the industrial development bank (Nacional Financiera), and the foreign commerce bank (Bancomext)—were all within the public financial sector.

Of these three organizations, the Banco de México had the highest degree of organizational autonomy and became the most important area for economists in postwar Mexican public administration. Legally, the Mexican central bank was not completely independent of the government and was in the final instance subject to the discretion of the president and the Ministry of Finance. In practice, however, after the devaluation of 1954 the Banco was granted a high degree of autonomy by the Mexican government as part of a conscious policy to try to control inflation. Evidence of the de facto independence of the Mexican central bank was Rodrigo Gómez's unusually long tenure as central bank director—from 1952 until 1970 (the nature and limitations of the Banco de México's autonomy will be discussed more extensively in chapter 5). During Mexico's famous "stabilizing development" period (1955–70), inflation averaged a meager 4.71% per annum (compared to over 10% for the period 1940–54) (Ayala Espino 1988: 315, 386).

Unlike government ministries offering high-level positions to the politically connected, the Banco de México guaranteed lifetime employment, and was characterized by meritocratic internal recruitment and advancement procedures. Its entrance examinations included both psychological and aptitude testing, and the Banco's renowned Department of Economic Studies had its own tests for recruiting economists beginning in the 1960s (interview, Solís 8/6/96). In contrast to the functionaries of other public bureaucracies, able Banco de México employees could start in low-level positions and spend their entire careers working their way to the top. An outstanding product of this system was Rodrigo Gómez, who assumed the position of director of the Banco after having ascended its ranks for eighteen years. Another feature of the central bank that made it particularly attractive was its impressive package of fringe benefits, which included low-interest loans, high-quality medical insurance and pension plans, a guaranteed package of food staples, and a scholarship program for studying abroad. The combination of the Banco's reputation for job stability, meritocratic advancement, and fringe benefits made it a magnet for Mexico's most talented young economists.

An equally important factor in making the Banco the most important "center of talent" within the Mexican government bureaucracy was its inherent interest as a place to work, as the source of basic information on the economy. In contrast to ministries where economists were put in charge of mundane tasks such as the processing of tax exemption applications for industries, economists at the Banco de México conducted studies on such broad macroeconomic issues as the rate of inflation, the rate of growth of the economy, and Mexico's trade deficit. Moreover, more than the other insulated areas of the financial bureaucracy (the industrial development bank and the foreign commerce bank), the Banco de México had some discretion in decisions over monetary policy, although it ultimately had to defer to the decisions of the Finance Minister. As a result, central bank economists could not only find a stable career with prospects for advancement but also participate in important policymaking decisions.

The Banco de México gained tremendous influence within the Mexican economic policymaking bureaucracy through its "personnel loan" program, which enabled employees to work in different positions within other branches of the public-sector bureaucracy (such as the Presidency and the Finance and Commerce Ministries) while maintaining their Banco positions and fringe benefits. Banco de México economists on loan to other public bureaucracies developed a reputation for professional excellence, both because of the Banco's meritocratic reputation (which enhanced Banco officials' legitimacy as professionals) and because Banco economists were not dependent on their superiors within other bureaucracies for their positions; they could, in other words, be relied on to present objective analyses without regard for internal political considerations (Camp 1977: 16). Camp (1977) noted that as a result of this loan program, Banco de México employees played a role analogous to that of the U.S. Council of Economic Advisors in executive decisionmaking: key Banco personnel in other ministries—notably Octaviano Campos Salas and Plácido García Reynoso in the Commerce Ministry—were instrumental in providing the advice that led to approval of the Latin American Free Trade Agreement (LAFTA) in 1960 (pp. 16–17). Thus, the Banco de México provided important organizational and institutional preconditions for the legitimacy of the economics profession within the Mexican

government: not only did it provide a framework for recruiting and certi-
fying experts, but it also provided a channel whereby their advice could
extend throughout Mexican public administration.

The Banco de México's role as a key organizational home for Mexican
economists made it influential in shaping the Mexican economics profession: the central bank was a crucial subconstituency within the public
sector that legitimated Mexican economics. One important feature of the
Banco that influenced Mexican economics was its unusual degree of international institutional isomorphism. Like many other economic bureaucracies, the Mexican central bank was called on to serve as an intermediary between the Mexican government and international economic
organizations; whereas Nacional Financiera was the Mexican government's link to the World Bank, the Banco de México was in charge of
dealing with the IMF and the Inter-American Development Bank. However, to a greater extent than other government organizations, the Banco
was also embedded in an international organizational field of central
banks, which met frequently through such forums as the 1946 meeting in
Mexico City on problems of central banks of the Americas (Banco de
México 1946).

Such frequent contact with its organizational counterparts in other
countries meant that the Banco de México was highly attuned to the techniques and professional standards of central banks around the world. As
part of its commitment to international standards, the Banco de México
had a scholarship program for sending its personnel to study abroad in
economics and other fields.[10] This was the first large-scale Mexican government scholarship program sponsoring foreign training in economics:
between 1941 and 1970, thirty-six Banco de México employees received
such training.[11] As part of the same scholarship program, many Banco
personnel were sent to study central banking techniques at the Washington and New York branches of the U.S. Federal Reserve, at the U.S. Department of Commerce (where they learned techniques for calculating
balance-of-payments and national income accounts), and at the Inter-
american Center for Statistical Training in Chile (a program sponsored by
the Organization of American States for training in statistical techniques)
(interviews, Urquidi 9/26/95; Durandeau 11/8/95).

Thus, the Banco de México was the single organization most responsible for the internationalization of the Mexican economics profession in
the postwar period. The isomorphism facilitated by the Banco de México,
however, was not generated by resource dependence but rather corresponds to what DiMaggio and Powell (1983) refer to as "mimetic" isomorphism, generated by uncertainty and the security that comes with emulat-
ing the apparent success of other organizations within an organizational
field. The Banco's adherence to worldwide standards was naturally ac-

companied by a proclivity toward the economic theories most internationally fashionable at the time. As a result, the ideology prevalent at the Banco de México during the postwar period was a hybrid of the conservatism of Mexican private bankers and the Keynesianism of postwar central bankers. The directors of the Banco de México from 1946 to 1952 and from 1952 to 1970 had both been private-sector bankers before they entered the central bank; extensive networks between private and public financiers in Mexico meant that Mexican central bankers were less sympathetic to inflationary monetary policy in the service of growth than other public-sector economists.[12] Nevertheless, the Mexican central bank was also clearly committed to state intervention in the service of industrial development. The Banco's Department of Industrial Research sponsored numerous feasibility studies on different areas of the Mexican economy and provided scholarships so that Mexico could acquire "human resources for specific tasks of national importance" (Bravo Jiménez 1982: 252). The postwar Banco de México also supported selective credit policies for financing projects that were seen as helpful to economic growth: for example, the Banco had trust funds for supporting projects in agricultural, tourism, and housing development (interview, Peralta Gómez 9/5/95). The prevailing ideology within the postwar Banco de México can therefore best be described as "conservative developmentalist": while the Banco may have been at the right of the postwar spectrum of developmentalist and Keynesian thinking, it still fell within this spectrum.

While there may not have been substantial ideological differences between Banco de México officials and other public-sector economists, it is clear that postwar Banco officials perceived a mismatch between the ideology of the UNAM School of Economics and the Banco's organizational needs. Even at its height of technicality during the 1950s and '60s, the National School of Economics continued to have strong Marxist tendencies, as well as problems with its system of student selection and certification (to be discussed in the following section). In his study of UNAM economics graduates from 1929 to 1952, Camp (1975) notes that the two most important professional destinations for UNAM economists were the Ministries of Commerce and Finance—and not, by implication, the Banco de México (p. 147).

As a result of this mismatch, Banco de México officials were involved in several efforts to create alternatives and supplements to UNAM education in economics. In 1958, Rodrigo Gómez sent central bank official Consuelo Meyer to reorganize the economics program at the University of Nuevo León in Monterrey; the Banco also provided the new program with some financial and infrastructural resources (Alanís Gómez 1969: 30–31; interview, Bolaños Lozano 11/8/95). The reorganized program at Nuevo León subsequently developed the reputation for being one of the most rigorous economics programs in Mexico and became an important source of central bank officials in the 1960s and '70s.

The original idea for creating Mexico's first postgraduate program in economics[13] at the Colegio de México in 1964 was conceived among a group of Banco de México functionaries and ex-functionaries including Ernesto Fernández Hurtado, Daniel Cosío Villegas, Víctor Urquidi, and Rodrigo Gómez. The program was intended to respond to the failure of many Banco de México scholarship recipients to complete their studies abroad because of deficient skills in English, mathematics, and neoclassical economics; it was believed that the Colegio program would be a cheaper alternative to studying abroad and would compensate for deficiencies in the training received by UNAM graduates (interview, Urquidi 9/19/95). The economics program at El Colegio was partly designed according to the recommendations of a report authored by the director of the Banco's Department of Economic Studies, Leopoldo Solís (interview, Solís 8/6/96). We will see in the following chapter that the Banco de México would also play a crucial role in the Americanization of the economics program of the ITM.

UNAM ECONOMICS DURING THE MEXICAN MIRACLE

The Banco de México's uneasy relationship with the National School of Economics notwithstanding, the evidence suggests that economics at the UNAM adapted itself reasonably well to the changing needs of the government after 1940, when government emphasis shifted from gaining the support of the masses through populist measures to the promotion of development. It was in keeping with the spirit of the times that in 1941 the director of the National School of Economics, Jesús Silva Herzog, revised its curriculum to be more technical and less contentiously leftist. Silva Herzog's revisions of the curriculum were intended to "suppress all those aspects of exaggerated radicalism that it contained, in order to achieve a more technical and complete teaching of economics" (words of UNAM rector De la Cueva cited in Pallares Ramírez 1952: 103). The Marxist theory class was maintained, but many other courses, such as the history of socialist doctrines, the agrarian problem, and the history of social movements, were canceled. Meanwhile, more technical courses such as industrial law and social security, cost accounting, and insurance techniques were introduced (Pallares Ramírez 1952: 105–6). The heyday of "social economics" was past, and the age of economics as policy technique had begun.

After this initial revision of the UNAM curriculum, there were three more major revisions, in 1946, 1951, and 1963. The changes implemented between 1941 and 1963, although not completely unidirectional,[14] all tended toward increasing technification. Thus, with respect to the curriculum of the 1930s, the 1963 plan had one more course in money and banking, one more in economic theory, one more in public finance, a new course in international commerce, and a new class in statistics. At the same time, the 1963 plan had three fewer classes in the history of economic thought and economic history, and had eliminated the old course in sociology. It was apparently the 1963 change in the curriculum (implemented under the directorship of Emilio Mújica Montoya) that was most intentionally directed toward making the National School of Economics more technical and academically rigorous (Petricioli and Reynolds 1967: 31); in the words of the school's 1967 Academic Organization, the revisions were aimed at "keeping up to date . . . [with] advances in economic theory and policy and to elevate . . . the academic level of the faculty" (Anaya Díaz 1979: 6). The 1963 revisions also responded to the new emphasis on economic planning within the government by adding a new three-hour course[15] on "Theory and Techniques of Economic Planning" (Fernández Lozano 1978: 21–26; Mancilla López 1980: 59). As part of the National School of Economics's new emphasis on the economist as a highly trained public-sector technician, in 1965 Director Horacio Flores de la Peña developed a scholarship program for sending promising students to study economics abroad with the commitment to return as UNAM professors (Torres Gaytán and Mora Ortíz 1978: 103).

Evidence of the postwar technification of UNAM economics is abundant in the sixteen theses[16] completed in 1958 (tables in appendix A), which differ in many respects from the earlier theses discussed in chapter 3. The theses from the first years of economics at the UNAM were written during the great social and political upheavals of the 1930s, and naturally dealt with such grand themes as whether communism or fascism were viable options for Mexico (Hornedo 1934) and the issue of agrarian reform (Mora 1935; De la Peña 1936; Vázquez 1936; Guerra Cepeda 1939). Other early theses presented highly detailed case studies of particular products that presented large quantities of statistical data but relatively little economic theory or analysis.

In contrast, the theses from 1958 focused less on social issues and more on the practical problems confronting the Mexican economic policymaking bureaucracy. With respect to the earlier group of theses, those written in 1958 displayed a much more sophisticated understanding of the institutions of a modern capitalist economy and dealt with such themes as the role of central banks in fostering economic development (Aguilera Schaufenberger 1958), the capital market in Mexico (Bravo Aguilero 1958), fiscal policy (Cervantes Delgado 1958), and the balance-of-payments problems of underdeveloped countries (Kahan Pintel 1958). There-

TABLE 4.1
Positions on State Intervention, UNAM 1934–45 and UNAM 1958

	UNAM 1934–45		UNAM 1958	
	N	(%)	N	(%)
Less intervention advocated	0	(0)	0	(0)
Existing interventions supported	30	(40)	6	(37.5)
More intervention advocated	21	(28)	10	(62.5)
No position on intervention	24	(32)	0	(0)
Total	75	(100)	16	(100)

$\chi^2 = 9.8, \alpha < .05$

fore, although students from this period were not methodologically or mathematically more sophisticated (1958 theses used no analytical statistics and little mathematical modeling), their theses are evidence of an increased level of *conceptual* sophistication.

In contrast to the leftist ideology of earlier years, the outstanding rhetorical themes of the 1958 theses reflected the postwar Keynesian and developmentalist consensus: it had been decided that Mexico would have a capitalist system of production, but a capitalist system guided and tempered by government intervention to promote development and compensate for market imperfections. In the words of one thesis author, "The abstentionist role that was traditionally demanded of the state has ceased to be valid. The supervision of the capitalist system depends in large measure upon state intervention in economic life, since government action tends to cover the system's deficiencies by maintaining the economy at adequate levels" (Cervantes Delgado 1958: 102). As a result of this new focus on the role of the government in the economy—and in contrast to the theses from 1934 to 1945—there were *no* 1958 theses that failed to mention state intervention either in theory or in practice (see table 4.1). At the same time, 1958 theses displayed a greater *degree* of support for state intervention, with more than 62% falling into the "strongly interventionist" category, as opposed to only 28% of the 1934–45 theses. And the idea that capitalism has grave defects for which the state must compensate appeared in 31% of the 1958 theses (as opposed to only 17% of the earlier ones).

The most notable contrast between the postwar and earlier theses was the dramatic appearance in 1958 of developmentalist thinking. As one author asserted, "The economic structure of [developing] countries is quite different from that of developed ones, if one considers that they are characterized by an economy based fundamentally on primary activities and with an incipient level of industrialization" (Hernández de la Mora 1958: 12). This idea that there were fundamental differences between developed and developing countries appeared in a striking 50% of the

TABLE 4.2
Most-Cited Authors, UNAM 1958
(Total N = 16, Theses with Theoretical Cites = 87.5%)

	N	%
J. M. Keynes	4	25.0
Ragnar Nurkse	4	25.0
J. Alienes Urosa	3	18.8
Horacio Flores de la Peña	3	18.8
Karl Marx	3	18.8
Juan F. Noyola	3	18.8
David Ricardo	3	18.8

1958 theses, as opposed to only 3% of the 1934–45 ones. As a result of these fundamental differences, developing countries needed to modify international prescriptions for state intervention so as to address the particular needs and deficiencies of underdeveloped economies: "In contrast to what occurs in highly industrialized economies, the economic policy of underdeveloped countries should tend fundamentally toward overcoming their reduced levels of production and income, which are a consequence of their economic and social structure, and particularly of their low productivity" (Cervantes Delgado 1958: 102). Evidence of the influence of ECLA can be seen in the three theses that cite Juan Noyola (a prominent ECLA economist), one of which explicitly used the ECLA theory of the deterioration in terms of trade (Herrera Domínguez 1958: 85).

A final important piece of evidence of the new technical focus of the National School of Economics was that the most-cited authors in 1958 (table 4.2) were John Maynard Keynes and Ragnar Nurkse[17]—in contrast to the earlier theses, which cited Marx most frequently. Whereas 4% of 1934–45 theses mentioned socialism approvingly, and about 3% disapprovingly, in 1958 *no* theses expressed either approval or disapproval; the debate over whether Mexico should or should not become a socialist country was apparently no longer a burning issue. Rather, the issue of the day was how to modify Mexican capitalism through government action to promote growth and development.

Clearly, the school had become more oriented toward training economic technicians to work within a developmentalist bureaucracy, and less oriented toward the formation of social and political thinkers. However, the degree to which the National School of Economics fulfilled its new role as a training ground for technicians should not be exaggerated. The dissatisfaction of Banco de México officials with the sorts of economists that the UNAM was producing—manifested in its support for the development of other programs—was evidence of several problems that the school encountered as a source of public-sector professionals. First, the school's ongoing leftist tradition created a potential contradiction between students' training in critical social and political theories, on the one hand, and their role as bureaucrats within a nondemocratic government and a capitalist economy, on the other. Second, problems of creating meritocratic selection processes within Mexican public universities, combined with exploding enrollments, created problems for recruiting UNAM economics graduates to public-sector positions.

Throughout its evolution toward increasing technification, the vision of "social economics" at the National School of Economics endured; concern with issues beyond the abstract theories and technical applications that were needed for bureaucratic work was a time-honored tradition upheld by students and professors alike. In a speech at the school's relocation to the new University City in 1955, the school's director Ricardo Torres Gaytán declared that "[t]he economist is a professional who should not be a stranger to, and remain indifferent to, social interests. . . . The economist needs to study, principally, the disjuncture between social production and social justice, since until today this . . . has dominated human life" (Escuela Nacional de Economía 1959: 48). Founding professors like Jesús Silva Herzog, who had contributed to the school's original populist flavor, continued to convey their points of view in the classroom. Meanwhile, a more recent group of leftists found a congenial institutional home at the school's Instituto de Investigaciones Económicas. The social commitment of economics as it was taught at the UNAM was also periodically revived by new generations of idealistic young students, who allied with sympathetic professors to keep the populist spirit of UNAM economics alive.

This tendency became more marked in the 1960s, as university students throughout Mexico became more radicalized. For example, at the 1962 Conference of Economics Students held at the National School of Economics, student delegates took the position that economists needed to be more than technicians, that worker and peasant solidarity should be upheld, and that all basic and public service industries should be nationalized; according to one source, the students' recommendations apparently had some effect on the 1963 Curriculum revision (Mancilla López 1980: 56).

This ideology of social responsibility and criticism had different effects. First, it created a certain amount of reluctance to hire UNAM graduates at the more conservative branches of public administration—most notably, the Banco de México—where leftist ideology was viewed unfavorably. Second, it created a certain amount of internal conflict for idealistic students who recognized that their employment prospects depended— literally—on working within the system. As one interviewee who attended the school in the early 1960s remarked:

The School taught us about reality: that in Mexico there was a great deal of misery. The explanation for this misery was the system, and the proposed alternative was the socialist system. So we studied the socialist system. The problem was that we young people had to go out into the world to work within the capitalist system. So on the one hand, the National School of Economics taught us these ideas, but it also taught us the technical instruments of an economist. So there was a basic disjuncture between what we had been taught to believe and the tasks we had to perform within the government. Horacio Flores de la Peña used to say, "I sell my labor, not my conscience." (Interview, Confidential 10/15/96)

As we will see in the following chapter, such contradictions between the school's leftist ideology and technical function would become most apparent in the late 1960s and early 1970s as a result of the student movement.

Another problem that the National School of Economics encountered in fulfilling its role as a training ground for government technicians was the difficulty in implementing and upholding standards of selection and certification within the Mexican public university system. In Mexico, as elsewhere in Latin America, the public university was originally an institution that reproduced elites by providing credentials for social status and economic rewards. However, beginning in the 1960s, governments throughout Latin America vastly expanded public university enrollments as a short-term way of defusing social discontent by fueling hopes for social mobility (Levy 1986: 38, 46).[18] Although such massification provided more opportunities for many, it also made it difficult to enforce formal standards of entrance and certification, as well as generally lowering the quality of public university education, since expanded enrollments were rarely accompanied by correspondingly expanded budgets. Another effect of massification was a phenomenon Collins (1979) refers to as "credential inflation" (p. 191): the mere fact of being more widely available cheapened the value of public university degrees and fueled efforts by elites to find new, more exclusive credentials. Levy (1986) notes that in many Latin American countries, massification provoked an exodus of the upper classes from public universities and increased enrollments in private ones. Thus, schools like the ITM ultimately benefited from more open public universities.

In Mexico, the relative absence of formal standards of selection and matriculation predated the explosion of enrollments: since its first decades, Mexican public universities were highly politicized and the focus of student discontent, especially regarding the implementation of meritocratic standards. In his history of student movements in Mexico, Mabry (1982) concludes by observing that—with a few notable exceptions, such as the 1968 student movement—Mexican public university students were rarely involved in movements that were revolutionary or antigovernment. Rather, "[T]hey more commonly rebel[led] against tuition increases, class attendance requirements, tougher admission or graduation standards, and more rigorous examination systems" (p. 285).

Whereas university students of all nations tend to grumble about these mundane sorts of oppression, Mexican university students were unusually likely to form effective protest movements based on these issues, thereby winning concessions that allowed more students to enter and more students to graduate, and prevented the implementation of more rigorous academic standards. For example, an important 1929 law-student strike was the result of an effort by National University authorities to implement more frequent and more difficult examinations (Mabry 1982: 59). In the 1960s, another such effort to raise academic standards and control university growth led to the resignation of the rector promoting the changes and the appointment of a new rector who pacified the students by uncapping enrollments (Mabry 1982: 221–33).

It is worth noting that in both cases the university officials promoting the changes and opposed by students were known as leftists: Law School director Narciso Bassols and rector Ignacio Chávez. Therefore, it is difficult to simplify these struggles as being between "reactionary" administrators and "democratic" students (particularly in the case of the first example, since the 1929 law students were renowned for their elite socioeconomic backgrounds and their right-wing politics). It is perhaps more useful to suggest that students' ongoing struggle to maintain open public universities made sense in a system where social stratification and mobility were linked to a powerful political system, which tended to distribute rewards on the basis of loyalty and connections, and not necessarily on the basis of ability. Since the public university was both the recruiting ground for political elites and the key place for the formation of both horizontal and vertical political ties, it was logical for students to fight against efforts to limit admissions and certification, so that all could have access to the possibility of forming these ties.

As a result of the political difficulty of imposing formal systems of control over public university access and certification, Levy (1980) observes that in general Mexican public universities have had lax entrance requirements and even less control over career matriculation (p. 67).[19] There was little control over admission to the National School of Economics, and grades gave a prospective employer only the roughest idea of how good a student was, since the relative difficulty of different professors varied widely (interview, Ibarra 11/5/95). However, this lack of formal selection systems at the National School of Economics was apparently compensated for by a relatively efficient informal system. In the intimate environment of the school's first decades (as late as 1948, the student population of the School of Economics was only 286) taxi professors teaching small classes could accurately distinguish the good students from the bad and recommend the former for posts in public administration (UNAM 1981: 257). Thus, the deficiencies of a formal system of credentials were made up for through personal networks.

However, rapid expansion of the student body reduced the efficiency of these informal selection mechanisms, making public-sector recruitment of UNAM economists more problematic. In contrast to the UNAM as a whole, which expanded most rapidly in the 1960s and '70s, the School of Economics experienced its biggest expansion from 1951 to 1962, when the number of students in the program increased more than fivefold (UNAM 1981: 257). Since during the same period the number of professors[20] increased only 163%, it is clear that class size must have grown substantially during this period (UNAM 1981: 267). Thus, the expansion of admissions to the National School of Economics made it more difficult for taxi professors to acquire the intimate knowledge of their students that had previously enabled them to recommend them for public-sector positions (interview, Confidential 11/5/96).

Moreover, the concomitant "credential inflation" resulting from this expansion reduced the value of an UNAM economics degree. In the absence of a fivefold increase in employment opportunities for economists corresponding to the increase in economics students, massification at the National School of Economics could have two possible effects: either selection measures (formal or informal) could be made more rigorous in order to select a smaller proportion of the student body for available positions, or credential inflation would result in the devaluation of the degrees of *all* students. Since massification was not accompanied by more rigorous formal selection mechanisms—and actually *decreased* the efficacy of informal ones—it was logical for credential inflation to result, and for elite students to seek alternatives to the public university for certification in economics.

In summary, it appears that by the 1960s, tendencies within Mexican public universities were harming the National School of Economics's ability to certify competent students for their subsequent employment in the government bureaucracy. These difficulties were rooted in the importance of such universities as a public resource for achieving social mobility: public universities were an openly contested territory, forced to respond to political pressures for expanded opportunities. As we will see in the following chapter, public universities would also become increasingly important centers of social and political criticism during the late 1960s and early 1970s, which would further impede the National School of Economics's ability to train and certify public administrators. Private universities, which were not subject to such pressures, would become an increasingly important source of public-sector economists during the 1970s and '80s.

PRIVATE SECTOR ECONOMICS AND THE ITM

The Mexican economics profession had originally been created by government functionaries for the purpose of staffing government bureaucracies, and the government was where economics graduates expected to work during the profession's first decades. By the 1960s, however, employment opportunities for Mexican economists in the private sector were becoming more significant. An UNAM economics thesis from 1961 noted that the utilization of the professional services of the economist in business was a relatively recent phenomenon, which had previously been hindered by Mexico's low level of economic development. In the old days, "the businessman designed his own plant, installed the machinery, acquired the raw materials, and bought the necessary materials and parts, and once the article was produced served as direct seller" (Barrosco Castro 1961: 43).

The simple and undifferentiated structure of these earlier businesses meant that economists were superfluous. But over time, Mexican firms came to take on some of the organizational characteristics associated with modern corporations in the United States (cf. Chandler 1977), leading to increased reliance on professional management.[21] Such professionalization was reflected in the growth of private university programs in accounting, economics, and business administration—perhaps best exemplified by the success of the Monterrey Tech, a university that has always catered primarily to the manufacturing firms for which the city of Monterrey is famous.

Two studies conducted in Monterrey provide useful descriptions of the prospects and problems faced by private-sector economists at the end of the 1960s. Alanís Gómez (1969) noted that whereas at the national level the best opportunities for economists were in the government, in Monterrey their best prospects were in the private sector. In his 1968 survey of graduates of the economics programs of the Monterrey Tech and the University of Nuevo León, the author found that over half of the graduates surveyed worked for the private sector, with 23% working in finance, 20% in manufacturing, and 8% in commerce. The author's survey among high-level administrators of Monterrey firms showed that the most-cited reason given by businesses for hiring economists was to carry out economic planning studies (Alanís Gómez 1969: 70–263). It therefore appears that the field of expertise of economists in the private sector was that of calculating long-term prospects, an area to which competing professionals—particularly accountants and administrators—had the least claim.

Nevertheless, the author concluded that the opportunities for economists in the private sector in Monterrey were still underexploited. Whereas 86% of the firm managers surveyed thought that an economist "could be useful," only 36% actually employed economists. The most pressing problem faced by economists in this area was private-sector officials' ignorance regarding what an economist was, and what services he or she could provide. When asked if they understood what an economist was, only 36% of the surveyed officials replied that they understood perfectly or well, while 43% replied that they "somewhat" understood, 18% had "notions," and 3% had no idea whatsoever (Alanís Gómez 1969: 261). This incomprehension of the function of economists among businessmen was also noted by Rico Samaniego (1971) in his study among financial-sector functionaries in Monterrey (p. 105). In keeping with Abbott's (1988) observations regarding professional systems, a second obstacle to private-sector employment of economists was competition with other professions. Of the financial-sector functionaries interviewed by Rico Samaniego (1971), 48% believed that the services of economists were easily replaceable. The professions most cited as replacing the services of economists were accountants and business administrators; engineers with economics "specializations" (economics "minors" in U.S. terminology) were also cited.

These factors limiting the private-sector employment of economists were noted in a place where the business need for experts was most highly developed (Monterrey), and among graduates of two programs with reputations for producing apolitical technicians—the Monterrey Tech and the University of Nuevo León.[22] It is reasonable to expect that these limitations were even more constraining in Mexico City, and for graduates of programs with a more leftist reputation. In particular, it appears that UNAM economics graduates were relatively unlikely either to seek or to obtain employment in private business, both because of the strong "pull" of government employment for those studying in Mexico City and because businesses were reluctant to hire graduates of a program known for cultivating Marxist views. This apparently led to a generalized but inaccurate perception among UNAM economics students that the only opportunities for economists were in government. In the words of one such student in 1961, "Due to the eminently social function of the licenciado in economics, the field of this profession appears to be limited to the [government] bureaucracy" (Barrosco Castro 1961: 34).

This perception notwithstanding, the evidence suggests that some private-sector opportunities for economists in Mexico City did exist. Graduates of the Department of Economics of the ITM were naturally more successful in securing private-sector employment than graduates of the National School of Economics. According to a study based on the database of the ITAM Ex-Students' Association, 45% of registered graduates before 1971 for whom data were available were working for the private sector in 1996, with 19% working in the public sector. One important factor that helped ITM graduates to secure private-sector employment was that many of them were sons and daughters of leading businessmen, and therefore simply worked for the family business.

Like the UNAM School of Economics during these years, ITM economics classes were taught mostly by professors with other full-time jobs and attended by many students who worked during the day as well; as a result, classes were held early in the morning and in the evening (interview, Bassols Zaleta 3/20/96). Where public-sector employment was concerned, a particularly important employer of ITM economics graduates appears to have been the Banco de México: among those employed in government in the database of graduates before 1971, the central bank was the single most important employer. The employment of early ITM economics graduates by the central bank was logical given their mutual disaffinity for leftist ideology, as well as the Banco's role in the school's foundation. Graduates from this period—notably Gustavo Petricioli, Miguel Mancera, and Francisco Gil Díaz—rose to high positions within the central bank and subsequently taught classes that provided more ITM graduates with the possibility of central bank employment. Even more important (and as we will see in the following chapter), these Banco officials would play a crucial role in reshaping the economics program at their alma mater, thereby creating a school of economics modeled in the image of international standards.

The ITM was founded to fulfill the ideological objective of providing economics training with a more conservative focus than the National School of Economics. In this sense, it differed from other private-sector economics programs founded before 1970, such as at the Monterrey Tech, which was founded in 1954 in the northern industrial state of Nuevo León. In contrast to the Depression era when UNAM economics was established, the mid-1950s was a time when Mexican industry had become sufficiently large, prosperous, and organizationally complex to begin to utilize economic professionals. Thus, the Tech's economics program was established to fulfill a technical rather than a political purpose, and required more technically oriented courses of its students. The Tech program's original curriculum required over 15% of total class hours in accounting, more than 21% in law, and over 16% in administration; in addition to their special skills as economists. Tech graduates were supposed to serve as versatile "jacks-of-all-trades" within the private sector (ITESM 1968: 63).

In contrast, the ITM economics program was less pragmatic and more academic than its counterpart in Monterrey. This was due particularly to the program's enormous debt to Miguel Palacios Macedo, a lawyer and conservative intellectual who had also assisted in the formation of the original economics curriculum at the UNAM. The ITM's 1951 curriculum[23] included two full-year classes in the history of economic thought, two in economic history, and a full-year class in sociology; students were also required to take two and a half years of law and two of accounting, but only half a year of business administration. As a result of its academic orientation, students were even required to take a full-year course titled "The Economic and Social Theory of Marxism." Significantly—and in contrast to its counterpart at the UNAM—the 1951 ITM curriculum also included two full years of English (ITM 1951: 27–28).

While the ITM and the Tech differed in *degree* of politicization, the ITM and the UNAM economics programs differed with respect to political *orientation*: while the UNAM had been founded as a statist, sometimes even Marxist program, the ITM had been established as an ideological bastion of a more conservative economic point of view. Sixteen theses written by ITM economics students from 1956 to 60 display revealing contrasts and similarities when compared with the UNAM theses from 1958. The most outstanding difference between the two groups is the complete absence of Marxism in the former: not only were there no Marxist theses and none approving of socialism in the ITM theses, but Marx was not cited once. Developmentalist ideas were also relatively weak at the ITM compared to the UNAM during the same period: only 12.5% of the ITM theses mentioned the fundamental differences between developed and developing countries.

However, the similarities between ITM and UNAM theses in the 1950s outweighed the differences. First, both groups displayed a comparable use of mathematical models and methods. This suggests that the apparent lack of mathematics in the UNAM program in the 1950s was not (as a contemporary reader might suppose) due to the UNAM's leftist focus but rather reflected the fact that economics in the 1950s was a less mathematized discipline than it is today. Second, the ITM theses resembled their UNAM counterparts in that the most-cited theoretical author from 1956 to 1960 was Keynes—with the second-most-cited author being Ragnar Nurkse, a Swedish development economist whose analyses were compatible with those of the ECLA developmentalists (Martinussen 1997: 57–58).

TABLE 4.3
Positions on State Intervention, UNAM 1958 vs. ITAM 1956–60

	UNAM 1958		ITAM 1956–60	
	N	(%)	N	(%)
Less intervention advocated	0	(0)	0	(0)
Existing interventions supported	6	(37.5)	6	(37.5)
More intervention advocated	10	(62.5)	8	(50)
No position on intervention	0	(0)	2	(12.5)
Total	16	(100)	16	(100)

$\chi^2 = 2.2, \alpha < .05$

The ITM theses did not use extravagant free-market and deregulatory rhetoric, except for a single article extolling private property. Most important, ITM theses took positions on state interventionism that were nearly identical to those taken in UNAM theses, with 50% strongly interventionist and 37.5% moderately interventionist (table 4.3). As one author explained, "I do not in any way uphold the traditional doctrine of laissez faire–laissez passer in its purest form, since although social and economic liberty should exist, one cannot deny the function of the state as a regulator and promoter of development. [I therefore] recognize certain social and economic intervention as necessary" (García Duarte 1959: 47). In summary, a comparison of theses from the UNAM and the ITM during this period reveals that whereas the ITM was not a center of Marxist economic thought, there was a basic agreement among the two schools regarding the need for state intervention in the economy; they shared a single policy paradigm.

CONCLUSION

The rhetoric, methods, and authors cited in the ITM theses of the 1950s show that there is no a priori reason for business groups to endorse liberal ideology and reject government intervention. In the 1930s Mexican business leaders saw their interests threatened by *cardenista* policies; their response was a turn to laissez-faire liberalism that culminated in the foundation of the ITM. After 1940, however, Mexican government policy toward business (both national and international) was consistently conciliatory: the government interventions of the 1950s and '60s were in the area of industrial promotion and infrastructural investment rather than the supporting of workers in strikes and peasants in land takeovers (and indeed independent labor and social movements were repressed). It is not surprising, therefore, that by the late 1950s, ITM economics had become

Keynesian and developmentalist; by this time it was abundantly clear that Mexican government intervention was good for business.

Thus, by the 1950s and '60s there appears to have existed a single Keynesian "policy paradigm" in Mexico, which was simultaneously upheld at the government-oriented UNAM, the privately funded ITM, and by renowned economic experts around the world. This common view of the role of the government in the economy was made possible by a certain level of agreement between the state and the private sector, economic growth that brought tangible improvements to many different sectors, and a political system that effectively managed demands from below. As a result, the economics profession in Mexico during the postwar period appears to have had legitimacy among both public and private constituencies, and few dissenting voices were raised to question this legitimacy.

This consensus was doubtless also made possible by the unique features of postwar Keynesianism noted by Skidelsky (1977). Unlike previous economic doctrines, Keynesianism had the virtue of appearing to "offer something to everybody": through the manipulation of abstract macroeconomic variables, governments were supposed to be able improve the general social welfare without making costly social trade-offs. Developmentalism was theoretically supposed to offer similar advantages: policies like import substitution could offer benefits to the protected private sector, the government, and its popular constituents.

However, Mexico's postwar policy paradigm could generate consensus only as long as it appeared to be working. The following chapter describes the breakdown of the Keynesian-developmentalist consensus in Mexico in the 1970s and the consequent division of Mexican economics.

CHAPTER 5

THE BREAKDOWN OF DEVELOPMENTALISM
AND THE POLARIZATION OF MEXICAN ECONOMICS

THE LATE 1960s represented a turning point for the Mexican developmentalist model. As in many parts of the world, in Mexico these years were a period of social upheaval and protest against the injustice of existing political and economic arrangements; moreover, by the early 1970s, signs of economic decline contributed to a general impression that the relatively peaceful, prosperous years of the postwar period were at an end and that something was going to have to change. Indeed, change was exactly what many young Mexican political activists expected; for some, a second Mexican revolution seemed to be right around the corner.

Of course, with historical hindsight we know that the great change that ultimately occurred in Mexico would bear little resemblance to what these young radicals anticipated. Although the student movement indirectly contributed to the "populist" policies of the 1970s, the debt crisis resulting from these policies would ultimately provide the conditions for austerity and neoliberalism. The market-oriented reforms of the 1980s and '90s would be implemented by a new generation of Mexican economists whose U.S.-style training predisposed them to look on the state interventionism of previous years with misgiving and to endorse market opening as the solution to Mexico's problems. This chapter discusses both how this new theoretical perspective came to predominate at the ITAM (the ITM's new name after it became officially autonomous in 1962), and the conditions leading to the adoption of a very different theoretical perspective at the National School of Economics.

THE CRISIS IN MEXICAN DEVELOPMENTALISM

In 1973, Mexican economist Leopoldo Solís observed in the introduction to his widely read book that all was not well with the Mexican economy:

> [G]radually great clouds have come to darken the optimism concerning Mexican economic evolution. The most important are those that indicate that, before the progress of some minority sectors, the poverty of many persists

tenaciously; and that the distribution of income not only resists being less unequal, but actually in certain periods has worsened notably. The incapacity of the system to provide employment to its growing labor force in the face of accelerated demographic growth—its lack of international competitiveness, expressed as lack of vigorous exporting and growing external debt, obliges many Mexican and foreign economists to reevaluate and rethink the characteristics and merits of the Mexican model of economic development. (Solís 1973: 7)

The problems of the Mexican economy, it was generally agreed, resulted from fundamental flaws in Mexican economic policymaking; the astounding growth rates of the 1950s and '60s had not been cost-free. Mexico's import substitution policy, originally designed to support "infant industries," had been institutionalized as a long-term subsidy to Mexican capitalists: although this policy had contributed to high rates of economic growth, it had also increased the cost of industrial inputs, raised domestic prices, and discouraged exports (Solís 1973: 8). The resulting lack of competitiveness of Mexican exports and reliance on imported inputs contributed to chronic and growing commercial deficits and balance-of-payments problems. Under these circumstances, the peso's fixed exchange rate—which was maintained under stabilizing development to help fight inflation and encourage domestic savings—resulted in an overvalued peso that had to be propped up by growing public debt. Thus, the fixed exchange rate amounted to a public subsidy to private consumption and production through cheap imports; the overvalued peso also discouraged exports, which could have ameliorated the resulting balance-of-payments deficits (Reynolds 1977b: 999–1001).

Mexico's notorious failure to implement a fully developed, progressive system of taxation also had negative long-term consequences. The Mexican government derived most of its resources from workers' income, indirect taxes (which were mostly regressive), and internal and external loans. The resulting fiscal restrictiveness put a permanent brake on government spending in areas such as social welfare (Reynolds 1977b: 1005–6). Hansen (1971) observed that in 1967 only 6.1% of the total Mexican population, or 18.9% of the workforce, was covered by social security benefits, which put Mexico behind all major Latin American countries (p. 86). Meanwhile—and in spite of twenty-five years of spectacular growth—long-standing, structural unemployment continued to plague the Mexican economy (Solís 1973: 8; Reynolds 1977b: 1005).

The resulting economic and social panorama had some discouraging features. Although income distribution did not worsen between 1958 and 1970, it showed no improvement, and the distribution of personal income *after taxes* had become worse because of the lack of significant fiscal reform (Izquierdo 1995: 139, 143). Although the period between 1940 and

1970 did witness a substantial growth in the Mexican middle class, in 1969, the poorest 30% of Mexican families still had an income equivalent to a third or less of the average Mexican family income (Hansen 1971: 180; Izquierdo 1995: 138). The combined effect of a post-*cardenista* agricultural policy that had favored large over small landowners,[1] on the one hand, and chronic unemployment, on the other, created a large demand for land reform that was not forthcoming. In the 1960s, Mexican social reformers began increasingly to talk about the "marginalization" of a rural population that had been left to stagnate in poverty and backwardness while urban Mexico moved into the modern era (González Casanova 1965: 62). The social deficiencies of the Mexican Miracle "sooner or later had to become incompatible with the popular image of the government" (Tello 1979: 34).

While the negative side effects of the Mexican Miracle were causing many to question the desirability of the economic and political models that had made it possible, historical events in Latin America caused a more general crisis for developmentalism. The military coup in Brazil in 1964 caused many to doubt that capitalist development could occur within a peaceful, democratic context as ECLA scholars had assumed: the developmentalist model was seen as having certain inherent "contradictions" that inevitably led to authoritarianism (a critique that was "confirmed" in the 1970s with the spread of military dictatorships throughout Latin America). At the same time, the early successes of the Cuban revolution provided an alternative model—some said the only alternative model—of economic development compatible with social equality (Zapata 1990: 217). A new school of thought known as "dependency theory" challenged developmentalism in general and the ECLA model in particular; many of its adherents proposed revolutionary change as the only way out of authoritarianism and chronic economic problems.

In Mexico, of course, these long-term historical trends played themselves out somewhat differently. As we saw in the preceding chapter, Mexican developmentalism was never formally theorized according to the ECLA model. Moreover, in Mexico the compatibility of government promotion of capitalist development with democratic rule appeared to be a vain illusion from the very beginning. The Mexican one-party political system, while certainly not as brutal as the South American dictatorships of the 1970s, had never been democratic by the standards of Western industrial democracies. The impressive growth of the Mexican Miracle was punctuated by incidents in which workers attempted to break free of the officially controlled union structure in order to demand a larger share of the growing economic pie, only to have their unions busted and their leaders thrown in jail (LaBotz 1988: 89). By 1970, the Mexican government was encountering significant and widespread opposition among a group that, on the surface, had relatively little to complain about: university students. The Mexican student movement that grew and evolved throughout the 1960s,[2] although overwhelmingly composed of young people of the middle classes, represented a challenge both to the inequalities that had accompanied postwar economic growth and to the repressive political system that had maintained these inequalities.

In keeping with the observations of resource mobilization theorists (cf. Tilly 1978), the relative strength of the student movement with regard to other Mexican social movements (such as organized labor) did not result from students' greater level of grievances. On the contrary, as Villegas (1993) points out, students were a relatively "spoiled" group in the postwar period: while independent labor movements were being crushed by the government, successive presidential administrations built a splendid new "University City" on the southern outskirts of the Mexican capital, and furnished and equipped it. A public university education in Mexico was not only practically free but also middle-class youths' gate of entry to a political career (Villegas 1993: 208). Moreover, the UNAM and other autonomous public universities constituted a unique space for freedom of expression: whereas independent leftist labor leaders were thrown in jail, Marxist professors and students were generally able to express their points of view with relative impunity. Thus, the university became the most important focal point of protest against the postwar economic and political models because it was an environment that provided the resources for such protest: students and professors possessed means for independent organizing that labor did not.

Social-scientific interpretation of the Mexican student movement is not yet sufficiently abundant to provide a definitive answer to the question of its most fundamental causes. Zermeño (1978) and Loaeza (1989) assert that the movement essentially represented a demand by middle-class youth for political participation. In Zermeño's view, the postwar Mexican political system attended to the interests of capitalists and controlled the demands of peasants and workers but failed to effectively incorporate the middle class (1978: 91). Thus, the 1968 movement represented an assertion of the "bourgeois" values of democracy and the rejection of authoritarian corporatism. Zermeño vigorously asserts that the radicalized students of 1968 were *not* primarily motivated by frustration stemming from "their expectations of professional employment"; good jobs still awaited students upon graduation (Zermeño 1978: 37–51).

Nevertheless, from a rational-choice point of view, at least, this interpretation of the student movement seems less than satisfactory. It is unquestionable that there was a great deal wrong with the Mexican social and political panorama in the late 1960s; students were right to protest. Moreover, it is likely that the movement offered great personal satisfaction and other selective incentives to those who participated. The question is neither why students felt they had grievances nor why movement participation appeared attractive, but rather why students would choose to undergo personal risk to express their grievances if the benefits from playing by the rules were considerable. This question seems especially salient for the Mexican student movement, the promised collective benefit of which (i.e., democracy) must have appeared rather abstract when contrasted with the individual benefits of the placid pursuit of a university degree, a political career, and a comfortable life.

The most obvious answer to this question is that playing by the rules was no longer enough: secure, middle-class employment was no longer guaranteed by a university degree. According to Collins's (1979) commonsense reasoning, in a system where the number of credentialed individuals increases at a faster rate than the number of desirable jobs, it inevitably follows that the possession of such credentials no longer invariably leads to the securing of desirable jobs. It is easy to imagine that the resulting "crisis of credentialism" could lower the relative costs associated with participation in social movements. Indeed, statistics suggest that the number of desirable "slots" in Mexican society did not increase at a rate commensurate with the increase in university degrees and that credential inflation must have resulted. Mabry (1982) calculates that the UNAM student population increased by 300% between 1944 and 1966 (p. 215). In contrast, according to Hansen (1971), between 1940 and 1963 the percentage of upper- and middle-class Mexicans of the total population increased by about 130%, from 13% of the population to over 30% (p. 180). Based on an analysis of historical data professionals, Lorey (1994) also concludes that "the Mexican economy has been unable to provide enough professional-level jobs for university graduates since at least the late 1950s" (p. 28). Thus, although there may still have been good jobs for Mexican university graduates, a university degree no longer *guaranteed* such a job.[3]

From the very beginning, the student movement's demand for political pluralism coexisted with a more radical agenda: the Mexican student movement was motivated by the repression of the labor movement of the late 1960s and inspired by the Cuban revolution (Guevara Niebla 1978: 12). As a result, its rhetoric was a sometimes incongruous combination of Marxist and pro-Cuba language, and more moderate demands for democracy. Such rhetorical diversity resulted in part from the diverse points of view that the movement represented: whereas some students were for the immediate revolutionary "removal of bourgeois domination," others hoped for future change through electoral battles. At the peak of the student movement in 1968, its dominant themes were prodemocratic rather than revolutionary: whereas few 1968 movement handbills demanded socialist revolution, many confined themselves to demands for democracy (Mabry 1982: 255–56).

The 1968 Olympics to be held in Mexico City symbolized the myth of the Mexican Miracle that the student movement wished to debunk. As the first developing country to host the Olympics, Mexico was supposed to be a model of economic progress and political liberties. While the movement was determined to use the Olympics to draw the world's attention to Mexican authoritarianism and social injustice, the government was determined to keep social disorder from creating a bad impression among the international community. Throughout the summer preceding the Olympics, the student movement asserted its power and scope through strikes and mass demonstrations, and the Mexican army was deployed to take over the UNAM on September 18 (Mabry 1982: 261). On October 2, 1968—ten days before the games were scheduled to be held—a movement rally at Tlatelolco Plaza was attacked by the army in a massacre that took the lives of as many as 350 (LaBotz 1988: 121). Government tolerance for dissent—even from elite university students— had been exhausted, and the Tlatelolco massacre became a national symbol of the government's lack of legitimacy.

THE POPULIST RESPONSE: 1970–1982

By 1970, the atmosphere in Mexico was highly charged and unstable. The student movement and the government's brutal response to it, along with growing guerrilla movements in the countryside, provoked a generalized fear of escalating social conflict and even civil war. The presidency of Luis Echeverría (1970–76) arrived to smooth over social turbulence through increased social spending and a policy of reconciliation with the university. Echeverría criticized the privileged position given to capital under the policies of stabilizing development and demanded the resignation of Antonio Ortíz Mena—the finance minister responsible for stabilizing development—several months before the end of the preceding presidential term. To replace the fiscal and monetary conservatism of his two predecessors, Echeverría proposed a new policy of "shared development," under which economic growth per se would no longer be the primary goal of economic development, and the role of the public sector would be expanded (Luna Ledesma 1992: 35). Issues of distribution rather than growth were to be emphasized, and a bigger government would address them. At the same time, the Echeverría administration promoted a democratic opening to address the government's legitimation crisis. Electoral reforms were carried out, the internal politics of the ruling party were modified, political prisoners from the student movement were liberated, and the formation of new political parties was encouraged (Latapí 1980: 57).

During the Echeverría administration, public expenditure was greatly expanded, and spending in areas such as health, housing, and education increased. Mexico's long-standing policy of import substitution was upgraded through more stringent import controls. Direct government intervention in the economy was expanded on an unprecedented scale: between 1971 and 1976 alone, 108 major public enterprises were created, as compared to only 83 between 1952 and 1970 (Bazdresch and Levy 1991: 241–42). To fund new and increased government interventions, the administration attempted to implement fiscal reform, but large-scale opposition from the private sector and threatened capital flight caused this initiative to be abandoned. The 1% sales tax increase that was successfully implemented was insufficient to cover the cost of increased public spending, and the government came to rely even more heavily on external borrowing (Bazdresch and Levy 1991: 239; Maddison et al. 1989: 26).

Mexico's foreign debt was also increased by Echeverría's adherence to the fixed exchange-rate policy of his predecessors, which meant that government resources were devoted to propping up the peso. Increased public spending and domestic credit contributed to higher levels of inflation, which averaged over 17% between 1973 and 1976. This inflation, in turn, increased the difference between the real and the official value of the peso, a difference that had to be financed by the government. By 1976, fears of an impending devaluation were fueling capital flight, which hastened the devaluation that investors feared. At the end of the Echeverría administration, the government was $29.5 billion dollars in debt and had to sign a standby agreement with the IMF (Bazdresch and Levy 1991: 232–23, 242).

Whereas the Echeverría administration threatened private investors with leftist rhetoric and talk of Third World solidarity, the López Portillo administration (1976–82) was seen as relatively friendly to business. López Portillo's answer to shared development was the Alliance for Production, a "new accord under which all social groups would participate in the process of economic recovery and political healing." What López Portillo had in common with his predecessor was the reliance on debt-financed government spending as a way of garnering political support. López Portillo vastly increased public investment in the oil industry and was also known for his investments in other infrastructure, health, and nutrition. The rising oil prices of the 1970s, combined with vast new discoveries of petroleum in Mexico, restored economic growth, but this temporary boom was ended with the fall in oil prices in 1981. At the same time, high rates of inflation in the early 1980s had consequences similar to those resulting from inflation during the Echeverría years: an overvalued peso and capital flight. López Portillo's response to capital flight was to nationalize the private banking industry. Like the administration of his predecessor, the López Portillo administration concluded with a devaluation and the signing of an IMF stabilization program; Mexico's foreign debt stood at $92.4 billion dollars (Bazdresch and Levy 1991: 246–49).

As critics of the Echeverría and López Portillo administrations, Bazdresch and Levy (1991) label the two presidents "economic populists" who relied on imprudent levels of government spending as a way of resolving Mexico's simultaneous economic, political, and social crises.[4] The populism of the 1970s had a high price, namely, the debt crisis of the 1980s. On the other hand, the policies of these two presidencies also helped restore of economic growth for a time, which averaged over 7% per annum for the years 1971–82 (Bazdresch and Levy 1991: 243). Whether or not the policies of the Echeverría and López Portillo administrations were the correct solution to Mexico's manifold problems, they had extremely significant implications for Mexican economics, which will be discussed in the following sections.

The 1970s Boom and Mexican Economics

Unlike the United States, where the 1970s were known as the decade of combined economic stagnation and high inflation ("stagflation"), in Mexico the decade was generally characterized by abundance and growth, albeit at the cost of rapidly increasing prices. The two factors most responsible for Mexico's flourishing economy were a surge in foreign borrowing and increased oil revenues, stemming from the discovery of new petroleum reserves combined with high oil prices (due to the actions of the OPEC cartel).

For Mexican economics, the abundance of resources during the 1970s had several outstanding consequences. First, the expansion of the public sector led to increased opportunities for economists of all sorts at all levels of government; from "structuralist" to "monetarist" and from lowly bureaucrat to powerful technocrat, the 1970s were a good decade to be an economist in Mexico. Second, the fact that the resources available were accompanied by a low level of conditionality made it possible for a new group of foreign-trained economists—those to the extreme left of the Mexican developmentalist consensus—to occupy certain prominent policymaking positions. Finally, the abundance of the 1970s meant that more government resources were available for higher education. This included both scholarships for foreign graduate study and increased funding for public economics programs—even those which, like the UNAM, were of progressively less use to the public sector.

As we saw in the previous chapter, during the postwar period, access to external resources—through the World Bank, IMF, Alliance for Progress, and others—had provided a strong impetus for the internationalization of Mexican economics. Foreign-trained economists in government, had been the ambassadors to a new world order that offered critical resources to the governments of developing countries, conditioned on certain policies and professional/administrative standards.

The 1970s were also a time of incredibly bountiful external financing, but of a different sort: in the 1970s loans from bilateral and multilateral organizations became progressively less important as borrowing on international financial markets increased dramatically. Mexico had been unusually successful among Latin American countries in regaining access to international financial markets after the 1954 devaluation of the peso. Nevertheless, Mexico's private external borrowing remained relatively moderate until the administrations of Echeverría and López Portillo. Figure 5.1 illustrates the increase in Mexico's external borrowing in the 1970s and early '80s, and contrasts it with the more prudent borrowing of the stabilizing development period: whereas the Mexican public external debt was equivalent to only 12.7% of gross domestic product in 1970, by 1982 it was equivalent to 36.5%.

Mexico was not alone: in general, the 1970s were a decade of immoderate lending by international banks and foreign investors, and immoderate external borrowing in Latin America and other parts of the Third World. As Frieden (1991) shows, although the destination of foreign loans was determined by domestic politics, as a more general phenomenon, heavy external borrowing was determined by international factors. These factors included the reglobalization of financial markets through a growing offshore banking sector (which eluded national banking regulations) and the glut of "petrodollars" from oil-exporting nations, which gave banks a surplus of investable funds. Led by Citibank president Walter Wriston, banks began to flock to developing countries to invest in both private- and public-sector projects.

In Mexico, public-sector borrowing predominated, and foreign loans were used by two successive presidential administrations to try to address Mexico's economic, political, and social problems. Whereas Echeverría's public spending went toward a diverse array of projects, during the administration of López Portillo the largest single destination of resources acquired through external financing was the public petroleum industry, embodied in the publicly owned company known as PEMEX. López Portillo saw in the petroleum industry the opportunity for renewed economic growth and rapid development in Mexico. By 1981, PEMEX had become

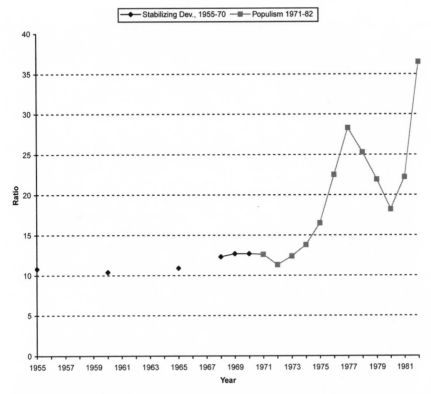

Fig. 5.1. Mexican Public External Debt/GDP Ratio, 1955–82. Source: Gil Díaz (1984).

the most important single source of government resources from domestic sources, accounting for 24.9% of federal taxes received (see table 5.1). Thanks to revenues from the rapidly expanding petroleum industry, Mexico was able to abandon its IMF agreement in 1976 simply by paying off its debt (Teichman 1988: 65–66).

The 1976–82 period in Mexico provides an interesting case study of how fluctuating resource dependence and independence affects the relative positions of different professions within the governments of developing countries. With the IMF safely out of Mexico's internal affairs once again, and with foreign investors climbing over one another to invest in Mexico's highly lucrative oil industry, the need to conform to the standards of powerful external actors was greatly reduced. As a result, the premium placed among Mexican officials on fluency in English and economese was reduced, while rising oil revenues made the engineers associated with the PEMEX bureaucracy more prominent and powerful. Thus,

TABLE 5.1
Petroleum and the Mexican Economy, 1976–82

	1976	1977	1978	1979	1980	1981	1982
Crude oil exports, 1000s bbl/day	94	202	365	533	828	1,098	1,492.1
Petroleum and products, % total							
value exports	16.8	22.4	29.7	43.8	67.4	74.4	73.6
% total taxes paid by PEMEX	5.0	8.3	9.6	13.8	24.0	24.9	47.3

Source: Teichman (1988).

for a brief period there were two different kinds of technocrats vying for control over economic policymaking in Mexico: the economists and the engineers. The leader of the rising engineer-technocrats was Jorge Díaz Serrano, a close friend of López Portillo who was director of PEMEX from 1976 to 1981 (and who was later imprisoned for fraud in 1983). According to Teichman (1988), during this period PEMEX engineers frequently came into conflict with the economist-technocrats of other branches of the Mexican public administration. Whereas the policy agenda of the engineers was rapid petroleum-output expansion at any cost, the economists tended to be more concerned with broader issues of economic development and price stability.

Such conflicts, however, were quickly ended by the fall in petroleum prices in the spring of 1981 and a mounting debt crisis that made economic expertise (and the ability to deal with foreign and international financial officials) ascendant once again; the economists had won. From 1982 onward, the focus of competition among Mexican technocrats would no longer be between engineers and economists, but among economists of different ideological persuasions. The nature and outcome of these battles will be discussed in chapter 7.

The dramatic expansion of the public sector during Echeverría's term led to a bonanza of employment possibilities for government economists; after a brief contraction in public finances at the beginning of the López Portillo administration, opportunities for public-sector economists expanded once again as the result of the oil boom (Lozano Hernández 1988: 25–26). Several areas of Mexican public administration stood out as institutions offering opportunities to young economists during the 1970s. Under Stanford-trained Davíd Ibarra's tenure as finance minister from 1977 through 1982, the Finance Ministry employed a team of rising young technocrats that included Pedro Aspe, an ITAM graduate who had only completed his Ph.D. at MIT in 1978. The Ministry of Budget and Planning (SPP), created in 1976, was simultaneously endowed with authority over both policymaking and resource allocation, and subsequently became a key organizational home for young Mexicans who had acquired foreign graduate credentials—both in economics and in other fields, such as public administration (Centeno 1994: 135). Meanwhile, the Banco de México—particularly its Department of Economic Studies—continued to be an important organizational base for economists with foreign training.

At the same time, economists came to occupy higher positions than ever before in the policymaking bureaucracy. In part, this reflected the agenda of the populist presidencies. If "economic planning" had been an important catchphrase in the 1950s and '60s, it became a mantra during the following decade, as the objectives of the public sector in the economy multiplied. Centeno (1994) has suggested that as direct government intervention in the economy became more common in the 1970s, "an administration's perceived success and legitimacy were increasingly based on its ability to *directly* foster economic growth rather than merely provide the political stability required to encourage and protect that provided by the private sector. . . . This redefinition of the role of the state obviously supported the rise in importance and influence of personnel with economic expertise" (p. 182). Moreover, the growing need to administer external debt put a particular premium on the understanding of international finance (p. 93). By 1980, the heads of the Ministry of Finance, the Ministry of National Patrimony, the development bank, and the central bank were all foreign-trained economists.

Nevertheless, it is well known among Mexican political scientists that the foreign-trained economists who came to control Mexican economic policymaking after 1970 did not share a single theoretical outlook. One common interpretation is that Mexican technocracy of this period was divided among "structuralists" and "monetarists"—a distinction I believe to be inexact and misleading in many ways, since it both overstates some distinctions in policy ideology and overlooks others.[5] I believe that a more useful analytical framework for understanding theoretical differences among Mexican economic policymakers is that used by Heredia (1996), who utilizes the policy ideologies of the stabilizing development period (1955–70) as a baseline for understanding subsequent trends in Mexican economic policymaking.

In Heredia's (1996) view, the stabilizing development period was a time of widespread consensus among Mexican economic policymakers, all of whom shared a roughly developmentalist outlook: the state needed to play an important role in economic development through such means as the protection of domestic industries from foreign competition.[6] The depth and breadth of this consensus was apparent in many of my conversations with the older generation of Mexican economists. For example, in an interview, Rafael Izquierdo (an economist who had been at the more conservative end of the developmentalist spectrum) recalled a discussion he had recently with Ifigenia Martínez (an economist who had been a more leftist developmentalist, and who later served as an elected representative with the opposition PRD):

> [T]he differences weren't that great; we all believed in sustained growth at a minimum of 6 percent per year. . . . I was talking to Ifigenia Martínez, and I said, 'Remember when we were enemies, you and I, because I believed in 6 percent growth and you believed in 7 percent growth?' There were differences but within a common framework: we were a poor country, and we needed to do something to stimulate growth. (Interview, Izquierdo 7/3/96)

Within this developmentalist spectrum, of course, there were some disagreements. Toward the right of the spectrum were economists and other policymakers from the Banco de México and other financial ministries, who tended to be more concerned with inflation. However, by today's standards, even the views espoused among this more "conservative" group in the 1960s appear quite statist and Keynesian, since they neither doubted the importance of the state's leadership in economic development nor questioned the necessity of some form of industrial protection (although some thought that it should be more selective).

During the 1970s, when external resources were relatively abundant and free of conditionality to the Mexican government, and oil revenues were at an all-time high, foreign-trained economists from the far left of the developmentalist consensus—the "structuralists" mentioned by Mexican political scientists (cf. Basañez 1991; Villarreal 1984)—came to hold important policymaking positions (Heredia 1996: 104). While the more conservative developmentalists remained in control of the Ministry of Finance and the Banco de México, the more radical group found institutional homes within sectors of the Ministry of National Resources (which was in charge of the rapidly expanding parastate industries) and the Secretary of the Presidency. These economists included José Oteyza and Carlos Tello, both of whom had pusued graduate studies at Cambridge University—a well-known center of Keynesian thinking. In general, the emphasis of these officials was on "deepening" Mexico's process of import substitution and accelerating Mexico's economic growth, even at the cost of inflation. Teichman (1988) has referred to them as the "quasi-populist tendency" within Mexican public administration [p. 94]). Conflict among these different tendencies became most intense during the López Portillo administration, when the more radical developmentalists effectively blocked the effort of more conservative technocrats to move toward trade liberalization (Heredia 1996: 108–41).

The left-leaning technocrats of the 1970s were affiliated with neither the UNAM nor the ITAM, but with the Center for Economics Education and Research (CIDE), created in the 1970s with public funding for the explicit purpose of training government economists. In keeping with this function, CIDE economists graduated with an M.A. in "public-sector economics" (Economía del Sector Público); undergraduate degrees were not offered. The CIDE became a bastion of Keynesian and left-developmentalist thinking in Mexico, and had important ties to the Department of Economics at Cambridge University, where several of the department's most notable professors had studied (interview, Alejo 2/13/97; Heredia 1996: 135–36). In this and the following chapters, we will see that the establishment of the CIDE as the government's source of left-developmentalist economists made sense given the radicalization of the UNAM during the 1960s and '70s—an evolution that would increasingly alienate UNAM economics from the public sector.

These highly visible trends in the profile of government policymakers were accompanied by a less visible trend that would have greater significance over the long term, namely, the vastly increased number of government scholarships to study abroad. One aspect of Echeverría's expansive higher education policy was the foundation of the National Council of Science and Technology (CONACYT) in 1970 for the purpose of funding training and research generally to benefit the cause of Mexican economic development. The council was able to fund graduate economics study abroad on a scale that dwarfed previous programs. For example, between 1941 and 1970, the Banco de México had provided scholarships for thirty-six of its employees to study economics abroad; in contrast, *in 1973 alone* there were forty-eight Mexicans studying economics abroad with Science and Technology grants (Banco de México 1961 and 1987; CONACYT 1973: 86).[7]

The Science and Technology scholarship program constitutes what is perhaps the most striking proof of the legitimacy of foreign standards of expertise within the Mexican government. Ironically, it was the nationalist-populist president Echeverría who was ultimately responsible for the foreign economics training of more Mexicans than any other scholarship program, either domestic or foreign. The resulting proliferation of foreign-credentialed economists in Mexican public administration would become extremely important as a source of training of the free-market-oriented policymakers of the 1980s and '90s.

A more immediate result of the proliferation of foreign credentials was credential inflation: by the late 1970s, it had become necessary to possess a graduate degree to be considered an "economist" in Mexico. Aspiring officials with mere undergraduate degrees had increasingly to compete with individuals with far more impressive credentials, a fact that effectively barred those with undergraduate degrees from reaching the upper levels of economic ministries. This credential inflation put UNAM economics graduates at a disadvantage because, throughout the 1960s and

'70s, UNAM economics was becoming increasingly radicalized and divorced from the public sector. On the other hand, the primary beneficiaries of credential inflation in Mexican economics were the graduates of the ITAM, which throughout the 1960s and '70s became Mexico's most internationalized economics program. The following sections examine the circumstances surrounding these simultaneous and thoroughly opposite evolutions.

The Student Movement and the Radicalization of UNAM Economics

The original economics program at the UNAM had been strongly influenced by *cardenismo* and the ideals of the Mexican revolution. After Cárdenas's term ended in 1940, however, and the government's most important goal became economic growth rather than social justice, UNAM economics became less political and more technical (discussed in chapter 4). In contrast, the student movement of the 1960s and '70s brought an end to this process of technification and reintroduced some of the radicalism that had characterized UNAM economics in the 1930s.

The highest rate of growth of the student population at the UNAM School of Economics occurred in the late 1950s and early 1960s (in contrast to the rest of the UNAM, which grew most rapidly in the 1970s). It was most likely partially a consequence of such massification that radicalism among UNAM economics students grew steadily throughout the 1960s, and students came increasingly to demand a greater say in the program's form and content. Under the directorship of Ifigenia Martínez de Navarrete[8] (1966–70), and with the intensive participation of students organized within a "cogovernment" of students and professors, a new program of studies was approved in 1967 and implemented in 1968 ("La Reforma" 1969: 660).

An outstanding theme among professors, students, and administrators in the discussions leading up to this new program was a critique of economics's pretension to neutrality, thus directly challenging the legitimacy of the profession of economics taught at the UNAM. A report on the new program criticized the tendency of economists ". . . to divorce economic from social reality and historical processes, removing it from the great problems of our times, robbing it of its scientific character and turning it into a supposedly neutral technique." In this view, by removing overt political and social content from its program of studies, the technification of economics at the UNAM achieved the opposite of the neutrality to which it aspired. In the 1968 program of studies, economics was conceived of "as political economy, and not apolitical" ("La Reforma" 1969: 660).

The new 1968 program of studies was significantly more leftist than the one that had preceded it, had an additional semester of Marxist theory, and included such new courses as "socialist economics" and "social accounting" (Mancilla López 1980: 141–44). At the same time, practical courses for training public functionaries were reduced: students were required to take only a year of public finance as opposed to two years in the previous program and were no longer required to take courses in cost accounting and financial analysis (Mancilla López 1980: 66; "La Reforma" 1969: 661). According to its statement of purpose, the 1968 program was for forming ". . . real economists and not simply technicians; that is to say, professionals with a rigorous theoretical foundation, with a deep knowledge of the national reality, with a consciousness of the social framework in which the economic process takes place, and who contribute to the independent development of the nation and the elevation of the people's standard of living" (Mancilla López 1980: 64). Among the other reforms of the 1968 program were its reduction in the number of required classes, an increase in the number of optional classes and seminars, and the institution of classes in the newly founded Center for Applied Economics, which was supposed to serve as a laboratory for training students in economic techniques, including mathematical methods and field studies (Facultad 1986: 7; Mancilla López 1980: 63).

It was not coincidental that this first round of radicalizing reforms at the National School of Economics was implemented the during the peak year of the Mexican student movement; the two events shared not only common causes but a common group of participants. As part of President Echeverría's (1970–76) policy of political opening and pacification toward the student movement, the government adopted a new attitude of tolerance and generosity toward public universities. With the notable exception of a 1971 incident in which leftist students were attacked by a progovernment gang in Mexico City, the Echeverría administration was generally known for its tolerance toward intellectual dissent and its declarations of respect for university autonomy (Latapí 1980: 89). Education was a key element in Echeverría's political philosophy, and was seen as both a means for the redistribution of wealth and creation of equal opportunity and as a way of promoting economic development. The fact that the relatively well-off higher education sector was favored in Echeverría's federal budgets over and above other areas of public education strongly suggests that increased funding for higher education was deliberately used as a political tool for defusing student discontent (Latapí 1980: 108).

The 1960s had been extremely lean years for the UNAM and other public universities, which suffered from a rapidly expanding student population and frozen budgets (Mancilla 1980: López 60). In contrast, between 1970 and 1975, there was a nearly sevenfold increase in the subsidies to public universities, while enrollment increased only 122%. According to Latapí's (1980) study on Echeverría's educational policy, funds were not withheld to "punish" schools that were centers of social discontent. On the contrary, Latapí suggests that greater subsidies were awarded to dissenting schools: funding was used as a carrot rather than a stick (Latapí 1980: 183–85).

As the crown jewel of the Mexican public university system, and one of the most important centers of student radicalism in Mexico, the UNAM was a clear beneficiary of Echeverría's educational policy. From 1971 to 1976, the number of students registered at the UNAM increased only 57%, while funding in real pesos nearly quadrupled (Padua 1988: 202; Noriega 1985: 75). The National School of Economics, a hotbed of student radicalism in the 1970s, had its budget increased from 11 million pesos in 1972 to 80 million pesos in 1977—a real increase of more than 168% (Torres Gaytán and Mora Ortíz 1978: 111; Gil Díaz 1984: 369–70). The increasing influence of the student movement within the National School of Economics resulted in part from the school's growth and the consequent hiring of new professors (some of them full-time), many of whom had been student participants in the 1968 movement and some of whom used their classrooms as political forums (interview, Aguirre 4/2/96).

An important difference between the UNAM student movement of the late 1960s and that of the 1970s was the inward focus of the latter: rather than directly demanding changes in the Mexican political system, the movement now focused on change within the university as the key to broader social change. Another apparent difference was that the 1970s movement was much more overtly radical and had replaced its prodemocratic rhetoric with a more revolutionary ideology. These changes were the product of circumstance: whereas the brutal repression of 1968 had radicalized the movement (while at the same time making open agitation for broad social and political reforms seem imprudent), Echeverría's relatively indulgent stance toward dissent within the university made public universities the most congenial environment in Mexico for political agitators.

Whether intentionally or unintentionally, Mexican government policy clearly contributed to the concentration of Mexican radicals within public universities and the leftward transformation of many different academic programs, including that of the National School of Economics. In the early 1970s, students who had lived through their political "initiation" in 1968 worked for the further reform of the governance and program of studies at the National School of Economics and in other areas of the UNAM, notably political science, philosophy and humanities (Guevara Niebla 1978: 13). These students' ideological tendencies were diverse, and included pro-Soviet communism, Maoism, focoism, Trotskyism, and social democracy. The two main tendencies that evolved in economics were apparently the pro-Soviet communists of the Mexican Communist Party (PCM) and the *cardenista* social democrats of the Popular Action Movement (MAP) (interview, Cabral Bowling 10/3/96).

In 1971, one-and-a-half-month student occupation of the school (with which workers and most professors cooperated) forced the resignation of the school's director, Ernesto Lobato López, who was criticized for his strong links to the ruling party and granting of university jobs as political favors (Brigada "José Carlos Mariátegui" 1971: 1–2; Comisión Organizada de Alumnos 1971). Shortly thereafter, a second "cogovernment" of professors and students was formed, and an academic boycott was held until the new director recognized the cogovernment's legitimacy (Arroyo 1975: 409). Under the sympathetic directorship of José Luis Ceceña (1972–77), radicalized students and professors were conceded the authority to bring about sweeping changes in the school's governance and study program. During Ceceña's tenure, students gained permanent parity representation with professors in the school's governing body (known as the Consejo Técnico) and organized for the promotion of academic reform (Torres Gaytán and Mora Ortíz 1978: 112). The cogovernment was reorganized into the Forum of Transformation (Foro de Transformación), which in December of 1974 held nine days of discussion on the direction of academic reform. According to reforms proposed by the forum at the end of 1974, the central focus of teaching at the National School of Economics should be Marxist ("Foro de Transformación" 1975).

Under the scrutiny of the student movement, the history of the National School of Economics acquired a new revisionist interpretation. We saw in chapter 4 that along with the new government focus on issues of growth rather than distribution, the school became more technically focused and less radical during the 1940s, '50s, and '60s—all the while maintaining enough of its original radical tradition to keep the private sector and the more conservative parts of public administration (especially the central bank) at a distance.

In contrast, the story the student movement told was that Mexican economics had sold its soul for material comfort. An article in the school's publication *Investigación económica* lamented the divergence of contemporary UNAM economics from the school's original revolutionary leftist tradition: as economists became incorporated into the government bureaucracy in the 1950s and '60s, "the economist became conformist, concerned only with the consequences of his everyday work" (Corona Rentería 1971: 11–12). Another article outlined a similar evolution: at the beginning, the National School of Economics had been "[c]onceived . . . as a center for the production of a technical-ideological corps for the revo-

lution which in that time was at its apogee. . . ." Later, the school had
betrayed its revolutionary origins through becoming more technical: "The
past three administrations [have promoted] programs . . . of 'technification' and 'updating' of the program, introducing or trying to introduce
new courses and projects aimed at bringing the School closer to the government and the private sector" (Arroyo 1975: 412).

Political pamphlets from the National School of Economics in the early
1970s questioned the notion of economics as neutral expertise in general
and the training of economists to be government bureaucrats in particular.
The increased emphasis on economics as technique put economists at the
service of an unjust authoritarian system. At best, these technocrats were
hypocrites:

> [T]he economist represents the most brittle variety of bureaucrat . . . and
> denounces in sensible studies such phenomena as imperialist penetration or
> the criminal distribution of income, none of which prevents him from receiv-
> ing a fabulous salary working tirelessly for the regime that gives rise to this
> state of affairs. (Rico Galán 1972: 69)

At worst, economics as it was taught at the National School of Economics
was an "apology for capitalism . . . in the service of the dominant class"
(Martínez, Ortega, and Molina 1972). In this sense, the technification of
economics at the UNAM created a mask of neutrality that disguised a
profoundly ideological function: the defense of the status quo. Mexican
technocracy presented itself as neutral but was actually the "ideological
expression of . . . authoritarianism" (Comisión Coordinadora del Foro
1974).

Thus, the movement criticized the school's role in propagating technocracy in the service of an unjust and authoritarian state. In contrast, the
movement proposed an explicitly political economics, which abandoned
the pretension of nonpartisan neutrality:

> [the teaching of economics at the UNAM] should be oriented toward criticiz-
> ing the system and the current situation of the country. *There can be no neu-
> tral position in this regard* [emphasis added]. Either we have plans and pro-
> grams that contain apologetic teaching that justifies the existing social order,
> or we decide to orient it toward the scientific understanding of the socioeco-
> nomic phenomena of our country. (Grupo Síntesis 1973: 7)

The movement advocated ". . . curricula that place professionals at the
service of the masses. . . . [This] . . . represents not only the conquest of
student revindication but also that of workers and peasants" (Rico Galán
1972: 12). The objective of the new program of studies was to train
"women and men capable of confronting, with a critical attitude, a na-

tional and international society whose development is based on exploitation" (Arroyo 1975: 413). The movement also advocated the participation of students in the popular struggles, the "democratization of teaching," and the linkage of such apparently "neutral" disciplines as mathematics and statistics to more political courses (Grupo Síntesis 1973: 1, 6; Brigada "Miguel Enríquez" 1974: 1).

Paradoxically, it was precisely through advocating the cause of the masses that economists could become "scientific" and objective: the movement's Marxist theoretical framework had the virtue of liberating its adherents from the appearance of subjectivity by claiming to be the theoretical expression of inexorable historical processes. As one pamphlet explained, the transformation of UNAM economics aimed at producing economists "trained in scientific study as the basis for social transformation and in revolutionary practice as the only means of achieving it" (Martínez, Ortega, and Molina 1972). Another tract published during the debates over the changes in the economics program similarly advocated the teaching of economics oriented "toward the scientific understanding of the socioeconomic phenomena of our country" (Grupo Síntesis 1973: 7).

In 1976 a new program of studies based on these proposals was implemented; this same year, the National School of Economics adopted a doctoral program and would henceforth be known as the Faculty of Economics. Under the new program of 1976, undergraduates at the Faculty of Economics were required to take *seven* semesters of "political economy," essentially Marxist courses that included the study of such themes as value and surplus value, the social relationships of production, imperialism, and socialist economics.[9] The political economy series contained a great deal of material that could easily have been taught in a course in sociology or political science; indeed the new program generally borrowed heavily from other social-scientific disciplines, a deliberate result of the movement's advocacy of teaching economics that was "integrated with that of the social sciences in general" (Facultad 1986: 11).

Like the political economy courses, the required courses in history and economic history had a strong Marxist content and included such topics as historical materialism, democratic-bourgeois revolutions, and twentieth-century socialist revolutions. Other required courses with significant Marxist content included the first semester introduction to economics and two courses on sociology and politics in the second and third semesters (Facultad 1986: 12–32). Under the new program, students were supposed to link learning in the classroom to real contexts and popular struggles, and students conducted field investigations in factories and the countryside (interview, Moguel Viveros 9/18/96).

Business, the Banco de México, and the Americanization of the ITAM

The policies of Echeverría—and to a lesser extent those of López Portillo—were designed to solve a legitimacy crisis originating from the left. While successfully ameliorating these problems of legitimacy, these policies simultaneously contributed to a breakdown of legitimacy on the right—both with respect to the private sector and with respect to more conservative factions within the Mexican government. Increasing disagreement over economic and social policies established extremely favorable conditions for the ITAM to return to its laissez-faire roots and become a bastion of American-style, neoclassical economic thought. The major impetus for this reform within ITAM economics, however, came not from disgruntled businessmen but rather from the Mexican central bank.

Echeverría's populism, like that of Cárdenas before him, threatened the private sector with its exaggerated leftist and anti-imperialist rhetoric and emphasis on "sharing" the benefits of development. The stymied tax reform of the 1970s meant that such sharing was actually quite limited; it was foreign borrowing rather than taxes on wealth and profits that funded Echeverría's social policies. Their limited redistributive effects notwithstanding, populist gestures and policies alienated the private sector and broke down postwar consensus between business and government. The attempted tax reform not only threatened to hurt private interests but also was carried out without the traditional "consultation" with private sector leaders (Luna Ledesma 1992: 42). Like Cárdenas, Echeverría encouraged peasant seizure of lands and supported workers against their employers in strikes (LaBotz 1995: 59). In 1975, when confronted with evidence that he was "losing the confidence" of the business community, Echeverría replied contentiously: "I prefer to be with the great mass of workers and campesinos of Mexico, than with my own cautious collaborators and with the businessmen" (Luna Ledesma 992: 45). In response to such threatening words and deeds, and under the leadership of the business group COPARMEX and the Monterrey firms that backed it, big Mexican businesses allied to form the Business Coordinating Council (CCE); this powerful group would subsequently become an important advocate for lessened state intervention in the economy (LaBotz 1995: 59; Luna Ledesma 1992: 45).

However, the rupture between business and government was not the most important breakdown generated by Mexican populism in the 1970s. Of equal significance were the conflicts generated within the Mexican government itself. The powerful Finance Ministry, always toward the right of the political spectrum within Mexican public administration, was not in agreement with many of Echeverría's policies, which often challenged the ministry's autonomy and authority; Echeverría became famous for declaring that economic policy was "made in Los Pinos" (the Mexican equivalent of the White House). In 1973 Finance Minister Hugo Margaín resigned and was replaced by López Portillo, a close personal friend of Echeverría's who would later assume the presidency. During the administrations of Echeverría and López Portillo, there would be six different ministers of finance (compared to a single finance minister for the previous two presidential administrations), a clear sign of the unwillingness of the executive to delegate economic policymaking authority.

Such conflicts between populist presidents and the Finance Ministry paled in comparison to those with the central bank (Banco de México). Unlike the Finance and other ministries, which tended to be highly politicized and subject to turnover in top- and medium-level personnel, the Banco de México had much more organizational stability and institutional autonomy in terms of its personnel.[10] On the other hand, before it was made legally autonomous in 1993, the Banco de México had state officials on its governing board and did not have final say in monetary policy matters, which had to be approved by the Finance Ministry. In one comparative international study of central bank independence, the Mexican central bank of the 1980s was ranked .36 on a scale of legal central bank independence ranging from 0 (least independent) to 1 (most independent), putting Mexico roughly on par with countries like Malaysia, Nigeria, and India (Cukierman 1992: 381).

Nevertheless, the extensive academic literature on central bank independence recognizes that legal autonomy is only one component of central bank independence; another important factor is the de facto autonomy of the central bank to select its own personnel free from political interference, as measured by the length of tenure of central bank directors (cf. Cukierman 1992; Eijffinger and de Haan 1996). Thus, although the Banco de México may not have acquired formal legal independence until 1993, during the stabilizing development years (1955–70) it was unofficially granted an important degree of autonomy, which was reflected in the extraordinarily long tenure of Rodrigo Gómez as central bank director from 1952 until 1970 (Maxfield 1997: 94–98).

Why did the Mexican government voluntarily cede authority to the central bank in this way, depriving itself of the valuable opportunity to finance itself through the inflation tax? Maxfield's (1990) answer is that Mexican policymaking was historically disproportionately influenced by a coalition of private bankers and financial policymakers. Another, perhaps more obvious, answer is that as a developing country sharing a two-thousand-mile border with the United States, Mexico was more subject than other countries to the risk of devaluation and capital flight, since exchange controls were more or less useless—a lesson Mexican policymakers learned well with the devaluation and subsequent IMF standby arrangement of 1954. In lieu of being able to implement exchange controls (which the border with the United States made impossible), it made sense for the Mexican government to do whatever it could to prevent inflation and devaluation, including granting policy autonomy to the central bank.

Whatever the ultimate reasons for de facto (if not de jure) central bank autonomy in Mexico, during the eighteen-year tenure of Rodrigo Gómez as central bank director the Banco de México was granted a fair amount of discretion in determining monetary policy, and inflation was correspondingly low (see figure 5.2). With the populist governments of the 1970s, however, the Banco found its semi-independent status trampled on by an increasingly powerful, centralized presidency. Both Presidents Echeverría and López Portillo were willing to sacrifice the integrity of the peso—the very thing the Banco was dedicated to defend—in favor of increased government spending and unorthodox monetary policies. Banco director Gustavo Romero Kolbeck had originally been approved by López Portillo in 1976 but resigned in 1982 because of disagreements with the president. Miguel Mancera, a traditional central banker who replaced Romero Kolbeck, lasted only a few months in the post before he was replaced by the left-leaning, unorthodox Carlos Tello, who immediately carried out López Portillo's controversial bank nationalization (which the conservative central bankers vehemently opposed). As Mancera would later recount it to the business press, "I resigned of my own free will, but I was fired at the same time" (Fuentes-Berain 1993: 15). Figure 5.2 documents the loss of central bank authority in the 1970s and early '80s, reflected in the drastic increase in the rate of inflation.

How did Mexican central bankers view such government encroachment on their autonomy aong with the undermining of monetary stability? Since discretion is the rule among Mexican public administrators, a foreign investigator posing this question to a central banker (or former central banker) inevitably receives such carefully worded answers as "[t]here were . . . problems under López Portillo, who appointed a not-very-formal central banker as director" (interview, Ghigliazza 7/19/94). Such understatements aside, it seems reasonable to assume that conflicts between the Mexican presidency and the central bank during the 1970s and early '80s must have both alienated Banco personnel from the government and solidified their bonds with central bankers and economists abroad. During the 1970s, Mexican central bankers found that they had more in common with central bankers and economists in other countries than with the Mexican government, which promoted policies antithetical to price stability.

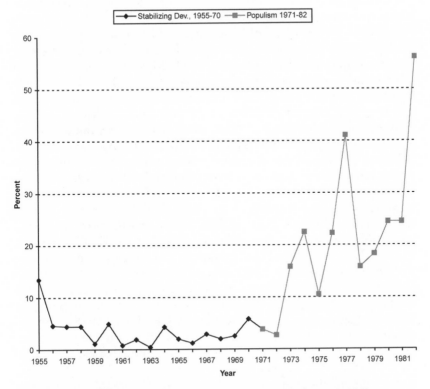

Fig. 5.2. Mexican Annual Inflation, 1955–82. Source: Gil Díaz (1984).

The ITAM[11] had always had a special institutional relationship with the Banco de México, for a number of reasons discussed in previous chapters, including the Banco's relatively conservative ideology and its links to private-sector bankers. This relationship naturally expanded and became more solid over time: ITAM graduates were recruited as Banco officials and sent to study abroad; Banco officials became leading professors and administrators within the ITAM economics department. For its part, the Banco de México was both highly attuned to international professional standards and in the 1970s increasingly threatened by an ideologically hostile government that curtailed its autonomy. As the international economic paradigm moved from Keynesian to neoclassical in the 1960s and '70s, Banco officials were the primary agents for transmitting these new economic ideas to the ITAM economics program. The ITAM, founded and funded by private-sector groups that were becoming more wary of state intervention, was the most fertile ground in Mexico in which these foreign ideas could take root and flourish.

The alienation of the Banco de México from the Mexican government had been preceded by the Banco's estrangement from the increasingly radicalized UNAM School of Economics—which throughout the 1960s became an ever more hostile environment for central bankers. Originally founded with central bank support, the ITAM became a new source of central bank economists, many of whom used Banco scholarships to study abroad. A central figure in the Banco's increasing reliance on the ITAM was Leopoldo Solís, an UNAM graduate who studied economics at Yale University with a Banco scholarship and subsequently became director of the Banco's Department of Economic Studies in 1964. As a taxi professor, Solís was able to recruit promising young economics students to the Banco, later sending them abroad to study with Banco scholarships. As a U.S.-trained central banker during an era of growing student radicalism, however, Solís chose to teach at the ITAM and the Colegio de México rather than the UNAM. Many of Solís's protégés would later be prominent public figures, including Francisco Gil Díaz (an ITAM graduate), Miguel Mancera (also an ITAM graduate), and former president Ernesto Zedillo (a graduate of the Polytechnic University).

Another prominent alumnus of the Banco scholarship program was Gustavo Petricioli, who had held a job at the Banco while attending the ITAM during its first decade of existence. Like Solís, Petricioli studied economics at Yale University; also like Solís, he returned to give classes at his alma mater while working full-time as a central bank official. During the early 1960s, the ongoing unprofitability of the ITAM was causing concern among those financing and governing the school; one proposal for increasing revenue was to become a Catholic university along the lines of the more profitable Iberoamerican University. Petricioli joined forces with Miguel Mancera (another Banco official, ITAM alumnus, and professor) and Alberto Bailleres (the son of one of ITAM's founders, Raúl Bailleres) to convince the governing board that the future of the school lay in becoming more modern and international rather than in imitating the private religious model; all three of these reformers had conducted graduate studies in economics abroad. The changes Petricioli subsequently oversaw as director of the School of Economics in 1965 were facilitated by the ITAM's recently granted autonomy, which freed it from the need to obtain government approval for its programs of studies (interview, Petricioli 2/3/97).

The new economics program implemented in 1965 (which was later slightly modified under the "integrated plan" of 1971)[12] was designed to resemble internationally prestigious economics programs, especially those in the United States. In contrast to the old program—and in striking contrast to the opposite tendency at the UNAM—economics at the ITAM was now treated as a science separate from other disciplines; rather than

extensive training in economic history, economic thought, and other assorted fields, ITAM students would now have a both narrower and deeper
grounding in economic theory. The expression of economic ideas through
mathematics was an important part of this new, more economic economics: students would master "the elements of economic analysis, using
wherever possible mathematical language both at the macroeconomic and
microeconomic levels" (*Boletín* 1970: 1).

An important and far-reaching change introduced with these academic
reforms was the requirement of full-time study: henceforth, the program
would accept only students able to attend classes during the day (interview, Bassols Zaleta 3/20/96). Under the new "full-time" program, students had weekly required hours library attendance, and upper-level students were recruited to be "tutors" who gave seminars and supervised
laboratories and study hours (an innovation copied from the system at
Oxford University) (Sección 1967: 6). In contrast to the earlier program
of studies, which consisted of a diverse mixture of different semester-long
classes, the full-time program included five more intensive yearly classes
(of five hours per week, as opposed to the earlier classes of two to three
hours per week). Economics students were also required to take two full
years of English and mathematics, in contrast to the earlier program,
which had no language requirement and only one required year of "applied mathematics"; two years of statistical methods were now required in
place of the single year of the earlier program. And whereas the previous
program had required only two years of economic theory, the new program demanded three. Classes eliminated to create room for new course
requirements included economic geography, demographic policy, sociology, and the economic and social theory of Marxism (ITM 1951: 26–28;
Escuela de Economía 1965: 4–5).

The new ITAM economics program was extremely rigorous: according
to one graduate of the first generation of students trained under the full-
time plan, of the entering cohort of forty-three in 1965, only twelve remained to graduate in 1969 (interview, Bassols Zaleta 3/20/96). To reduce
dropout rates, several years after the introduction of the full-time plan
the program restricted its yearly admissions to thirty-five students, thus
replacing selectivity through attrition with selectivity through admissions
procedures (Petricioli and Reynolds 1967: 37). The requirement of full-
time study also made the already elite ITAM economics program more
socially selective, since students without access to substantial family resources could no longer work full-time to finance their education: a study
of ITAM economics in 1967 noted that "[o]wing to the yearly tuition of
2,800 pesos [$224] and the requirement of full-time study, the majority
of students are from middle or upper income families" (Petricioli and
Reynolds 1967: 37).[13]

Thus, whereas in the early 1960s the population of UNAM economics students was growing rapidly, the ITAM was undergoing the opposite process: for example, while there were 152 economics students at the ITAM in 1965, in 1969 there were only 110 (Petricioli and Reynolds 1967: 28; ANUIES 1969). A concomitant and surely intended effect of this process of "minification" (as opposed to the "massification" at the UNAM) was to increase the market value of an ITAM economics degree: in the language of Collins (1979), whereas UNAM economics credentials were becoming "inflated" during the 1960s, ITAM economics credentials were becoming "deflated," and hence more valuable in the job market. However, during the late 1970s the ITAM economics program began to expand rapidly, leading to a doubling of the student population in just a few years (ANUIES 1977–80). Unlike the massification of the UNAM, which was driven by political considerations, the expansion of ITAM economics was clearly driven by the expanding job opportunities for its graduates; these opportunities will be discussed extensively in the following chapter.

After the implementation of the full-time plan in 1965, ITAM economics underwent an important subsequent theoretical evolution. In the late 1960s there was an ideological battle between "some professors of the left" and ". . . others who wanted the school to be more technical"; whereas the former group included professors of diverse disciplines, ITAM economists were among the latter. The more conservative group apparently won this debate, which led to the resignation of C. P. Gómez Morfín as the school's rector in 1971; his rectorship was briefly followed by that of Antonio Carrillo Flores (1971–72) and that of Javier Beristáin (1972–91). ("Un Chicago Boy . . ." 1978: 2). Early in Berstáin's tenure (1973), a young Banco de México official named Francisco Gil Díaz became director of ITAM economics.

Professor Gil Díaz had graduated from the ITAM in 1966 and subsequently acquired a job in the Banco de México's Department of Economic Studies with the help of Leopoldo Solís, a Yale-educated Banco official who had been Gil Díaz's professor at the ITAM in the early 1960s (interview, Solís 8/6/96). With funding from a Banco de México scholarship, Gil Díaz acquired a Ph.D. in economics from the University of Chicago in 1970. His Chicago-school perspective came to permeate the ITAM economics program through his recruitment of a sizable number of Chicago graduates—particularly those who had worked at the Banco de México and the Finance Ministry[14]—to give classes at the ITAM. Monetary theory taught from a monetarist perspective became one of the ITAM's strongest areas (interviews, Espíndola 9/15/96 and Katz 3/27/96). Gil Díaz also selected promising students to recommend for graduate study at the University of Chicago and utilized the personal networks he had acquired there to facilitate their admission. As one ITAM professor put it:

> The entrance of one ITAM graduate into a particular graduate program can
> have a snowball effect, through both direct and indirect relations. Letters of
> recommendation from a graduate of a particular school could be important,
> but especially because of personal relations developed between individuals.
> So for example, for an applicant to the University of Chicago a letter from
> Gil Díaz to Harberger was practically a letter of acceptance to the program.
> (Interview, Confidential 9/15/96)

Thus, just as the "taxi professor" system at the UNAM gave economics
students access to the personal networks necessary to obtain public-sector
employment, student-professor relationships at the ITAM gave its students a special advantage in gaining admission to foreign economics
programs.

The financing of foreign graduate education was less problematic in the
abundant, free-spending 1970s than it had been in previous decades;
rather than having first to enter the central bank in hopes of receiving a
scholarship, ITAM students now could go directly to graduate school
funded by Science and Technology scholarships. While scholarship recipients from other universities selected diverse options for their postgraduate
study abroad, ITAM students in the 1970s displayed a marked preference
for Chicago-school economics. Table 5.2 shows that after 1971, Chicago
was the single most important destination for ITAM graduates studying
economics abroad, accounting for 20% of those who chose such study.
This bias toward Chicago was much more pronounced in the late 1970s,
when Gil Díaz was director of the ITAM economics program; in 1978,
an ITAM economics professor remarked that there were seven or eight
ITAM graduates studying at the University of Chicago, and that ITAM
graduates accounted for nearly *all* the Mexicans studying there ("Un Chicago Boy" 1978: 2). The second-largest group from this period studied
at MIT, apparently the result of MIT graduate Pedro Aspe's tenure as
director of the Economics Department from 1978 to 1982.[15]

In summary, during the 1960s and '70s, the ITAM economics program
became thoroughly Americanized. The evidence overwhelmingly suggests
that the source of this Americanization was not the businessmen who
financed the ITAM and sat on its governing board but rather the Mexican
central bank. The Banco de México constituted a professional "subconstituency" within the Mexican state that provided the ITAM with resources
by supplying its professors and hiring its graduates. It was principally
through the Banco de México that new foreign models were transmitted
to the ITAM in the 1960s and '70s. Whereas the Banco de México provided the crucial organizational bridge that brought new international
theoretical trends in economics to Mexico, the ITAM provided fertile institutional soil where these theories could prosper and spread.

TABLE 5.2
ITAM Economics Graduates, Top Universities
Attended for Graduate Study Abroad in
Economics, Date of Graduation 1971–96

University	Number Attending
U. Chicago	20
MIT	7
London S. Econ.	5
Yale	5
Harvard	4
Cambridge	3
Columbia	3
U. of London	3

The Banco's sponsorship of Americanized economics made sense within the context of the final divorce between the Banco and the always somewhat left-leaning UNAM economics progam, which became even more radical in the 1960s and '70s. It also made sense for the Banco to sponsor the Americanization of a Mexican economics program at a time when there was growing estrangement between the central bank and the Mexican state, and when American economics was becoming decreasingly statist. Ironically, Nixon's statement ("We are all Keynesians now") was made precisely at a time when the pendulum in American economics was moving in the opposite direction (Krugman 1994: 15). Rational expectations theory and monetarism—both of which viewed central government involvement in monetary policy with horror—were coming into their height of fashionability, and the University of Chicago was becoming a top source of Nobel prizewinners. If the reigning economic orthodoxy in mainstream U.S. universities had resembled that of Cambridge (the alma mater of Mexico's free-spending left developmentalists during the 1970s), it is doubtful that the Americanization of ITAM economics would have seemed as quite so appealing a project to central bank officials. As it happened, however, the central bankers' project to increase the quality of Mexican economics graduates coincided nicely with the rise of a particularly congenial doctrine in the United States.

If the businessmen who financed the ITAM were not responsible for the school's Chicago-school focus in the 1970s, they certainly did not oppose it—especially at a time when government intervention was beginning to appear as a threat rather than a boon to business interests. The role of the ITAM as a congenial receptacle for—rather than an active promoter of—neoclassical economic ideas mirrored a remarkably similar process that occured at the Catholic University in Chile in the 1950s and '60s, which "presented a vacant space in the field [of economics] . . ."

According to Valdés (1995), officials of the Catholic University had been "greatly interested in establishing a department of economic studies that could be competitive and capable of serving the business class. However, the university's capacity to resist and/or select the contents of the message transferred was virtually nonexistent" (pp. 49–50).

The apparently insignificant fact that neoclassical economics in Mexico took root at a private university becomes more significant if we consider the hypothetical opposition that any effort to implement such a program would have encountered at the UNAM: the force of revolutionary tradition, the influence of leftist faculty, the power of the student movement, to say nothing of opposition from interventionist government functionaries—all these would have nipped any such effort in the bud. Of course, to become a center for foreign economic ideas it is not sufficient that a university be private: lack of resistance must be combined with means of transmission. A particularly revealing case in this regard is the Department of Economics at the Monterrey Technological Institute, which lacked the ITAM's institutional relationship with the Banco de México.[16] Even today, the "Tech" program in economics is much less oriented toward abstract neoclassical economic theory and much more toward practical business skills; required courses in 1996 include several in accounting and even one in "leadership." Those differences notwithstanding, it is safe to say that private economics programs in Mexico have historically tended to be more internationalized and less leftist than economics programs at public universities—a trend that continues through the present day.

CONCLUSION

Although the most profound break with previous political, social, and economic arrangements would not occur until at least a decade later, it was during the 1970s that the Mexican Miracle began to break down. While radical students questioned the justice of a system that promoted economic growth at the cost of growing inequality, marginalization, and political exclusion, two successive presidents sought to solve problems of declining legitimacy and a flagging economy through debt-financed spending and other populist measures. Although somewhat ameliorating the crisis of legitimacy on the left, this new interventionism brought about conflicts with business and among different branches of the Mexican government.

Economic, political, and social crises brought about changes in the educational institutions responsible for training public-sector economists. Whereas the Keynesian consensus of the 1950s generated remarkably similar, interventionist economics programs at the state-funded UNAM and the private ITAM, the 1970s witnessed a radical divergence. The actual events bringing about this divergence, however, defy facile interest-group-based explanations. The UNAM was radicalized neither by the long-suffering masses nor by a populist state, but rather by a movement of relatively privileged students; the ITAM was not "neoliberalized" by disgruntled private-sector groups but by foreign-trained central bankers attempting to re-create their international vision of a quality program in economics during a time of grave threat to central bank autonomy. Therefore, and unlike the first division of Mexican economics in the 1940s, the divergence of the 1970s was not a direct reflection of disagreements between the state and the private sector but rather resulted from a set of more varied and complex institutional or structural factors.

Although the respective transformations of the UNAM and ITAM economics programs in the 1960s and '70s catapulted them in completely opposite directions, their respective evolutions were both driven by social conflict—conflict that was ultimately rooted in disagreements about how to deal with the breakdown of Mexican developmentalism. These changes had direct and divergent consequences for the two programs' professional prospects. The nature of these consequences will be explored in the following chapter.

Chapter 6

THE UNAM AND THE ITAM AFTER 1970

D$_{URING}$ THE 1970s, a vocal student movement advocated the adoption of socialism to resolve the contradictions of Mexico's highly unequal process of economic development. While the UNAM economics program was being radicalized by the movement and its supporters, very little attention was paid to the ITAM, a relatively obscure night school in economics that was quietly being remade into a bastion of American and Chicago-school thought. As it turned out, the ITAM represented the future of Mexican economics.

In contrast to the paradigmatic consensus of the postwar period, after 1970 there was a marked divergence between the UNAM and the ITAM economics programs, in terms of theory, method, and employment prospects. Two historical factors stand out as having caused this divergence, one domestic and the second international. The first of these factors was the "breakdown" of Mexican developmentalism discussed in the previous chapter, which ended the political consensus that had previously facilitated the two programs' convergence. The second factor was more incremental and difficult to measure but was equally important to the fate of the two economics programs: namely, postwar changes in international standards of economic expertise that gave rise to a more quantitative, theoretical, and neoclassical discipline. As international standards changed, the ITAM changed along with them. Meanwhile, a vocal student movement pushed the UNAM program along a completely opposite trajectory. Thus, while the ITAM evolved to become one of the most Americanized economics programs outside the United States, the UNAM became increasingly divorced from international standards.

POSTWAR CHANGES IN THE ECONOMICS PROFESSION

Throughout its history, Mexican economics was heavily influenced by international models of economic expertise. The very idea of founding an economics program at the UNAM in 1929 was inspired by the foreign travels and readings of Mexican officials working for government ministries—organizations like the Finance Ministry and the central bank, which had been modeled in the image of their preexisting foreign counterparts. UNAM economics theses rarely cited indigenous theories in their theses but rather drew on the ideas of Marx, Keynes, Smith, and a host of other foreign authors. In short, at the most general level, Mexican economics illustrates world-cultural theory, which postulates that nation-states make up an organizational field that shares a common culture, which leads them to imitate one another and become more similar over time.

On the other hand, the history of Mexican economics also shows that there was not a monolithic, all-determining model of economics toward which the Mexican profession converged. Rather, there were a *variety* of possible interpretations of international models of economic expertise, and different Mexican constituencies were prone to support different sorts of economics professions. In the 1930s, the Mexican state was willing to foster a profession with populist and even socialist undertones; the Mexican private sector was emphatically not willing to support such a profession, and participated in the founding of the ITAM economics program to rival that of the UNAM (the ITM became the autonomous ITAM in 1962, and for purposes of simplification will be referred to as ITAM for the remainder of this chapter).

The diversity of "interpretations" of economics in Mexico during its first decades was undoubtedly facilitated by the heterogeneous state of the profession at that time: during the first decades of the UNAM program, economics was a much more pluralistic discipline than it is today, without a single clearly defined orthodoxy. For one thing, in the 1930s, economics was not dominated by the ideas emanating from a single nation: various schools of thought flourished in different nations, such as the Stockholm school in Sweden and the Oslo school in Norway (Sandelin and Veiderpass 1996). Mexican economists and public officials must have been aware that UNAM economics in the 1930s was quite different from the discipline as it was taught at prestigious universities in England or the United States.[1] However, even in the United States, economics in the 1930s was a relatively ecumenical discipline, in which various methods and models coexisted (Yonay 1998; Backhouse 1998). In the United States, the institutionalist school was a highly visible rival to neoclassical economics. The institutionalists were suspicious of the formal deductive models of neoclassical economics and questioned the assumptions on which these models rested; the institutionalists emphasized applied empirical research and the variable nature of economic institutions (Yonay 1998: 52).

In short, during the 1930s, the international standards on which UNAM economics was drawing were a mixed bag. Over the course of the postwar years, however, this pluralistic panorama began to change, and the discipline of economics converged toward a more uniform model in at least two respects. The first was the emergence of a single country—the United States—as world leader in the field of economics (Coats, ed., 1996). Although national differences were not entirely obliterated, economics as it was taught in the United States came to "set the standard" for the discipline in many countries. This postwar Americanization of economics will be discussed at length in chapter 8.

The second way international models of economic expertise became more uniform was that *within* the core of the discipline—increasingly located at elite universities in the United States—there was a convergence on a much more agreed-upon set of topics and techniques. Several recent studies provide convincing evidence that the great transition in American economics around the middle of the twentieth century was not—as is commonly believed—the rise of Keynesianism. Rather, of greater significance was the move from a pluralistic discipline, in which several competing schools and methods were seen as intellectually valid, toward a more uniform orthodoxy of theory and method (Yonay 1998; Morgan and Rutherford, eds., 1998; Backhouse 1998; Goodwin 1998). Based on the formalized models of marginal analysis and the assumptions of rational utility maximization, the version of economics that emerged victorious after the Second World War was clearly more indebted to the neoclassical than to the institutionalist tradition. However, Yonay (1998) contends that what triumphed was essentially a third version of economics—what he refers to as "mathematical economics," which was far more technical and quantified than "old-fashioned neoclassical economics" (pp. 184–85).

During the postwar period, American economics became more mathematical both in terms of formal theoretical modeling and in terms of practical empirical application. At the theoretical level, there was a growing emphasis on the sort of formal mathematical modeling that has become standard fare in introductory microeconomics classes today. At the empirical level, there was an increased use of econometrics, or statistical analysis of economic data, that made use of relatively sophisticated summary measures, such as standard deviations and regression coefficients. These measures were not new in themselves, but ever expanding sources of data, as well as computer facilities that made the analysis of such data much more convenient, were widening their application.

Backhouse (1998), who surveys a sample of articles published in the *American Economic Review*, the *Journal of Political Economy*, and the *Quarterly Journal of Economics* from 1920 until 1960, identifies and measures the defining features of the postwar transformation of American economics. First, these data document the progressive decline in the percentage of atheoretical, empirical articles, from over 50% to under 30%. At the same time, there was an increase in the incidence of articles that were either theoretical or employed formal economic theory, from about 15% to about 45%. Articles using some form of mathematics (excluding statistical techniques) rose from 0% in 1920 to 40% in 1960. In addition to this use of formal mathematical modeling, econometric analysis of data became a common feature of American economics articles, and gradually supplanted the large tables of descriptive data that had prevailed in the earlier period. Regression analysis began to be widely used as a tool for empirical research in the 1950s (Backhouse 1998: 105).

Why did postwar American economics departments provide such fertile ground for the rise of quantitative, neoclassical economics? Goodwin (1998) suggests that universities, the government, and the private sector all played a role in the fostering of a more neoclassical, mathematical economics in the United States. One of the effects of McCarthyism at American universities was to make economists seek refuge in highly quantified economics, at a time when even Keynesians were considered suspect by the American right-wing establishment. The U.S. government also played an ongoing part in the technification of American economics—not only through the well-known employment of economists to work under Keynesian administrations but also through its policy of hiring academic economists during the Second World War. Finally, the American private sector, along with the organizations it supported (such as the Ford Foundation and the Cowles Commission) helped promote a more technical discipline, which would be of greater use to business than previous varieties. American business also supported economists whose ideas were congenial to the free enterprise system—such as the nucleus of the group that became the Chicago school (Goodwin 1998: 70).

Another important factor in the postwar quantification of American economics was undoubtedly the increased availability of computers as a tool for econometric analysis. Computers enabled users to perform more complex calculations with larger data sets—without having to spend prohibitively long hours performing calculations with pencil and paper. Economists working at American universities were more likely to have access to these computers—which were large, slow, and enormously expensive—than economists working at European universities, because by the late 1950s, the United States had become the world leader in computer technology (Ceruzzi 1998: 11). This American lead in computing was strongly related to Cold War military spending, which provided the resources for expensive initial research that could later be used for nonmilitary applications. As an indirect result of the Cold War, therefore, American economists had a technological "comparative advantage" in econometric research.

In summary, during the postwar period, American economics became more mathematical, more theoretical, and more neoclassical. At the same time, American economics increasingly "set the standard" for economics in other countries. Some Mexican economics programs found it easier to conform to these new international standards, which were most easily emulated within economics programs that could require heavy doses of mathematical training and that had relatively apolitical student bodies. The following sections show how the UNAM and the ITAM fared within this new environment.

DIVERGENT CURRICULA AT THE UNAM AND ITAM

In chapter 5, we saw how the relative social and political consensus of the postwar period was shattered in the late 1960s, creating an environment that fostered new trends at the UNAM and the ITAM. While the UNAM economics department was taken over and transformed by the ever more radical student movement, the ITAM program was revived and remade by several key central bankers. Thus, the "breakdown" of developmentalism in the late 1960s and in the 1970s revived the historical division between the UNAM and ITAM economics programs, creating two separate subdisciplines speaking different languages.

The UNAM

As part of Echeverría's program of political pacification, funding for public universities was expanded, and student movement demands for curriculum changes were allowed in many public university departments, including the UNAM School of Economics (which became the UNAM Facility of Economics with the addition of a graduate program in 1976). The radicalization of UNAM economics in the 1970s was merely the best-known example of similar processes that occurred in the economics programs of other public universities, notably the Polytechnical University in Mexico City and numerous provincial public universities.

As a result of similar histories of radicalization and reform, the faculty and students of these public university programs came to hold congruent views on a variety of issues. Participants from various public programs attended periodic meetings at which the fundamental similarity of their views was affirmed. For example at the 1976 National Meeting of Economics Schools and Research Centers, participants agreed that the core of economics teaching should "generally be determined by the logical structure of the theory expressed in *Capital* by Karl Marx"; the meeting had participants from thirteen different universities, including the UNAM, the Polytechnical University, the Autonomous University of Sinaloa, the Autonomous University of Zacatecas, and the Autonomous University of Puebla ("Encuentro . . ." 1976: 1–2). Notably absent from this meeting were representatives not only from the ITAM but also from other important private schools of economics, such as those of the Monterrey Tech, the Iberoamerican University, and the Anahuac; representatives from the public Autonomous University of Nuevo León (discussed in chapter 4) were also absent.

The radicalization of UNAM economics was a trend that would not be reversed until 1993 (when there would be an attempt to make the curriculum more practical and technical once again). What was the ultimate result of the radicalization of the UNAM program for students and graduates? Did a curriculum saturated with Marxism and dependency theory lead to the creation of a generation of economist-revolutionaries?

Based on my sampling of fifty UNAM undergraduate economics theses from 1976 and another fifty theses from 1994 (see table 6.1 and complete tables of results in Appendix A), it appears that radicalization had a relatively weak effect. Although a core group of students embraced radical ideas in their theses, the vast majority adhered to the time-honored UNAM tradition of picking a concrete issue or problem within the Mexican economy and compiling copious statistics on the subject. However, UNAM theses from 1976 differed in at least one important respect from their counterparts in the 1950s; namely, they were less likely to have developmentalist diagnoses of underlying economic problems (such as the inherent defects of capitalism) and became less likely to prescribe government intervention as the solution to these problems.

In other words, the most visible effect of changes within the UNAM economics program after 1968—at least on the undergraduate theses— was the decline of developmentalism rather than the ascent of radicalism per se. In 1958, the UNAM's revolutionary ideals and Marxist leanings had been discernible, but the primary focus of the theses had been statist and Keynesian rather than revolutionary and Marxist: in 1958, only 6.25% of the theses used Marxism as their central theoretical framework. In contrast, in 1976 12% of the theses could be characterized as Marxist. In keeping with the prescriptions of some of the dependency theorists, the most radical students advocated socialism; in 1976, 4% mentioned socialism approvingly and 2% disapprovingly. In 1958, socialism had not even been mentioned as a possible alternative. Other evidence of increased radicalism in the 1976 UNAM theses included anti-imperialist rhetoric, which occurred in 12% of the theses from 1976 as compared to 6.25% of the theses in the 1950s.

These relatively small numbers, however, show that the revolutionary firebrands were in the minority. This makes sense if we assume that the true student radicals were greatly outnumbered by students more interested in social mobility than social change. The enormous expansion of the UNAM in the 1960s and '70s may have helped fuel the student move-

TABLE 6.1
Most-Cited Authors, UNAM 1976 and UNAM 1994

UNAM 1976, n = 50 (Theses with Theoretical Cites = 76%)		
	N	%
Karl Marx	5	10.0
Paul Baran	4	8.0
Raymand Barre	4	8.0
Freidrich Engels	3	6.0
Celso Furtado	3	6.0
Oswaldo Sunkel	3	6.0

UNAM 1994, n = 50 (Theses with Theoretical Cites = 58%)		
Karl Marx	9	18.0
J. M. Keynes	5	10.0
Adam Smith	4	8.0
René Villarreal	4	8.0
F. Fajnzlyber	3	6.0
Milton Friedman	3	6.0
A. Guillén Romo	3	6.0
David Ricardo	3	6.0
M. A. Rivera Ríos	3	6.0

ment (see chapter 5), but it also brought in new cohorts of students who were the first in their families to receive a university education, and for whom studying at the UNAM was the opportunity of a lifetime. Unfortunately (as we will see in the following sections), at the same time that the UNAM economics program was expanding, its efficacy as a route to a government job and social mobility was diminishing.

The citations of theoretical authors by UNAM economics students also exhibited important changes over time. The most-cited theoretical author of the randomly selected theses from 1976 was Marx, who appeared in 10% of the theses; the second most-cited authors were Marxist theorist Paul Baran and the French economist Raymond Barre,[2] a French government official who had written a popular textbook on economics. Other important theoretical authors included Celso Furtado and Oswaldo Sunkel, indicating the increasing influence of dependency theory—a more radical alternative to ECLA developmentalism. Most significantly, Keynes—who had been cited in a quarter of the theses from the 1950s— was cited in only 4% of the theses from 1976.

However, the majority of the UNAM theses from 1976 did not cite revolutionary or *dependentista* authors; on the contrary, 24% of these

theses did not make any theoretical citations *at all*. When we examine
UNAM economics theses from 1958, 1976, and 1994, we can see a trend
toward progressively less theory: whereas 87% of the 1958 theses had
theoretical citations, only 76% of the 1976 theses had such citations; by
1994, the proportion of UNAM economics theses making theoretical citations had gone down to a mere 58%.

Related to the trend of the declining importance of theoretical citations
was the decreasing propensity to identify problems that government intervention could solve. In the 1950s, UNAM students were taught to believe
that government intervention was a viable remedy to the defects of capitalism in general and the defects of capitalism in developing countries in
particular. In contrast, the principal problems recognized by the student
movement of the 1970s were not underdevelopment and stagnant growth
but rather authoritarianism and social injustice.

The consequent assumption of the need for radical political and economic change in Mexico posed something of a dilemma for the thesis
writers of 1976. The state that was lauded in the 1950s as the solution
to problems of underdevelopment was condemned by the 1970s student
movement as the authoritarian promoter of an unjust economic and political system. In the UNAM of the 1970s, to advocate the intervention of
this one-party state on the behalf of development was not only to misdiag-
nose but actually to implicitly endorse part of the problem. Although the
1970s theses that endorsed state intervention tended to call for a much
stronger variety than those of 1958, a substantial group of the 1976 theses
(22%) were silent on the issue of state intervention. Whereas in 1958,
31.25% of the theses had discussed the defects of capitalism and the need
for state intervention, in 1976, only 4% of the theses utilized this sort of
rhetoric. Strikingly, whereas an overwhelming proportion (50%) of the
1958 theses had emphasized the fundamental differences between developed and developing countries (table 6.2) a meager 4% of the theses discussed these differences in 1976. By 1994, theses no longer observed that
developed and developing countries were fundamentally different.

By 1994, the trend away from developmentalism within the UNAM
economics program was complete. After 1982, the Mexican government
took a dramatic turn away from the developmentalist assumptions that
had guided it before, and a new set of free-market assumptions came to
take their place (see chapter 7). By 1994, there were no UNAM theses
discussing either the defects of capitalism or the fundamental differences
between developed and developing countries. Several theses even praised
the benefits of free markets and free trade, as well as calling for less government intervention in the economy. Theses endorsing the new market
wisdom sat incongruously alongside other theses that were clearly Marx-

TABLE 6.2
Presence of Rhetorical Element, "Developed and developing
countries are fundamentally different"

	UNAM 1958 N (%)	UNAM 1976 n (%)	UNAM 1994 n (%)
Yes	8 (50)	2 (4)	0 (0)
No	8 (50)	48 (96)	50 (100)
Total	16 (100)	50 (100)	50 (100)

$\chi^2 = 40.9$, $\alpha < .005$

TABLE 6.3
Position on State Intervention, UNAM 1958, 1976, and 1994

	UNAM 1958 N (%)	UNAM 1976 n (%)	UNAM 1994 n (%)
Less intervention advocated	0 (0)	0 (0)	7 (14)
Existing interventions supported	6 (37.5)	19 (38)	16 (32)
More intervention advocated	10 (62.5)	20 (40)	5 (10)
No position on intervention	0 (0)	11 (22)	22 (44)
Total	16 (100)	50 (100)	50 (100)

$\chi^2 = 32.9$, $\alpha < .01$

ist, which accounted for 12% of the 1994 theses in my sample. The citations of Marx reflected the ongoing presence of Marxist professors hired in the 1970s, whose influence on newer generations of UNAM students was waning but had not disappeared.

The theoretical citations in theses from 1994 similarly illustrate some of the contradictory features of the UNAM economics program during the 1990s. By this time, Marxism at the UNAM Faculty of Economics had been fully institutionalized, and Marx was cited even more frequently than in 1976. At the same time, however, the 1990s were the decade during which Mexican neoliberalism was in full swing, and free markets and free trade were more fashionable than ever before in the history of Mexican economics. As a result, Smith, Ricardo, and even Milton Friedman appear in the 1994 theses, along with Keynes. Whereas the citations from both 1958 and 1976 displayed a certain measure of internal theoretical coherence, by the 1990s the UNAM Faculty of Economics seemed to be torn by conflicting theories.

Most interestingly, the 1994 theses followed the earlier trend of being less likely to take any position on the issue of state intervention. Table 6.3 shows that in 1958 there was not a single thesis that failed to take some sort of stand on the issue of government involvement in the econ-

omy. However, in 1976, 22% of the theses failed to address the issue of
government intervention, and by 1994, 44% failed to deal with the issue.
The decline of Keynesianism and developmentalism at the National
School of Economics seems to have left behind a theoretical and ideological vacuum, which Marxism and neoliberalism alike failed to fill. Revolutionary Marxism was most likely too radical a doctrine for most UNAM
economics students, intent as they were on getting a university degree as
a route to a job. But developmentalism, which had previously been the
ideology of choice—both for framing one's thesis and for getting a job
in the public sector toward which developmentalism was oriented—was
considered "selling out" in the UNAM of 1976, and thoroughly unfash-
ionable by 1994. Small wonder that only 58% of the 1994 theses contained theoretical citations. Without the central ideas of developmentalism to guide them, many UNAM economics theses came to have no
central idea at all.

The ITAM

While the student movement of the 1970s made the UNAM economics
program into a center for the teaching of Marxism and dependency theory, at the ITAM the influence of a group of central bankers was having
the opposite effect, namely, to remake ITAM economics into a highly
rigorous, full-time, Americanized program. As we saw in chapter 5, the
University of Chicago was the most frequent destination for ITAM economics graduates studying economics abroad after 1971. However, to say
that the ITAM became a center for the training of Chicago boys would
be just as simplistic—and as incorrect—as to say that the UNAM was
made into a center for the training of revolutionary Marxists. Certainly,
the Chicago influence was very strong during the mid-1970s, under the
influence of Chicago-trained central banker Francisco Gil Díaz, who was
ITAM's director from 1973 to 1978. Ultimately, however, the most salient
long-term trend at the ITAM was its Americanization, rather than its af-
filiation with any particular school.

By the mid-1970s, the Chicago influence on economics students at the
ITAM was strongly apparent in undergraduate theses, particularly in the
theoretical citations (see table 6.4). The most-cited author from 1974 to
1978 was the University of Chicago's Gary Becker, who appeared in 19%
of the theses. Other University of Chicago authors included Milton Friedman and Harry Johnson, who each appeared in 16% of the theses. Paul
Cagan, cited in 9% of the theses, was a well-known, Chicago-educated
crusader against inflation and for more austere monetary policy. Another
frequently cited author was Heinz Robert Heller, an economist who was

TABLE 6.4
Citations from ITAM Theses, 1974–1978, 1994

ITAM 1974–79, N = 43
(Theses with Theoretical Cites = 86.1%)

	N	%
Gary Becker	8	18.6
Milton Friedman	7	16.3
Harry Johnson	7	16.3
J. M. Keynes	5	11.6
Paul Cagan	4	9.3
Heinz Robert Heller	4	7.0
Robert Musgrave	4	9.3
Paul Samuelson	4	9.3
J. M. Buchanan	3	7.0
Alvin Hansen	3	7.0
R. A. Mundell	3	7.0
David Ricardo	3	7.0
T.W. Schultz	3	7.0

ITAM 1994, N = 37
(Theses with Theoretical Cites = 86.5%)

	N	%
Hal Varian	4	10.8
Kenneth Arrow	3	8.1
Robert Barro	3	8.1
Robert Lucas	3	8.1
Paul Samuelson	3	8.1

chief of the Department of Financial Studies at the IMF during this period, and who authored a book titled *The Monetary Approach to the Balance of Payments*. Some theses also addressed Keynesian theory; Keynes and his follower Samuelson appeared in 12 and 9% of the theses, respectively. As the author of an oft-reprinted textbook on public finance, Richard Musgrave was also cited in 9% of the theses. As in previous years, the works of Marx were not cited in any theses.

Nevertheless, the theoretical citations from 1994 show that rather than adhering dogmatically to the single theoretical subparadigm of the Chicago school, the ITAM economics program eventually diversified its focus. Both the 1976 and the 1994 ITAM theses tended to be theory-driven: in both periods, 86% of the ITAM theses contained theoretical citations. In contrast to the declining use of theory at the UNAM, the ITAM clearly had no lack of ideas to stand behind its empirical inquiry. However, between 1976 and 1994, these ideas became less theoretically one-sided. Of the assortment of most-cited theoretical authors in 1994,

TABLE 6.5
Position on State Intervention, ITAM 1956–60, 1974–78, and 1994

	1956–60		1974–78		1994	
	N	(%)	N	(%)	N	(%)
Less intervention advocated	0	(0)	4	(9.3)	4	(10.8)
Existing interventions supported	6	(37.5)	12	(27.9)	12	(32.4)
More intervention advocated	8	(50)	5	(11.6)	1	(2.7)
No position on intervention	2	(12.5)	22	(51.2)	20	(54.1)
Total	16 (100)		43 (100)		37 (100)	

$\chi^2 = 19.6, \alpha < .005$

only one—Robert Lucas—was a Chicago scholar. The rest were a diverse array of mainstream American economists, including Hal Varian (a Berkeley economist who authored a popular microeconomics textbook) and Kenneth Arrow (who won a Nobel prize in 1972 for his contributions to the study of general equilibrium theory). The most-cited theoretical authors of 1994 were cited less frequently than those of 1976, each appearing in about 8–10% of the theses (in contrast to Becker, Friedman, and Johnson in 1976, who were cited in 16–18% of the theses).

Three major trends stand out when we compare the ITAM theses of the 1970s and 1990s, on the one hand, and those of 1956–60, on the other: the heightened use of formal economic theory, the shift away from Keynesianism, and the dramatic increase in mathematical sophistication. Of the late–1950s theses, only 44% had contained theoretical citations, in contrast to over 80% in 1974–78 and 1994. Moreover, the Keynesian and developmentalist rhetoric of the late 1950s was dwindling in the theses of 1974–78, and completely absent in the theses of 1994; by the 1990s, thesis authors were discussing neither the fundamental differences between developed and developing countries nor the fundamental defects of capitalism that required government intervention. Positions on state intervention in the economy were similar in the 1976 and 1994 theses, but in 1994 proportionately more theses made explicit statements supporting free trade and free markets (8 and 11%, respectively).

Nevertheless, as table 6.5 demonstrates, overt, rhetorical endorsements of free markets and free trade were surprisingly scarce in the ITAM theses of 1994, the year marking the height of the popularity of President Salinas and his neoliberal reforms. This lack of free-market triumphalism seems doubly strange if we contrast it with the clear rhetorical endorsement of developmentalism at the UNAM in the 1950s. In 1958, a substantial proportion (62.5%) of UNAM thesis writers had endorsed increased government intervention; half had commented on the fundamental differences between developed and developing countries, and more than a third had commented on the weaknesses of capitalism as an economic system.

In contrast, in the 1994 ITAM theses, only 11% supported less government intervention, only 8% praised free trade, and only 11% supported free markets or deregulation.

How can we account for this apparent silence on issues of such overwhelming contemporary relevance? The answer, I believe, is that the use of highly sophisticated mathematical language and tools at the ITAM replaced or perhaps even precluded the use of normative statements. In discussing postwar trends in American economics (the ITAM's model), Morgan and Rutherford (1998) observe that the neoclassicism that appeared "offered answers but without the accompanying advocacy of the earlier period. These answers were naturally 'correct' because they were the result of 'objective' methods and because by that stage economists were beginning to spurn intervention and to turn to their new love: the belief of neoclassical economics in the market, in competition, and in the primacy of the self-interested individual" (Morgan and Rutherford, eds., 1998: 13).

This was a marked departure from the earlier way of "doing economics." The Keynesian/developmentalist paradigm of the 1950s presupposed a social consensus regarding both the means and the ends of economic policy, which encouraged the open endorsement of state intervention as the means to a greater social good. In contrast, the highly mathematized economics of the ITAM after the 1970s was framed as pure, objective technique because it did not recognize political and social contracts as an important basis for a functioning economy. Political-sounding statements of what "should" be done were irrelevant in this context; the greater good was best served by the proper application of technique, which would liberate the beneficial forces of the market. While the theories utilized may have had important value-laden presuppositions, the nature of these presuppositions was invisible to the nonexpert observer: mathematical language gave (and still gives) ITAM economics an impenetrable appearance of objectivity. The evolution of the ITAM toward mathematical economics as it was practiced in the United States—and the failure of the UNAM to evolve in this way—is explored further in the following section.

The New Mathematical Economics: UNAM vs. ITAM

If we look retrospectively on the history of the ITAM economics program, the most striking change over time was the dramatic increase in level of methodological sophistication between the late 1950s and 1994. Tables 6.6 and 6.7 show that whereas in 1956–60 there had been no ITAM economics theses utilizing econometric methods (as opposed to merely descriptive statistics),[3] and only a single thesis utilizing mathematical models to express economic concepts, between 1974 and 1978, *more than half of*

TABLE 6.6
ITAM Theses Use of Statistics, 1956–60, 1974–78, and 1994

	1956–60		1974–78		1994	
	N	(%)	N	(%)	N	(%)
Descriptive statistics only	13	(81.2)	18	(41.9)	13	(35.1)
Descriptive and econometrics						
or only econometrics	0	(0)	23	(53.5)	22	(59.5)
No statistics	3	(18.8)	2	(4.6)	2	(5.4)
Total	16 (100)		43 (100)		37 (100)	

$\chi^2 = 18.1$, $\alpha < .005$

TABLE 6.7
ITAM Theses Use of Formal Mathematical Modeling,
1956–60, 1974–78, and 1994

	1956–60		1974–78		1994	
	N	(%)	N	(%)	N	(%)
Formal math models used	1	(6.2)	32	(74.4)	35	(94.6)
Formal math models not used	15	(93.8)	11	(25.6)	2	(5.4)
Total	16 (100)		43 (100)		37 (100)	

$\chi^2 = 42.7$, $\alpha < .005$

ITAM economics theses utilized analytical statistical methods, and *nearly three-quarters* utilized mathematical models; by 1994, these numbers had increased even further. Thus, the ITAM economics program faithfully represented the shifts in international professional standards toward a more quantitative and theoretical approach; the ITAM was very much on the "cutting edge" of economics as it was being practiced in the United States.

Increased mathematical sophistication over time at the ITAM erased any resemblance that it had once borne to the UNAM. Economics at the UNAM had been inaugurated as a profession in the service of an emerging nation-state, one of the primary tasks of which had been to begin to gather quantitative data to be used in the application of new techniques, such as the calculation of national income. The compiling and presentation of descriptive statistics had always been a central part of the ritual of writing an UNAM economics thesis. In the 1930s, this practice was in keeping with mainstream economics in the United States: Backhouse (1998) finds that a typical format for an American economics journal in the 1920s and '30s was the coverage of an applied topic (such as the application of railroad tariffs during a certain period) and the presentation of copious descriptive statistics on that topic.

This relatively atheoretical presentation of descriptive statistics was one of the few features of UNAM theses that remained constant over time.

TABLE 6.8
UNAM Theses Use of Statistics, 1934–45, 1958, 1976, 1994

	UNAM 1934–45 N (%)	UNAM 1958 N (%)	UNAM 1976 n (%)	UNAM 1994 n (%)
Descriptive statistics only	63 (84)	14 (87.5)	42 (84)	43 (86)
Descriptive and analytical or only analytical	0 (0)	0 (0)	2 (4)	4 (8)
No statistics	12 (16)	2 (12.5)	6 (12)	3 (6)
Total	75 (100)	16 (100)	50 (100)	50 (100)

$\chi^2 = 9.2 \; \alpha > .05$

TABLE 6.9
UNAM Theses Use of Formal Mathematical Modeling, 1934–45, 1958, 1976, 1994

	UNAM 1934–45 N (%)	UNAM 1958 N (%)	UNAM 1976 n (%)	UNAM 1994 n (%)
Formal math models used	7 (9.3)	2 (12.5)	5 (10)	10 (20)
Formal math models not used	68 (90.7)	14 (87.5)	45 (90)	40 (80)
Total	75 (100)	16 (100)	50 (100)	50 (100)

$\chi^2 = 5.8 \; \alpha > .1$

Table 6.8 shows that during the populist *cardenismo* of the 1930s, the peaceful Keynesianism of the 1950s, or the student radicalism of the 1970s, descriptive statistics remained a reliable feature of the UNAM economics thesis. Over time, the presentation of such statistics could reliably be found in about 85% of the theses written within the UNAM economics program. Econometrics, in contrast, was notably absent throughout the UNAM's history: even as late as 1994, only 8% of the UNAM theses were using econometric methods.

Thus, the UNAM economics program was standing in place as international standards moved in a new direction. As we saw at the beginning of this chapter, American economics underwent a theoretical and methodological revolution during the postwar period, which would change the face of the discipline. By the mid 1970s, the ITAM had placed itself at the cutting edge of these trends; the UNAM, in contrast, fell increasingly further behind. The lack of change in the methods used at the UNAM over time is exemplified by the statistically insignificant results in tables 6.8 and 6.9.

The growing disparity between the UNAM economics program and international trends and techniques was noted early on by some Mexican economists—particularly those with strong ties to the public sector. In 1968, there was a proposal to inaugurate a more technically and theoretically up-to-date program in economics at the UNAM, supported by Stanford-trained Davíd Ibarra (a technocrat who would later become minister of finance). However, this proposal appeared precisely at a time when the student movement was beginning to voice its well-founded criticisms of the Mexican political, economic, and social orders—and was increasingly turning to Marxist analysis. The student movement and their supporters within the School of Economics criticized the Ibarra proposal as reactionary (interviews, Ramírez 10/15/96 and Ibarra 11/5/95). The Ibarra proposal was defeated, and the first round of radicalizing reforms in the study program of the School of Economics was implemented instead.

Indeed, the idea that UNAM economics could ever have been reformed in line with international trends seems inconceivable. As we saw in chapter 5, the student movement explicitly opposed economics as a technical discipline oriented toward the training of government functionaries; after all, the government was responsible for the Tlatelolco massacre, the repression of the labor movement, and innumerable other instances of social and political injustice.[4] Even more important, the movement had a strong anti-imperialist bent and would have been utterly against the adoption of a theoretical agenda from the United States.

The highly politicized and socially aware student body that opposed the technification of the UNAM economics program had no counterpart at the ITAM. The ITAM was an expensive private school that was disproportionately attended by students from Mexico's highest income brackets; the class consciousness of ITAM students did not predispose them toward radical ideas. If there was any student opposition to the increasing mathematical rigor of the ITAM program in the 1960s and '70s, I have been able to find no record of it. But perhaps even more important, the ITAM did not share the UNAM's liability of being *the* national university of Mexico—such an institution of higher education was inevitably the focus of political struggles over the destiny of the Mexican nation. The evidence suggests that the Echeverría administration may even have deliberately used the UNAM as a safety valve for political discontent; allowing students to take over UNAM programs like that of the School of Economics was a less costly alternative to having them demonstrating in the streets or organizing guerrilla movements in the country. In contrast, politically troublesome students at the ITAM could be quietly expelled.

The political climate of the UNAM was the most important reason for its failure to stay in line with international methodological trends in economics. Nevertheless, another likely factor was the lack of resources. Good statistical training comes at a relatively high price, because potential professors with statistical competence tend to have other employment possibilities. As a school financed by expensive private tuitions, the ITAM could afford to pay the salaries necessary to attract competent teachers of quantitative methodology. At the UNAM, tuitions were so small as to be of merely symbolic value. The UNAM was entirely dependent on funding from the federal government—funding which was heavily dependent on the vagaries of politics and the government's own financial situation. Even during the best of times, the salaries for full-time UNAM economics professors were hardly a foundation for supporting a middle-class family. During the worst of times, they were a pittance—and the worst of times became more or less a permanent state of affairs beginning with the debt crisis of the 1980s, when inflation devalued professors' salaries to a fraction of their former value. Moreover, as one of the most radicalized programs on campus, the UNAM Faculty[5] of Economics was not favored by the neoliberal presidential administrations that oversaw the UNAM budget from 1982 onward (in spite of the fact that President Salinas was an UNAM economics graduate).

In summary, the decline of Mexican developmentalism occurred not just at the abstract level of ideas but also at the very tangible level of institutional transformation, at both the public UNAM and the private ITAM. By the late 1970s, it appeared that developmentalism was being replaced by two ideologically polar extremes: revolutionary Marxism at the UNAM and Chicago-school monetarism at the ITAM. However, a closer examination of undergraduate theses from the two programs in the late 1970s and mid-1990s reveals that their respective institutional transformations were much more subtle. Marxism and dependency theory never came to play the same defining role in shaping students' thinking at the UNAM as developmentalism had for previous generations. At the same time, the Chicago-school focus of the ITAM was ultimately diluted by other mainstream, American perspectives. Nevertheless, these institutional evolutions would have an enormous impact on the professional prospects of UNAM and ITAM economics graduates.

Professional Opportunities for UNAM and ITAM Economists

In the 1950s, the ITAM was a night school that hardly anyone had heard of; young Mexicans who were interested in studying economics were encouraged to study at the UNAM's better-known program. By the 1970s, however, the respective positions of the two institutions within the profession began to reverse. The ITAM became notably successful—not only within the private sector but also within the Mexican government. In contrast, the UNAM economics program suffered from a progressive process of deprofessionalization—understood not in the normative sense we use in everyday language ("her behavior that day was shockingly unprofessional") but rather in the descriptive sense that UNAM graduates could no longer find work.

The UNAM

The Mexican student movement of the 1960s and 70s generated a network or field of economics departments at public universities with similar perspectives on the proper subjects and methods of economic inquiry. The best graduates of the most prestigious of these institutions (particularly of the UNAM) were able to utilize their training to become career professors—a relatively new category in Mexico—because state resources for public universities had increased. During Echeverría's presidential term public university professors' salaries increased between 35 and 58%[6] and there was a considerable growth in academic jobs, particularly in the social sciences (Zermeño 1978: 66; Latapí 1980: 141). For the first time in the history of Mexican public higher education, full-time social science professors began to appear in significant numbers, and they included among their numbers some 1968 movement leaders who had been granted amnesty during the 1970s (Ayala, Blanco, and Paz 1978: 33). At the same time, new institutions of higher education were founded to relieve the UNAM of the excessive burdens of a growing student body. The Autonomous Metropolitan University (UAM)[7] was founded in 1973, and the graduate Center for Economics Education and Research (CIDE) was founded in 1974 to train personnel for the expanding government bureaucracy.

Unfortunately, such opportunities for full-time academics in the economics departments of public universities were limited. The majority of public university economics graduates would still have to count on employment in the public sector, where opportunities for such graduates were dwindling. Three factors contributed to the decline of UNAM economics (and those of other public universities) in the Mexican government. First, the massification of the 1960s decreased the efficacy of informal selection mechanisms for recruiting students to public-sector jobs and devalued UNAM credentials in the job market. Second, radicalization in the 1970s eliminated government employment as the principal objective of UNAM economics and contributed to the flight of "taxi professors" capable of finding public-sector jobs for their students. Third, and finally, the growing indispensability of foreign training put UNAM students at a disadvantage, because they were less able than their ITAM counterparts to acquire admission to and funding for foreign studies in economics.

The massification of economics at the UNAM occured primarily between 1951 and 1962 and between 1970 and 1979, and was not accompanied by a commensurate increase in the number of professors. By 1978 there were nearly five thousand students enrolled in the UNAM economics program (ANUIES 1979). Although many Mexican observers contend that the expansion of enrollments brought about a decline in the academic quality of public universities, there are no standardized measures of such declining quality over time. Rather than evaluating the program's quality, I wish to point out that the production of more graduates by an educational system—no matter how high its quality—also inevitably brings about a phenomenon Collins (1979) refers to as "credential inflation." Levy (1986) notes that massification in Latin American education in the 1960s and '70s caused a "crisis of credentialism" in Latin American public universities, not only because of the sheer increase in the number of degrees—in itself enough to cause the devaluation of credentials—but also because a public university education no longer certified socioeconomic elite status, since massification had opened higher education to the lower and middle classes. The result was a widespread class-based exodus to private universities (Levy 1986: 46–47). In the area of economics in Mexico, this tendency was doubtless exacerbated by public programs' radical reputations.

Moreover, massification also made it more difficult to recruit students into government through the informal "taxi professor" system (also discussed in chapter 4). This system had worked particularly well at the National School of Economics due to the program's small size, which made it relatively easy to identify promising students. When the School of Economics expanded, however, informal recruitment became more difficult in a system where formal mechanisms—such as rigorous examinations and entrance requirements—were in relatively short supply.[8]

During the 1930s and '40s, the handful of students who graduated as economists from the UNAM had been relatively likely to acquire prominent public-sector positions (Camp 1980: 159). By the 1970s, however, not only was an UNAM economics graduate statistically less likely to acquire a government job (since the School of Economics expanded more rapidly than the public sector, meaning that fewer jobs were available per graduate), but the means for sorting out those best qualified for these jobs had been substantially weakened. Whereas massification decreased the efficacy of the selection process at the UNAM and the value of its credentials, radicalization decreased the utility of the program's *content* for public-sector jobs. During the first decades of UNAM economics, students had viewed the prospect of government employment with a certain degree of Mexican revolutionary idealism; one UNAM economics graduate of the 1930s, for example, recalled that she studied to be an economist "in the service of [her] country" (interview, Meyer L'Epée 7/15/96). In contrast, during the 1970s, the idea that to be a government economist was to serve the Mexican people had all but disappeared. In the words of one UNAM economics graduate of the 1970s:

> When I was studying, the people who went to work in the government were seen very negatively. Nobody thought in those terms, nobody thought about what they were going to do after graduating. Working in the public sector was seen as the worst option of all. (Interview, Aguirre 4/2/96)

In keeping with this rejection of the goal of a government career, the concessions won by the student movement in the UNAM economics curriculum from the late 1960s through the mid-1970s led to its steadily decreasing utility for public-sector employment. This was the exact opposite of what had occurred from 1940 through 1968, when UNAM economics had become progressively more technical. The failure to identify problems that government intervention could solve, as well as the tendency to abstain from prescribing the solution of government intervention, constitute evidence that as early as 1976, pressure from the student movement was having the intended effect: the focus of UNAM economics was no longer the training of government functionaries, and the link between the UNAM and the Mexican economic technocracy had become more tenuous.

The delinking of public university curricula from government employment was noted with concern by members of the National College of Economists, the official professional organization of Mexican economists and formal bridge between the economics profession and the Mexican government. In 1978, the organization held a meeting to discuss the shortcomings of the curricula at the UNAM and other public economics programs. Some participants complained of the dogmatism of programs that excluded mainstream theoretical tendencies and even modern Marxist authors (Ramírez Hernandez 1978: 12). Others complained that UNAM graduates had deficient preparation in economic theory, mathematics, and research skills, and lacked foreign language proficiency, "an indispensable instrument for the study of current works, and of great use in professional life" (Fernández Lozano 1978: 24–25).

Two years later, one UNAM economics undegraduate dissertation similarly documented (and lamented) the irrelevance of the curriculum to the public sector (Mancilla López 1980). Keenly aware of the rising fortunes of competing institutions, the author compared a list of required courses at the UNAM to those required at the private programs of the ITAM, the Monterrey Tech, and the Anáhuac in Mexico City—and found the UNAM sorely lacking. By 1976, UNAM economics students were required to take seven semesters of Marxist economics, but there were only two required courses directly addressing public-sector topics (public finance, and monetary theory and policy), a "situation [that] puts the Faculty of Economics at a notorious disadvantage with respect to other undergraduate institutions . . ." as well as with respect to previous UNAM curricula (Mancilla López 1980: 86).

The UNAM's radicalization not only affected the content of the material covered in the classroom but also saturated the very atmosphere of the Faculty of Economics. Revolutionary posters plastered the walls, and student strikes and demonstrations frequently prevented normal classroom activities. Professors with high-level government jobs were openly challenged in class by students who accused them of being agents of the authoritarian state. These professors—who, as one interviewee pointed out, were not paid particularly well for their time but rather taught because of their sense of loyalty to their alma mater—began to abandon their teaching positions in the late 1960s and early 1970s, an exodus that some claim was accelerated during the Echeverría presidency when many left-leaning UNAM graduates were put into high-level government posts (interview, Cabral Bowling 10/3/96).

The result was the further weakening of the taxi professor system of recruitment—already diminished by the effects of massification. Economic policy officials who wanted to give classes increasingly turned to the ITAM and the Colegio de México, if they were conservative, or to the Center for Economics Education and Research (CIDE), if they were further to the left. The CIDE became important in the 1970s because it was seen as an institution with ideology congenial to the populist administrations of Echeverría and López Portillo; it had been founded by the Echeverría administration for the explicit purpose of training public-sector functionaries.[9] Officials who taught at the CIDE included some of the left-developmentalist technocrats who worked within the populist presidential administrations of the 1970s, such as Javier Alejo and José Oteyza, and subsequently pursued graduate studies in economics at Cambridge University in England. Both Alejo and Oteyza were UNAM economics graduates who nevertheless chose the CIDE over the UNAM as the location from which to recruit aspiring functionaries.[10]

Unlike the ITAM, the UNAM does not maintain a database on the career trajectories of its graduates (which would be a formidable task, given the enormous numbers of graduates since the mid-1960s). However, all the available evidence strongly suggests that beginning in the 1970s, the majority of more ordinary UNAM economics graduates faced either unemployment or jobs as very low-level government bureaucrats. As early as 1973, an UNAM economics publication noted "a lowering in the level of salaries" of the typical economics graduate, "who often begins as an auxiliary in the collection of statistics, staying in routine jobs of this nature due in part to his lack of preparation in areas such as the monetary, the fiscal and the statistical" (Yarza 1973: 183). Several years later, an American observer of Mexican economics noted that public university economics graduates were "more often found at the lower salary levels and at the technical positions in these public bodies, rather than among the policy-makers," as opposed to ITAM and other private university graduates, who found places in the upper ranks of economic policymaking ministries (Labarge and Osborn 1977: 24).

When the oil boom of the 1970s gave way to the austerity of the 1980s, the employment panorama for public university economics graduates became even bleaker. During the 1970s, the public sector had been expanded in part to provide jobs for the graduates of Mexico's increasingly massified public university system (Lorey 1994: 14). But with the government downsizing of the 1980s, public university graduates found themselves in increasingly dire straits. One Mexican economist lamented "the crisis" of UNAM economics:

> [T]oday [the early 1990s] graduates [of the UNAM Faculty of Economics] cannot find work. Nobody wants them or hires them because unfortunately they have not been trained to solve concrete problems but rather to preach popular leftist slogans. In contrast, the graduates of the ITAM are in demand in the skilled labor market and obtain with relative ease scholarships for their graduate studies at MIT, the University of Chicago, and other top North American and British universities. (Flores n.d.)

There were, of course, important exceptions—as there are bound to be in a program producing hundreds of graduates per year. Some outstanding students went on to jobs as academics within public universities. A handful managed to win scholarships to study abroad and subsequently had successful government careers: former president Salinas (UNAM economics '71) and current central bank director Guillermo Ortíz (UNAM economics '72) are the most well-known examples.[11] However, it is worth noting that both Salinas and Ortíz started studying at the UNAM *before* the first round of radicalizing reforms in 1968—and therefore were able to benefit from the mentorship of government officials who subsequently ceased giving classes at the UNAM. For example, Salinas's thesis committee at the UNAM included Jesús Silva Herzog Flores (who stopped giving classes at the UNAM in 1969) and Davíd Ibarra (who stopped giving classes at the UNAM in 1970) (Camp 1994).

A study commissioned by the UNAM economics department in 1993 confirmed empirically what was already common knowledge: potential employers were not interested in hiring UNAM graduates. The fifty-seven employers surveyed (88% from the public sector and all in Mexico City) saw the UNAM as being overly Marxist in its theoretical orientation but were even more concerned about its graduates' low level of practically applicable knowledge (Consultores 1993: 22). In contrast, employers' perception was that the best economists came from the ITAM, followed by the Iberoamerican University and the Anáhuac (both also private programs in Mexico City) (Consultores 1993: 25). Under the leadership of a new director, the UNAM Faculty of Economics implemented a major change in its curriculum in 1993, among the explicit aims of which was to increase the employability of UNAM economics graduates. As of the completion of this book, it is still unclear whether these changes have increased the marketability of an UNAM economics degree.

The ITAM

While the UNAM economics program was losing ground professionally, graduates of the ITAM program were increasingly successful, both in their admission to foreign graduate programs and in the labor market. Most ITAM economics graduates did not go on to graduate studies and pursued private-sector careers. Meanwhile, ITAM graduates who acquired foreign graduate degrees in economics tended to go on to careers either in academia or in the government—where they became visible and powerful during the 1980s and '90s.

The ITAM department had "a curriculum designed to be like a U.S. college" (Labarge and Osborn 1977). It comes as no surprise, therefore, that ITAM students were unusually successful in gaining admission to foreign graduate programs—particularly in economics, and particularly in the United States. A study of economics graduates registered in the ITAM Alumni Society shows that after 1971, a substantial proportion of those registered with the society (18.44%) completed graduate study the United States or other foreign countries; a little more than half of those who studied abroad (about 10% of total graduates) studied economics.[12]

ITAM students' success in gaining admission to foreign economics programs both attested to and helped further build the program's growing and formidable reputation abroad. As consecutive generations of ITAM graduates excelled within U.S. graduate programs, social networks linking the ITAM to U.S. universities proliferated: the first ITAM graduates to gain admission to foreign graduate economics programs were pioneers who were able to ease the passage of subsequent generations by becoming ITAM professors and recommending their own students to particular programs. The close personal relationships between prominent ITAM graduates such as Pedro Aspe and famous economics professors in the United States like Jagdish Bhagwati and Rudiger Dornbusch were among the ITAM's most important assets.[13]

In addition to their notable ability to secure admission to foreign economics programs, ITAM economics graduates were also overwhelmingly successful in procuring grants to finance such international study, particularly from Fulbright. Of a total of ninety-six Mexicans who completed graduate studies in economics with funding from Fulbright from 1970 to 1995, 60 were graduates of private universities—an extraordinary figure when one considers that even as late as 1994, four times more economics students graduated from public than from private universities (Fulbright-García Robles 1996; ANUIES 1994). Even more impressive, *more than 40%* of the total ninety-six Fulbright scholars in economics were graduates of the ITAM. In contrast, fewer than 10% were UNAM economics graduates (Fulbright 1996).

The obvious explanation for the ITAM's extraordinary rate of success in acquiring Fulbright grants is that its graduates possessed the sorts of formal academic skills that were rewarded by Fulbright and U.S. universities; for example, ITAM students were well versed in mathematical methods and had a solid preparation in neoclassical economic theory. As it turns out, however, these formal academic attributes were *not* the factor accounting for ITAM students' extraordinary rate of success with Fulbright. To qualify for Fulbright scholarships, applicants were required to take neither field examinations nor GREs; rather, their acceptance was based solely on grades, letters of recommendation, a biographical statement, a minimum TOEFL score, and a general personal interview in English in which factors such as "maturity" and "leadership ability" were stressed.

According to a Fulbright administrator who oversaw this application process in the late 1970s, ITAM graduates tended to have far better English skills than their public university counterparts, both because of the ITAM's emphasis on English skills and also because the socioeconomic backgrounds of ITAM graduates favored international travel and the study of English at an early age (interview, Partearroyo 4/23/96). Not all scholarship opportunities for Mexicans to study economics abroad had such rigorous language requirements; for example, recipients of scholarships from the government's National Council on Science and Technology (CONACYT) often attended a well-known English program at Boulder, Colorado, as preparation for their attendance of graduate programs in the United States. In general, however, the possession of language skills gave ITAM graduates an advantage in the scholarship market.[14] This advantage became particularly important in the 1980s, when funding cuts in the Science and Technology scholarship program meant that applicants had increasingly to rely on foreign-funded scholarship programs, such as Fulbright and the British Consulate program (interview, Espíndola 9/15/96). It is certain, moreover, that the class background of ITAM students provided them with a level of confidence and competence in face-to-face interviews that generally placed them far ahead of their publicly educated counterparts.

In addition to being English-fluent, confident, and well-spoken, ITAM economics graduates benefited from their membership in a community that shared and understood the criteria of foreign economics programs, since a large proportion of ITAM professors had studied abroad themselves. An ex-Fulbright administrator recalled that

> ITAM applicants . . . became so good at writing applications, it was almost as if they had had a course in application writing. The letters of recommendation showed a big difference. Most Mexican public universities at the time . . . didn't generate the kind of letter that we were looking for. We were looking for letters that showed a knowledge of the candidate and of their specific strengths and weaknesses. . . . The ITAM . . . became very good at writing letters, although at the beginning there were very few who were good. . . . And of course as time went on, many of the professors were people who had been through the application process themselves. (Interview, Partearroyo 4/23/96)

Understanding how to write effective applications and letters of recommendation was a form of international cultural capital that, in addition to helping ITAM graduates gain access to funding, no doubt also contributed to their success in being admitted to foreign economics programs.

Thus, whereas the UNAM economics department became part of an organizational field of Mexican public university economics departments influenced by the radicalizing ideologies of the 1960s and '70s, the ITAM economics department became more or less fully integrated with mainstream economics as an international profession. ITAM students participated in meetings of AIESEC (the International Association of Students in Economics and Commercial Sciences), and the ITAM economics department hosted meetings attended by U.S. economists of international renown. For example, in March of 1981 the ITAM jointly sponsored a conference with the U.S. National Bureau of Economic Research on financial policy and capital markets in Latin America; notable participants included Professors Rudiger Dornbusch of MIT and Thomas Sargent of the University of Minnesota. In this way, the social networks established between ITAM graduates and their mentors at prestigious graduate programs in the United States culminated in a major international academic event; ITAM professors proudly saw the meeting as "an international recognition of the academic quality" of the ITAM (*Boletín* 1970: 1; "Entrevista: 1981: 6–7).

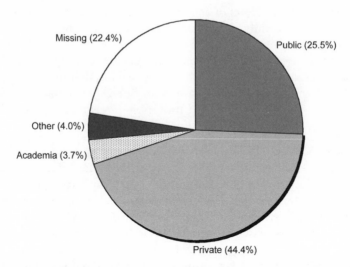

Missing (22.4%)

Public (25.5%)

Other (4.0%)

Academia (3.7%)

Private (44.4%)

Fig. 6.1. 1996 Place of Employment of ITAM Economics Graduates, Date of Graduation 1971–95.

In contrast to the UNAM, which was always primarily oriented toward training economists to work in the government, the focus of the ITAM had always been more eclectic. The results of my study of ITAM alumni (see appendix B) show that of the individuals registered in the database who graduated between 1971 and 1995, the largest group of graduates (44%) were working in the private sector in 1996, with a substantial proportion (25.5%) working for the public sector, and a small minority (4%) working in academia (see fig. 6.1).

Data on ITAM economics graduates before 1971 reveal a similar pattern: more than half of graduates for whom data were available were working in the private sector. Many among the ITAM's first generations of economics students were children of privilege who were simply planning for a lifetime of working for the family firm. Given the enormous expansion of private economics programs over subsequent decades, however, such "ruling class" students must have come to constitute a smaller percentage of the total number of private economics graduates over time. This implies that there were more private-sector jobs for economics "professionals" in the modern sense of the word, hired on the basis of their expertise rather than their family connections.

Within the manufacturing sector, the graduates of private economics programs benefited from a series of historical changes in both government policy and the Mexican economy. One development was a trend toward increased firm size and complexity, and the enhanced reliance on the services of professionals that resulted. Firms run and controlled by families became more open to public ownership and professional management (Camp 1989: 206–7). According to one study conducted during the late 1970s, economists in the northern industrial city of Monterrey were more than three times more likely to work within large (presumably professionalized) firms than they were to work within small or medium firms (Universidad de Nuevo León 7/78).

Another important factor was the increased macroeconomic insecurity of post-1970 Mexico. Unlike the years of stabilizing development, the 1970s and '80s were characterized by inflation, sudden devaluation, and drastic changes in the relative prices of domestic and imported goods. As a result, manufacturing firms looked increasingly to the services of economists to help predict future developments and their effects on profitability—ironically, at a time when economists were less able than ever to predict future developments. One economist who worked for the Monterrey glass firm Vitro in the 1970s recalled:

> I was the first person in the glass group to whom it occurred to do a study of what would happen if the currency was devalued. Why? Because it was the year 1973, and the currency hadn't been devalued in Mexico since 1954. . . . People thought at the time that if there is a devaluation, the prices adjust themselves. . . . What they didn't see is that the impact of the devaluation could translate into prices, and that is where there could be a problem of economic harm to the corporation. (Interview, Sada González 11/10/95)

Another recalled that "we had very difficult times in the 1976 Echeverría devaluations and all that; it was hell trying to price our machines, to establish where we were. . . . So I worked with economists . . . and we did our five-year projections, our three-year projections based on economic outlook" (interview, Garza 11/9/95). Thus, by the late 1970s economists had a palpable presence in the Mexican manufacturing sector. However, it appears that this presence was not extensive: of 1,125 firms surveyed in Monterrey in 1977, only 81 (7%) had economists working for them (Universidad de Nuevo León 1978).

Although the liberalization of the Mexican economy over the past two decades has doubtless produced changes in opportunities for economists in the manufacturing sector, it is not clear whether on balance the impact has been positive or negative. As one business economist rather amusingly recalled, while import substitution was in full effect during the 1970s, the need for economists was everywhere limited by the fact that Mexican businesses were subject to very little competitive pressure:

[T]he importance of the economist was very little; what's more, in the glass market, there was very little importance given to the market. Everything got sold! Moreover, whatever the manufacturer wanted to sell got bought. They never asked the customer what it was that they wanted: do you want a glass like this [round] or do you want it square? No, the glasses are round because it's easier to make them that way, so we're going to make round glasses. They didn't need economics, they didn't even need marketing. This was because of the protection that we had in Mexico then, which meant that we didn't have competition. (Interview, Sada González 11/10/95)

The stiffer competition faced by Mexican firms in the neoliberal era may be having contradictory effects on Mexican business economics. On the one hand, the need for good, long-term information pertaining to future profitability is greater than ever. On the other hand, the comfortable margin of profit that previously financed firms' departments of economic studies (which several interviewees seemed to view as a sort of fad) has disappeared. As a result, many Mexican businesses may be relying more on consulting firms—a relatively new development in Mexico—rather than having their own staff of in-house economic experts (interview, Garza Valle 5/22/96).

However, it seems that the most significant increase in private-sector demand for economists occurred not in manufacturing but within the financial sector. Bankers were key actors in the founding of the ITAM, and from very early in the ITAM's history, Mexican banks hired ITAM graduates to work within their departments of economic studies (interview, Maldonado 11/8/95). As the financial sector became bigger and more complicated, opportunities for ITAM economists proliferated. In response to both financial instability and increased opportunity, the 1970s saw numerous legislative reforms intended to make the Mexican financial system more flexible, resulting in the formation of numerous brokerage houses (Johnson [Hazel] 1995: 105–6).[15] Even more important, the liberalization of Mexican banking under Salinas has contributed to booming opportunities for economics graduates from private universities—perhaps in part because the reprivatized system has been highly unstable (Johnson [Hazel] 1995:107–39).

Thus, among ITAM economics graduates registered in the Alumni Association's database, there is a marked difference between the earlier group (who graduated between 1951 and 1970) and the later group (who graduated between 1971 and 1995). Among those working for the private sector, only 25% of the earlier graduates were working in finance—as opposed to about half of the later graduates.

Part of the success of this more recent cohort in the world of finance doubtless has to do with the technical content of an ITAM economics education. Not only are ITAM students thoroughly schooled in the workings of public and private finance, but they are also well trained in mathematics and statistics. There is also reason to believe that the *cultural* content of the ITAM program has contributed to its graduates' success in finance and banking. Financial-sector liberalization has meant that more Mexican firms have come to rely on foreign portfolio investment. This means that Mexican banks and brokerage houses have greater use for economists who are fluent in English and schooled in the United States. Recently, a group of ITAM economists founded a brokerage house specifically aimed at bringing Mexican firms in contact with foreign investors (interview, Sales 8/2/99).

Although most of its graduates were destined for private-sector careers, the recent fame and prestige of the ITAM economics program has reflected the high-profile careers of graduates who entered the public sector. During the Salinas administration (1988–93), the meteoric rise of the ITAM within the government began to attract public attention, even in the United States.

Table 6.10 shows that ITAM graduates' success in the Mexican government occurred not only at the very top of economic policy ministries but also at lower levels. The success of ITAM graduates in government has been extraordinary, considering the comparatively small size of the ITAM economics program—which in 1980 accounted for only 2.7% of Mexican economics graduates (ANUIES 1981). Although under the subsequent Zedillo administration, ITAM graduates lost ground at the very top of the policy bureaucracy under the Fox administration, an ITAM graduate—Francisco Gil Díaz—is once again at the head of the Finance Ministry.

The proliferation of ITAM graduates in government seems surprising in light of the well-known tendency for Mexican politics to work according to *camarillas*, or political networks. During the 1970s, it was observed that the links holding these networks together were formed primarily at the UNAM, where law students formed long-lasting friendships with their peers and found political mentors among the taxi professors who taught their classes (cf. Camp 1980; Smith [Peter] 1979). As a graduate of the UNAM School of Economics, Salinas could have been expected to recruit his economic cabinet from among his university comrades. Instead, we find that his economic cabinet was stacked with graduates of the ITAM and other private schools, such as the Anáhuac and the Universidad of the Americas.

How did these privately educated individuals "break into" the public sector? A list of some of Salinas's most important political associates, as well as how these individuals made contact with Salinas, helps shed light on this puzzle.

TABLE 6.10
Top and Medium Economic Policymaking Positions in Mexico, October 1994

Name	Position/Year	Undergraduate Degree	Graduate Degree
Carlos Salinas de Gortari	President	UNAM economics, 1969	Ph.D. political economy and government, Harvard, 1978
Pedro Aspe Armella	Minister of finance	ITAM economics, 1974	Ph.D. economics, MIT, 1978
Guillermo Ortíz Martínez	Deputy minister of credit (Finance Ministry)	UNAM economics, 1972	Ph.D. economics, Stanford, 1977
Francisco Gil Díaz	Deputy minister of revenues (Finance Ministry)	ITAM economics, 1966	Ph.D. economics, U. of Chicago, 1972
Carlos Ruiz Sacristán	Deputy minister of budget control (Finance Ministry)	Anáhuac economics, 1972	Ph.D. economics, Northwestern U., 1974
Antonio Sánchez Gochicoa	Oficialia mayor (Finance Ministry)	ITAM economics, 1974	M.A. economics, Cambridge U., 1977
Carlos Jarque	Director of National Bureau of Statistics (INEGI—Finance Ministry)	Anáhuac accounting, 1976	M.S. and M.A. statistics, London S. of Econ. 1977, 1978; M.A. economics, Australian National U., 1981
Jaime Serra Puche	Minister of commerce	UNAM political science, 1973	Ph.D. economics, Yale, 1979
Pedro Noyola de Garagorri	Deputy minister of foreign trade (Commerce Ministry)	No information available	No information available
Fernando Sánchez Ugarte	Deputy minister of industry and foreign investment (Commerce Ministry)	ITAM economics, 1973	Ph.D. economics, U. of Chicago, 1977

TABLE 6.10 (*cont.*)
Top and Medium Economic Policymaking Positions in Mexico, October 1994

Name	Position/Year	Undergraduate Degree	Graduate Degree
Eugenio P. Carrión Rodríguez	Deputy minister of domestic trade and foodstuffs (Commerce Ministry)	UNAM business administration, 1972	M.A. economics, Colegio de México, 1975; Ph.D. economics, U. of Grenoble, France, 1980
Miguel Mancera Aguayo	Central bank director	ITAM economics, 1956	M.A. economics, Yale, 1960
Ariel Buira Seira	Director of international organisms and agreements (central bank)	B.A. economics, U. of Manchester, England, 1963	Ph.D. economics, U. of Manchester, England, 1966
Agustín Carstens Carstens	Assistant to the director (central bank)	ITAM economics	Ph.D. economics, U. of Chicago
Marín Maydón Garza	Director of development credit (central bank)	Autonomous University of Nuevo León (UANL) economics, 1965	Ph.D. economics, MIT, 1967
Angel Palomino Hasbach	Director of monetary programming and financial systems analysis (central bank)	UNAM economics, 1966	M.A. economics, Colegio de México, 1971
José Julian Sidaoui Dib	Director of central bank operations (central bank)	University of the Americas economics, 1973	M.A. economics, UPenn, 1974; Ph.D. economics, George Washington U., 1978

Sources: Camp (1995), Unidad de la Crónica Presidencial (1994), and interviews particularly for the central bank).
Note: Top positions include president, finance minister, commerce minister, and central bank director.

168 CHAPTER SIX

TABLE 6.11
Salinas's *Camarilla*

Politician	Place of Contact with Salinas
Pedro Aspe Armella	MIT student, Finance Ministry
Manuel Camacho Solís	UNAM student
Patricio Chirinos Calero	PRI—Institute of Political and Economic Studies (IEPES)
Luis Donaldo Colosio	IEPES
José Córdoba Montoya	Ministry of Budget and Planning, Finance Ministry
Marcela González Salas	Finance Ministry
Otto Granados Roldán	Bureaucracy
Emilio Lozoya Thalmann	UNAM student
María Moreno Uriegas	Finance Ministry
Andrés Massieu Berlanga	Presidency
Carlos Mier y Terán	Ministry of Budget and Planning
Gonzalo Martínez Corbala	PRI
Rogelio Montemayor Seguy	Finance Ministry
Juan José Páramo Díaz	Finance Ministry
Sócrates Rizzo García	Ministry of Budget and Planning
José Ruiz Massieu	UNAM student
Jaime Serra Puche	Finance Ministry
María Vásquez Nava	Finance Ministry
Ernesto Zedillo	Ministry of Budget and Planning

Source: Camp (1994).

Table 6.11 illustrates a number of interesting features of Salinas's political network. For one thing, the UNAM does not appear to be a particularly important site for recruitment to Salinas's network. On the other hand, two government ministries appear to have been tremendously important, namely, the Ministry of Finance and the Ministry of Budget and Planning. Indeed, these trends have been observed by a number of scholars as important characteristics of the presidential administrations of the 1980s and '90s (Hernández Rodríguez 1987, Camp 1995; Centeno and Maxfield 1992; Centeno 1994).

In light of these tendencies in Mexican political recruitment, the colonization of economic policy ministries by the ITAM and other private schools seems less surprising. During earlier decades, when political networking was carried out primarily at the UNAM, and primarily through the political channels of the state bureaucracy, ITAM graduates were excluded from the highest levels of power. But in an emerging system in which the most important site of political networking was increasingly the planning and banking bureaucracies, ITAM graduates could become more influential.

Throughout the history of the ITAM, graduates who entered public-sector careers overwhelmingly did so through the financial bureaucracy. The ITAM's initial "point of entry" into the public sector was the Banco de México—an institution with important historical ties to the ITAM and with a pronounced ideological disincentive to hire the graduates of the better-known UNAM School of Economics. The Banco de México was relatively (although not absolutely) insulated from the six-year cycle of presidential appointments and turnover: central bank functionaries could be hired with more technical criteria in mind. Moreover, being from a privileged economic background, a liability in other sectors of the Mexican government, could be an asset in the central bank, where there was a long tradition of networking between public- and private-sector financiers (Maxfield 1990).

Thus, three ITAM graduates who were able to enter the Banco de México early on were Gustavo Petricioli, Miguel Mancera, and Francisco Gil Díaz. Through teaching part-time classes at their alma mater, these ITAM graduates were able to help new generations into public-sector careers. ITAM graduates were also helped into the financial bureaucracy by government officials who graduated from the UNAM but whose distaste for the radicalization of the UNAM program drove them to give part-time classes at more congenial institutions. A particularly important ITAM recruiter was Leopoldo Solís, an UNAM graduate who subsequently studied economics at Yale and became director of the Banco de México's Department of Economic Studies. ITAM graduates mentored by Solís included Pedro Aspe and Francisco Gil Díaz.

As a result, during the 1970s, ITAM graduates were able to acquire a firm foothold in the Mexican government. At the Banco de México, many upper-level policymaking officials were ITAM graduates. In the Ministry of Finance, Davíd Ibarra worked with a team of young economists that included ITAM graduate Pedro Aspe. Under the de la Madrid administration, Aspe moved to the Ministry of Budget and Planning, where he worked under an UNAM graduate whom he had initially met while both were pursuing graduate studies in Cambridge, Massachusetts: Carlos Salinas de Gortari. When Salinas came to power several years later, he appointed Aspe as minister of finance, thus providing ITAM graduates with a point of entry to all branches of the ministry. This was a historic moment, since as Centeno and Maxfield (1992) point out, Mexican government officials prefer to appoint subordinates who share their own characteristics.

Conclusion

The breakdown of the developmentalist consensus in Mexico had enormous implications for the Mexican economics profession. Under the influence of the student movement, the UNAM economics program was deliberately and systematically deprofessionalized, in the sense that it was delinked from the most important source of employment of its graduates, namely, the Mexican government. Changes in the ideal content of an UNAM economics education had very real implications for students' career prospects, which after the late 1970s became increasingly bleak. Meanwhile, graduates of the newly Americanized ITAM program were becoming quite sucessful—not only within the private sector (where most graduates were destined to work) but also within the government. The reason was a system of incentives that increasingly rewarded technical expertise, and the ability to deal with the world of international finance. The following chapter looks at how the outbreak of the debt crisis in 1982 facilitated the rise of U.S.-trained economists—including many from the ITAM—within the Mexican government.

Chapter 7

NEOLIBERALISM AND THE RISE OF
THE NEW TECHNOCRATS

WHEN Miguel de la Madrid was selected to be the ruling party's official candidate in 1981, the international business press initially viewed him with a certain pessimism. "Those who forecast a conservative administration between 1982 and 1988 forget that Mr. de la Madrid will inherit a powerful nationalist and populist tradition. He seems likely to preserve the new fashion of economic planning," the *Economist* magazine predicted ("The New Hero" 1981: 68). A *Business Week* article similarly forecast that de la Madrid's cryptic reference to "a change of course" in Mexican economic policy was a veiled reference to "more government intervention" ("Mexico: An Economic Tornado" 1982: 41).

These grim expectations notwithstanding, de la Madrid would not follow in the footsteps of his populist predecessors. The terms of Miguel de la Madrid (1982–88), Carlos Salinas (1988–94), and Ernesto Zedillo (1994–2000) would be known for the promotion of free-market reforms by a new kind of economic technocrat in place of the older generations of self-taught economic policymakers with law degrees. Under the guidance of foreign-trained economists in top policy positions, Mexico underwent a free-market revolution that utterly transformed the developmentalist policies of previous years. Thus, the presidential succession of 1982 turned out to be a watershed for Mexican economic policymaking, simultaneously marking the rise of technocracy, the blossoming of the debt crisis, and the dawning of neoliberalism.

This chapter focuses the relationship between three historical processes in Mexico: international financial pressures, the rise of foreign-trained technocrats in government, and the implementation of neoliberal reforms. This historical account of the process of liberalizing reforms in Mexico suggests that Mexican market reforms were not just the imposition of international financiers (coercive isomorphism). Rather, a key factor was a group of technocrats whose training in mainstream neoclassical economics predisposed them to look favorably on the dismantling of the developmentalist state. Thus Mexico's neoliberal transition illustrates the power of professionals to transform the organizations within which they are embedded, through a process of "expert" or "normative" isomorphism. However, the rise of these economic experts within the government is itself a phenomenon requiring further explanation. This chapter reviews evidence suggesting that both mimetic and coercive pressures contributed to the proliferation of U.S.-trained technocrats at the highest level of Mexico's policymaking bureaucracy.

MEXICO'S POLICY PARADIGM SHIFT

Neoliberal reforms in Mexico proceeded in two stages. The first was the stage of "structural adjustment"—a generalized downsizing of government and an implementation of fiscal and monetary austerity, conducted under the watchful eyes of the IMF from 1982 through the mid-1980s. During this stage, Mexico's policies were consistently so respectful of creditors and conforming to the exacting standards of the IMF that even international business observers were impressed by the severity of the measures the new technocrats were willing to impose. "Turning the screws on just about everybody, President Miguel de la Madrid has reined in inflation, slashed imports and public spending, and boosted exports. Under a grinding austerity program real wages have dropped 30% in two years," reported an article in *Business Week,* going on to quote the head of an economic forecasting group in Mexico City: "Mexico wasn't lucky to find the banks. The banks were lucky to find Mexico" ("Will Mexico Make It?" 1984: 74). During the de la Madrid presidency, real GDP growth was negative, while inflation averaged over 80% (Maddison et al. 1989: 159).

The second stage was a series of institutional reforms that dismantled the developmentalist policy framework of previous decades, which began during the final years of the de la Madrid administration and came to full fruition under the administration of Carlos Salinas (1988–94). Whereas de la Madrid's privatizations had been relatively modest, and seemed to be more a matter of fiscal expediency than ideological commitment, Salinas made a virtue of privatizing some of the Mexican government's largest and most important parastate industries, including the state telephone monopoly, television station, and airline. The banking system that had been nationalized in 1982 was reprivatized, and the financial system liberalized; interest rates and deposits were no longer regulated by the government, and reserve requirements were eliminated (Córdoba 1994: 252). Policy toward foreign investors was liberalized such that foreign firms could acquire up to 100% ownership in publicly traded Mexican firms (Moffett 1989: A11). The central bank was granted formal independence from the government in 1993.

Another policy shift of historic proportions was the revision of Article 27 of the Mexican Constitution. The 1992 amendments to Article 27 effectively ended Mexico's long postrevolutionary history of land reform through redistribution and opened the *ejidos* to purchase by private investors, both domestic and foreign (Córdoba 1994: 256–57). The crown jewel of liberalization under Salinas was the North American Free Trade Agreement (NAFTA), effective as of 1994.

Why did the Mexican government embark on this dramatic course of policy reform after 1982? To some observers—particularly those associated with the international business press—the answer was merely common sense: neoliberal reforms occurred because they were the most efficient policy available. On further consideration, however, this explanation seems thoroughly inadequate. For one thing, sociologists have shown that a host of considerations other than efficiency determine the behavior of organizations—including the behavior of national governments (cf. DiMaggio and Powell 1983; Meyer et al. 1997). For another thing, even enthusiastic supporters of liberalizing reforms recognize that governments often pursue policies that are neither good nor efficient but rather serve the selfish interests of politicians and their rent-seeking private-sector collaborators (Krueger 1974; Buchanan et al. 1980). Given these considerations, it is useful to frame the question in historical terms, namely, why did the Mexican government implement liberalizing reforms after 1982—but not before? The following section considers some potential answers.

Policy Reform—External Imposition or Inside Job?

It is impossible to understand neoliberal reforms in Mexico and other developing countries without taking international context into account. The beginning of the 1980s represented the start of an international political sea change that had a critical effect on the economic policy options of Mexico and other developing countries. From the very outset, the debt crisis was recognized by the Reagan administration as an opportunity to leverage policy reforms. An initial rescue plan coordinated by U.S. Treasury Secretary James A. Baker III offered debt rollover in exchange for the adoption of market-oriented and investor-friendly policies by developing countries (Miller 1986: 16). World Bank director Tom Clausen appointed University of Minnesota economist Anne Krueger as the World Bank's chief economist. Krueger was a well-known theorist of the harmful "rent-seeking" effects of protectionism in the Third World and a vociferous advocate of free trade. Under Clausen, "structural adjustment loans"— loans conditioned on the implementation of policy reforms—became a tool utilized repeatedly for the promotion of market-friendly policies in developing countries (George and Sabelli 1994: 58). Meanwhile, the perennially conservative International Monetary Fund, too, saw the debt crisis as an opportunity and began a new era of "policy-based lending," in which financial support was offered in return for commitment to government downsizing and conservative monetary policy.

In Mexico, and around the developing world, there have been countless instances of such policy-based lending since 1982—deliberate interventions of the U.S. government and international financial institutions on behalf of market-oriented policy reform. To a casual observer, therefore, it would seem that the radical paradigm shift in developing countries during the 1980s and '90s was quite simply the result of coercion by powerful external agents—not the result of a "social learning" process at all.

On closer inspection, however, this picture becomes substantially more complicated. For one thing, there are many instances of liberalizing reforms that have no apparent connection to direct pressures from any single organization. One outstanding example is central bank independence, recently adopted by developing nations around the world, but with little connection to direct pressures levered by international financial institutions. Rather, the reason for the widespread adoption of independent central banks appears to be the overwhelming need to foster investor confidence in an era of rapid international capital mobility (Maxfield 1997).

Even more interesting, in many developing nations, neoliberal reforms have been almost joyfully embraced by a new and internationally credentialed group of policymakers: technocrats with Ph.D.'s from foreign universities—usually American universities, and usually in economics. In other words, in many respects, neoliberalism looks much more like an inside job than an external imposition.

Since neoliberal policy reforms in any developing country are necessarily a complex phenomenon, serious investigators writing about Mexico's neoliberal transition have tended to focus on either domestic or international factors in their accounts. One sort of account emphasizes international pressures, including the influence exerted by foreign investors, foreign governments, and/or international financial institutions (cf. Stallings 1992; Maxfield 1997). Another group focuses on domestic factors, such as the influence of national interest groups or developments within the Mexican state (cf. Centeno 1994; Heredia 1996; Thacker 1999). Whereas the first story is about policy reforms imposed from the outside, the second story is about neoliberal "revolution from within."

However, there is no inherent reason for these two kinds of explanation to be mutually exclusive. In fact, the evidence suggests that both domestic and international factors played an important part in the implementation of liberalizing reforms in Mexico. It appears that at the domestic level, the critical impetus for Mexican neoliberalism came from the Mexican state rather than from organized domestic interest groups. The Mexican system of single-party corporatism was always unusually good at managing and repressing popular demands (cf. Middlebrook 1995). However, during the period of neoliberal reforms, this system of control was compounded by the extreme centralization of power within the presidency and the culmination of a historical process whereby elected officials systematically lost ground to other groups within the ruling party. As a result, "while the union of party-government remain[ed] strong, the role of the former as a conduit for protest from below and for communication from above [had] virtually been abandoned, and replaced by a greater emphasis on manipulation of revolutionary symbols and control of opposition" (Centeno and Maxfield 1992: 71). In short, by the time of the Salinas administration, organized popular interests were not playing a major role in the negotiation and formulation of government policy. Similarly, the demands of small- and medium-size Mexican businesses were effectively prevented from interfering with the negotiations leading up to the North American Free Trade Agreement—an agreement that ran directly counter to the interests of many such businesses (Shadlen 1999).

In contrast, the most elite, powerful sector of Mexican business did play an important part in negotiating the terms of liberalizing reforms in Mexico—particularly (although not exclusively) around the terms of the North American Free Trade Agreement (NAFTA). However, the impetus for NAFTA and other liberalizing reforms did not originate from domestic big business. Rather, actors within the Mexican state first chose to implement liberalizing reforms and *later* successfully mobilized big business as their allies in pursuing a course of free-market reforms (Thacker 1999). Liberalizing reformers within the government were not puppets of the Mexican bourgeoisie but were always at the vanguard of Mexico's neoliberal revolution.

In summary, both national and international factors can be implicated in Mexico's liberalizing reforms. At the national level, the most important agents in this policy transformation were government officials rather than organized domestic interest groups. At the international level, important players included multilateral institutions (e.g., the IMF, the World Bank), U.S. government officials, and international investors. An examination of the events leading up to Mexican neoliberal reforms reveals how external pressures and internal politics interact to produce neoliberal outcomes in developing countries.

FROM POPULISM TO STRUCTURAL ADJUSTMENT. . .

In 1981, rising international interest rates and falling international petroleum prices were leading to speculation about the impending devaluation of the peso and widespread capital flight. Different factions of foreign-trained economists within the Mexican policy bureaucracy favored distinct approaches to the debt crisis: there was a group of "radical developmentalists" associated with the López Portillo government, on the one hand, and on the other, an opposing group of fiscal and monetary conservatives. This latter group was mostly comprised of individuals who had had long careers within the financial-sector bureaucracy—particularly the central bank—and who had received graduate training in economics in the United States. The radicals, in contrast, had worked in the Ministry of National Resources (which was in charge of the rapidly expanding parastate industries) and other areas of the Mexican government, and often had studied economics at Cambridge University—a hotbed of Keynesian and "post-Keynesian" thinking.

A crucial event in determining which group of technocrats prevailed was President López Portillo's selection of Miguel de la Madrid as the ruling party's official candidate for the presidency—which essentially anointed him to be Mexico's future president. De la Madrid—like Salinas and Zedillo after him—had never held public office but had impeccable technical credentials: a master's degree in public administration from Harvard university. He was initially described in the foreign business press as "a technocrat, adept at modern economics but out of touch with Mexico's revolutionary traditions," "a friend of bankers and businessmen," and "a liberal capitalist, not a revolutionary firebrand" ("The New Hero" 1981: 68; "Mexico's New Man 1982: 14).

Why did López Portillo select de la Madrid and not another, more politically experienced candidate? Until very recently, the PRI candidate was selected by the outgoing president through a process shrouded in mystery known as the *destape* (or "unveiling"). It is therefore impossible to know with certainty why de la Madrid was selected. Given the dire situation of Mexico's finances by the end of 1981, however, it seems reasonable to assume that López Portillo's selection was based on his perception that Mexico's most pressing problems at the time were financial rather than political (Centeno 1994: 158–59).[1] It was no longer peasants, workers, and radicalized students that the party needed to impress but multilateral agencies, foreign lenders, and government officials—all of whom needed to be mobilized to help bail Mexico out.

In deference to the incoming president, two top-level economic policymakers were appointed even before de la Madrid's accession to the presidency. One was Finance Minister Jesús Silva Herzog Flores, the son of the famous cofounder of the UNAM school who had a masters' degree in economics from Yale University. In terms of ideology, Jesús Silva Herzog Flores differed substantially from his father, and had a reputation for prudence and conservatism that made him a favorite among international bankers, who were reputed to smile ". . . at the mere mention of Mexico's charismatic finance minister," in the words of one *Wall Street Journal* account (Kraft 1984: 1). With typical dryness, the *Economist* remarked that Silva Herzog Flores seemed to be ". . . more popular with the New York bankers than he is with some of the folks back home" ("Mexico's Happy Creditors" 1984: 60). De la Madrid's other prepresidential appointment was central bank director Miguel Mancera, an ITAM graduate, also a Yale M.A. in economics, and a conservative central banker to the core.

The intervening months between de la Madrid's selection as candidate in September of 1981 and his ascension as president in December of 1982 were marked by the blossoming of Mexico's debt problems into a full-blown debt crisis, and an extraordinary and fascinating struggle between different camps of government economists with similar foreign credentials but very different ideologies. On one side were "radical" economists inspired by developmentalism and its more radical cousin, dependency theory—most important, Carlos Tello, formerly director of the Ministry of Budget and Planning (and briefly head of the central bank), and José Andrés de Oteyza, the minister of national resources. These economists had reached the peak of their careers during the populist presidencies of Echeverría and López Portillo, had both been UNAM economics undergraduates, and had both studied at Cambridge University, known for its Keynesian tendencies. On the other side were the more orthodox, Yale-educated economists, Jesús Silva Herzog Flores and Miguel Mancera, along with their numerous allies within Mexican public administration.

The battle between the Yale and the Cambridge economists came to a head over how to deal with Mexico's external debt crisis. On August 18, 1982, Finance Minister Jesús Silva Herzog Flores informed the U.S. government, the IMF, and the world financial community that Mexico would be unable to meet its debt payments. To negotiate with the banks, the IMF, and the U.S. government, Mexico put its best foot forward: a team of English-fluent, foreign-trained technocrats whose close personal connections within international financial circles were an important asset.[2] These technocrats included Silva Herzog Flores and Mancera, as well as José Angel Gurría and Alfredo Phillips Olmedo (Kraft 1984: 5).

After initially declaring its inability to pay, Mexico faced the critical choice of whether to attempt to meet its obligations to its creditors or to default. For Jesús Silva Herzog Flores, a Yale M.A. who had spent his formative professional years at the Mexican central bank, the latter course was not an option: Mexico would behave as a responsible debtor. Knowing well that default was a very real possibility, international businessmen and financiers breathed a collective sigh of relief. In the words of an article in the *Economist* magazine, "Mexico, always an inward-looking country, could have defaulted, snubbed its nose at the bankers, turned its back on the United States and used its oil wealth—Qaddafi-style—to stoke the revolutionary fires of central America" ("Mexico under the IMF" 1983: 19).

Instead, Silva began immediately to steer Mexico toward a negotiated settlement with the banks, for which he would have to enlist the support of the U.S. Treasury, Paul Volcker of the Federal Reserve, the Bank for International Settlements, and the International Monetary Fund. In order to meet its obligations, Mexico needed bailout funds from the U.S. Treasury and IMF, both of which demanded uncomfortable concessions in return for their support: the U.S. Treasury wanted to buy Mexican oil at a heavy discount (the equivalent of a loan at over 30%); the IMF, on the other hand, wanted Mexico to commit to the usual package of structural adjustment austerity measures. The oil deal was finalized over the objections of Oteyza and with bitter criticism from Mexico's left-opposition press (Kraft 1984: 15–16).

But it was the IMF deal that was the most difficult for the leftist economists to swallow. The widespread capital flight preceding the debt crisis was diagnosed by these economists as a effect of the exaggerated ease with which the rich could move their capital out of Mexico. As a remedy, Oteyza and other like-minded Mexican economists advised the imposition of capital controls. These controls were thoroughly opposed not only by the IMF but also by orthodox Mexican government economists like Silva and Mancera; in an overt sign of disagreement, in 1982 Mancera published a pamphlet titled "The Disadvantages of Capital Controls." The leftist economists also advised the nationalization of the Mexican banking system—an idea that must have particularly appalled Mancera as a traditional central banker. On August 31, 1982, López Portillo took their advice and signed capital controls, and the nationalization of the Mexican banks, into law; at the same time, Mancera was deposed as head of the central bank and Carlos Tello put in his place (Kraft 1984: 38).

Whether or not these heterodox measures were the correct solution to Mexico's problems, they direcly contradicted Silva's strategy of committing to debt repayment and compliance with the requirements of foreign governments and international financial institutions. López Portillo's decree represented a severe setback for Silva's negotiations with the IMF; matters were made even worse by the fact that Tello had replaced Mancera on Mexico's negotiation team. But Tello was isolated, and the policies he favored were not only opposed by Silva, the IMF, and foreign negotiators like Paul Volcker of the Federal Reserve but also precluded by the harsh fact that Mexico's funds were running out; unless Mexico was willing to default on its debt, it would have to accept the IMF's terms, which Volcker also required as a precondition for his ongoing intermediation on behalf of Mexico with private banks. Tello attempted to hold his ground in negotiations with the IMF, insisting on exchange controls, a generous wage policy, and high government spending; rumors abounded that he was attempting to strengthen his position by entering into a debtors' cartel with Argentina and Brazil (Kraft 1984: 44–45).

However, IMF negotiators knew Tello was outnumbered on the negotiating team and that de la Madrid's ascension to the presidency would solidify their position. On November 10, 1982, Silva announced the terms of the IMF deal: Mexico was committed to cutting the budget deficit from 16.5% of the GNP in 1981 to 8.5% in 1983, to drastically reducing foreign borrowing, and to lowering government subsidies dramatically (Kraft 1984: 46). The IMF and the fiscal and monetary conservatives within the Mexican government had won.

. . . AND FROM STRUCTURAL ADJUSTMENT TO INSTITUTIONAL REFORMS

On December 1, 1982, Miguel de la Madrid assumed the Mexican presidency; Oteyza was replaced by a new minister of national resources, Mancera was reinstated as central bank director, and Silva was kept on as minister of finance. The de la Madrid cabinet was stacked with foreign-trained M.A.'s and Ph.D.'s to an extent never before seen in the Mexican government, and nearly one in four officials in the administration had studied in the United States (Centeno 1994: 117). Indeed, officials in de la Madrid's cabinet were much more likely to have received graduate training than officials in the concurrent Reagan administration (Camp 1995: 103).

From the very beginning, this administration was committed to carrying out IMF structural adjustment measures to the letter. Under the Programa Inmediato de Reordenamiento Económico (PIRE) of 1983, which was negotiated with the IMF, government budgets were slashed, the peso radically devalued, subsidies eliminated or reduced, and the real wages of government workers lowered. Unprofitable and smaller government firms were sold off to private investors (Heredia 1996:154–60).

The stage was set for the next phase of Mexican post-debt-crisis policy: structural adjustment was now to be followed by deeper and more long-term liberalizing reforms. The officials in de la Madrid's administration shared a similarly conservative position with respect to policy toward Mexico's creditors and the IMF. However, the economists and other officials in the de la Madrid cabinet were by no means unanimously convinced of the desirability of a broader liberalizing program. De la Madrid himself is described by Heredia (1996) as a "liberal developmentalist" of the sort that abounded in Mexico—particularly in the central bank—during the 1950s: although fiscally and monetarily conservative, these individuals also firmly believed in the necessity of state intervention to promote development, including such measures as import substitution to protect domestic industry (p. 159).

Until the mid-1980s, de la Madrid put forward a moderate policy of gradual and selective opening to free trade. But later, disagreements developed regarding the speed and depth of the trade opening: on one side were the "liberal developmentalists" within the Ministry of Commerce, and on the other the "free traders" in the Mexican central bank. Commerce Minister Héctor Hernández Cervantes was a graduate of the UNAM economics program who had done his graduate work at the University of Melbourne in Australia rather than in the United States. Hernández advocated only gradual and selective opening to international free trade, and was generally in favor of an active state in a mixed economy. At the same time, there existed a small group of radical rent-seeking protectionists within the ministry, whose position undermined the credibility of Hernández and his team (Heredia 1996:170–72).

On the opposite end of the debate was a younger generation of foreign-trained officials at the Banco de México who were much more fervent believers in market forces than fiscal conservatives and old-style liberal developmentalists. The most important of these was a young University of Chicago graduate named Francisco Gil Díaz—the same Gil Díaz who had helped remake the ITAM into a center of U.S.-style neoclassical economics in the 1970s. Gil Díaz had numerous U.S.-trained allies outside the Banco de México, including Pedro Aspe, an ITAM graduate working at the Budget and Planning Ministry, and Jaime Serra Puche of the Colegio de México. A joint seminar series that had brought together U.S.-trained economists from the ITAM and the Colegio de México since 1977 was an influential source of free-market ideas in the Mexican government during this period. At the same time, the President's Office of Economic Advisers brought together yet another team of U.S.-trained economists to support free-trade ideas, which included Chicago-trained Herminio Blanco. The position of these economists was strengthened by the ongoing deterioration of Mexico's finances, hastened by the earthquake of 1985 and the fall in oil prices in 1986 (Heredia 1996:173–80).

The Ministry of Finance occupied an intermediate position between the Banco de México and the Ministry of Commerce, since it was divided between officials who supported free trade and those who opposed it. But in 1985, an administrative reform eliminated two subministries and created a new subministry headed by Pedro Aspe; later, in 1986, Silva resigned as minister of finance (for internal political reasons). These developments, according to Heredia, pushed the Finance Ministry into the free-trade camp: Silva's successor as finance minister was Gustavo Petricioli, the man responsible for the renovation and Americanization of ITAM economics in the mid-1960s, who brought in other free traders, notably Yale-educated Jaime Serra Puche (Heredia 1996:168–69, 238–39).

Aided by their alliance with World Bank and IMF officials espousing similar policies—and opposed by Commerce Ministry officials and private-sector interests—the free-trade coalition within Mexican public administration prevailed. In 1984, the Banco de México began to disseminate policy proposals in favor of accelerated trade opening. A World Bank trade policy mission was sent to Mexico in November of 1984, which negotiated and collaborated closely with officials in the central bank and Finance Ministry; later that year, the World Bank granted Mexico the first "Trade Policy Loan" in the bank's history, which provided Mexico with a series of loans in return for comprehensive trade liberalization. In March 1985, a letter from Silva and Mancera to the IMF agreed to "a complete revision of trade policy," beginning with the replacement of quantitative import controls with tariffs (Buchanan and Rhein 1985: 61). In 1986, the Reagan administration further strengthened the hand of international financial institutions and free traders within the Mexican government by announcing that it would not negotiate on Mexico's behalf with international banks unless Mexico "implemented substantive structural reforms" and arrived at a new agreement with the IMF ("Silva Lining" 1986: 81).

But Mexico needed very little prompting; from the very beginning, Mexican and World Bank officials saw eye to eye on trade policy. Describing Mexico as "the darling" of the World Bank's economists, a *Financial Times* article written in 1992 claimed that Mexico had been able to secure more nonpoverty loans from the World Bank than any other country. The reason for such preferential treatment[3] was a collaboration beginning in the mid-1980s, when World Bank officials had discovered Mexican officials to be so like-minded that "Mexico went much further in reducing its trade barriers than the bank required. . . . The two sides agree on almost everything. . . . World Bank economists and Mexican officials often spend weekends together brainstorming on policy issues. Many are graduates of the same US universities, and friends" (Fraser 1992: 7). Similarly, Heredia argues that the victory of free trade in Mexico was not driven by external pressures but rather reflected the unabashedly free-market views of the officials who had taken control of policymaking (Heredia 1996: 224–57).

Collaboration between Mexico and the World Bank led Mexico to join the General Agreement on Tarriffs and Trade (GATT) in 1986, resulting in the elimination of a host of licensing requirements and quantitative controls. In 1987 the Mexican government implemented a program of trade liberalization that went even beyond GATT requirements. These collaborations culminated in the North American Free Trade Agreement (NAFTA), implemented during the Salinas administration (1988–94).

NAFTA pledged Mexico to lowering tariffs and eliminating nontariff barriers on goods imported from the United States and Canada. In some
respects, NAFTA is a much more doctrinaire free-trade document than
GATT: whereas GATT recognizes the right of governments temporarily to
restrict imports in cases of balance-of-payments crises, NAFTA effectively
denies access to such restrictions (Nadal Egea 1996: 14).[4]

When Carlos Salinas assumed the presidency in 1988, he gave prominent positions to the same U.S.-trained economists who had pushed for
trade liberalization under the de la Madrid presidency. Pedro Aspe (MIT),
an ITAM graduate, became Mexico's new minister of finance. Jaime Serra
Puche (Yale) of the Colegio de México became minister of commerce.
Miguel Mancera (Yale), another ITAM graduate, remained at the head of
the central bank. Free traders were also appointed at the next-to-highest
level of economic policymaking: Francisco Gil Díaz (the University of
Chicago) was appointed deputy minister of revenues in the Finance Ministry; Herminio Blanco (the University of Chicago) became deputy minister
of foreign trade in the Commerce Ministry. Under Salinas, the entire
upper and medium strata of all economic policymaking ministries became
dominated by U.S.-trained economists.

Throughout the Salinas administration, Mexico's liberalizing policies
were rewarded by generous loans from international financial institutions. At the same time, the Brady negotiations of 1989 led to the effective
reduction of Mexico's public external debt with the commercial banks
from $52.6 billion to about $48 billion (Gurría and Fadl 1995: 134). Not
surprisingly, Salinas's probusiness policies restored investor confidence:
between 1987 and 1994, foreign investment in Mexico totaled over $100
billion (Santiso 1999: 52).

Of course, it is well known that subsequent developments tarnished
Salinas's golden reputation. The peso crisis of 1994–95 showed Salinas's
policies to be driven by political as well as technical considerations; in
1999, his brother Raúl was condemned to life imprisonment for his
involvement in a political assassination. As a result, Carlos Salinas had
to retreat into semiexile in Ireland, his ambitions to become director of
the World Trade Organization shattered.

Nevertheless, the policies associated with *salinismo* outlived Salinas.
Under the presidency of Yale-trained economist Ernesto Zedillo (1994–
2000), Mexico maintained its commitment to the market-oriented model
and relied on the same sort of U.S.-trained technocrats that had prevailed
under the previous administration. Even the astonishing election of an
opposition candidate—Vicente Fox, of the right-wing PAN—in the summer of 2000 promises to maintain the same economic policies. Mexico's
move to free markets cannot be associated with the agenda of a particular

political leader nor even with a particular political party. Rather, neoliberalism in Mexico has become the new policy paradigm, a set of taken-for-granted assumptions that all serious contenders for power must take into account.

Making Sense of Mexico's Move to Free Markets

The history of Mexico's neoliberal transition shows that policy reforms in developing countries can be complex and multifaceted, involving the interplay of internal and external factors. The result has brought Mexican economic policy in line with global trends, as more nations adopt a more "Anglo-Saxon" mode of economic governance. Mexico is one piece of a larger picture of global institutional isomorphism.

In their observations of the evolution of organizations within "organizational fields" (such as nation-states within a global system of similar institutions), DiMaggio and Powell (1983) observe three different sorts of isomorphic processes: mimetic, coercive, and normative (which I have termed "expert"). Whereas mimetic isomorphism consists in the voluntary adoption of organizational models (to minimize uncertainty), coercive isomorphism occurs when organizations conform to the demands of powerful external actors, sometimes under conditions of resource dependence. Normative or expert isomorphism is the transformation of organizations by powerful actors *within* the organization—namely, certified experts with their own ideas of how best to run the organization.

In Mexico, the evidence strongly suggests that both coercive and expert isomorphism helped propel free-market reforms. On the one hand, external pressures clearly had something to do with Mexico's economic policies after 1982. On the other hand, another key factor was the presence of a large and powerful cohort of U.S.-trained economists within the Mexican government, who were able to use external pressures as a way of leveraging the dismantling of a developmentalist governance regime.

But how did these economists come to dominate the top levels of Mexico's economic policymaking bureaucracy in the first place? There is little doubt that external pressures also played an important role in the empowerment of U.S.-trained technocrats within the Mexican government. Stallings (1992) has developed a useful distinction between different ways that international pressures can influence the policies of developing countries. One is leverage, or the direct imposition of policies by foreign and international organizations, such as the U.S. government and the IMF. A second mechanism is markets, or the need to foster the confidence of foreign investors in a world of highly volatile capital movements. Finally, there is linkage, or "the tendency of certain groups in the Third World to identify with the interests and outlook of international actors"—particularly foreign-trained technocrats (Stallings 1992: 52). In Stallings's view, international pressures help cause policy reform in developing countries not only directly, as when loans from international agencies are conditioned on liberalizing reforms, but also indirectly, through the influence of foreign-trained economists in government.

In the Mexican case, it is possible to see all three variables at work in complicated and interacting ways. Particularly noteworthy is the extent to which linkage was promoted and strengthened through the combined force of leverage and markets. In other words, at a time when resources were scarce and external organizations and actors (such as the IMF and nervous foreign investors) were controlling access to these resources, the Mexican government was under great pressure to comply with the substantive preferences of these organizations and actors (i.e., by accepting the initial IMF structural adjustment package). However, there was also a simultaneous tendency toward "ceremonial conformity" to the standards of powerful external actors, achieved by adopting their language, rituals, and standards (Markoff and Montecinos 1993; Schneider 1998). To negotiate with the U.S. Treasury and the IMF and to inspire the confidence of foreign investors, it made tremendous sense to staff the top levels of government with English-fluent economists trained at American universities. External creditors' approval supported "those internal candidates who not only share the same economic perspectives, but perhaps most importantly, speak the same language, both literally and metaphorically" (Centeno 1993: 325). These economists, in a sense, became the Mexican government's diplomats to the international financial community.

Of course, the Cambridge-trained economists were presumably also fluent in English and familiar with macroeconomic models. In contrast to their U.S.-trained colleagues, however, the Cambridge-school economists disappeared from Mexican economic policymaking after 1982. There are some compelling commonsense reasons why U.S.-trained economists would prevail over Cambridge-trained economists during the first years of the debt crisis. For one thing, by the early 1980s, American economics was indisputably the leader in the field of (Coats, ed., 1996). More important, Mexico's U.S.-trained technocrats shared a common ideological framework with the powerful international actors with whom they were dealing. Unlike the Keynesian paradigm that prevailed in Cambridge, by the 1970s, mainstream American economics complemented rather than contradicted the orthodox prescriptions that emanated from multilateral institutions following the outbreak of the debt crisis.

For these reasons, the U.S.-trained technocrats were doubtless the intermediaries preferred by representatives of the international financial community. Since the World Bank, IMF, et al. had the lion's share of the power

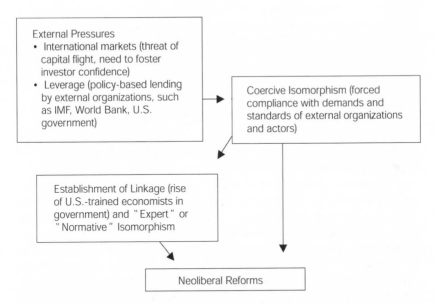

Fig. 7.1. The Role of External Pressures in Mexican Neoliberal Reforms.

in this bilateral negotiating situation, it is easy to see why they got their preferred intermediaries. After all, had the Mexican government continued to rely on the Cambridge economists, the outcome would have been either stalemate or default—both highly risky scenarios for the government in power. Once the U.S.-trained technocrats reached the helm of policymaking, they were able to remake Mexico's governance regime from the inside out. Thus, leverage and markets promoted neoliberal reforms not only directly (e.g., the imposition of structural adjustment measures by the IMF) but also indirectly, by pushing neoliberal-friendly, internationally linked experts to the top of the policy hierarchy, where they could privatize, deregulate, and liberalize to their hearts' content.

In summary, it appears that both coercive isomorphism and expert isomorphism were implicated in Mexico's move to free markets. Neoliberal reform in Mexico was not only imposed by the discipline of international markets and the requirements of powerful external organizations but was also promoted by a group of economic experts within the Mexican government who believed that market reforms were the correct policy course. On the other hand, the empowerment of these particular government officials was in large measure brought about by external pressures. The relationship between these different variables is illustrated in figure 7.1.

However, the rise of U.S.-trained economists within the Mexican government cannot solely be attributed to coercive isomorphism and international pressures. In keeping with world-cultural theory (cf. Scott and

Meyer, eds., 1994; Boli and Thomas 1997), there has also been much voluntary adoption of foreign standards of economic expertise, based in transnational standards of legitimation. The following section reviews how both voluntary and coercive processes shaped the Mexican economics profession after 1929.

Mexican Economics in Historical Perspective

The Mexican economics profession was not invented "from scratch" but rather from the very beginning was self-consciously modeled in the image of international standards of economic expertise. However, both the nature of these international standards and the role of economists in Mexico were very different half a century ago than they are today. During the 1930s, economics was a nationally and internationally heterogeneous discipline, and a discipline struggling to make sense of global economic crisis. The standards on which the initial UNAM economics program drew, while international in origin, had little or nothing in common with the neoclassical economics being taught at most universities in the United States at the time.

Aided by their "taxi professors" in government ministries, the first generations of economists graduating in the 1930s did not have trouble finding work. Initially, however, the positions they occupied were of quite a low level (recall the UNAM graduate who described his first job as the production of "yards and yards of adding tape"). Economics in Mexico was immediately a successful profession, in the sense that economics graduates had ample employment opportunities. It was not, however, influential in the field of economic policy, a professional "jurisdiction" that economists would conquer only later, and much more gradually (see table 7.1).

In the 1940s, Mexican economic policymaking was indisputably in the hands of amateurs. These amateurs were mostly (although not exclusively) lawyers, as were Mexican political elites more generally until the 1980s (Camp 1980). Table 7.1 shows that over time, economists began to rise to the top levels of economic policy ministries. Unlike the earlier proliferation of lawyers, the flourishing of economists at the top of economic policymaking apparently depended on a much higher level of training. Although many lawyers with mere undergraduate degrees have occupied top policy posts between 1940 and 2000, only two economists[5] with only undergraduate degrees came to occupy such posts. The vast majority of economists who came to power had graduate training, of necessity from abroad (since Mexico's first graduate program in economics was not founded until the 1960s) and increasingly from the United States. Economic experts within the Mexican government were foreign-trained experts.

TABLE 7.1

Characteristics of Top Economic Policymaking Slots by Presidential Administration

Presidency (Term)	No. Top Econ. Policy Slots	Undergrad. Econ. Degree N (%)	Undergrad. at Private Mex. School N (%)	Foreign Grad. Training N (%)	Foreign Grad. Training, Econ. N (%)
Avila Camacho (1940–46)	5	0	1 (20)	0	0
Alemán (1946–52)	5	0	0	0	0
Ruiz Cortínez (1952–58)	4	1 (25)	0	0	0
López Mateos (1958–64)	5	1 (20)	1 (20)	1 (20)	1 (20)
Díaz Ordaz (1964–70)	5	1 (20)	0	1 (20)	1 (20)
Echeverría (1970–76)	9	2 (22)	0	4 (44)	2 (22)
López Portillo (1976–82)	12	4 (33)	0	7 (58)	4 (33)
De la Madrid (1982–88)	7	6 (86)	2 (29)	7 (100)	4 (33)
Salinas (1988–94)	5	4 (80)	2 (40)	5 (100)	5 (71)
Zedillo (1994–2000)	8	7 (87.5)	2 (25)	8 (100)	7 (87.5)

Source: Camp (1994) and assorted news media for more recent information.

Note: Total number of slots for each presidential administration equal the number of top policy positions multiplied by the number of individuals who occupy those positions during a given administration. Thus, the data for an individual who occupies two positions at different times during the same administration are counted twice. Top policy positions are defined as the president of the republic, minister of finance, minister of commerce, and central bank director (throughout the entire period), and minister of the presidency (from 1958 to 1976) and minister of budget and planning (from 1976 to 1992).

Thus, when analyzing trends in the Mexican government, it is impossible analytically to separate the issues of the legitimation of economic expertise, on the one hand, and the legitimation of foreign standards of economic expertise, on the other. But to whom, precisely, were these foreign credentials legitimate? Two parallel processes contributed to the rise of foreign-trained economists within the Mexican government: the legitimation of economic expertise by domestic actors within the Mexican state (mimetic or world-cultural isomorphism) and its legitimation by powerful resource-bearing external actors (coercive isomorphism).

Mimetic Isomorphism and Internal Legitimation

Acceptance of the professional prescriptions of Mexican government economists was apparently not universal within Mexican public administration. On the contrary, the conflict Vernon (1963) identified between the "políticos" and the "técnicos" was based in very real disputes in the Mexican government over economists' prescriptions, which were sometimes questioned by the lawyers who worked as their superiors. Until the mid-1970s or so, it was the políticos (the lawyers) who had final say over policymaking, and the suggestions of the técnicos (the economists) could be ignored; the tax reform effort of the early 1960s represented an important test of the professional authority of economists in government—a test that the economists ultimately failed.

Such intrabureaucratic conflict notwithstanding, it appears that Mexican economics never had to go through intraprofessional battles of the sort discussed by Abbott. There are at least two obvious reasons for the gradual and apparently peaceful conquering of the field of economic policymaking by economists. The first is that from the mid-1930s through the early 1980s, the Mexican state was in continuous expansion and was therefore able to provide ample employment opportunities for all professional contenders. The second reason is that rapid turnover within the Mexican public sector provided a means through which economists—particularly those with foreign training—could come to occupy more important positions through mobility rather than through struggle.

As a result, Mexican economists did not have to take the castle of economic policymaking by storm from the amateurs who had previously occupied it. On the contrary, Mexican economics was actively promoted by the older generation of amateur economic policymakers, such as Jesús Silva Herzog Flores, Rodrigo Gómez, and Antonio Ortiz Mena, because it was *legitimate* among these policymakers: they believed that assistants trained specifically to deal with economic matters would be able to increase the efficacy and prestige of the economic policy ministries of which they were in charge. As economists moved up the hierarchy by impressing their superiors, they acquired decisionmaking power over successive strata of officials in the bureaucratic hierarchy.

The official most devoted to the promotion of Mexican economics and the advancement of Mexican economists was probably Banco de México director and accountant Rodrigo Gómez, who supported the development and internationalization of Mexican economics in manifold ways, from supporting Banco scholarships, to helping renovate the economics program at the Autonomous University of Nuevo León, to supporting the foundation of a program at the Colegio de México (see chapter 4). Amateur economic policymakers like Gómez not only tolerated economic expertise in their ministries but systematically created and nurtured it. A substantial body of evidence reviewed in this book suggests that the Banco de México was the branch of public administration within which foreign economics credentials had the greatest weight and legitimacy. This was doubtless due to the Banco's location within the international organizational field of central banking, which gave central bankers around the world common standards for economic policymaking.

From a historical perspective, the Banco was the government organization most responsible for the Americanization of Mexican economics. The central bank was responsible for Mexico's first foreign scholarship program for economists, and played a key role in the founding of economics at the ITM and the Colegio de México and the renovation of economics at the University of Nuevo León. Furthermore, Banco de México officials were instrumental in the remaking of ITAM economics into a much more Americanized program oriented toward sending students to postgraduate study in the United States. There is evidence that central banks in other countries have had similar roles in the internationalization of local economics professions (see Dagnino Pastore 1989 on Italy [pp. 196–99] and Urrutia 1994 on Colombia [p. 304]).

Thus, the recognition of the value of international credentials among domestic actors was a critical factor contributing to both the internationalization of Mexican economics and the ascent of foreign-trained economists in the Mexican government. Perhaps no better evidence of this exists than the large-scale government funding that was made available to study economics (among other fields) through the National Council for Science and Technology (CONACYT) grants in the 1970s. The council was founded in 1970 for the purpose of the promotion of higher education and research in the natural and social sciences. Funding for the council expanded rapidly, making scholarships to study economics abroad available on a tremendous scale.[6] Graduates of this scholarship program were so conspicuously prominent among the neoliberal reformers of the 1980s and '90s that former Chicago professor Arnold Harberger has called the council "a secret weapon without which Mexico's economic transformation would never have been accomplished" (Harberger 1996: 311).

Coercive Isomorphism and External Legitimation

At the same time, Mexican government support for internationalized economics also reflected Mexico's historically fluctuating subjection to external pressures. A rough way of gauging these pressures incorporates both the *flow* of international resources to the Mexican government and the *conditionality* attached to these resources. Kahler (1992) defines conditionality as "the bargains struck between . . . outside agencies . . . and national governments" (p. 89). Conditionality encompasses such factors as interest rates and the policies required by institutions such as the IMF in exchange for loans. During different historical periods, there have been varying levels of international pressures on the Mexican government.[7]

THE COLLAPSE OF INTERNATIONAL CAPITAL MARKETS

In Mexico, as in many other Latin American countries, government external indebtedness was high during the first decades of the twentieth century—a time when financial markets were highly internationalized and the Mexican government had heavy debts to foreign creditors. The conditionality of these resources, while not officially enforced by multilateral institutions like the IMF (which did not yet exist), was still relatively high, since many nations ran into problems with refinancing their loans. This was the era during which "money doctors"—orthodox foreign economists, such as Edwin Kemmerer of Princeton University—were invited to give advice to Latin American governments and certify the soundness of their policies, all in the interest of inspiring foreign investor confidence. Like other mainstream economists of his day, Kemmerer "sought primarily to promote gold-based convertible currencies as the basis for a self-adjusting and self-regulating international economic trading and investment order" (Rosenberg and Rosenberg 1994: 67).

With the collapse of financial markets in the early 1930s, Mexico was one of the earliest Latin American countries to withdraw from the world of global finance. Ongoing social conflict, along with ominously populist-sounding provisions of the newly drafted Mexican Constitution, made international investors wary of Mexico after the revolution. Mexico went in and out of default throughout the 1920s and remained in default from 1932 until 1942, when Mexico began negotiations with its creditors under the auspices of a U.S.-led initiative (Eichengreen 1994: 122–23). In part because of U.S. concern with maintaining Mexico as an ally during World War II, the result was a dramatic reduction of Mexican bonded debt—the debt for which government securities were issued—to less than 10% of its original sum (Bazant 1968: 214–21).

THE POSTWAR INTERNATIONAL ORDER

This period of relative autonomy from global financial markets was gradually ended by the construction of a new postwar financial order with the United States as its captain and new global financial institutions—especially the World Bank and the IMF—as its lieutenants. A host of new international organizations (such as the World Bank, IMF, and IADB[8]) and programs (such as the Alliance for Progress) began to reward Third World governments that conformed to the standards of expertise set in the core.

After the resumption of external borrowing following the 1954 peso devaluation, the credentials of foreign-trained economists became more desirable assets for Mexican economic policymaking ministries. By this time, Mexico was actively producing foreign-trained economists, particularly through the Banco de México scholarship program. The first top economic policymaker with foreign graduate credentials in economics—Raúl Salinas Lozano—became commerce minister in 1958, only four years after Mexico's devaluation and consequent IMF standby arrangement. From 1954 to 1958, Salinas Lozano had been director of the National Investment Commission, which was created under the joint recommendation of the Mexican government and the World Bank, and which gave Salinas Lozano a working familiarity with the staff of international development agencies. Even more significant, from 1956 to 1958, Salinas had served as an alternate governor of the IMF (Camp 1994).

In retrospect, however, the Mexican government's postwar level of external indebtedness during this period was quite low (Gil Díaz 1984). This was partly because Mexican investment was increasingly financed through the growth of domestic savings—encouraged by the simultaneous occurrence of economic growth and monetary stability (Thompson 1979: 148). Moreover, loans from multilateral institutions were accompanied by relatively low levels of conditionality. The IMF standby loan of 1954 was accompanied by structural adjustment measures, but was repaid within a few years. The World Bank—Mexico's largest creditor by 1965—would not begin its era of conditional, policy-based lending until the 1970s.[9] Most important, the bulk of Mexican external debt during stabilizing development was to private sources (more than 70.9% of all borrowing in 1965) (Thompson 1979: 175). Far from attempting to impose their policy preferences on the Mexican government, by the late 1960s private lenders were competing for the privilege of having politically and monetarily stable Mexico as a creditor (Thompson 1979: 174–85).

Although external pressures during the populist period (1970–82) were also moderate in level, they were of a qualitatively different kind. During this period, the flow of external resources was tremendous but conditionality exceedingly low. The reglobalization of financial markets, combined with low international interest rates and a surplus of investable "petrodollars," made it possible for Third World governments to access loans from private foreign lenders at variable interest rates. Although a devaluation and IMF standby loan in 1976 required the Mexican government to implement structural adjustment measures, attempts by the IMF to increase loan conditionality were undermined by the free availability of foreign financial resources, as well as the enormous revenues that the Mexican government was receiving through petroleum sales. Because of the oil boom, Mexico was able to pay off its IMF loan of 1976 in advance (Teichman 1988: 65).

The Third World lending boom of the 1970s appears to have had a number of consequences for the role of economists in the Mexican government. On the one hand, easy money made it possible for the government to pursue populist policies and therefore aided the rise of economists to the left of the developmentalist consensus within the Mexican government. These economists received their undergraduate training at the UNAM but subsequently studied at Cambridge University. The academic institution with which they were associated was not the UNAM but the CIDE, which became the new bastion of developmentalist thinking after the UNAM became radicalized.

However, the influence of the Cambridge economists was limited. The Finance Ministry and central bank were always bastions of conservatism; the Ministry of Budget and Planning, although briefly under the directorship of Carlos Tello, was increasingly dominated by U.S.-trained technocrats (among whom were Miguel de la Madrid and Carlos Salinas). Meanwhile, U.S.-educated technocrats, increasingly from private schools such as the ITAM, were assuming government posts in ever greater numbers.

Although Mexico's borrowing and level of indebtedness were high throughout the 1970s, its need to conform to the demands of external organizations was low until 1982, when Mexico signed another IMF standby agreement in the context of lowered international oil prices and raised international interest rates. After 1982, external pressures on the

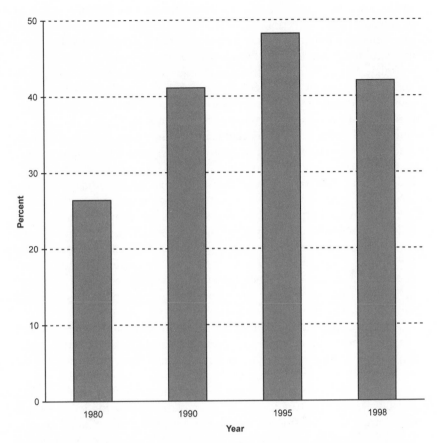

Fig. 7.2. Total Mexican External Debt as Percentage of GNP. Source: World Bank (2000).

Mexican government were extraordinarily high, as Mexico struggled to finance its large external debt. Figure 7.2 shows how Mexico's ratio of debt to gross national product evolved over time.

With the debt crisis in full swing, Mexican dependence on external resources was higher than at any time since the revolution, and the need to cater to the professional standards and policy preferences of external actors intense. It is not surprising, therefore, that 1982 marked the definitive ascent of economists to the pinnacle of policymaking—economists, moreover, who were very different from the radical developmentalists who had gained some influence during the 1970s. During the first forty-odd years of Mexican economics, resource dependence was a contributing factor to the rise of foreign-trained economists in government. After

1982, however, the extreme resource dependence brought on by the debt crisis resulted in a selection *among* foreign-trained economists in government: first, for the most fiscally and monetarily conservative technocrats, and later for those most likely to favor free markets and free trade.

Today, Mexico's foreign debt is no longer officially considered to be of "crisis" proportions. As figure 7.2 shows, however, high levels of external debt have become an institutionalized context of Mexican economic policymaking. Under these circumstances, it is not surprising that a U.S.-trained technocracy has also become institutionalized, since "ceremonial conformity" to the wishes of international investors is an absolutely necessary (if not sufficient) condition for successful macroeconomic policy. Indeed, it is important to note that in promoting liberalizing reforms, U.S.-trained technocrats have perpetuated and strengthened the conditions that make their presence so necessary. Thanks to neoliberal reforms, today the Mexican economy is far more open to free trade and foreign investment than it was twenty years ago. Trade imbalances resulting from the elimination of protectionist barriers result in current-account imbalances, which in turn are financed by highly volatile foreign indirect investment. International investor confidence has become the sine qua non of successful macroeconomic policy in Mexico.

Therefore, although since 1982 the Mexican government has followed the prescriptions of international financial institutions to the letter, capital flight remains an ever present concern, to which every policymaker—no matter how scrupulously neoliberal—must attend. A striking reminder of this state of affairs occurred in the form of the 1994–95 peso crisis. The nervousness of investors fearing an impending devaluation led to capital flight, a drastic reduction in the value of the peso, and yet another joint U.S. Treasury–IMF bailout plan. The man widely (if perhaps incorrectly) vilified for this disaster was Yale-trained finance minister Jaime Serra Puche. However, Serra Puche's resignation was followed neither by the reevaluation of the neoliberal economic model nor the appointment of a different kind of official. Instead, the disgraced technocrat Jaime Serra Puche was replaced by Guillermo Ortíz Martínez, a Stanford-trained economist with the same commitment to neoliberal reforms. Indeed, at a moment when Mexico's future depended on the combined goodwill of the IMF, the U.S. Treasury, and jumpy foreign investors, it is hard to imagine how the Mexican government could have done otherwise.

Even more important, Mexico's recent transition to multiparty democracy has led to little change in the realm of economic policy. President Vicente Fox of the National Action Party (PAN) is a businessman rather than a "technopol" of the sort that rose to power in the 1980s. In general, Fox's cabinet looks less technocratic than the previous three PRI administrations, with fewer foreign postgraduate degrees per capita.

However, the *economic* policymakers of the Fox administration look quite similar to their predecessors. They include Luis Derbez at the head of the newly renamed Economy Ministry (formerly the Trade Ministry), who has an economics degree from the University of Iowa, and Economic Coordinator Eduardo Sojo, whose economics Ph.D. is from the University of Pennsylvania.

For the purposes of this book, the most striking Fox appointee is Francisco Gil Díaz at the head of the Finance Ministry—the same Chicago boy who was instrumental in the revision of the ITAM curriculum in the 1970s and the promotion of liberalizing reforms in the 1980s. A former student of Milton Friedman, Gil Díaz quickly acquired a reputation for being the "fiscal terrorist" within the Fox administration, committed both to rationalizing Mexico's tax structure and to trimming fat from the government budget. He is also known for being extremely devoted to his alma mater; during Fox's term as president, the ITAM is likely to maintain its privileged position within the Mexican economics profession.

Thus, although the Fox administration represents a historic break with the past in a number of respects, it also revisits some important and well-established themes. Neoliberalism and the rise of the new economists represent broad, international trends that transcend national peculiarities. Although Mexico's single-party political system has been irreversibly changed, both the profiles of economic policymakers and the policies they support remain essentially the same.

A New Mexican Miracle?

The purpose of this book has been to describe, rather than to evaluate, changes in economic ideas, policies, and policymakers in Mexico over time. Given the widespread fanfare accompanying neoliberal reforms around the world, however, it seems appropriate to mention some of the evidence regarding the results of neoliberalism in Mexico. Has Mexican neoliberalism "worked" to produce growth and prosperity for the Mexican population?

The fact is that after eighteen years of structural adjustment, liberalization, privatization, and deregulation, the evidence suggesting that Mexican neoliberalism is a success is surprisingly weak. In terms of macroeconomic performance—that is to say, in the terms in which the neoliberal technocrats themselves measure success and failure—the record of Mexican neoliberalism is mixed and certainly not exceptional. Figure 7.3 shows that under the developmentalist regimes—including both the "conservative" developmentalism of the 1950s and the "populist" developmentalism of the 1970s—the Mexican economy grew substantially. Even

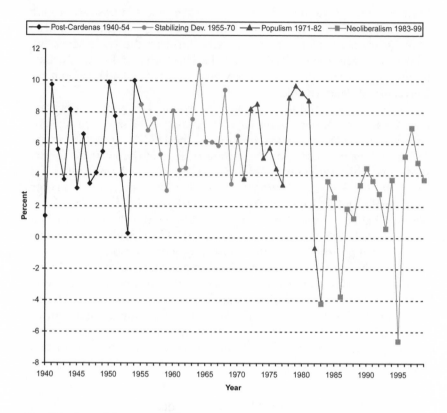

Fig. 7.3. Annual Percentage Change in Mexican GDP, 1940–99. Sources: 1940–94 data calculated from Cárdenas (1944, 1996). Cárdenas's data are from the Banco de México. 1995–99 data from INEGI 2000.

during the more conservative, less inflationary period (1955–70), real economic growth averaged 6½%. From 1983 to 1999, in contrast, growth has averaged a disappointing 2%.

Of course, defenders of the new economic model can rightly object that the populist presidencies of the 1970s left behind a tremendous mess for subsequent administrations to clean up. The stagnant or even negative growth of the "lost decade" (the 1980s) was produced in the context of an enormous external debt, large inherited macroeconomic imbalances, and draconian IMF stabilization measures. However, as Mexico approaches the twentieth anniversary of the outbreak of the debt crisis, this defense is beginning to wear thin. How many more decades must past before the benefits of the new model are clearly established? During the early 1990s, there was a brief period when it was hoped that the Mexican economy was getting back on track. These hopes were dashed by the 1995 peso crisis and subsequent round of austerity measures, which pulled the economy into a deep recession. A few years later, due to financial-sector deregulation and inadequate institutional safeguards, the government has had to bail out the Mexican banking system, at an estimated cost of up to $100 billion. Thus, after repeatedly being subjected to budget-slashing and austerity measures, the Mexican public has been treated to the spectacle of a massive government intervention on behalf of the banks.

The past several years have seen some renewal of economic growth (after the disastrous 6% shrinkage of the economy in 1996). However, serious questions remain about whether the neoliberal model is improving Mexican living standards. According to one calculation, in 1996 real wages in manufacturing were only 64% of their 1980 level, and real wages among *maquila* production workers were only 54% of their 1980 level (Larudee 1999: 278–81). Such poor performance in terms of wages can partly be attributed to two disastrous peso devaluations (in the early 1980s and in 1995) and consequent rounds of austerity measures. However, there are also compelling theoretical reasons for believing that some of the central tenets of the new model—free trade and privatization— have contributed to declining real wages. As Mexican firms are privatized, or put out of business by foreign competition, there has been a corresponding weakening of unions and collective-bargaining power. At the same time, the combined impact of free trade and diminished government subsidies has put thousands of former farmers on the labor market, contributing to downward pressures on wages (Larudee 1999).

In terms of social welfare, recent studies indicate the record of Mexican neoliberalism is not good, although perhaps not so strikingly poor as some of its harshest critics might have expected. In 1992, 36% of Mexican households were living below the poverty line—as compared with 34% in 1984 (which we may assume is higher than the poverty rate for the years prior to the outbreak of the debt crisis in 1982). During the same period, the share of monetary income of the lowest 40% of Mexicans descended from 12.7% to 11% (Sheahan 1997: 24). Household income distribution also deteriorated between 1984 and 1992, although there was some recuperation between 1994 and 1996 (Cortés 2000: 82).

In summary, thus far the track record of neoliberalism in Mexico has not been stellar. Economists who support Mexico's economic model are likely to point to a number of circumstances that have kept the model from succeeding. Perhaps the years to come will bring economic performance that empirically justifies faith in the current paradigm. In the meantime, it seems that the best argument for the neoliberal model is not that it works but that there is no other choice.

Conclusion

This chapter has reviewed evidence suggesting that the role of foreign-trained economists in the Mexican government has historically been shaped by both domestic and international factors. During the past two decades, however, international pressures have become far more salient, contributing to the rise of a new kind of "global expert" in the Mexican government who serves as an intermediary between the government, on the one hand, and the international financial community, on the other.

This transformation within the state has led to broader transformations in the Mexican economics profession. The ongoing demand for foreign-trained technocrats to serve at the top of government ministries, in turn, has transformed the Mexican economics profession beyond recognition. The following chapter examines some of the broader implications of the transformation of Mexican economics for other developing nations.

Chapter 8

THE GLOBALIZATION OF
ECONOMIC EXPERTISE

MARKETS have broken out all over. From the nations of the former Soviet Union to South America, governments have been privatizing state industries, removing government regulations, and liberalizing foreign trade. Throughout the developing world, these policies have been implemented by technocrats trained in the United States—the country that is widely identified as the source of the market model being adopted around the globe. Meanwhile, economics professions in developed and developing nations alike have converged toward American standards of expertise, and regional or national schools of thought have been largely eclipsed.

As an ideal-typical case of technocratic policymaking, neoliberal reforms, and Americanized economics, Mexico provides theoretical insights on a number of fronts. First, the Mexican case shows how changing historical-material factors can be reflected in national systems of economic expertise. Second, the Mexican case highlights how different processes may be behind neoliberal policy reforms in developed versus developing countries. And third, the Mexican case exemplifies how the kind of institutional convergence we associate with neoliberalism and globalization can actually mask very different institutional underpinnings across national settings—as well as different types of "social learning." This chapter brings the story of Mexican economics to its conclusion and suggests some aspects of the Mexican story that may be generalizable to other Latin American countries.

THE AMERICANIZATION OF MEXICAN ECONOMICS

During its first decades of existence, the Mexican economics profession was characterized by the selective use of international standards of expertise—a sort of nationalist adaptation of foreign technique. UNAM economics students in the 1950s and '60s may have read Keynes, Smith, and Marx; they may even have been sent to study economics in the United States with UNAM scholarships. However, the central tenets of mainstream, neoclassical economics as it was emerging in the United

States during these years never penetrated the walls of the UNAM—even while the UNAM program was becoming more technical in the 1950s and early 1960s.

A mixture of admiration for and caution toward foreign economic ideas was a recurring theme among an earlier generation of economists. As one elderly Mexican economist remarked to me several years ago: "[I]t is easy to send people to study in the United States; the problem is that they come back thinking that Mexico is the United States. I studied to be an economist in the service of my country" (interview, Meyer L'Epée 7/15/96). In his book providing advice to "a young Mexican economist," Jesús Silva Herzog wrote in even stronger terms that "the native economist of a peripheral country . . . who follows the writings of a foreign author to the very letter . . . resembles the servant who grotesquely imitates the fine manners of his master" (Silva Herzog 1967: 36).

Today, in contrast, Mexican economics has become a profession dominated by standards of expertise set in the United States. These standards, moreover, are far less relativistic than they were in the days of Keynesianism, when the "ice" of neoclassical economics had been broken and heterodox prescriptions for developing economies proliferated. Mainstream Mexican economics today is built on a core of universalistic assumptions; as one ITAM economist put it to me, "A demand curve is the same here, in China, in the United States, in Russia, and wherever. And where prices are higher, the producers will produce a higher quantity, it doesn't matter where" (interview, Confidential 3/27/96).

One way of gauging the extent of the Americanization of the Mexican economics profession over time is to chart the historical trajectory of the *Trimestre económico,* Mexico's first and most important economics journal. The *Trimestre* is institutionally dependent on the Fondo de Cultura Económica, a government-supported but nominally autonomous organization. During the 1950s and '60s, the *Trimestre* was a bastion of the sort of economics endorsed by the United Nations Economic Commission for Latin America, with Raúl Prebisch and other well-known developmentalists on its editorial board, along with a number of important government officials. This reflected the state of the economics profession in Mexico: developmentalist in ideology and bureaucratic by vocation.

In 1987, however, there was a significant change in the *Trimestre*'s masthead. Its directorship was assumed by Carlos Bazdresch, a graduate of the Monterrey Tech who had pursued graduate studies at Harvard and who had ties to the Salinas administration and the Banco de México. Along with the change in directorship was a total overhaul of the editorial board, which since that time has been dominated by economists trained in the United States and to an extraordinary extent, by economists associated with the ITAM. From 1987 through 1999, eleven different economists who had either graduated from or taught at the ITAM served on the *Trimestre*'s editorial board—in contrast to two UNAM graduates (both of whom had studied abroad) and a handful of people from other institutions (including the Colegio de México and the CIDE). Moreover, over time the masthead included a growing proportion of full-time academic economists rather than the public officials of the earlier phase of Mexican economics.

Of course, it could be objected that the *Trimestre económico* does not reflect the state of the Mexican economics profession but rather the state of the Mexican government, which promotes and supports a particular version of economics. However, the point is precisely that Mexican economics and the Mexican government are inextricably intertwined. The *Trimestre*'s changing profile reflects the fact that government resources are being channeled toward perpetuating and furthering a U.S.-style, neoclassical discipline—thereby maintaining the Mexican economics profession in its currently Americanized form. Although the theoretical content of Mexican economics may have changed dramatically over time, the most active and important constituency of the Mexican economics profession remains the same: the Mexican state.

Far from detracting from the trend toward Americanization, the government has been its most enthusiastic supporter. Throughout the history of Mexican economics, government officials contributed to Americanization in various ways, from hiring U.S.-trained economists in the government to participating in the foundation and remolding of economics programs to promoting the financing of foreign scholarships.

Perhaps the most dramatic instance of such government patronage of Americanized economics occurred when a small group of central bankers remade a second-rate night school into the world-famous bastion of neoclassical economics known as the ITAM. This unusual project (for the time) turned into a highly visible professional success story. During the 1980s, successful negotiation with international financial markets became a necessary, if not sufficient, precondition for successful economic policy; having U.S.-schooled economists at the head of policy ministries was one important facet of such negotiation. As Mexico's most ideal prep school for graduate study in the United States, the ITAM was well positioned to benefit from this trend. Although most ITAM economics graduates went on to careers in the private sector, those who pursued foreign graduate training in economics were much more likely to work in government than in business (see figure 8.1). The promise of government jobs for foreign-trained economists, in turn, created demand for U.S.-trained economists to work as academics in private universities. Academic economists accounted for the smallest group of ITAM economics graduates, but these were the graduates most likely to have received foreign graduate training

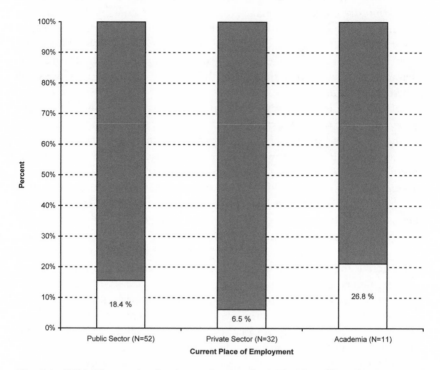

Fig. 8.1. ITAM Economics Graduates: Postgraduate Training Abroad in Economics by 1996 Place of Employment, Date of Graduation 1971–95.

in economics. Under the Fox administration, ITAM graduates will undoubtedly continue to proliferate in govermnent posts, since Fox's finance minister, Francisco Gil Díaz, is a graduate of the ITAM.

The lesson to be learned from the ITAM's success was not lost on other private economics programs, which came to emulate the ITAM's highly Americanized format—and even to hire professors away from the ITAM. Today, U.S.-trained economists dominate the faculties of a number of private economics programs, including the Monterrey Tech, the Anáhuac, the Ibero-American University, and the University of the Americas. Graduates of these private programs are enjoying some success within the Mexican government technocracy, although the ITAM is still the leading institution. Mexican government data show that the number of private university economics students more than doubled between 1965 and 1977; by 1994, their number had approximately doubled again. In contrast, the number of public university economics students decreased by about a third from 1988 to 1994, presumably reflecting the perceptions of potential students of their employment possibilities (ANUIES 1984–95).

The Mexican state also contributed to the ongoing dominance of Americanized economics in more political ways. When U.S.-trained technocrats assumed the helm of the Mexican state after 1982, they acquired the political power to perpetuate and nurture their own brand of expertise. One example of how this power is wielded can be found in the history of the Center for Economics Education and Research (CIDE). Once a bastion of left-developmentalist thinking associated with Cambridge University, in the early 1990s , the publicly financed CIDE was taken over by a director linked to the Salinas administration (the same individual who reformed the *Trimestre económico* in the 1980s). Its economics program was subsequently thoroughly Americanized, and today the reputation of CIDE economics graduates rivals that of the ITAM.

Even more important, the Mexican government has ensured the ongoing availability of financing for academic economics through the National Council for Science and Technology (CONACYT). Although the council was established during the populist spending boom of the 1970s, its greatest flourishing occurred during the 1980s and '90s. The neoliberal technocrats were generous in their support for higher education, but the emphasis of this support began to change significantly. The structural adjustment measures and radical devaluation of the peso in the mid-1980s led to a 60% decline in professors' salaries. Meanwhile, public universities were subjected to strong public criticism by government officials questioning their relevance and viability (Lorey 1994: 17). Rather than broadly increasing funding for public universities (as the administrations of the 1970s had done), the de la Madrid, Salinas, and Zedillo administrations developed various forms of *targeted assistance* to higher education—many of which were administered through the council—which gave government officials significantly more control over the kinds of disciplines they were supporting.

Legally dependent on the Secretariat of Public Education (but in fact an independent bastion of much more modern, foreign-trained technocrats), CONACYT channels resources toward the most highly Americanized sector of Mexican economics through a number of different programs, the best known of which is its scholarship program. In 1995 alone, there were nearly two hundred Mexicans studying economics abroad with funding from the council (CONACYT 1995). However, it is important to note that the council's scholarship program is biased neither toward the study of economics nor toward studying abroad but rather provides financing for study at both Mexican and foreign universities, and within a range of disciplines, including medicine, engineering, pure sciences, and a range of social sciences.

In addition to funding scholarships to study abroad, the council also provides financing for the Colegio de México and the CIDE (among other relatively small, prestigious public institutions), thereby supporting these institutions' staffs of full-time professors. Another important source of funding is a council program known as the National System of Researchers, or SNI, which since 1984 has subsidized the salaries of Mexican academics in different fields based on their research and publications (Lorey 1994: 18). In a nation where most universities pay low salaries that force academics to seek secondary employment, the SNI creates a space and incentive for academic research. In 1997, more than six thousand academics were registered within the SNI (CONACYT 1997: 41). Mexican graduate programs that are listed in the council's "List of Excellence" are eligible for council-funded scholarships. Other council programs include subsidized professorships (*cátedras*) for outstanding teachers and "repatriation" scholarships to bring Mexicans studying abroad back to Mexico.

The council is the cornerstone of an edifice of government-sponsored support for higher education that has enabled social sciences to flourish in Mexico perhaps more than in any other Latin American country. Financing for the council increased throughout the 1990s, with the exception of a dip in 1995–96 due to the peso devaluation. In 1998, the council administered a budget of about $260 million U.S. dollars at the current exchange rate (CONACYT 1998). The council's generosity has meant that Mexico has generally not suffered from the same degree of "brain drain" as other Latin American countries; indeed, academics have come to live and work in Mexico from around the world (including the United States and Europe) because of the agreeable working conditions.

Such generous funding for the council is undoubtedly related to the educational profiles of the policymakers at the helm of the government: Mexico's foreign-educated technocrats are naturally sympathetic to government projects for fostering higher education. It is worth emphasizing that the targeted nature of council assistance makes it possible for the government to selectively support and encourage academics who conform most closely to mainstream international standards. Thus, for example, council scholarships to study abroad are not offered for study at any institution, but are limited to those listed in its "Padrón de Excelencia" (List of Excellence), which has a "mainstreaming" affect on studies abroad. In 1994, for example, of the thirty-nine institutions listed as belonging to the Padrón for economics, twenty-one were in the United States. The American institutions listed included the Ivies and such universities as Rochester and Northwestern but did not include the New School for Social Research or the University of Massachusetts at Amherst (both bastions of leftist economics). Similarly, the SNI provides salary subsidies to academics based on publication records, with more weight given to publications in mainstream and internationally prestigious journals.

Thus, although academic economists of all ideological stripes were harmed by the devaluations and inflation of the 1980s, since 1984 the government has intervened selectively to support the academic production of some—but not all—of these economists. The winners tended to be the neoclassically oriented economists linked to an international community of like-minded academics; among the losers were leftist economists at institutions like the UNAM.

Thus, at a number of different levels, the government has proved to be a very generous constituency for U.S.-style economics in Mexico. Largely as a result of this patronage, an elite sector has emerged within the Mexican economics profession that strongly resembles its counterpart in the United States, namely, academic professionals teaching university courses to undergraduates and conducting research to publish in academic journals—often in the United States. Forty years ago, there was essentially no such thing as an academic economist in Mexico, because resources were too scarce to support such a profession. Today, however, most economics classes at the Colegio de México and the CIDE are taught by full-time academics, most of whom have received graduate training in the United States. Although the figure of the "taxi professor" continues to play an important role at the ITAM (and continues to be an indispensable element in political recruitment), today the ITAM has a core of eleven full-time professors in its Department of Economics. The ITAM also has fourteen economists in its Center for Economic Research (CIE)—almost all of whom have American Ph.D.'s. The center's professors routinely publish in prestigious international journals, such as the *Journal of Economic Theory, The International Economic Review,* and *Econometrica.*[1]

As this book goes to press, it is still not entirely clear how the end of PRI rule will affect Mexican economics. On the one hand, the fact that U.S.-trained economists still dominate the economic cabinet bodes well for the Americanized mainstream of the profession, since government jobs will continue to proliferate for those with the right kind of background. In particular, the appointment of Francisco Gil Díaz to the head of the Finance Ministry will serve as a tremendous boost to the ITAM, both by providing a direct channel to provide jobs for its graduates and by increasing its visibility and reputation.

On the other hand, there is some reason to believe that more direct government subsidies to the profession could become less abundant than they were under the hypertechnocratic PRI administrations of the 1980s and '90s. The Fox administration is noticeably less homogeneous than its predecessors, and clearly reflects a different set of social and political networks: this cabinet has fewer fancy foreign degrees and more business connections. Such an administration is likely to have a more pragmatic set of priorities, and to look less favorably on financing for pure academic economic research and study abroad.

In keeping with this trend toward pragmatism, the new director of CONACYT is Jaime Parada Avila, an engineer trained at the UNAM with a long career in the private sector. In an interview for the newspaper *Reforma*, Parada repeatedly expressed the need to forge alliances between government-sponsored education and the needs of business. However, he also emphasized that the council would "be judicious and careful to not destroy what we have spent so many years constructing . . . we are not going to abandon primary research, we have areas of excellence that we are going to continue to cultivate and push forward" (Barba 2001). He also expressed that CONACYT would continue to strongly support its foreign scholarship program. Thus, although over the long run Mexico's democratic transition may end up eroding the edifice of government support for U.S.-style economics, in the short run it seems unlikely that there will be major changes: the state will continue to be its most important constituency.

The crucial importance of the state as the sustaining constituency of Mexican economics is most apparent in comparative perspective. In Mexico, a strong framework of state-financed institutions—from the Fondo de Cultura Económica to the Banco de México to the National Council on Science and Technology—has allowed the economics profession to thrive. By contrast, in Peru—a nation with significantly less state capacity and weaker government institutions—the economics profession is in a far more precarious position. Conaghan (1998) characterizes Peruvian economists as "floating experts," eking out an existence with multiple and often overlapping jobs in the government and private sector, and generally unable to make a living giving university classes. Surprisingly, this is even true of Peruvian economists with prestigious foreign credentials. In Peru, "Economists, like other professional groups, struggle to make a living and many talented professionals are lured off into pursuits out of the discipline" (Conaghan 1998: 150).

In contrast, economists in Mexico are both materially comfortable and politically influential. Their striking professional success, although aided by a certain level of private-sector demand, is fundamentally owed to the state. There is a wonderful irony inherent in this situation. In the United States, the defining constituency of economics is a decentralized network of private and state universities, subject to comparatively little federal government control. As Klamer and Colander (1990) observe, in the United States, economics is a popular major because many students are interested in going on to study business—but business is not viewed as an acceptable liberal arts undergraduate major. The demand for academic economists, therefore, is market driven—sustained by economics's status as a "proxy" major for business-bound students (p. 197). In Mexico, by contrast, economics is sustained by the state at every level—from the financing of foreign scholarships to the hiring of government economists to the subsidizing of academic salaries. At the most superficial level, the Mexican economics profession resembles its counterpart in the United States; its institutional moorings, however, are very different—and indeed are more reminiscent of the Continental European model. The economics behind the dismantling of Mexican government intervention in the economy is very much a creature of the state.

Social Learning in Mexico

Economic globalization has not only changed Mexican economic policy, but also the way Mexicans collectively think about economic policy. One manifestation of this ideal change can be seen within the Mexican economics profession, which has evolved from nationalism to neoliberalism. But it is also possible to see broader changes in public discourse about economic issues in Mexico, which are symptomatic of a new way of thinking. Public universities that followed the UNAM's radicalizing trajectory in the 1970s are either in the process of reform or languishing in relative obscurity. There are still a number of UNAM professors who remain important public figures in economic policy debates, as well as many top specialists in particular economic subfields. Nevertheless, there is a widespread (if somewhat inaccurate) impression among the educated Mexican public that highly Americanized institutions like the ITAM are home to Mexico's most reliable economic experts, whereas public institutions such as the UNAM are home to a much more politicized, less "objective" sort of economist.

Today, Mexico seems to be a country that is saturated in foreign-trained economic experts, some of whom are interested in bringing their views from the halls of academe to a more public forum. Elite discourse in Mexico has a long tradition of "public intellectuals," whose literary fame and political involvements qualify them to speak authoritatively on a range of issues, from democracy to development to cultural affairs. More recently, however, a new sort of expert has appeared on the editorial pages of Mexican newspapers, namely, the individual with a profound knowledge of a circumscribed topic (such as monetary policy), often with a degree from a prestigious U.S. university. The increased visibility of these experts has been promoted by the growth in the number of business-oriented publications, such as *El Economista, El Financiero,* and *Reforma.*

Evidence of changes in public discourse around economic policy issues was also evident during the 2000 presidential race that led to the election of Vicente Fox of the right-wing PAN—the first opposition candidate to win a presidential election in over seventy years. During their campaigns, all three of the major presidential candidates used the ITAM as a public forum to air their views on economic policy. In an editorial commenting on this phenomenon, a prominent Mexican political analyst opined that the ITAM had become a civic forum for discussion of economic issues because the UNAM (at the time embroiled in a ten-month student strike) had become too politicized. Moreover, "the increasingly accepted fact is that the academic level of the ITAM, at least in the field of economics, left the UNAM behind a long time ago" (Sarmiento 2000).

Another notable feature of this electoral contest was that issues of economic policy played a relatively minor role. Exit polls suggested that the pro-Fox vote was largely founded in political issues—in particular, a desire to end the institutionalized corruption of decades of PRI rule ("Vicente Fox" 2000). The months leading up to the election were mostly characterized by rhetoric about "change" and accusations of electoral foul play. With the exception of the thorny issue of the privatization of Mexico's still-public oil industry, there was little debate over the future of the Mexican economy. Indeed, as one business publication observed:

> The three main presidential candidates agree on the great need for foreign investment, credit recovery, and fiscal discipline. It is difficult to find differences in their economic policies since there is little room to make drastic changes when the nation is in the process of consolidating policies established over the past decade by former President Carlos Salinas and his successor President Ernesto Zedillo. (Fernández 2000).

Whereas the economic policy proposals of PRI candidate Francisco Labastida and right-wing PAN candidate Vicente Fox were almost identical, the economic platform of left-wing PRD candidate Cuahtémoc Cárdenas had some distinguishing features, including the renegotiation of some provisions of NAFTA and an emphasis on progressive tax reform. Nevertheless, these distinguishing features did not add up to paradigmatic differences. Cárdenas called neither for a return to the populism of the 1970s nor to the more conservative developmentalism of the postwar period. There was neither a proposal to make the central bank politically accountable nor any hint at a reimplementation of import substitution. The PRD platform called for the reform of the neoliberal model, not for its revolutionary transformation.

Interestingly, it was at the ideological epicenter of Mexican neoliberalism that Cárdenas made the essential continuity of his policy proposals most apparent. To a packed auditorium at the ITAM, he emphasized that "structural change should be conceived as based on the opening of the economy, and the global operation of markets and capital flows. Nobody with their feet on the ground [i.e., in their right mind] would propose isolationist or ultra-protectionist policies" (Cárdenas quoted in Zúñiga 2000). When Cárdenas initially ran for president in 1988, the ITAM was viewed as "enemy terrain," the source of the technocrats against whom Cárdenas and his allies were waging a popular struggle. Today, in contrast, U.S.-trained economists at universities like the ITAM are being acknowledged—albeit grudgingly—as experts rather than mere ideological mouthpieces for vested interests.

At the same time, Cárdenas's speech at the ITAM reflects the contradictions of being a social democratic politician in a globalized national economy (cf. Kitschelt 1999). In Mexico and other developing nations, one central fact about economic globalization overshadows all others, namely, that political success depends fundamentally on macroeconomic stability, which in turn depends on maintaining the confidence of the international financial community. Any major shaking of this confidence can lead to capital flight, currency devaluation, the enlargement of dollar-denominated debt, and the imposition of multilateral structural adjustment packages. As a result, even social democrats must be appear to be good neoliberals. A central outcome of Mexico's collective process of "social learning," therefore, seems to be the depoliticization of economic policy. The economy is no longer framed as an arena for social and political struggle but rather as a matter for the experts. As we will see in the following section, such depoliticization is one of many features that Mexico shares in common with other Latin American nations.

SOCIAL KNOWLEDGE AND SOCIAL LEARNING IN THE DEVELOPING WORLD

The theoretical premise of this book has been that national systems of expert knowledge are shaped by constituencies—organizations and social groups that provide professionals with resources. To flourish, professions do not need a majority of citizens to believe in their expertise. Rather, they require a source of payment for their services and/or support for professional training. The nature of professions' constituencies in diverse national contexts can have significant consequences for professional ideology and practice. One central cross-national difference where professional constituencies are concerned is whether the state or private individuals and organizations provide the most important source of financing.

Professional constituencies are particularly important in shaping social science professions, since social sciences tend to approach the normative issues of how states should intervene in the economy, polity, and society at large. Whereas in many European nations, social sciences have historically argued "from the point of view of the state" (Weir and Skocpol

1985: 143), in other nations (most notably the United States), social sciences have developed a more autonomous point of view. To the distinction between state-centered versus Anglo-American social science professions, this book has raised another basis of contrast, namely, the difference between social science professions in developed versus developing countries.

Examining social science professions in developing countries highlights the importance of resources for professional success. In the poorest developing nations, social science professions tend to be weak (cf. Conaghan 1998 on Peru) or nonexistent. In medium-income developing nations, social sciences tend to depend heavily on the state for resources, since the state is the only constituency willing and able to finance social-scientific expertise. However, a critical feature of social sciences in developing countries is also the importance of *external* or *international* constituencies, which provide resources either directly or indirectly through the state. When the governments of developing countries become more dependent on external resources, external constituencies become more important in shaping social science professions in the developing world.

International Isomorphism and Third World Economics

In the United States, professions have been shaped by the existence of a large middle class (i.e., with resources to pay for the services of professionals) and a liberal "governance regime," in which state intervention in the economy tends to be indirect rather than direct (Campbell and Lindberg 1990). As a consequence, American professionals tend to receive payment from private individuals and organizations, and the training of American professionals occurs within the framework of a university system consisting of institutions that are either partially or entirely funded by private resources, in the form of endowments and tuitions.

But the conditions shaping professions in Latin America and other developing regions have been very different. In many late-developing nations of the twentieth century, states adopted distinctly illiberal governance regimes, in the hopes of compensating for relative economic backwardness. The nurturing of systems of expert knowledge constituted one aspect of developmentalist projects, which also included state-owned industries and the protection of domestic business from foreign competition. Programs for the training of professionals were sponsored at government-funded "National" universities, in the Continental tradition. States also played leading roles in hiring professionals.

There are also a number of reasons why professions in developing countries gravitate toward standards of expertise set in the developed world. For one thing, late-developing professions are not free to invent themselves "from scratch"—any more than late-developing economies are free to reinvent the steam engine, internal combustion, and the microchip. Rather, latecomers are bound to draw upon already existing standards and technologies set in other countries and at other times. From engineering to medicine to economics, professions in developing countries are bound to model themselves in the image of standards of expertise borrowed from more technologically advanced, developed countries. At the broadest level of theoretical analysis, we can say that such imitation occurs because there is a shared transnational world culture that fosters an ongoing process of imitation (Scott and Meyer, eds., 1994; Boli and Thomas 1997; Boli and Thomas, eds. 1999).

However, whereas some forms of imported expertise are compatible with a wide variety of political ideologies (witness the Soviet Union's adoption of Western techniques of industrial engineering in the 1920s and '30s), others are likely to be more controversial. As the science that lays claim to the understanding of the best way to employ and distribute the resources of a society, economics is perhaps the single most contested form of professional knowledge. As a result, different "versions" of economics may appear, founded in the contrasting (or even conflicting) visions of different professional constituencies. Historical divisions of the sort exemplified by the UNAM and the ITAM economics programs have been noted in other Latin American nations (cf. Valdés 1995 on Chile and Loureiro (1996) on Brazil).

Furthermore, these inherently political implications of economic expertise mean that economics professions in late-developing nations are likely to have a complicated relationship to international standards of economic expertise. On the one hand, international standards are admired by the educated elites of developing nations and seen as worthy of emulation. But intellectuals affiliated with developmentalist states in peripheral or semiperipheral countries may also view the threat of imperialism—whether of the economic or cultural variety—as a reason to take the prescriptions of the core with a grain of salt. This was certainly the case with Mexico's first generations of economists. Selective interpretations of Western economics also prevailed in postwar Japanese economic thinking, which drew on the ideas of Marx, Ricardo, Schumpeter, and Keynes—but also represented "a different tradition of economic thinking" from those which predominated in the West. Indigenous Japanese economists and policymakers modified the Ricardian notion of "comparative advantage" to mean something that could be systematically built up rather than simply based on natural endowments (Gao 1997: 64–65, 210). Contrastingly, in Taiwan, academic economics was Americanized, but U.S.-trained economists were excluded from economic policymaking positions, which were monopolized by engineers with more interventionist ideologies and practices (Wade 1990: 217–27).

These ambivalent relationships notwithstanding, today Latin American economics professions have achieved an astounding level of convergence with mainstream neoclassical economics as it is taught in the United States. The following section describes how resource dependence helped foster this convergence.

Coercive Isomorphism and External Constituencies

As Abbott (1988) observes, professions triumph in their struggles over jurisdictions through "abstraction"—by making their knowledge seem so technical as to be beyond the understanding of amateurs and the lay public. Such abstraction can be seen as an invaluable tool professions use to convince constituencies that their services are worth paying for. If economics is merely common sense, why would anyone bother to hire economists? If, on the other hand, economists are able to mobilize economic formulaes and mathematical models that are indecipherable to the lay public, it may be easier to convince constituencies that economists have a monopoly over a body of scientific knowledge that is worth financial recompense and support.

During the postwar period, American economics evolved to become a singularly abstract discipline, founded in mathematical models that became increasingly inscrutable to outsiders (Johnson [Harry] 1977). During the same period, economics professions around the world converged toward American standards (Coats, ed., 1996). One reason for the adoption of U.S.-style economics in diverse national contexts may have been that American economics was the best endowed with the abstract characteristics that enable professions to succeed. For example, a recent account of the postwar trajectory of British economics suggests that the characteristically abstract and scientific nature of U.S. economics inspired emulation among British economics departments beginning in the late 1960s (Backhouse 1996). In neoinstitutionalist terms, the professional success of American economics inspired voluntary imitation abroad and generated an international process of mimetic isomorphism.

This book has suggested that economics professions in developing countries are shaped by a somewhat different constellation of forces. Mimetic isomorphism has certainly played a part in the Americanization of economics professions in developing countries. As members of a transnational "organizational field" of similar institutions in ongoing communication, central banks seem to have been particularly important in this regard. However, the resource dependence that characterizes developing countries has also been a critical factor. One easily overlooked variety of such "coercive" isomorphism is the impact of scholarships offered by organizations of wealthy nations to the denizens of poor ones. Although it might be objected that a gift can hardly be characterized as "coercive," it should be remembered that neoinstitutionalists use this term in the loosest possible way. Aspiring young economists from Chile and South Korea did not attend economics programs at Harvard and the University of Chicago because they were threatened with incarceration if they failed to do so. Rather, they were attracted by the prestige and resources of the leading economics programs of the wealthiest country in the world. Had universities in their own nations possessed the extensive libraries, generous scholarships, and high faculty salaries that prevailed in the United States, the interest in studying abroad would doubtless have been much less.

During the postwar period, U.S.-trained economist were seeded throughout the developing world; one reason was the availability of scholarships for graduate study in the United States. These scholarships were destined to have their greatest effect on the economics professions of developing countries, where the scarcity of resources meant that local graduate programs were either nonexistent or likely to be of lower quality than programs in the industrialized countries. Many scholarships were provided by U.S. economics departments themselves, which were prospering under the G.I. Bill and the general postwar expansion of higher education in the United States: more undergraduates meant more tuitions and therefore more funding for graduate study. As a result, many foreign graduate students were able to study economics in the United States with funding from American economics departments (Johnson [Harry] 1973: 66 and 1977: 102–3). At the same time, U.S. government funding was provided through Fulbright and USAID. Private foundations, particularly Ford and Rockefeller, offered both funding for congenial Third World universities and scholarships for Third World natives to study in the United States (cf. Valdés 1995, Rosen 1985).[2]

The incentives for Third World scholars to study economics in the United States were magnified by the emergence of new career opportunities in the context of the postwar international order. Foreign-trained economists in the governments of developing countries became the ambassadors to a new set of multilateral institutions, negotiating with their counterparts in the IMF, USAID, and the Inter-American Development Bank, and gathering the sorts of data that these organizations required. In Latin America, for example, the Alliance for Progress offered external financing to governments that came up with development "plans," the development of which was facilitated by the services of professional economists (Izquierdo 1995: 48). Third World economists with prestigious foreign credentials frequently worked for a period at the World Bank or International Monetary Fund and, upon returning to their home countries, were seen as valuable assets in negotiating with these organizations (cf. Ambirajan 1996 for the case of India).

However, the single most important event for the Americanization of economics professions in developing countries was the outbreak of the Third World debt crisis in 1982. In the poorest developing nations—such as Haiti and many sub-Saharan African countries—the consequence of the debt crisis was "leverage": neoliberal reforms were simply imposed by international financial institutions like the World Bank and the IMF. But there was also an important group of medium-income developing nations with relatively strong states and well-institutionalized economics professions. In these nations, the debt crisis had an important and transformative impact on local economics disciplines, since it dramatically increased the premium Third World governments attached to foreign economics credentials in general but to American economics credentials in particular. As noted in chapter 7, economists trained in the United States shared not only a common language with the international financial community but also a common set of theoretical presuppositions.

The result has been the "ubiquitous rise of economists" in top policy positions (Markoff and Montecinos 1993). This has had consequences for economic policies in medium-income developing countries, which have increasingly been made in keeping with the "common core of wisdom embraced by all serious economists" (Williamson 1994: 27–28). At the same time, it has contributed to the Americanization of local economics professions, as finance ministers with Ph.D.'s from prestigious foreign universities hire subordinates with similar training (and these subordinates hire similar subordinates, and so on down the line), and as internationalized undergraduate economics programs gain prestige from the highly visible careers of alumni. It also seems likely that Mexican government support for academic economics and studying abroad may be paralleled in some of the wealthier Latin American nations, such as Chile, Argentina, and Brazil (although my impression is that such financing is far more abundant in Mexico).

For better or for worse, today the governments of developing countries are inextricably embedded in global financial markets. Large external debts, it seems, have become an institutionalized fact of life for Latin American governments. The confidence of foreign investors is required not only to continue to service these debts but also to help stimulate growth and maintain macroeconomic equilibrium. With trade barriers and capital controls reduced or eliminated, heavily indebted "emerging markets" are continuously exposed to balance of payments crises, as well as crises of confidence and capital flight. Thus, in promoting free-market reforms, the technocrats have perpetuated the conditions that make their presence indispensable. In an era in which there is always another crisis of investor confidence and IMF negotiation around the corner, the services of these technocrats will always be needed. As a result, whereas individual technocrats may be replaced, the general technocratic profile—and the economic model it represents—remain the same.

THE ROLE OF TECHNOCRACY IN SOCIAL LEARNING

Market-oriented reforms have become so ubiquitous around the world that it is easy to forget that both the processes through which neoliberal reforms have been implemented—and the results of these processes—have differed significantly in different places. As this book nears completion, the literature comparing neoliberal transitions in diverse national contexts is still too sparse to be able to draw many definitive conclusions. Nevertheless, one notable difference is that whereas U.S.-trained economists have been at the helm of Third World governments implementing neoliberal reforms, in wealthier, OECD nations, foreign-trained technocrats have been notably absent. A 1993 cross-national survey by the *Economist* magazine found that almost all central bank directors and finance ministers in large developing countries had degrees in economics; in contrast, lawyers still prevailed as top economic policymakers in the developed world ("Economic Policy: Qualified" 1993). Economists who do manage to reach the highest levels of power in Europe, for example, are trained domestically rather than in the United States.

Thus, while foreign-trained technocrats dominate top policy posts in Latin America, European national governments still tend to be run by politicians served by teams of nationally trained experts. This fact is particularly striking considering that European economics professions have not been exempt from the worldwide trend toward Americanization (cf. Fourcade-Gourinchas 2000; Backhouse 1996; Sandelin and Veiderpass 1996). Today, U.S.-trained economists proliferate in academic departments throughout Europe, and many local programs have been remade in the image of American economics departments. However, in contrast to their Latin American colleagues, U.S.-trained economists in Europe have generally not penetrated the top levels of European governments; Latin American economics professions have been much more successful at conquering the top levels of economic policymaking. Whereas normative or "expert" isomorphism may have been an important factor in propelling neoliberal reforms in Mexico and other developing countries, such isomorphism does not appear to have played the same role in Europe.

How can we account for this striking difference between Latin American and European policymaking? A functionalist might suggest that developing countries have an objectively greater need for foreign expertise.

In nations in which universities have historically been deficient at producing the sort of expert that is needed to staff government ministries (witness
the UNAM in the 1970s, for example), Latin American governments must
look to foreign-trained economists to fill top government posts, and to
help solve large and ongoing economic problems.

However, there are a number of ways that this explanation falls short.
First, there are, in fact, a number of elite national institutions in Latin
America that produce extremely competent economists with highly internationalized graduate training. Why are top government ministries not
headed by economists with M.A.'s from the Colegio de México or the
CIDE (in Mexico), or from the Getulio Vargas Foundation (in Brazil)?
Moreover, in many Latin American nations, the rigorous study of a specialized field occurs at the undergraduate level. Individuals with undergraduate degrees in economics from programs like the ITAM already have
highly specialized training in economics—why should top government
officials have graduate training at all?

Second, the proposition that an academic economist is naturally better
equipped to manage economic policy than, say, a lawyer with twenty
years' experience in banking, or a public official with a background in
business, is hardly unassailable. The graduate training leading up to a
Ph.D. is as esoteric in economics as it is in any other academic discipline;
unlike preprofessional programs like law, engineering, or business, graduate economics programs tend toward the theoretical rather than the practically applicable. This is particularly true of U.S. programs, in which
academic employment is the implicit and most highly valued goal of graduate training in most social sciences (see Colander and Klamer 1990: 181;
Frey and Eichenberger 1993). This not to say that economics Ph.D.'s cannot play a useful role in economic policymaking, but merely to note that
there is no particular reason for them to be finance ministers and central
bank directors—rather than assistants to these top policy officials.

Because functional necessity provides such an unsatisfactory explanation for the rise of economists in Latin American and other Third World
governments, a growing number of authors have resorted to more sociological arguments (cf. Markoff and Montecinos 1993; Schneider 1998).
As Markoff and Montecinos (1993) put it, "To some extent the infusion
of economic expertise into positions of public authority has indeed been
a response to issues of effective management of complex problems. . . .
But accession to the *highest* levels of government . . . cannot be explained
without regard to the *ceremonial* meanings of expertise" (p. 41). In keeping with the observations of neoinstitutionalist sociologists, the profiles
of the new Third World technocrats appear to have an importance that
is more symbolic than functional. Ph.D.'s from Harvard and MIT may

not provide the most efficient solution to policy problems, but they serve an indispensable symbolic function with respect to the international financial community.

However, this merely leads to a reframing of the original question: if foreign-educated technocrats have such an important symbolic function, then why are they not exploited for their symbolic value in European governments? I believe that the answer may have to do with the relative symbolic trade-offs between national and international political constituencies. To put it more simply: relative to European governments, Latin American governments have more reason to be concerned with the meanings they project to the international financial community and less reason to be worried about the symbolic statements they are making to domestic political supporters.

Money doctors have both positive and negative symbolic value. Their positive value as diplomats to the international financial community has been amply discussed in this and previous chapters. Their negative symbolic value, however, is also an important factor to consider. In Mexico, the symbolic risks of heavy reliance on U.S.-trained technocracy became particularly apparent after the peso crisis of 1994–95, a massive technocratic failure that was followed by the implementation of IMF structural adjustment measures and a severe recession. Antitechnocratic rhetoric subsequently became a staple of Mexican political discourse. A 1995 political cartoon appearing in the left-wing newspaper *La Jornada* depicted a scene of urban devastation, with a beggar woman and her child in the foreground, and toward the back a pair of smart-suited technocrats wearing buttons with the logo of the ruling PRI. Gesturing at the scene around them, one technocrat remarks, "It took me years of study at Harvard and Yale to understand that all this means that we [i.e., the Mexican economy] are doing well" (El Fisgón 1995). Recognizing the political problem the technocrats were creating for the ruling party, the PRI National Committee passed antitechnocratic legislation in 1996 that prohibited the nomination of presidential or gubernatorial candidates who had never held elected office.

Foreign-trained technocrats are vulnerable to bombardment by all manner of heavy political artillery. At best, they can be lambasted for being out of touch with the national reality. At worst, they are easy targets for accusations of betraying the national interests to American imperialism. Therefore, one reason why U.S.-trained economists may not be featured in top government posts in France and Germany is that their presence could potentially undermine electoral support.

On the other hand, these technocrats may be able to thrive in Latin American governments, in spite of political attacks, because of both the stronger influence of international finance in domestic politics and the weaker influence of domestic political constituents—in other words, because their positive symbolic value outweighs their negative symbolic value. There are some very simple and commonsensical reasons why the governments of developing countries need to be more concerned with pleasing international financiers than their European counterparts need to be. For one thing, heavily indebted Third World governments run the risk of having their policies being directly determined by multilateral agencies, something that seldom occurs in the developed world (the experience of Britain in 1976 being one of the rare exceptions). For another thing, developing markets represent an area of uncertainty for international investors. For example, as this book is being completed, the long-term government securities of most Latin American nations are rated as below investment grade by Moody's and Standard and Poor's; all Western European nations are rated investment grade, and more than half in the highest category of Aaa (Moody's). As a result of such expectations, Third World borrowers must both pay a higher price for investment and disproportionately suffer the consequences of investor nervousness and capital flight. Sometimes, financial markets can punish developing nations for simply belonging to a particular region of the world—resulting in so-called samba or tequila effects. Developing nations rely on the symbolic capital of foreign-trained "money doctors," quite simply, because they desperately need any advantage they can get.

While there is little doubt that Latin American countries are more subject to these sorts of financial pressures than their European counterparts, the notion that Latin American governments are less subject to the pressures of domestic electorates is more controversial, and certainly goes against current conventional wisdom. During the past ten years, Latin America has witnessed simultaneous trends toward economic liberalization, the opening of political systems to electoral participation, and the rise of foreign-educated technocrats in government. It is therefore easy to arrive at the prima facie conclusion that these phenomena are both related and mutually complementary—that markets, democracy, and technocracy are part of a single package. The idea that Latin American technocracies are compatible with democratic participation is supported by recent scholarship on Chile, where the "technocratization" of policy debates contributed to the smoothness of Chile's democratic transition in 1989 (cf. Silva 1991; Montecinos 1993; Puryear 1994; Montecinos 1998).

However, there are also some less optimistic signs about the compatibility of markets and democracy in Latin America. For one thing, democracy seems to allow for little variation where economic policy is concerned. As we have seen, in Mexico, democratic transition promises to transform neither neoliberal policies nor the technocratic profile of economic policymakers. Similarly, in 1999, Argentina's notoriously technocratic Menem administration was replaced by the opposition government of Fernando de la Rúa—who appointed José Luis Machinea, a Minnesota-trained economist and former central bank president, as minister of the economy. The following year, the administration's IMF-inspired structural adjustment measures caused widespread protests in Buenos Aires. In Chile, the Socialist Ricardo Lagos assumed the presidency in 2000 and immediately pledged his commitment to upholding market reforms. He also appointed former IMF director and Harvard graduate Nicolás Eyzaguirre as finance minister and José de Gregorio, an MIT-trained economist, as minister of the economy. President Lagos himself is an economist with a degree from Duke University.

One interpretation of these policy continuities is that the electorate at large has endorsed the continuing presence of foreign-trained technocrats and the policies they prefer: social learning has made Latin Americans across the class spectrum into neoliberals. However, given the tremendous problems of social inequality and social injustice that continue to plague the continent, it seems more likely that economic policy is being placed beyond the reach of democratic institutions—that economic policy choices are moving ever further from the ballot box and ever more into the hands of experts. Some scholars have recently raised concerns that in the new "democratic" Latin American politics, elections are becoming suspiciously depoliticized (Barrera 1998; Silva 1999). There is an accompanying risk that citizens will become increasingly apathetic and disillusioned about party politics (cf. Montecinos 1998: 138).

Thus, although the brutality of military dictatorships is fading in the collective memory, Latin American democracy may be weakened by a sort of "tracking" or "tiering" of politics. Some political issues—such as corruption, drugs, and the prosecution of human rights abuses—are subject to popular discussion and electoral contention. However, the core of issues pertaining to economic policy may be increasingly insulated from popular discussion and debated only among foreign-educated policymakers, economic elites, and the international financial community. Whereas neoliberal reforms in wealthier nations may be mediated through democratic mechanisms and national electorates, in Latin America they are much more prone to mediation by technocratic mechanisms and international constituencies (Centeno 1994). This suggests that social learning in Latin America may be based on a consensus that excludes a significant portion of the population—a state of affairs that would not bode well for the region's political future.

Conclusion

The globalization of economic expertise is not a new phenomenon. Economically backward nations have always borrowed ideas from more developed ones, whether out of genuine admiration for these ideas or because taking foreign advice opened access to foreign resources. What is new is the extent to which foreign ideas are both reproduced domestically and directly involved at the highest levels of political power. In a number of developing countries, it is no longer necessary to invite foreign money doctors to oversee policy reforms; global experts are produced domestically and placed in charge of economic policy.

Has economic policy in the developing world reached the end of history—never again to deviate from its technocratic form and neoliberal content? If the past serves as any guide, it would take an economic upheaval of the scope of the Great Depression for a major change to come about, although some observers hope that a global social movement will produce a similar result with less drastic costs. In any case, it will take a powerful force indeed to challenge the authority of the experts presiding over the new global economy.

Appendix A

STUDY OF UNAM AND

ITM/ITAM THESES

A MAJOR PORTION of this book is based on my analysis of 287 undergraduate theses from the public Autonomous National University of Mexico (UNAM) and the Autonomous Technological Institute of Mexico (ITAM, but called the ITM before being made officially autonomous in 1962). The UNAM was home to Mexico's first—and for more than a decade, only—economics program. The ITAM was founded in 1945, as a private-sector response to the perceived leftist bias at the UNAM School of Economics. Today, the ITAM has arguably become home to Mexico's most important economics program, and for more than a decade its graduates have been disproportionately represented among government technocrats.

My decision to look at undergraduate theses was originally motivated by the scarcity of archival records from Mexican economics programs: I was unable to find collections of syllabi that documented what economics students were exposed to in the different programs over time. In contrast, the undergraduate theses of Mexican economics programs are freely available to the public in university libraries. Although doubtless a less valid reflection of the content of the courses taken by economics undergraduates (this discrepancy is particularly notable in the UNAM theses of 1976), the theses do have the advantage of reflecting, however imperfectly, what the students "got out" of their economics education. Rather than describing course content, the theses are exercises in applied theory and method, and indicate the general approach to economic problems that students learned during their five years of undergraduate education, and generally what skills they would bring to the job market.

In Mexico, there are two ways to graduate with an undergraduate degree: as a *titulado*, which requires the completion of an undergraduate thesis, or as a *pasante*, which merely requires the completion of course work. Titulados make up a larger proportion of graduating students in Mexico than "honors" graduations make up in the United States; for example, in 1993, there were a total of 1,082 economics titulados graduating in Mexico, compared with 2,019 economics pasantes (ANUIES 1994). It is safe to say that the titulados are on average better and more

motivated students than the pasantes, since like honors students in the
United States, they must complete a thesis. Since my study is based on
undergraduate theses, it is these higher-quality students whose ideas and
methods are being reflected.

My method was to thoroughly read the introduction and conclusion of
each thesis, where main theoretical points and citations were made, and
skim the middle for methodological approaches. I coded each thesis for
theoretical citations, methodology, application (to private or public sector), and various rhetorical features (most important, position on government intervention in the economy).

Selection of Theses for Investigation

I selected years from four key periods in the history of Mexican economics
for consideration in my study, to show the evolution of the economics
programs over time: (1) the first years of the UNAM program (or rather,
the years when the first UNAM economics theses were submitted), from
1934 to 1945; (2) the stabilizing development period of the 1950s and
'60s; (3) the period of populism and social conflict of the late 1970s; and
(4) the neoliberal period, which began approximately in the mid-1980s
and continues through the present.

Due to the very small size of the ITM/ITAM during its first decades, I
chose to review theses from a range of years during the developmentalist
and populist periods. Thus, UNAM theses from the year 1958 are compared with ITM theses from the years 1956–60, and UNAM theses from
the year 1976 are compared with ITAM theses from the years 1974–78.
By 1994, the ITAM program was producing graduates in sufficient quantities that I opted to investigate theses from a single year rather than a
range of years.

In contrast, the UNAM economics program became so large after the
1970s that to look at all the theses from any given year would have been a
dauntingly time-consuming and tedious process. Therefore, for the years
1976 and 1994, I chose a random sample of 50 UNAM economics theses
(I assigned all the theses from each year a number, and then selected according to a table of random numbers). Table A.1 shows how the 287
theses I selected from the UNAM and ITM/ITAM are broken down.

Theoretical Citations

I defined a theoretical citation as a citation referring to a theoretical point
made by any author, rather than to an author's empirical observation
or methodological recommendation. The decision to code for theoretical
citations only (rather than substantive or methodological citations) was

Table A.1
Undergraduate Theses Coded by Institution and by Year

	UNAM		ITM/ITAM	
	Year(s)	N or n	Year(s)	N or n
Founding decades of Mexican economics	1934–45	75		
Stabilizing development	1958	16	1956–60	16
Populism	1976	50	1974–78	43
Neoliberalism	1994	50	1994	37
Total		191		96

based on time considerations (in what was already an extraordinarily time-consuming process). I listed only the works actually cited in the text, rather than those listed in the bibliography, which often seemed "padded" with authors who were not cited in the text and footnotes. Authors from before the eighteenth century were not included (in some of the earlier theses, authors like Aristotle were cited, albeit infrequently).

In documenting the presence or absence of certain theoretical citations, my data do not take into account whether these authors were cited in a positive, negative, or neutral way. For the most part, I do not think that this detracts from the accuracy of the portrait I have painted of the UNAM and ITM/ITAM economics programs over time. Although citations were mostly positive, their greatest value was to show shifting theoretical "maps" or "frames of reference," rather than approval for an idea per se. Whether authors were cited positively or negatively, the fact of citation shows that their ideas were considered important and worthy of mention. In the early UNAM theses, for example, there were a few authors who cited Marx in a disapproving way; in the UNAM theses from 1994, there was at least one author who cited Milton Friedman disapprovingly. In contrast—and despite the fact the ITM was founded in part to combat the leftist ideology of the UNAM—the ITM (later ITAM) theses did not cite Marx at all, a clear demonstration of the theoretical irrelevance of Marx at the ITM/ITAM.

Codes

The following are the codes for the rhetorical elements I tracked in the theses:

1. Tables of empirical statistics:
    a. Descriptive statistics only

224 APPENDIX A

b. Both descriptive statistics and econometric methods, or only econometric methods
c. No statistics

2. Formal mathematical modeling:
   a. Yes
   b. No

3. State intervention in economy:
   a. Less state intervention in specific areas advocated (e.g., get rid of tariffs or get rid of subsidies), or ideological justification for less state intervention mentioned
   b. Tinkering with or expanding existing state interventions advocated (e.g., calls for studies, reduced paperwork, raising or lowering existing tariffs/taxes)
   c. Introduction of major new interventions advocated, or ideological justification for state intervention mentioned
   d. None of the above

4. Discussion of socialism:
   a. Mentioned approvingly
   b. Mentioned disapprovingly
   c. Not mentioned

5. Goals of the Mexican revolution extolled:
   a. Yes
   b. No

6. Capitalism/free markets have grave defects, serious problems that must be compensated for:
   a. Yes
   b. No

7. Marxist theory/rhetoric at center (e.g., surplus value, etc.):
   a. Yes
   b. No

8. Place limits on foreign investment or other anti-imperialist rhetoric:
   a. Yes
   b. No

9. Developed vs. developing countries are fundamentally different, different paths to development:
   a. Yes
   b. No

10. Private property extolled:
    a. Yes
    b. No

11. Competition or free trade extolled:
    a. Yes
    b. No

12. Free markets or deregulation supported:
   a. Yes
   b. No

Codes 1 and 2 are based on a brief review of the entire contents of the thesis to determine the methods used in the author's investigation. A thesis received a 1a if it contained descriptive but not econometric statistical information (e.g., tables of agricultural output over time). The distinction between descriptive statistics and econometric methods can be ambiguous; for example, the calculation of a mean is straightforward and does not require any statistical analysis beyond adding a column of figures and dividing them by N. To avoid including such calculations as "econometric methods," I categorized a thesis as containing econometric methods if it utilized summary measures of dispersion, such as standard deviations. Under this definition, t-tests and bivariate regressions counted as "econometrics" but means did not. These theses (including those that contained nonanalytical statistical information) received a code of 1b. In contrast to code 1, code 2 is designed to identify theses that utilized the nonempirical mathematical formulas used by economists (particularly after the 1950s) to model their theories.

Unlike codes 1 and 2, which pertain to thesis methodology and are based on an assessment of the content of the entire body of the thesis text, codes 3–12 are an analysis of the rhetoric of: (1) the introductory statement of purpose and theoretical section; and (2) the conclusion. I decided that reading through and coding entire theses would be an overly time-consuming project. Such considerations of feasibility aside, the introductions and conclusions were generally the most rhetorically rich sections of the theses from all different departments over time; the content in between tended to be dry, technical, and rhetorically uninteresting.

Code 3 was both the most problematic and the most interesting of the codes. At the beginning, I was faced with the problem of how to "measure" an author's position on state interventionism. Many authors who failed to make explicit endorsements or condemnations of state intervention in the abstract made concrete recommendations that clearly marked their position on the interventionist–laissez-faire continuum. Thus, each coding value (i.e., 3a, 3b, or 3c) contained both cases of explicit theoretical position-taking as well as cases that were defined by their positions on particular issues.

The "interventionist" authors (3c) can broadly be thought of as those who enthusiastically supported a mixed economy or supported even more state intervention. They include:

1. Authors who made theoretical statements supporting a strong role for government in the economy and/or against a laissez-faire role

2. Authors who actively criticized neoliberalism and/or its consequences
3. Authors who suggested substantial and new state interventions in the economy (e.g., starting a new government credit program for a specific industry)

In contrast, "anti-interventionist" authors (3a) include:

1. Those who actively endorsed neoliberal lessening of state intervention
2. Those who made suggestions for substantial and new lessened interventions in the economy (e.g., privatizing social security)
3. Those who endorsed replacing direct interventions with more regulatory functions

A third "position" on state interventionism, which must be distinguished from those that took no position on state interventionism whatsoever, is the "neutral" category (3b). Unlike the 3a's and the 3c's, which advocated substantial increases or decreases in state intervention in the economy, and 3d's, which failed to take any position on state intervention, 3b's represent technical approaches to existing interventions. Thus, whereas a 3c might have suggested a new government program to finance small producers in a given industry, a 3b might have suggested how to improve the performance of existing programs; whereas a 3a might suggest that the social security system be privatized, a 3b (while generally approving of banking liberalization) might suggest that regulations should have been better applied in the privatization of Mexican banks. These authors include:

1. Those who suggested modest changes within the existing policy framework (consolidation of functions of a particular department, call for a study, etc.), or approved of particular programs
2. Those who suggested less modest changes that nevertheless could be categorized as "minimal" state functions (e.g., build a particular highway)
3. Those who suggested that the government "do something" but who failed to offer details as to what the government should do
4. Those few who made suggestions that fall into both the "a" and "c" categories (therefore, an average between the two makes a "b").

Tables A.2–A.7 are based on analysis of the theses. Tables included in earlier chapters have been excluded from this appendix.

TABLE A.2
Rhetorical Elements from UNAM Theses, 1934–45 (Total N = 75)

Code	N	%
1. Tables of empirical statistics:		
a. Descriptive statistics only	63	84
b. Both descriptive statistics and econometric methods, or only econometric methods	0	0
c. No statistics	12	16
2. Formal mathematical modeling:		
a. Yes	7	9.3
b. No	68	90.7
3. State intervention in economy:		
a. Less state intervention in specific areas advocated (e.g., get rid of tariffs or get rid of subsidies), or ideological justification for less state intervention mentioned	0	0
b. Tinkering with or expanding existing state interventions advocated (e.g., calls for studies, reduced paperwork, raising or lowering existing tariffs/ taxes)	30	40
c. Introduction of major new interventions advocated, or ideological justification for state intervention mentioned	21	28
d. None of the above	24	32
4. Discussion of socialism:		
a. Mentioned approvingly	3	4
b. Mentioned disapprovingly	2	2.7
c. Not mentioned	70	93.3
5. Goals of the Mexican revolution extolled:		
a. Yes	9	12
b. No	66	88

TABLE A.2 *(cont.)*
Rhetorical Elements from UNAM Theses, 1934–45 (Total N = 75)

Code	N	%
6. Capitalism/free markets have grave defects, serious problems that must be compensated for:		
a. Yes	13	17.3
b. No	62	82.6
7. Marxist theory/rhetoric at center (e.g., surplus value, etc.):		
a. Yes	4	5.3
b. No	71	94.7
8. Place limits on foreign investment or other anti-imperialist rhetoric:		
a. Yes	3	4
b. No	72	96
9. Developed vs. developing countries are on fundamentally different paths to development:		
a. Yes	2	2.7
b. No	73	97.33
10. Private property extolled:		
a. Yes	0	0
b. No	75	100
11. Competition or free trade extolled:		
a. Yes	0	0
b. No	75	100
12. Free markets or deregulation supported:		
a. Yes	0	0
b. No	75	100

TABLE A.3
Rhetorical Elements from UNAM Theses, 1958 (Total N = 16)

Code	N	%
1. Tables of empirical statistics:		
a. Descriptive statistics only	14	87.5
b. Both descriptive statistics and econometric methods, or only econometric methods	0	0
c. No statistics	2	12.5
2. Formal mathematical modeling:		
a. Yes	2	12.5
b. No	14	87.5
3. State intervention in economy:		
a. Less state intervention in specific areas advocated (e.g., get rid of tariffs or get rid of subsidies), or ideological justification for less state intervention mentioned	0	0
b. Tinkering with or expanding existing state interventions advocated (e.g., calls for studies, reduced paperwork, raising or lowering existing tariffs/taxes)	6	0
c. Introduction of major new interventions advocated, or ideological justification for state intervention mentioned	10	37.5
d. None of the above	0	62.5
4. Discussion of socialism:		
a. Mentioned approvingly	0	0
b. Mentioned disapprovingly	0	0
c. Not mentioned	16	100
5. Goals of the Mexican revolution extolled:		
a. Yes	4	25
b. No	12	75
6. Capitalism/free markets have grave defects, serious problems that must be compensated for:		
a. Yes	5	31.3
b. No	11	68.8

TABLE A.3 (*cont.*)
Rhetorical Elements from UNAM Theses, 1958 (Total N = 16)

Code	N	%
7. Marxist theory/rhetoric at center (e.g., surplus value, etc.):		
a. Yes	1	6.2
b. No	15	93.8
8. Place limits on foreign investment or other anti-imperialist rhetoric:		
a. Yes	1	6.2
b. No	15	93.8
9. Developed vs. developing countries are on fundamentally different paths to development:		
a. Yes	8	50
b. No	8	50
10. Private property extolled:		
a. Yes	0	0
b. No	16	100
11. Competition or free trade extolled:		
a. Yes	0	0
b. No	16	100
12. Free markets or deregulation supported:		
a. Yes	1	6.2
b. No	15	93.8

TABLE A.4
Rhetorical Elements from UNAM Theses, 1976 and 1994

Code	1976 (n=50)		1994 (n=50)	
	n	%	n	%
1. Tables of empirical statistics:				
a. Descriptive statistics only	42	84	43	86
b. Both descriptive statistics and econometric methods, or only econometric methods	2	4	4	8
c. No statistics	6	12	3	6
2. Formal mathematical modeling:				
a. Yes	5	10	10	20
b. No	45	90	40	80
3. State intervention in economy:				
a. Less state intervention in specific areas advocated (e.g., get rid of tariffs or get rid of subsidies), or ideological justification for less state intervention mentioned	0	0	7	14
b. Tinkering with or expanding existing state interventions advocated (e.g., calls for studies, reduced paperwork, raising or lowering existing tariffs/taxes)	19	38	16	32
c. Introduction of major new interventions advocated, or ideological justification for state intervention mentioned	20	40	5	10
d. None of the above	11	22	22	44

TABLE A.4 *(cont.)*
Rhetorical Elements from UNAM Theses, 1976 and 1994

	1976 (n=50)		1994 (n=50)	
Code	N	%	N	%
4. Discussion of socialism:				
a. Mentioned approvingly	2	4	0	0
b. Mentioned disapprovingly	1	2	0	0
c. Not mentioned	47	94	50	100
5. Goals of the Mexican revolution extolled:				
a. Yes	2	4	0	0
b. No	48	96	50	100
6. Capitalism/free markets have grave defects, serious problems that must be compensated for:				
a. Yes	2	4	0	0
b. No	48	96	50	100
7. Marxist theory/rhetoric at center (e.g., surplus value, etc.):				
a. Yes	6	12	6	12
b. No	44	88	44	88
8. Place limits on foreign investment or other anti-imperialist rhetoric:				
a. Yes	6	12	1	2
b. No	44	88	49	98
9. Developed vs. developing countries are on fundamentally different paths to development:				
a. Yes	2	4	0	0
b. No	48	96	50	100
10. Private property extolled:				
a. Yes	0	0	0	0
b. No	50	100	50	100
11. Competition or free trade extolled:				
a. Yes	0	0	5	10
b. No	50	100	45	90
12. Free markets or deregulation supported:				
a. Yes	0	0	1	2
b. No	50	100	49	98

TABLE A.5
Rhetorical Elements from ITM Theses, 1956–60

Code	N	%
1. Tables of empirical statistics:		
a. Descriptive statistics only	13	81.2
b. Both descriptive statistics and econometric methods, or only econometric methods.	0	0
c. No statistics	3	18.8
2. Formal mathematical modeling:		
a. Yes	1	6.2
b. No	15	93.8
3. State intervention in economy:		
a. Less state intervention in specific areas advocated (e.g., get rid of tariffs or get rid of subsidies), or ideological justification for less state intervention mentioned	0	0
b. Tinkering with or expanding existing state interventions advocated (e.g., calls for studies, reduced paperwork, raising or lowering existing tariffs/taxes)	6	37.5
c. Introduction of major new interventions advocated, or ideological justification for state intervention mentioned	8	50
d. None of the above	2	12.5
4. Discussion of socialism:		
a. Mentioned approvingly	0	0
b. Mentioned disapprovingly	1	6.2
c. Not mentioned	15	93.8
5. Goals of the Mexican revolution extolled:		
a. Yes	3	18.8
b. No	13	81.2

TABLE A.5 (*cont.*)
Rhetorical Elements from ITM Theses, 1956–60

Code	N	%
6. Capitalism/free markets have grave defects, serious problems that must be compensated for:		
a. Yes	0	0
b. No	16	100
7. Marxist theory/rhetoric at center (e.g., surplus value, etc.):		
a. Yes	0	0
b. No	16	100
8. Place limits on foreign investment or other anti-imperialist rhetoric:		
a. Yes	0	0
b. No	16	100
9. Developed vs. developing countries are on fundamentally different paths to development:		
a. Yes	2	12.5
b. No	14	87.5
10. Private property extolled:		
a. Yes	1	6.2
b. No	15	93.8
11. Competition or free trade extolled:		
a. Yes	0	0
b. No	16	100
12. Free markets or deregulation supported:		
a. Yes	0	0
b. No	16	100

TABLE A.6
Most-Cited Authors, ITM 1956–60
(Total N = 16, Theses with Theoretical Cites = 43.8%)

	N	%
J. M. Keynes	3	18.8
Ragnar Nurkse	2	12.5
Lionel Robbins	2	12.5
Alfredo Weber	2	12.5

TABLE A.7
Rhetorical Elements from ITAM Theses, 1974–78 and 1994

Code	1974–78 (N = 43)		1994 (N = 32)	
	N	%	N	%
1. Tables of empirical statistics:				
a. Descriptive statistics only	18	41.9	13	35.1
b. Both descriptive statistics and econometric methods, or only econometric methods	23	53.5	22	59.5
c. No statistics	2	4.6	2	5.4
2. Formal mathematical modeling:				
a. Yes	32	74.4	35	94.6
b. No	11	25.6	2	5.4
3. State intervention in economy:				
a. Less state intervention in specific areas advocated (e.g., get rid of tariffs or get rid of subsidies), or ideological justification for less state intervention mentioned	4	9.3	4	10.8
b. Tinkering with or expanding existing state interventions advocated (e.g., calls for studies, reduced paperwork, raising or lowering existing tariffs/taxes)	12	27.9	12	32.4
c. Introduction of major new interventions advocated, or ideological justification for state intervention mentioned	5	11.6	1	2.7
d. None of the above	22	51.2	20	54.1

TABLE A.7 (*cont.*)
Rhetorical Elements from ITAM Theses, 1974–78 and 1994

	1974–78 (N = 43)		1994 (N = 32)	
Code	N	%	N	%
4. Discussion of socialism:				
a. Mentioned approvingly	0	0	0	0
b. Mentioned disapprovingly	0	0	0	0
c. Not mentioned	43	100	37	100
5. Goals of the Mexican revolution extolled:				
a. Yes	0	0	0	0
b. No	43	100	37	100
6. Capitalism/free markets have grave defects, serious problems that must be compensated for:				
a. Yes	0	0	0	0
b. No	43	100	37	100
7. Marxist theory/rhetoric at center (e.g., surplus value, etc.):				
a. Yes	0	0	0	0
b. No	43	100	37	100
8. Place limits on foreign investment or other anti-imperialist rhetoric:				
a. Yes	2	4.7	0	0
b. No	41	95.4	37	100
9. Developed vs. developing countries are on fundamentally different paths to development:				
a. Yes	2	4.7	0	0
b. No	41	95.4	37	100
10. Private property extolled:				
a. Yes	1	2.3	0	0
b. No	42	97.7	37	100
11. Competition or free trade extolled:				
a. Yes	2	4.7	3	8.1
b. No	41	95.4	34	91.9
12. Free markets or deregulation supported:				
a. Yes	1	2.3	4	10.8
b. No	42	97.7	33	89.2

Appendix B

STUDY OF DATABASE OF SOCIEDAD
DE EX-ALUMNOS OF THE ITAM

THE SOCIEDAD de Ex-Alumnos (Alumni Society) of the ITAM is a voluntary organization of ITAM graduates. I was fortunate to gain access to their database, which provides a general view of the career trajectories of ITAM graduates, including information about current place of employment and graduate study. No equivalent database exists for the UNAM, which lacks the ITAM's financial resources. My study includes data on all ITM/ITAM economics graduates registered with the Sociedad through the spring of 1996 (when I obtained the database), a total of 1,193 individuals. As implausible as it sounds here in the United States, I was unable to find out the total number of ITM/ITAM graduates for the same period (which would have given me the proportion of my sample to the population of ITM/ITAM economics graduates at large). Data supplied by the ANUIES (the Mexican government agency that keeps records of statistics on higher education) include statistics on ITAM graduates since the late 1970s, but the numbers are apparently inconsistent (sometimes presenting separate numbers for titulados and pasantes, and sometimes counting titulados among the pasantes).

The most important limitation involved in using data from the database of the Sociedad de Ex-Alumnos is sampling bias. As a voluntary association, the Sociedad has information only on graduates who have chosen to enroll and thus does not constitute a random sample of graduates of ITAM economics. This sampling bias is particularly troublesome for the graduates of earlier years, of whom a smaller proportion are currently enrolled in the Sociedad de Ex-Alumnos.

Another problem is that existing information is only on graduates' *current* place of employment rather than their first place of employment on graduation. Thus, an important assumption of this study is that ITAM graduates in economics generally remained within the sector within which they originally chose to work: for example, graduates who began working in government tended not to move to the private sector. However, Camp's (1980, 1984) work on Mexican political and economic elites suggests that this assumption is tenable.

Since some graduates were unemployed or between jobs at the time that data was last updated, there is missing employment data for over 20% of graduates, which may also introduce bias to the sample (since government workers may be more likely to be unemployed than private-sector workers, for example). Finally, these data do not distinguish between pasantes and the more rigorously prepared titulados.

Since a fundamental hypothesis of my book is that the economics profession in Mexico has changed over time, I divided the ITAM economics graduates in the database into two groups: those graduating before 1971 and those graduating after (who studied under the improved full-time program implemented by Gustavo Petricioli in the mid-1960s). Despite the numerous problems previously mentioned, this database provides the only available source on the career trajectories of ITAM economics graduates. In addition to suggesting patterns of employment and graduate study for ITAM economics graduates, it also provides important clues to certain aspects of the Mexican economics profession in general.

Findings Pertaining to ITAM Economics Graduates

In stark contrast to the dominance of government employment among the UNAM economics graduates, over 40% of ITAM economics graduates for whom data are available were working for the private sector in 1996 (see tables B.1 and B.2). Among both earlier and later graduates, a relatively small proportion were working for academic institutions (9.0% and 3.7%, respectively).

The low percentage of graduates working for academic institutions is somewhat misleading, since full-time Mexican government officials frequently teach university classes part-time. This does, however, demonstrate that Mexico differs substantially from the United States in that full-time academic employment of economists is still a relatively limited field (primarily because of the limited number of institutions offering attractive salaries).

The difference between the proportion of graduates working for the private sector before and after 1971 is nearly nonexistent, but public-sector employment of graduates seems to have increased somewhat between the two periods. The breakdown of graduates working in the public sector by area of employment (tables B.3 and B.4) must be considered in context, since it is well known that public-sector officials in Mexico move among different branches of government with great rapidity. Thus, an ITAM economics graduate who initially works for the Commerce Ministry is likely to find himself or herself working for the Finance Ministry six years later, and is likely to be in yet another ministry six years after that. However, it is worth noting that a substantial proportion of both earlier and later ITAM economics graduates working in government (17.6% and 12.4%) are currently working in the coveted and relatively stable positions within the central bank. It is also worth noting that the most popular public-sector place of employment for post-1971 graduates was the Finance Ministry (19.5% of government employees).

Tables B.9 and B.10 suggest that in both periods, the majority of ITAM economics graduates who undertook graduate study abroad chose to study economics or econometrics, and that administration has gained in popularity as a field of graduate study. The relative probability of graduate study abroad in general appears to have increased slightly: 14.3% of pre-1971 graduates and 18.4% of post-1971 graduates (see tables B.11 and B.12). However, given the number of cases with missing data on 1996 place of employment (over 20%), this apparent increase should probably not be taken at face value.

Tables B.13 and B.14 show that graduate study abroad in *economics* has tended toward different institutions over time. Whereas before 1971 the most popular institutions for graduate study abroad were Harvard and Yale, after 1971 the University of Chicago has been overwhelmingly the most popular institution, accounting for 17.9% of all those studying economics abroad.

Findings Pertaining to Mexican Economists in General

The results of this study suggest a number of trends for the economics profession in Mexico. First, tables B.5 and B.6 suggest that for graduates working within the private sector, there has been an important change in career prospects: whereas only 25% of ITAM economics graduates before 1971 with private-sector jobs were working within the financial sector in 1996, of the post-1971 graduates *nearly half* were working within this sector. This finding complements interview data I have collected suggesting that the growing complexity of financial transactions has led banks, insurance companies, brokerage houses, and other financial businesses to hire economists in larger numbers than before. Since this shift implies that fewer private-sector economists are working for industry and other branches of the private sector, it seems safe to assume that financial institutions have been offering comparatively more attractive salaries for economists.

Tables B.7 and B.8 provide a means of gauging the relative importance of graduate training abroad for employment in different sectors over time. A minority of ITAM economics graduates subsequently conducted graduate studies abroad: about 14.% of the graduates between 1951 and 1970, and about 18% of the 1971–95 graduates, subsequently pursued such study. Of those who did choose to study abroad, however, there was a disproportionate concentration in academia and the public sector, with the private sector being the area that apparently offered the fewest rewards (pecuniary or otherwise) to economics graduates with foreign training. Tables B.11 and B.12 show more specifically the career trajectories of individuals who undertook foreign training in *economics*, and show an even greater contrast among sectors. Not surprisingly, foreign graduate study in economics was a most important prerequisite among ITAM graduates who went into academia. These results confirm the widely held impression that foreign graduate training in economics is an important prerequisite for government technocrats (and academic economists) but is substantially less important for working in the private sector.

TABLE B.1
ITAM Economics Graduates, 1996 Place of Employment
(Date of Graduation 1951–70)

	N	%
Public	17	19.1
Private	40	44.9
Academia	8	9.0
Other	5	5.6
Missing	19	21.3
Total	89	100.0

TABLE B.2
ITAM Economics Graduates, 1996 Place of Employment
(Date of Graduation 1971–95)

	N	%
Public	282	25.5
Private	490	44.4
Academia	41	3.7
Other	44	4.0
Missing	247	22.4
Total	1104	100.0

TABLE B.3

ITAM Economics Graduates Working in Public Sector
1996, by Place of Employment
(Date of Graduation 1951–70)

	N	%
Commerce Min.	1	5.9
Central bank	3	17.6
Finance Min.	1	5.9
Fed. district	1	5.9
Other	11	64.7
Total	17	100

TABLE B.4

ITAM Economics Graduates Working in Public Sector
1996, by Place of Employment
(Date of Graduation 1971–95)

	N	%
Nac. Financiera	6	2.1
Commerce Min.	19	6.7
Central bank	35	12.4
Finance Min.	55	19.5
Presidency	9	3.2
Fed. district	12	4.3
Bancomext	19	6.7
Other	127	45.0
Total	282	100

TABLE B.5

ITAM Economics Graduates Working in Private Sector
1996, by Place of Employment
(Date of Graduation 1951–70)

	N	%
Financial sector	10	25
Other private sector	30	75
Total	40	100

TABLE B.6

ITAM Economics Graduates Working in Private Sector
1996, by Place of Employment
(Date of Graduation 1971–95)

	N	%
Financial sector	240	49
Other private sector	250	51
Total	490	100

TABLE B.7

ITAM Economics Graduates, Graduate Study Abroad by 1996
Place of Employment (Date of Graduation 1951–70)

Employment	Foreign Grad. Studies N (%)	No Foreign Grad. Studies N (%)	Total N (%)
Public sector	5 (29.4)	12 (70.6)	17 (100)
Private sector	3 (7.5)	37 (92.5)	40 (100)
Academia	2 (25)	6 (75)	8 (100)
Other	0 (0)	5 (100)	5 (100)
All places of employment	10 (14.3)	60 (85.7)	70 (100)

Note: Tables B.7 and B.8 include only those graduates for whom current employment information was available.

TABLE B.8

ITAM Economics Graduates, Graduate Study Abroad by 1996
Place of Employment (Date of Graduation 1971–95)

Employment	Foreign Grad. Studies N (%)	No Foreign Grad. Studies N (%)	Total N (%)
Public sector	71 (25.2)	211 (74.8)	282 (100)
Private sector	65 (13.3)	425 (86.7)	490 (100)
Academia	16 (39.0)	25 (61.0)	41 (100)
Other	6 (13.6)	38 (86.4)	44 (100)
All places of employment	158 (18.4)	699 (81.6)	857 (100)

TABLE B.9

ITAM Economics Graduates with Foreign Graduate
Training by Subject Studied (Date of Graduation 1951–70)

	N	%
Economics/econometrics	8	61.5
Administration	1	7.7
Finance	0	0
Other	4	30.8
Total	13	100

TABLE B.10

ITAM Economics Graduates with Foreign Graduate
Training by Subject Studied (Date of Graduation 1971–95)

	N	%
Economics/econometrics	112	61.9
Administration	40	22.1
Finance	5	2.8
Other	24	13.3
Total	181	100

TABLE B.11

ITAM Economics Graduates, Graduate Study Abroad in Economics by
1996 Place of Employment (Date of Graduation 1951–70)

Employment	Foreign Grad. Studies N (%)	No Foreign Grad. Studies N (%)	Total N (%)
Public sector	3 (17.7)	14 (82.4)	17 (100)
Private sector	1 (2.5)	39 (97.5)	40 (100)
Academia	1 (12.5)	7 (87.5)	8 (100)
Other	0 (0)	5 (100)	5 (100)
All places of employment	5 (7.1)	65 (92.9)	70 (100)

Note: Tables B.11 and B.12 include only those graduates for whom current employment
information was available.

TABLE B.12

ITAM Economics Graduates, Graduate Study Abroad in Economics by
1996 Place of Employment (Date of Graduation 1971–95)

Employment	Foreign Grad. Studies N (%)	No Foreign Grad. Studies N (%)	Total N (%)
Public sector	52 (18.4)	230 (81.6)	282 (100)
Private sector	32 (6.5)	458 (93.5)	490 (100)
Academia	11 (26.8)	30 (73.3)	41 (100)
Other	3 (6.8)	41 (93.2)	44 (100)
All places of employment	98 (11.4)	759 (88.6)	857 (100)

TABLE B.13

ITAM Economics Graduates, Universities Attended for
Graduate Study Abroad in Economics
(Date of Graduation 1951–70)

University	N	%
Yale	2	25.0
U. Chicago	1	12.5
Harvard	2	25.0
Stanford	1	12.5
Other	2	25.0
Total	8	100

TABLE B.14

ITAM Economics Graduates, Universities Attended for
Graduate Study Abroad in Economics
(Date of Graduation 1971–95)

University	N	%
Yale	5	4.5
U. Chicago	20	17.9
Columbia	3	2.7
Harvard	4	3.6
U. of London	3	2.7
Oxford	2	1.8
Stanford	1	.9
MIT	7	6.3
London S. Econ.	5	4.5
Cambridge	3	2.7
Other	59	52.7

NOTES

CHAPTER ONE
NEOLIBERALISM AND THE GLOBALIZATION OF ECONOMIC EXPERTISE

1. Silva Herzog's own son (of the same name) had completed his M.A. in economics at Yale University only a few years before, and was working in the Mexican Central Bank; he would later become finance minister, and the official in charge of overseeing the implementation of IMF austerity measures in the 1980s.

2. According to a recent study, more than 50% of U.S. doctoral students in economics were foreigners (Aslanbeigui and Montecinos 1998).

3. Some American readers may be puzzled by the notion of economics as a "profession," since in the United States it could be seen as a subset of a larger profession of "academicians." I would argue that even in the United States, the fact that economists have their own professional association, as well as journals that are inaccessible to noneconomist academicians, both suggest that economics is a separate profession in its own right. Moreover, as chapter 2 shows, in many other nations (including Mexico), economics has historically been a state-based rather than an academic profession—in such cases the prototypical economist is a government official rather than a full-time academic.

4. The term *coercive* is something of a misnomer, in that it confounds processes that are coercive in the strong sense (as when an administrative apparatus is imposed by an occupying army) with processes that are voluntary within externally determined constraints (as when developing countries make their central banks independent in order to foster investor confidence). This is roughly analogous to the difference between an army draftee who must wear a uniform or be thrown in jail, on the one hand, and a job applicant who must dress conservatively for a job interview, on the other.

CHAPTER TWO
THE ORIGINS OF MEXICAN ECONOMICS

1. This generalization must be made only with qualifications; for example, it is possible to document private-sector participation in the formation of Continental European professions (e.g., Guillén 1989), as well as direct government involvement in professionalization in England and the United States (e.g., Halliday and Carruthers 1996; Bernstein 1990). Nevertheless, these exceptions assume importance only against the general pattern of statist versus nonstatist professions.

2. The Mexican degree of "licenciado" corresponds roughly to the B.A. in the United States but is dissimilar in that it is based on five rather than four years of course work and a much greater degree of specialization. It also requires the completion of a thesis.

3. The original source for all indexes of Mexican inflation—and therefore of real growth—are the annual reports of the Mexican central bank (Banco de México). An important recent debate among economists has addressed problems with conventional measures of inflation (cf. Moulton 1996). However, to my knowledge there is no literature addressing potential problems with price indexes historically used in Mexico, which forces me to take the Banco data at face value. Social scientists from across the political spectrum cite these historical data, which are presented in summary form by organizations ranging from the IMF to the United Nations Economic Committee on Latin America.

4. At this time, the finance minister had discretion over monetary as well as fiscal policy. This de jure (if not de facto) discretion was terminated in 1993, when the Banco de México was made officially autonomous.

5. This ministry was actually known as the "Ministry of the Economy" during the 1930s and underwent several changes in name before it arrived at its current name (the Ministry of Commerce and Industrial Development). For the purposes of simplification, I will refer to it as the Ministry of Commerce throughout this book.

6. Interestingly, there is no mention in Pallares of economists working in the parastate sector (e.g., in the nationalized petroleum company). This is perhaps because the parastate sector had been staked out as the professional "turf" of engineers rather than economists.

CHAPTER THREE
MARXISM, POPULISM AND PRIVATE SECTOR REACTION: THE SPLITTING
OF MEXICAN ECONOMICS

1. In 1801, Thomas Jefferson tried (and failed) to inaugurate a project for such a university (Seabury 1979: 15).

2. A recent study shows that state funding of American public higher education is on the wane, accounting for 40.3% of revenues in 1990–91 and only 35.9% in 1993–94 (Callan and Finney, eds., 1997: 32).

3. From this it should *not* be inferred that there is a clear functional connection between the content of an undergraduate economics education and the practical needs of private-sector employers. In discussing the prevalence of economics majors among investment bankers, Michael Lewis remarked as follows: "Economics satisfied the two most basic needs of investment bankers. First, bankers wanted practical people, willing to subordinate their education to their careers. Economics seemed designed as a sifting device. Economics was practical. It got people jobs. And it did this because it demonstrated that they were among the most fervent believers in the primacy of economic life. Economics allowed investment bankers directly to compare the academic records of the recruits. The only inexplicable part of the process was that economic theory (which is what, after all, economics students were supposed to know) *served almost no function in an investment bank*" (quote from *Liar's Poker* by Michael Lewis in Ormerod 1994).

4. Although economics in the United States was divided between laissez-faire neoclassicals and more interventionist institutionalists, the former group predominated, with the University of Wisconsin at Madison and Columbia University being the only bastions of institutionalist thought (Yonay 1994: 47).

5. For a detailed description of government-labor relations in Mexico, see Middlebrook (1995) and La Botz (1992).

6. It must also be considered that Keynesian theories did not become popularized in the United States until the postwar period, through the efforts of more accessible writers such as Paul Samuleson.

7. Interestingly, the director of the private National Bank of Mexico, Luis Legoretta, was also persuaded to donate one thousand pesos to the cause (Chumacero 1980: 10).

8. Unfortunately, course syllabi from the National School of Economics have not been preserved in any historical archive I was able to find.

9. This was particularly true of Alemán, under whose presidency the ruling party began to purge itself of communists and communist sympathizers, leading one U.S. diplomat to observe that Alemán clearly "knew which way the wind was blowing," a clear reference to the Cold War (Carr 1992: 147). Although the presidency of Avila Camacho foreshadowed these developments, it did not show the same overt hostility to leftism as did that of Alemán, and incorporated leftists into cabinet positions.

10. These changes are discussed further in chapter 4.

11. Rather than the letter grade system, almost all Mexican universities grade on a scale of one to ten.

12. Salinas Lozano later went on to pursue graduate studies in the United States and was the most important economist of his generation to reach high-level public office (secretary of commerce). He was also the father of Carlos Salinas de Gortari, who was president of Mexico from 1988 to 1994.

13. A more complicated governance system established in 1944–45 removed power from professors and students to choose rectors and department heads, who were chosen instead by an internally renewed governing board (Mabry 1982: 189–90). Since that time, the most important link between government and university has been the president's ultimate control over the university purse strings—with the consequence that university rectors have generally been on good terms with the president (Levy 1980: 77). Nevertheless, in his work on Mexican public universities, Levy (1980: 97, 115–17) noted a high degree of autonomy from the government.

14. This confirms Maxfield's (1990) observation of a high degree of overlap between public and private financiers in Mexico.

15. Unfortunately, I was unable to find material on the courses required at the ITAM during its first years.

CHAPTER FOUR
THE MEXICAN MIRACLE AND ITS POLICY PARADIGM, 1940–1970

1. Alemán's 1947 visit to Washington was the first such visit since 1836; his commitments to protecting the rights of foreign investors and to fighting communism (particularly in Mexican unions) earned Alemán the popular title of "Mister Amigo" (Krauze 1997: 162–63).

2. Overall during this period, however, per capita incomes rose because of the movement of agricultural workers to urban industrial centers; so while Mexican

workers were relatively worse off than they were before, Mexicans in general were better off (Hansen 1971: 50).

3. However, a more recent analysis shows that industrial workers benefited absolutely from the Mexican Miracle: for example, between 1958 and 1970, average real hourly wages increased from 3.27 to 7.45 pesos per hour (Izquierdo 1995: 129).

4. Interestingly, Hirschman's article utilizes the term "programming" in place of "planning," a choice of words that, according to a reliable source, was a by-product of the Cold War, which caused Western economists to eliminate terminology smacking of socialism.

5. Raúl was the brother of Antonio Ortíz Mena, who later became famous as the long-reigning finance minister of the stabilizing development period.

6. A notable exception was the economist Raúl Salinas Lozano (the father of President Carlos Salinas), who was minister of commerce from 1958 to 1964.

7. These economists were Rafael Urrutía Millán, Agustín López Munguía, Ernesto Fernández Hurtado, Ifigenia Navarrete, and Víctor Urquidi (Urquidi 1987: 923).

8. Another example of the same phenomenon is the conflict that arose within the Reagan administration when Surgeon General Koop's position as a doctor on cigarette smoking created problems for a party with strong support from the tobacco lobby.

9. Of course, this applies only to professionals in government who are behaving *as* professionals, not to all government employees with professional titles. For example, although law has long been the standard professional training for elected officials in many countries, lawyers in office are generally expected to behave as politicians rather than as professionals serving a collective client.

10. A separate scholarship program for training non-Banco employees in skills related to economic development (notably engineering and medicine) was simultaneously run by the Banco de México's Industrial Studies Department.

11. Data on Banco de México economics scholarships are from a database I constructed based on information from the following documents: Banco de México, Departamento de Investigaciones Industriales 1961; Banco de México, Departamento de Capacitación de Personal 1987.

12. A Banco official who worked with Gómez described him as ". . . a pragmatic monetarist rather than an automatic one in the rigid sense of Milton Friedman . . ." (Pérez López 1991: 163).

13. The original program in 1964 combined postgraduate studies in economics and demography.

14. For example, in 1959 the course in Marxist theory was expanded from one to two hours (interview, Ramírez 10/15/96).

15. Courses that met three hours per week were the shortest offered in the 1963 plan (except for laboratories and optional seminars); in a typical semester, students were required to take eighteen hours of courses, and particularly difficult courses (such as mathematics) met five hours per week.

16. The fact that only sixteen economics theses were defended at the UNAM in 1958 attests to the small size of the program, which only began its phase of rapid expansion in the 1960s.

17. Nurkse was a Swedish development economist specializing in the problems of capital formation of developing countries.

18. Collins notes that these policies were adopted in many universities in many parts of the world during the 1960s and '70s; he refers to this strategy as "credential radicalism" (Collins 1979: 196).

19. To avoid repeating this well-known deficiency of the UNAM, the 1958 reforms supported by the Banco de México at the Economics Department of the University of Nuevo León included the implementation of a rigorous entrance examination (interview, Bolaños Lozano 5/29/96).

20. None of these professors were full-time, and all were paid by the hour; the first two full-time positions at the school did not appear until 1962.

21. Camp (1984) suggests that this movement away from family control and toward professional management was slow in Mexico in part because of a strong family-oriented cultural tradition (pp. 198–99).

22. As in most public universities, there was apparently a certain degree of radicalization among the students of the economics program of the University of Nuevo León (which became the Autonomous University of Nuevo León in 1969) during the 1960s and '70s, but the program still maintained a more technical reputation than that of the National School of Economics (interview, Bolaños Lozano 5/29/96).

23. The original 1946 curriculum was not available.

CHAPTER FIVE

THE BREAKDOWN OF DEVELOPMENTALISM AND THE
POLARIZATION OF MEXICAN ECONOMICS

1. After 1940, Mexican agricultural policy focused on creating viable commercial agriculture in the form of largeholdings rather than small farms, and the government distributed newly irrigated land in much larger units than previously, and to private owners rather than *ejidos* (Reynolds 1977a: 142–43).

2. In 1963, a national student organization was founded in Morelia, Michoacán, largely as a result of the organizing efforts of the Mexican Communist Party (PCM). Conceived as a broad student front, the rhetoric of this group was essentially prodemocratic; significantly, its second national congress was held at the UNAM School of Economics in 1964. This group was an important nucleus for the famous 1968 movement, although by 1968 political sectarianism had caused its decline (Guevara Niebla 1978: 12).

3. It should not be inferred from this, however, that all movement participants were unemployed. Indeed, one interviewee recalled that many participants worked full-time in government jobs and subsequently arrived in suits at after-hours university protests (interview, Ramírez 10/15/96).

4. Bazdresch and Levy distinguish between the "economic" populism of the 1970s and the "political" populism of earlier politicians such as Lázaro Cárdenas, who relied on the support of workers and peasants but not on profligate and inflationary spending.

5. The popularly cited division between the interventionist "structuralists" and more conservative "monetarists" is problematic in several respects. First, it is not clear that such individuals as Horacio Flores de la Peña, Carlos Tello, Javier Alejo, Davíd Ibarra, and José Andrés Oteyza can be grouped together under a single ideological label. Nor were there yet many individuals in Mexican public administration who could rightfully be called "monetarists" in the strong sense of Chicago-school orthodoxy. For example, Basañez (1991) characterized Finance Minister Antonio Ortíz Mena as a "monetarist" when he was neither an economist nor an advocate of free-market radicalism, but rather a lawyer and a fiscal and monetary conservative.

6. For an outline of the major theoretical tenets on which this consensus was based, see Heredia 1996: 81.

7. Indeed, it has been suggested that one of the reasons for such dramatic funding of opportunities for studying abroad was a deliberate government strategy for getting 1968 radical students out of Mexico (Centeno 1994: 152). Also in contrast to Banco de México scholarship recipients—almost all of whom studied economics at the best-known universities of the United States and England—council scholarships funded study at a much more diverse and probably more heterodox group of institutions, which in 1973 included the Nederlandse Economishe in Holland, the University of Napoli in Italy, and the University of Paris (CONACYT 1973: 98–110).

8. Martínez later became a prominent politician for the left opposition party, the Party of the Democratic Revolution (PRD).

9. It has been pointed out to me that although the official course titles and descriptions were Marxist in character, the frequent teaching of these courses by non-Marxist professors (particularly in the 1980s and '90s) meant that their content was not necessarily as Marxist as their titles implied (interview, Alvarez Bejar 1/17/97).

10. Between 1950 and 1989, the Banco had a lower than average level of turnover in its directorship (when compared with other central banks), equivalent to that of France and Sweden, and dramatically lower than the average among developing countries (Eijffinger and de Haan 1996: 28).

11. For stylistic reasons, I will refer to this university as the ITAM for the duration of this chapter, although technically the ITM became the autonomous ITAM in 1962.

12. The primary modification of the integrated plan was to develop a common core of required courses for economics, accounting and administration students.

13. In this respect, it is important to note that in contrast to the United States, widespread student loan programs for undergraduates do not exist in Mexico. Scholarship programs for private universities like the ITAM exist but obviously benefit only the most brilliant students from nonelite backgrounds.

14. These individuals included Socrates Rizzo, Manuel Cavazos, and Aurelio Montemayor. Interestingly, many of these individuals were graduates of the University of Nuevo León, which had a rigorous, non-Marxist economics department developed in large measure through the efforts of Banco de México officials (interview, Katz 3/27/96).

15. The relative scarcity of funding in the 1980s and '90s, according to one ITAM professor interviewed, has more recently led to more diverse patterns of postgraduate study in economics, as students are forced to attend programs on the basis of scholarship availability rather than admissions alone. As a result, there has been a recent surge in the proportion of Mexican economists choosing to study in England, with a scholarship program offered through the British Consulate (interview, Espíndola 9/15/96).

16. Although the most-cited theoretical author in theses at the Tech between 1971 and 1975 was Milton Friedman, this author appeared proportionately about half as frequently as he appeared in theses at the ITAM between 1975 and 1977, and other important monetarist and/or Chicago-school authors were not cited.

CHAPTER SIX
THE UNAM AND THE ITAM AFTER 1970

1. Indeed, two foreign-trained economists who studied at the Swarthmore and the London School of Economics recall the UNAM School of Economics as a somewhat uncongenial place to teach (interviews, Sáenz 10/6/95; and Urquidi 9/19/95).

2. This is the same Raymond Barre who is a prominent French politician.

3. The distinction between descriptive statistics and econometric methods can be ambiguous; for example, the calculation of a mean is straightforward and does not require any statistical analysis beyond adding up a column of figures and dividing them by "N." To avoid including such calculations as "econometric methods," I categorized a thesis as containing econometric methods if it utilized summary measures of dispersion, such as standard deviations. Under this definition, t-tests and bivariate regressions counted as "econometrics" but means did not.

4. Moreover, as Mabry (1982) has noted, powerful student organizations have blocked attempts to raise academic standards within the UNAM at several times in Mexican history, and regardless of political predilections.

5. Upon incorporating a graduate program in 1976, the UNAM School of Economics officially became the Faculty of Economics.

6. Given the high rate of inflation in the 1970s, I have assumed that Zermeño refers to a real rather than a nominal increase in professors' salaries, since a nominal increase on this order would amount to a real decrease!

7. Many Mexican academics allege that the UAM was aimed at co-opting ex-student radicals by incorporating them as full-time professors (interview, Aguirre 4/2/96).

8. A illuminating discussion of formal selection mechanisms (and their absence) in public versus private Mexican economics programs can be found in Labarge and Osborn (1977).

9. Although I have no documentation for this, it seems highly likely that the increasing radicalization of the UNAM School of Economics was a key reason for

the CIDE's foundation in the 1970s, since the UNAM was no longer a reliable center for the recruitment of public-sector economists.

10. The CIDE served as a center of Keynesian and left-developmentalist thinking in Mexico until the early 1990s, when it was taken over by U.S.-trained economists associated with the Salinas administration. Since then, the CIDE economics department has developed a reputation for being a top-quality, neoclassically oriented economics program, very much like the ITAM; its graduates go on to prestigious government, business, and academic jobs.

11. President Zedillo was an economics graduate from the "Poli" (the Polytechnical University), a public school that underwent a process of radicalization similar to that of the UNAM. For reasons unknown to me, the central bank economist Leopoldo Solís gave classes at the Poli (and not at the UNAM); Zedillo became Solís's protégé, obtaining a job at the Banco de México and studying economics at Yale (although apparently not with a Banco scholarship).

12. Such study was particularly concentrated among those students who subsequently made their careers in the public sector and in academia (see appendix B).

13. There were also, however, liabilities inherent in these relationships. When Dornbusch began to criticize his former student Aspe's exchange-rate policy in the years leading up to the peso crisis, the Salinas administration allegedly did everything it could to keep Dornbusch from airing these criticisms in Mexico.

14. Foreign language skills were also crucial for applicants for Ford Foundation grants, since Ford required previous acceptance to a foreign program in order to be eligible for the grant (interview, Schreiver 6/18/96).

15. Dezalay and Garth (1998) observe that a parallel process of increasing complexity in financial markets occurred in the United States during the 1970s, leading to the increased private-sector hiring of economics Ph.D.'s from elite universities (pp. 8–9).

16. Observant readers may recall that another ITAM graduate, Gustavo Petricioli, was finance minister during the last years of the De la Madrid administration. However, Petricioli was not known for maintaining such strong old school ties and therefore did not provide as many opportunities to ITAM graduates as did Aspe.

CHAPTER SEVEN
NEOLIBERALISM AND THE RISE OF THE NEW TECHNOCRATS

1. Centeno and Maxfield (1992) point out, however, that de la Madrid was not the only potential candidate with a profile pleasing to foreign investors; domestic politics played into why de la Madrid was selected over technocratic competitors such as Davíd Ibarra.

2. For example, one of Mancera and Silva's former professors at Yale was a director on the board of the Federal Reserve. Paul Volcker, the Federal Reserve's chair, was also familiar with Silva and Mancera from previous Mexican debt negotiations; Volcker subsequently became a mediator between Mexico, on the one hand, and the IMF, U.S. Treasury, and private banks, on the other (Kraft 1984: 8).

3. Preferential treatment of Mexico by the U.S. government and international financial institutions during crisis years, such as 1982 and 1995, can plausibly be

explained as resulting from Mexico's proximity to the United Stgates and the perceived need to keep economic crisis from turning into economic and political chaos. The 1985–92 period, however, was one of economic stagnation rather than economic crisis in Mexico. Therefore, the World Bank's preferential treatment of Mexico during this period is more difficult to explain as resulting from geographical proximity to the United States.

4. Nadal Egea (1996) argues that balance-of-payments exceptions could significantly have diminished the negative effects of the peso crisis of 1994–95.

5. This was Gilberto Loyo, commerce minister from 1952 to 1958. Indeed, according to a reliable source (Víctor Urquidi), Loyo had not studied economics at all.

6. For example, in 1995 alone, 194 Mexican students were studying abroad with Science and Technology funding (CONACYT 1995).

7. Pfeffer and Salancik (1977) observe that the dependence of one organization on another for resources can be gauged based on three factors: (1) the importance of the resource for the receiving organization; (2) the extent to which the donor organization has discretion over the resource; and (3) the extent to which there are alternatives to that resource (p. 45). This theory is useful for considering the dependence of the Mexican state on external finance. Beginning in the 1970s, external debt became more important for the financing of Mexican development. The expansion and institutionalization of external indebtedness during the 1970s and '80s essentially magnified the first condition. Moreover, the third condition—lack of alternatives—was magnified by the activism of the International Monetary Fund, which organized the creditors into a single bloc (Cline 1995: 206).

8. The Inter-American Development Bank was not founded until the 1960s.

9. In reviewing World Bank lending to Mexico in the mid-1950s, Thompson (1979) shows that the World Bank "implied" that its support was contingent on Mexico's adoption of sound financial policies; he also concludes that these proposed requirements ". . . were probably not inflexible. Considering the close and developing relationship between Mexico and the World Bank, the essential requirement was that Mexico convince the World Bank that its policies were sound from the points of view of development and stability" (p. 117).

CHAPTER EIGHT
THE GLOBALIZATION OF ECONOMIC EXPERTISE

1. The most recent trend at the ITAM has been for the professors without Ph.D.'s from U.S. universities to be concentrated in the Department of Economics, where they are responsible for the bulk of undergraduate teaching; economists with more prestigious credentials are concentrated in the ITAM's Center for Economic Research (CIE), where they are sheltered from undergraduate teaching responsibilities.

2. Another goal realized by the foundations was the promotion of area studies in the United States, to help create a corps of academic experts on developing nations (Berman 1983: 99–125).

REFERENCES

Abbott, Andrew. 1988. *The System of Professions: An Essay on the Division of Expert Labor.* Chicago: University of Chicago Press.

Aguilera Schaufenberger, Evangelina. 1958. "El banco central en la política de desarrollo." Undergraduate thesis, School of Economics, UNAM.

Alanís Gómez, Elmo. 1969. "Monterrey y sus economistas." Undergraduate thesis, School of Economics, Autonomous University of Nuevo León.

Alemán, Ricardo. 1996. "Confía Zedillo en los logros que se alcancen en Chiapas." *La Jornada,* February 17: 8.

Ambirajan, S. 1981. "India: The Aftermath of Empire." In Coats, ed., 1981: 98–132.

———. 1996. "The Professionalization of Economics in India." In Coats, ed., 1996: 80–96.

Anaya Díaz, Alfonso. 1979. "Ponencia sobre la Facultad de Economía." Paper read at UNAM Congreso de Docencia Universitaria, 8–11 October 1979.

Andrade Muñoz, Carlos. 1945. "La tributación en México y la función social del impuesto sobre la renta." Undergraduate thesis, School of Economics, UNAM.

"Aníbal de Iturbide, fundador de la Asociación Mexicana de Cultura." 1988. *Opción* 8 (40): 8.

ANUIES (Asociación Nacional de Universidades e Institutos de Educación Superior). Various years. *Anuario estadístico.*

———. Various years. *La enseñanza superior en México.*

Aranda Izguerra, Carlos José. 1976. "La economía chilena de 1964 a 1973." Undergraduate thesis, School of Economics, UNAM.

Arroyo, Pablo. 1975. "Introducción." *Investigación económica* 34 (135): 409–14.

Aslanbeigui, Nahid, and Verónica, Montecinos. 1998. "Foreign Students in U.S. Doctoral Programs." *Journal of Economic Perspectives* 12 (3): 171–82.

Ayala Espino, José. 1988. *Estado y desarrollo: La formación de la economía mixta mexicana (1920–1982).* México: Fondo de Cultura Económica.

Ayala Espino, José, José Blanco, and Pedro Paz. 1978. "Consideraciones sobre la investigación de la economía mexicana." *El economista mexicano* 12 (3): 31–35.

Azis, Iwan J. 1994. "Indonesia." In Williamson, ed., 1994: 385–425.

Babb, Sarah. 1998. "The Evolution of Economic Expertise in a Developing Country: Mexican Economics, 1929–1998." Ph.D. dissertation, Department of Sociology, Northwestern University.

Babb, Sarah, and Marion Fourcade-Gourinchas. 2000. "Social Learning in the Global Village: Paths to Neoliberalism in Four Countries." Paper presented at the Globalization and Politics: Opening the Black Box miniconference, cosponsored by the Political Economy of the World System and Political Sociology sections of the American Sociological Association, August 11, 2000, Washington, D.C.

Backhouse, Roger E. 1996. "The Changing Character of British Economics." In Coats, ed., 1996: 33–60.

——. 1998. "The Transformation of U.S. Economics, 1929–1960, Viewed through a Survey of Journal Articles." In Morgan and Rutherford, eds., 1998: 85–107.

Baker, Stephen, and Elizabeth Weiner. 1992. "Latin America: The Big Move to Free Markets." *Business Week*, June 15: 50–55.

Banco de México. 1946. *Memoria: Primera reunión de técnicos sobre problemas de banca central del continente americano.* México: Banco de México.

——. 1999. Official Website.

Banco de México, Departamento de Capacitación de Personal. 1987. "Estudios de posgrado en el extranjero patrocinados por el Banco de México para formar a sus funcionarios y técnicos de 1944 a 1986." Unpublished internal document.

Banco de México, Departamento de Investigaciones Industriales. 1961. *Programas de becas y datos profesionales de los becarios.* México: Banco de México.

Barba, Arturo. 2001. "Ciencia para prioridades nacionales: Entrevista con Jaime Porada Avila, Director General del CONACYT." *Reforma*, February 16.

Barber, William. 1981. "The United States: Economists in a Pluralistic Policy." In Coats, ed., 1981: 180.

Barrera, Manuel. 1998. "Macroeconomic Adjustment in Chile and the Politics of the Popular Sectors." In Oxhorn, Philip D., and Graciela Ducatenzeiler, eds., *What Kind of Democracy? What Kind of Market? Latin America in the Age of Neoliberalism.* University Park, Pa.: Penn State Press: 127–50.

Barrosco Castro, Francisco José. 1961. "El papel del licenciado de economía como asesor técnico en la iniciativa privada." Undergraduate thesis, School of Economics, UNAM.

Basañez, Miguel. 1991. *La lucha por la hegemonía en México 1968–1990.* México, D.F.: Siglo XXI.

Bazant, Jan. 1968. *Historia de la deuda exterior de México.* México, D.F.: El Colegio de México.

Bazdresch, Carlos, and Santiago Levy. 1991. "Populism and Economic Policy in Mexico, 1970–1982." In Dornbusch, Rudiger, and Sebastian Edwards, eds., *The Macroeconomics of Populism in Latin America.* Chicago: University of Chicago Press: 223–62.

Bennett, Douglas, and Kenneth Sharpe. 1980. "The State as Banker and Entrepreneur: The Last-Resort Character of the Mexican State's Economic Intervention, 1917–76." *Comparative Politics* 12 (2): 165–89.

Berg, Trond. 1981. "Norway: The Powerful Servants." In Coats, ed., 1981: 133–74.

Berman, Edward H. 1983. *The Ideology of Philanthropy: The Influence of the Carnegie, Ford, and Rockefeller Foundations on American Foreign Policy.* Albany, N.Y.: SUNY-Albany.

Biersteker, Thomas J. 1992. "The 'Triumph' of Neoclassical Economics in the Developing World: Policy Convergence and Bases of Governance in the International Economic Order." In Rosenau, James N., and Ernst-Otto Czempiel, eds.,

Governance without Government: Order and Change in World Politics. Cambridge: Cambridge University Press: 102–31.

Biggart, Nicole Woolsey, and Mauro Guillén. 1999. "Developing Difference: Social Organization and the Rise of the Auto Industries of South Korea, Taiwan, Spain, and Argentina." *American Sociological Review* 64: 722–47.

Blair, Calvin P. 1964. "Nacional Financiera: Entrepreneurship in a Mixed Economy." In Vernon, Raymond, ed., *Public Policy and Private Enterprise in Mexico.* Cambridge, Mass.: Harvard University Press.

Boletín ITAM. 1970. November–December.

Boletín ITAM. 1976. January.

Boli, John, and Francisco O. Ramírez. 1986. "World Culture and the Institutional Development of Mass Education." In Richardson, John G., ed., *Handbook of Theory and Research for the Sociology of Education.* New York: Greenwood Press: 65–90.

Boli, John, and George M. Thomas. 1997. "World Culture in the World Polity: A Century of International Non-Governmental Organizations." *American Sociological Review* 62 (2): 171–90.

———, eds. 1999. *Constructing World Culture: International Nongovernmental Organizations since 1875.* Stanford, Calif.: Stanford University Press.

Botas Santos, Eduardo. 1944. "Teoría económica y liberalismo." Undergraduate thesis, School of Economics, UNAM.

Bravo Aguilera, Luis. 1958. "El mercado de capitales de México." Undergraduate thesis, School of Economics, UNAM.

Bravo Jiménez, Manuel. 1982. "Con Gonzalo Robles, 1946–1980." In Baldovinos Gabriel, René Becerra, et. al., eds., *Economía e industrialización,* México: Fondo de Cultura Económica: 244–48.

Brigada "José Carlos Mariátegui." 1971. *Ante la destitución del Lic. Lobato como Director de la ENE.* Political pamphlet from the Collection of the Library of the UNAM Faculty of Economics.

Brigada "Miguel Enríquez." 1974. *Proposiciones para la transformación de la ENE.* Political pamphlet from the Collection of the Library of the UNAM Faculty of Economics.

Buchanan, James M., Robert D. Tollison, and Gordon Tullock, eds. 1980. *Toward a Theory of Rent-Seeking Society.* College Station: Texas A&M University Press.

Buchanan, Ron, and Reginald Rhein, Jr. 1985. "A First Step toward Freer Trade with the U.S." *Business Week,* February 6.

Burrage, Michael, and Rolf Torstendahl. 1990. *Professions in Theory and History: Rethinking the Study of the Professions.* London: Sage Publications.

Callan, Patrick M., and Joni E. Finney, eds. 1997. *Public and Private Financing of Higher Education: Shaping Public Policy for the Future.* Phoenix, Ariz.: Oryx Press.

Camp, Roderic A. 1975. "The National School of Economics and Public Life in Mexico." *Latin American Research Review* 10 (3): 137–51.

———. 1977. *The Role of Economists in Policy-Making: A Comparative Case Study of Mexico and the United States.* Tucson: University of Arizona Press.

Camp, Roderic A. 1980. *Mexico's Leaders: Their Education and Recruitment.* Tucson: University of Arizona Press.

———. 1984. *The Making of a Government: Political Leaders in Modern Mexico.* Tucson: University of Arizona Press.

———. 1985. "The Political Technocrat in Mexico and the Survival of the Political System." *Latin American Research Review* 20 (1): 97–118.

———. 1989. *Entrepreneurs and Politics in Twentieth-Century Mexico.* New York: Oxford University Press.

———. 1991. *Mexican Political Biographies, 1884–1935.* Austin: University of Texas Press.

———. 1994. *Mexican Political Biographies, 1935–1993.* Austin: University of Texas Press.

———. 1995. *Political Recruitment across Two Centuries.* Austin: University of Texas Press.

Campbell, John L., and Leon N. Lindberg. 1990. "Property Rights and the Organization of Economic Activity by the State." *American Sociological Review* 55 (10): 634–47.

Caplow, Theodore. 1954. *The Sociology of Work.* Minneapolis: University of Minnesota Press.

Cárdenas, Enrique. 1994. *La hacienda pública y la política económica, 1929–1958.* México, D.F.: Fondo de Cultura Económica.

———. 1996. *La política económica en México, 1950–1994.* México, D.F.: Fondo de Cultura Económica.

Cardoso, Fernando Henrique, and Enzo Faletto. 1979. *Dependency and Development in Latin America.* Translated by Marjory Mattingly Urquidi. Berkeley: University of California Press.

Carr, Barry. 1992. *Marxism and Communism in Twentieth-Century Mexico.* Lincoln: University of Nebraska Press.

"La carrera de economista." 1929. *El economista*, February 16: 6.

Cassidy, John. 1996. "The Decline of Economics." *The New Yorker* 2 (37): 50–60.

Centeno, Miguel Angel. 1993. "The New Leviathan: The Dynamics and Limits of Technocracy." *Theory and Society* 22: 307–35.

———. 1994. *Democracy within Reason: Technocratic Revolution in Mexico.* 1st edition. College Station: Pennsylvania State University Press.

———. 1997. *Democracy within Reason: Technocratic Revolution in Mexico.* 2nd edition. University Park: Pennsylvania State University Press.

Centeno, Miguel Angel, and Sylvia Maxfield. 1992. "The Marriage of Finance and Order: Changes in the Mexican Political Elite." *Journal of Latin American Studies* 24 (1): 57–85.

Centeno, Miguel Angel, and Patricio Silva, eds. 1998. *The Politics of Expertise in Latin America.* New York: St. Martin's Press.

Ceruzzi, Paul E. 1998. *A History of Modern Computing.* Cambridge, Mass.: MIT Press.

Cervantes Delgado, Alejandro. 1958. "Aspectos del gasto público y de la tributación en México." Undergraduate thesis, School of Economics, UNAM.

Chandler, Raymond. 1977. *The Visible Hand: The Managerial Revolution in American Business*. Cambridge, Mass.: Belknap Press.

"Un Chicago boy entre nosotros." 1978. Interview with Prof. Fernando Sánchez Ugarte. *Intramuros* (ITAM student newsletter) 1 (3): 2–3.

Choi, Young Back. 1996. "The Americanization of Economics in Korea." In Coats, ed., 1996: 97–122.

Chumacero, Alí. 1980. "Breve historia." In *Libro conmemorativo del 45° aniversario del Fondo de Cultura Económica*. México, D.F.: Fondo de Cultura Económica: 9–12.

Cleaves, Peter S. 1987. *Professions and the State: The Mexican Case*, Tucson: University of Arizona Press.

Cline, William R. 1995. *International Debt Reexamined*. Washington, D.C.: Institute for International Economics.

Coase, Ronald H. 1983. "The New Institutional Economics." *Journal of Institutional and Theoretical Economics* 140: 229–31.

Coats, A. W. 1996. Introduction. In Coats, ed., 1996: 1–11.

Coats, A. W., ed. 1981. *Economists in Government: An International Comparative Study*. Durham, N.C.: Duke University Press.

———. 1986. *Economists in International Agencies: An Exploratory Study*. New York: Praeger.

———. 1992. *On the History of Economic Thought: British and American Economic Essays*. Vol. 1. London: Routledge.

———. 1996. *The Post-1945 Internationalization of Economics*. Durham, N.C.: Duke University Press.

Cockcroft, James D. 1968. *Intellectual Precursors of the Mexican Revolution, 1900–1913*. Austin: University of Texas Press.

Cocks, Geoffrey and Kondrad H. Jarausch, eds. 1990. *German Professions, 1800–1950*. New York: Oxford University Press.

Colander, Arjo, and David Klamer. 1990. *The Making of an Economist*. Boulder: Westview Press.

Collins, Randall. 1979. *The Credential Society: An Historical Sociology of Education and Stratification*. Orlando: Academic Press.

Combined Mexican Working Party. 1953. *The Economic Development of Mexico*. Baltimore: The Johns Hopkins University Press.

Comisión Coordinadora del Foro de Transformación de la ENE. 1974. Political pamphlet from the Collection of the Library of the UNAM Faculty of Economics.

Comisión Organizada de Alumnos de la ENE et al. 1971. *La verdad en el problema de la Escuela Nacional de Economía*. Political pamphlet from the Collection of the Library of the UNAM Faculty of Economics.

CONACYT. 1973. *Informe de labores*. México: CONACYT.

———. 1974. *Consideraciones sobre el papel del CONACYT en el sistema nacional de ciencia y tecnología*. México: CONACYT.

———. 1995. *Becarios del CONACYT en el extranjero*. México: CONACYT.

———. 1997. *Indicadores de actividades científicas y tecnológicas*. México: CONACYT.

————. 1998. *Indicadores de actividades científicas y tecnológicas*. México: CONACYT.

Conaghan, Catherine. 1998. "Stars of the Crisis: The Ascent of Economists in Peruvian Public Life." In Centeno and Silva, eds., 1998: 142–64.

Consejo Universitario archives. 1931a. January 21.

Consejo Universitario archives. 1931b. January 26.

Consultores de Estudios y Proyectos, S.C. 1993. *Perfil del economista demandado en el mercado de trabajo*. México: Consultores de Estudios y Proyectos.

Contla Caceres, Raúl. 1976. "La importancia económica del los distritos de riego en México, el caso del distrito de riego de Valsequillo, Puebla." Undergraduate thesis, School of Economics, UNAM.

Cordera, Rolando, and Carlos Tello. 1981. *México: La disputa por la nación*. México, D.F.: Siglo XXI.

Córdoba, José. 1994. "Mexico." In Williamson, ed., 1994: 232–84.

Córdova, Arnaldo. 1973. *La ideología de la revolución mexicana: La formación del nuevo régimen*. México: Ediciones Era.

Corona Rentería, Alfonso. 1971. "Crónica de la revista Investigación económica." *Investigación económica* 1 (21): 7–12.

Cortés, Fernando. 2000. *Procesos sociales y desigualdad económica en México*. México, D.F.: Siglo XXI.

Cosío Villegas, Daniel. 1977. *Memorias*. México: Joaquín Mortíz.

Cueto, Marcos, ed. 1994. *Missionaries of Science: The Rockefeller Foundation and Latin America*. Bloomington: Indiana University Press.

Cukierman, Alex. 1992. *Central Bank Strategy, Credibility, and Independence: Theory and Evidence*. Cambridge, Mass.: MIT Press.

Dagnino Pastore, José María. 1989. "Argentina." In Pechman, Joseph A., ed., 1989, *The Role of the Economist in Government: An International Perspective*. New York: New York University Press.

De la Peña, Moisés. 1936. "El problema agrícola nacional." Undergraduate thesis, School of Economics, UNAM.

————. 1942. "Los economistas: Los técnicos y los espontáneos." *Revista de economía*: January 20: 32–34.

Dezalay, Yves, and Bryant Garth. 1990. "The *Big Bang* and the Law: The Internationalization and Restructuration of the Legal Field." In Featherstone, Mike, ed., *Global Culture: Nationalism, Globalization and Modernity*. London: Sage Publications: 281–93.

————. 1995. "Building the Law and Putting the State into Play: International Strategies among Mexico's Divided Elite." American Bar Foundation Working Paper #9509.

————. 1996. "Political Crises as Professional Battlegrounds: Technocratic and Philanthropic Challenges to the Dominance of the Cosmopolitan Lawyer-Statesman in Brazil." American Bar Foundation Working Paper #9612.

————. 1997. *Dealing in Virtue*. Chicago: University of Chicago Press.

————. 1998. "Le 'Washington consensus': Contribution à une sociologie de l'hégémonie du néolibéralisme." *Actes de la recherche en sciences sociales* 121–22 (March): 3–22.

Díaz Alejandro, Carlos F. 1984. "Latin America in the 1930s." In Thorp, Rosemary, ed., *Latin America in the 1930s*. London: Macmillan Press: 17–49.

Díaz Martínez, Gabino. 1943. "Algunas consideraciones sobre el fomento industrial de México." Undergraduate thesis, School of Economics, UNAM.

DiMaggio, Paul J., and Walter W. Powell. 1983. "The Iron Cage Revisited: Institutional Isomorphism and Collective Rationality in Organizational Fields." *American Sociological Review* 48: 147–60.

Dobbin, Frank. 1994. *Forging Industrial Policy: The United States, Britain, and France in the Railway Age*. New York: Cambridge University Press.

Domínguez, Jorge I., ed. 1997. *Technopols: Freeing Politics and Markets in Latin America in the 1990s*. University Park, Pa.: Pennsylvania State University Press.

Drake, Paul W., ed. 1994. *Money Doctors, Foreign Debts, and Economic Reforms in Latin America from the 1890s to the Present*. Wilmington, Del.: Jaguar Books.

"Economic Policy: Qualified." 1993. *The Economist*, August 14: 63.

"Economistas, ¿Veleidad de Banqueros?" 1988. Reprinted in *Opción* 8 (40): 13–14.

Edelman, Lauren B., Stephen Petterson, Elizabeth Chambliss, and Howard S. Erlanger. 1991. "Legal Ambiguity and the Politics of Compliance: Affirmative Action Officers' Dilemma." *Law and Policy* 13 (1): 73–97.

Edwards, Sebastian. 1995. *Crisis and Reform in Latin America: From Despair to Hope*. New York: Oxford University Press.

Eichengreen, Barry. 1994. "House Calls of the Money Doctor: The Kemmerer Missions to Latin America, 1917–1931." In Drake, ed., 1994: 110–132.

Eijffinger, Sylvester C. W., and Jakob de Haan. 1996. "The Political Economy of Central-Bank Independence." In *Special Papers in International Economics* 19. Princeton, N.J.: International Finance Section, Department of Economics, Princeton University.

El Fisgón. 1995. "Optica Neoliberal." Political cartoon in *La Jornada*, August 17.

"Encuentro nacional de escuelas de economía y centros de investigación económica." 1976. *Economía informa* 3 (21): 1–4.

"Entrevista al Señor Rector." 1981. *Opción* 5: 6–7.

Escobar Cerda, Luis. 1953. "El desarrollo de la enseñanza de la economía." *Panorama económico* 92: 385.

Escuela de Economía, ITAM. 1965. *Plan de estudios*. México, D.F.

Escuela Nacional de Economía, UNAM. 1959. *Anuario*. UNAM Escuela Nacional de Economía. México D.F.

Esping-Anderson, Gösta. 1990. *The Three Worlds of Welfare Capitalism*. Princeton, N.J.: Princeton University Press.

Evans, Peter. 1979. *Dependent Development: The Alliance of Multinational, State, and Local Capital in Brazil*. Princeton, N.J.: Princeton University Press.

———. 1992. "The State as Problem and Solution: Predation, Embedded Autonomy, and Structural Change." In Haggard and Kaufman, eds., 1992: 139–81.

———. 1995. *Embedded Autonomy: States and Industrial Transformation*. Princeton, N.J.: Princeton University Press.

Evans, Peter B., Dietrich Rueschemeyer, and Theda Skocpol, eds. 1985. *Bringing the State Back In.* Cambridge: Cambridge University Press.

Facultad de Economía, UNAM. 1986. *Plan de estudios.* México, D.F.

Felix, David. 1982. "Income Distribution Trends in Mexico and the Kuznets Curves." In Hewlett, Sylvia Ann, and Richard S. Weinert, eds., *Brazil and Mexico: Patterns in Late Development.* Philadelphia: ISHI: 265–316.

Fernández, José. 2000. "Down to Business: Mexico's Economic Future as Seen through the Presidential Candidates' Eyes." *Business Mexico,* April 1.

Fernández Lozano, Ma. Teresa. 1978. "La formación del economista en México." *El economista mexicano* 12 (3): 21–26.

Filgueira, Fernando. 2000. "Economic and Social Development in the Southern Cone of Latin America: Revisiting Politics." Ph.D. dissertation, Department of Sociology, Northwestern University.

Flores, Edmundo. n.d. "La facultad de economía de la UNAM y el ITAM, crónica de una dolorosa autodestrucción." Unpublished paper. México, D.F.

"FMI: La recuperación mexicana va 'sorpredentemente bien.'"

Fondo de Cultura Económica. 1988. *Libro conmemorativo del 45° aniversario del Fondo de Cultura Económica.* México: Fondo de Cultura Económica.

———. 1996. *La Jornada* July 1: 54.

"Foro de transformación." 1975. *Economía informa* 2 (7): 2.

Fourcade-Gourinchas, Marion. 1998. "Identity Construction in Nineteenth Century Economics: National Trajectories and the Structure of Western Polities." Paper presented at the annual conference of the Social Science History Association, Chicago.

———. 2000. "The National Trajectories of Economic Knowledge: Discipline and Profession in the United States, Great Britain and France." Ph.D. dissertation, Department of Sociology, Harvard University.

Franko, Patrice. 1999. *The Puzzle of Latin American Economic Development.* New York: Rowman and Littlefield.

Fraser, Damian. 1992. "Mexico's Growing Intimacy with World Bank." *Financial Times,* March 3: 7.

Freidson, Eliot. 1970. *Profession of Medicine.* New York: Dodd, Mead.

Frey, Bruno S., and Reiner Eichenberger. 1993. "American and European Economics and Economists." *Journal of Economic Perspectives* 7 (4): 185–93.

Frey, Bruno S., Werner W. Pommerehne, Friedrich Schneider, and Guy Gilbert. 1984. "Consensus and Dissension among Economists: An Empirical Inquiry." *American Economic Review* 74 (5): 986–94.

Frieden, Jeffrey A. 1991. *Debt, Development, and Democracy: Modern Political Economy in Latin America, 1965–1985.* Princeton, N.J.: Princeton University Press.

Fuentes-Berain, Rossana. 1993. "Miguel Angel Mancera: Banco de México Head Has Spent a Lifetime Bucking Economic Currents." *El financiero inernational,* August 9: 15.

Fulbright-García Robles, Mexico City Office. 1996. Unpublished database of Mexican scholarship recipients, 1970–1995.

Furner, Mary O. 1975. *Advocacy and Objectivity: A Crisis in the Professionalization of American Social Science.* Lexington: University of Kentucky Press.

Furner, Mary O., and Barry Supple. 1990. *The State and Economic Knowledge: The American and British Experiences.* New York: Cambridge University Press.

Gao, Bai. 1997. *Economic Ideology and Japanese Industrial Policy.* New York: Cambridge University Press.

García Duarte, Alberto. 1959. "El desarrollo económico de los países subdesarrollados." Undergraduate thesis, School of Economics, ITM.

Geddes, Barbara. 1990. "Building 'State' Autonomy in Brazil, 1930–1964." *Comparative Politics* 22 (2): 217–35.

George, Susan, and Fabrizio Sabelli. 1994. *Faith and Credit: The World Bank's Secular Empire.* London: Penguin.

Gerschenkron, Alexander. 1962. *Economic Backwardness in Historical Perspective.* Cambridge, Mass.: Belknap Press.

Gil Díaz, Francisco. 1984. "Mexico's Path from Stability to Inflation." In Harberger, Arnold C., ed., 1984. *World Economic Growth.* San Francisco: Institute for Contemporary Studies: 333–76.

Golob, Stephanie R. 1997. "Making Possible What Is Necessary: Pedro Aspe, the Salinas Team, and the Next Mexican 'Miracle.'" In Domínguez 1997: 95–143.

González, Luis. 1981. *Los días del presidente Cárdenas.* Historia de la Revolución Mexicana, vol. 15. México: El Colegio de México.

González Casanova, Pablo. 1965. *La democracia en México.* México: Ediciones Era.

Goodman, John B. 1992. *Monetary Sovereignty: The Politics of Central Banking in Western Europe.* Ithaca, N.Y.: Cornell University Press.

Goodwin, Crauford. 1998. "The Patrons of Economics in a Time of Transformation." In Morgan and Rutherford, eds., 1998: 53–81.

Gray, John. 1999. "Bursting Bubbles." *The Guardian*, January 26: 16.

Grindle, Merilee. 1977. *Bureaucrats, Politicians, and Peasants in Mexico.* Berkeley: University of California Press.

Groenewegen, Peter. 1996. "The Australian Experience." In Coats, ed., 1996: 61–79.

Grupo Síntesis. 1973. *Projecto de restructuración de planes y programas y formas de gobierno de la ENE.* Political pamphlet from the Collection of the Library of the UNAM Faculty of Economics.

Guerra Cepeda, Roberto. 1939. "El ejido colectivizado en la Comarca Lagunera." Undergraduate thesis, School of Economics, UNAM.

Guevara Niebla, Gilberto. 1978. "Antecedentes y desarrollo del movimiento de 1968." *Cuadernos Políticos* 17: 8–33.

———. 1990. *La rosa de los cambios: Breve historia de la UNAM.* México: Cal y Arena.

Guillén, Mauro F. 1989. *La profesión de economista: El auge de economistas, ejecutivos y empresarios en España.* Barcelona: Ariel.

———. 1994. *Models of Management: Work, Authority, and Organization in a Comparative Perspective.* Chicago: University of Chicago Press.

Gurría, José Angel, and Sergio Fadl. 1995. "Mexico's Strategy for Reducing Financial Transfers Abroad." In Grosse, Robert, ed., *Government Responses to the Latin American Debt Problem.* Miami: North-South Center Press: 121–58.

Gutiérrez, Gumaro N. 1944. "Algunos aspectos de los seguros." Undergraduate thesis, School of Economics, UNAM.

Haber, Stephen H. 1989. *Industry and Underdevelopment: The Industrialization of Mexico, 1890–1940*. Stanford, Calif.: Stanford University Press.

Haggard, Stephan. 1990. *Pathways from the Periphery: The Politics of Growth in the Newly Industrializing Countries*. Ithaca, N.Y.: Cornell University Press.

Haggard, Stephan, and Robert R. Kaufman, eds. 1992. *The Politics of Economic Adjustment: International Conflicts and the State*. Princeton, N.J.: Princeton University Press.

Haggard, Stephan, and Sylvia Maxfield, eds. 1993. *The Politics of Finance in Developing Countries*. Ithaca, N.Y.: Cornell University Press.

Hall, Peter. 1993. "Policy Paradigms, Social Learning, and the State: The Case of Economic Policymaking in Britain." *Comparative Politics* 25 (3): 275–96.

———, ed. 1986. *Governing the Economy: The Politics of State Intervention in Britain and France*. Cambridge: Polity Press.

——— ed. 1989. *The Political Power of Economic Ideas: Keynesianism across Nations*. Princeton, N.J.: Princeton University Press.

Halliday, Terence C., and Bruce G. Carruthers. 1996. "The Moral Regulation of Markets: Professions, Privatization and the English Insolvency Act 1986." *Accounting, Organizations, and Society* 21 (4): 371–413.

Hamilton, Gary G., and Nicole Woolsey Biggart. 1988. "Market, Culture, and Authority: A Comparative Analysis of Management and Organization in the Far East." *American Journal of Sociology* 94 (supplement): S52–S94.

Hamilton, Nora. 1982. *The Limits of State Autonomy: Post-revolutionary Mexico*. Princeton, N.J.: Princeton University Press.

Hansen, Roger D. 1971. *The Politics of Mexican Development*. Baltimore: The Johns Hopkins University Press.

Harberger, Arnold. 1996. "Good Economics Comes to Latin America, 1955–95." In Coats, ed., 1996: 301–11.

Harrison, Ann, and Gordon Hanson. 1999. "Who Gains from Trade Reform? Some Remaining Puzzles." *Journal of Development Economics* 59: 125–54.

Heidenheimer, Arnold J. 1989. "Professional Knowledge and State Policy in Comparative Historical Perspective: Law and Medicine in Britain, Germany and the United States." *International Social Science Journal* 122: 529–53.

Heimer, Carol A., and Mitchell L. Stevens. 1997. "Caring for the Organization: Social Workers as Frontline Risk Managers in Neonatal Intensive Care Units." *Work and Occupations* 24 (2): 133–63.

Helleiner, Eric. 1994. *States and the Reemergence of Global Finance*. Ithaca, N.Y.: Cornell University Press.

Heredia, Blanca. 1996. *Contested State: The Politics of Trade Liberalization in Mexico*. Ph.D. dissertation, Department of Political Science, Columbia University.

Hernández de la Mora, Jenaro. 1958. "Los gastos corrientes del gobierno federal." Undergraduate thesis, School of Economics, UNAM.

Hernández Rodríguez, Rogelio. 1987. "Los hombres del presidente de la Madrid ." *Foro internacional* 109: 5–38.

Herrera Domínguez, José. 1958. "Excedentes, mercado común e integración económica." Undergraduate thesis, School of Economics, UNAM.

Hirschman, Albert O. 1961. "Ideologies of Developmentalism in Latin America." In Hirschman, Albert O., ed., *Latin American Issues and Comments*. New York: The Twentieth Century Fund: 7–24.

———. 1971. *A Bias for Hope: Essays on Development and Latin America*. New Haven, Conn.: Yale University Press.

———. 1981. *Essays in Trespassing: Economics to Politics and Beyond*. Cambridge: Cambridge University Press.

Hollingsworth, J. Rogers, and Robert Boyer, eds. 1997. *Contemporary Capitalism: The Embeddedness of Institutions*. Cambridge: Cambridge University Press.

Hollingsworth, J. Rogers, Philippe C. Schmitter, and Wolfgang Streeck, eds. 1994. *Governing Capitalist Economies: Performance and Control of Economic Sectors*. New York: Oxford University Press.

Holloway, Nigel, Ahmed Rashid, Rigoberto Tiglao, and Timothy Maples. 1996. "Home Truths." *Far Eastern Economic Review*, December 5: 60–63.

Hornedo, Eduardo. 1934. "La desorientación económica de México." Undergraduate thesis, School of Economics, UNAM.

Hutt, W. H. 1936. *Economists and the Public: A Study of Competition and Opinion*. London: Jonathan Cape.

Ikeo, Aiko. 1996. "The Internationalization of Economics in Japan." In Coats, ed., 1996: 123–41.

INEGI. 1994. *Estadísticas históricas de México*. Vol. 1. México, D.F.

———. 2000. Sistema de cuenatas nacionales de México. México, D.F.

Institute for International Education (IIE). 1953. *Open Doors*. Washington, D.C.: IIE.

———. 1954. *Education for One World*. Washington, D.C.: IEE.

———. 1970. *Education for One World*. Washington, D.C.: IEE.

ITESM. 1968. *Facultad de Economía, XIII aniversario*. Monterrey, Nuevo León, México.

ITM. 1951. *Catálogo*. México, D.F.

Izquierdo, Rafael. 1964. "Protectionism in Mexico." In Vernon, Raymond, ed., *Public Policy and Private Enterprise in Mexico*. Cambridge, Mass.: Harvard University Press: 243–85.

———. 1995. *Política hacendaria del desarrollo estabilizador, 1958–1970*. México: Fondo de Cultura Económica.

Johnson, Harry G. 1973. "National Styles in Economic Research: The United States, the United Kingdom, Canada, and Various European Countries." *Daedalus* 102 (2): 65–74.

———. 1977. "Economics and the Radical Challenge: The Hard Social Science and the Soft Social Reality." In Ben-David, Joseph, and Terry Nichols Clark, eds., *Culture and Its Creators*. Chicago: University of Chicago Press: 97–118.

Johnson, Hazel J. 1995. *Banking without Borders: Challenges and Opportunities in the Era of North American Free Trade and the Emerging Global Marketplace*. Chicago: Probus Publishing.

Kahan Pintel, Alejandro. 1958. "Inestabilidad de los mercados de exportación y desarrollo económico (el caso de México)." Undergraduate thesis, School of Economics, UNAM.

Kahler, Miles. 1990. "Orthodoxy and Its Alternatives: Explaining Approaches to Stabilization and Adjustment." In Nelson, ed., 1990: 33–61.

———. 1992. "External Influence, Conditionality, and the Politics of Adjustment." In Haggard and Kaufman, eds., 1992: 89–138.

Keohane, Robert O., and Helen V. Milner, eds. 1996. *Internationalization and Domestic Politics.* Cambridge: Cambridge University Press.

King, Timothy. 1970. *Mexico: Industrialization and Trade Policies since 1940.* New York: Oxford University Press.

Kinney Giraldo, Jeanne. 1997. "Democracy in Chile: Aljeandro Foxley." In Domínguez, ed., 1997: 229–75.

Kitschelt, Herbert. 1999. "European Social Democracy between Political Economy and Electoral Competition." In Kitschelt et al., eds., 1999: 317–45.

Kitschelt, Herbert, Peter Lange, Gary Marks, and John D. Stephens, eds. 1999. *Continuity and Change in Contemporary Capitalism.* New York: Cambridge University Press.

Klamer, Arjo, and David Colander. 1990. *The Making of an Economist.* Boulder: Westview Press.

Knight, Alan. 1986. *The Mexican Revolution.* Vol. 2. Cambridge: Cambridge University Press.

———. 1991. "The Rise and Fall of Cardenismo." In Bethell, Leslie, ed., *Mexico since Independence.* Cambridge: Cambridge University Press: 241–88.

Kolko, Gabriel. 1997. *Vietnam: Anatomy of a Peace.* New York: Routledge.

Kolm, Serge-Christophe. 1988. "Economics in Europe and the U.S." *European Economic Review* 32: 207–12.

Kraft, Joseph. 1984. *The Mexican Rescue.* New York: Group of Thirty.

Krause, Elliott A. 1996. *Death of the Guilds: Professions, States, and the Advance of Capitalism, 1930 to the Present.* New Haven, Conn.: Yale University Press.

Krauze, Enrique. 1980. *Daniel Cosío Villegas.* México: Editorial Terra Nova.

———. 1985. *Caudillos culturales en la revolución mexicana.* México: Siglo XXI.

———. 1997. *La presidencia imperial: Ascenso y caída del sistema político mexicano (1940–1996).* México: Tusquets.

Krueger, Anne O. 1974. "The Political Economy of the Rent-Seeking Society." *American Economic Review* 64 (3): 291–303.

Krugman, Paul R. 1994. *The Age of Diminished Expectations: U.S. Economic Policy in the 1990s.* Cambridge, Mass.: MIT Press.

Kuhn, Thomas. 1962. *The Structure of Scientific Revolutions.* Chicago: University of Chicago Press.

Kuhnle, Stein. 1996. "International Modeling, States, and Statistics: Scandinavian Social Security Solutions in the 1890s." In Rueschemeyer and Skocpol, eds., 1996: 223–63.

Labarge, Richard A., and T. Noel Osborn. 1977. "The Status of Professional Economics Programs in Mexican Universities." *Interamerican Economic Affairs* 31 (1): 3–24.

La Botz, Dan. 1988. *The Crisis of Mexican Labor.* New York: Praeger.

———. 1992. *Mask of Democracy: Labor Suppression in Mexico Today*. Boston: South End Press.

———. 1995. *Democracy in Mexico: Peasant Rebellion and Political Reform*. Boston: South End Press.

Larson, Magali Sarfatti. 1977. *The Rise of Professionalism: A Sociological Analysis*. Berkeley: University of California Press.

Larudee, Mehrene. 1999. "Integration and Income Distribution under the North American Free Trade Agreement: The Experience of Mexico." In Baker, Dean, Gerald Epstein, and Robert Pollin, eds., *Globalization and Progressive Economic Policy*. New York: Cambridge, University Press: 273–92.

Latapí, Pablo. 1980. *Análisis de un sexenio de educación en México, 1970–76*. México: Editorial Nueva Imagen.

Latour, Bruno. 1987. *Science in Action: How to Follow Scientists and Engineers through Society*. London, United Kingdom: Open University Press.

League of Nations. 1920. *International Financial Conference*. Vol. 1. Brussels: Th. Dewarichet.

Levy, Daniel C. 1980. *University and Government in Mexico: Autonomy in an Authoritarian System*. New York: Praeger.

———. 1986. *Higher Education and the State in Latin America*. Chicago: University of Chicago Press.

Lindenfeld, David F. 1990. "The Professionalization of Applied Economics: German Counterparts to Business Administration." In Cocks and Jarausch, eds., 1990: 213–31.

Loaeza, Soledad. 1989. *El llamado de las urnas*. México: Cal y Arena.

Lorey, David. 1994. *The Rise of the Professions in Twentieth-Century Mexico: University Graduates and Occupational Change since 1929*. Los Angeles: UCLS Latin American Center Publications.

Loriaux, Michael. 1991. *France after Hegemony: International Change and Financial Reform*. Ithaca, N.Y.: Cornell University Press.

Loureiro, María Rita. 1996. "The Profession and Political Impacts of the Internationalization of Economics in Brazil." In Coats, ed., 1996: 184–207.

Love, Joseph. 1990. "The Origins of Dependency Analysis." *Journal of Latin American Studies* 22: 143–68.

———. 1996. "Economic Ideas and Ideologies in Latin America since 1930." In Bethell, Leslie, ed., *Ideas and Ideologies in Twentieth Century Latin America*. New York: Cambridge University Press: 207–34.

Loyo, Engracia. 1988. "La lectura en México, 1920–1940." In *Historia de la lectura mexicana*. Mexico: El Colegio de México: 243–94.

———. 1991. "La difusión del Marxismo y la educación socialista en México, 1930–1940." In Hernández Chávez, Alicia, and Manuel Miño Grijalva, eds., *50 años de historia en México*. México: El Colegio de México.

Loyo, Gilberto. 1946a. Letter to Carlos Novoa, April 12. Fondo Universitario, Sección Rectoría, Box 71, Folder 752.

———. 1946b. Letter to Gustavo R. Velasco, July 10. Fondo Universitario, Sección Rectoría, Box 71, Folder 752.

———. 1949. "La profesión de economista." *Investigación económica* 9 (4): 393–402.

Lozano Hernández, Wilfrido. 1988. "La época que nos ha tocado vivir." In *30 años de la vida profesional: generación 1953–1957*. México: UNAM.

Luna Ledesma, Matilde. 1992. *Los empresarios y el cambio político: México, 1970–1987*. México: Ediciones Era.

Lustig, Nora. 1992. *Mexico: The Remaking of an Economy*. Washington, D.C.: The Brookings Institution.

Mabry, Ronald J. 1982. *The Mexican University and the State: Student Conflicts, 1910–1971*. College Station: Texas A&M University Press.

Maddison, Angus, and Associates. 1989. *Brazil and Mexico: The Political Economy of Poverty, Equity and Growth*. New York: Oxford University Press.

Madison, Christopher. 1982. "Exporting Reaganomics—The President Wants to Do Things Differently at AID." *National Journal*, May 29: 960–63.

Mancilla López, Esteban Luis. 1980. "La formación de economistas para el sector público." Undergraduate thesis, Faculty of Economics, UNAM.

March, James G., and Johan P. Olsen. 1984. "The New Institutionalism: Organizational Factors in Political Life." *American Political Science Review* 78: 734–49.

Mares, David R. 1993. "State Leadership in Economic Policy: A Collective Action Framework with a Colombian Case." *Comparative Politics* 25 (4): 455–73.

Markoff, Jonathan, and Verónica Montecinos. 1993. "The Ubiquitous Rise of Economists." *Journal of Public Policy* 13 (1): 37–38.

Márquez Gómez, Juan. 1944. "Estudio económico del garbanzo." Undergraduate thesis, School of Economics, UNAM.

Martínez, Luis, Joel Ortega, and Carlos Molina. 1972. *Proposiciones de trabajo para 1972*. Political pamphlet from the Collection of the Library of the UNAM Faculty of Economics.

Martinussen, John. 1997. *Society, State, and Market: A Guide to Competing Theories of Development*. London: Zed Books.

Maxfield, Sylvia. 1990. *Governing Capital: International Finance and Mexican Politics*. Ithaca, N.Y.: Cornell University Press.

———. 1997. *Gatekeepers of Growth: The International Political Economy of Central Banking in Developing Countries*. Princeton, N.J.: Princeton University Press.

McCarthy, John D., and Mayer N. Zald. 1977. "Resource Mobilization and Social Movements: A Partial Theory." *American Journal of Sociology* 82 (6): 1212–41.

McKeown, Timothy J. 1999. "The Global Economy, Post-Fordism, and Trade Policy in Advanced Capitalist States." In Kitschelt et al., eds., 1999: 11–35.

McNamara, Kathleen R. 1998. *The Currency of Ideas: Monetary Politics in the European Union*. Ithaca, N.Y.: Cornell University Press.

McNeely, Connie L. 1995. *Constructing the Nation-State: International Organization and Prescriptive Action*. Westport, Conn.: Greenwood Press.

Mekler, Ana. 1942. "El impuesto del doce porciento sobre el valor de aforo: Sus repercusiones en la exportación." Undergraduate thesis, School of Economics, UNAM.

"Mexico: An Economic Tornado Devaluation Can't Tame." 1982. *Business Week*, August 23: 40–41.

"Mexico Cuts a Deal That's a Victory for Latin Debtors." 1984. *Business Week*, September 10: 58.

"Mexico under the IMF." 1983. *The Economist*, August 20: 19.

"Mexico's Happy Creditors." 1984. *The Economist*, August 4: 60.

"Mexico's New Man." 1982. *The Economist*, November 27: 14.

Meyer, John W. 1994. "Rationalized Environments." In Scott and Meyer, eds., 1994: 28–54.

Meyer, John W., John Boli, George M. Thomas, and Francisco Ramírez. 1997. "World Society and the Nation-State." *American Journal of Sociology* 103 (1): 144–81.

Michaels, James W. 1992. "We Don't Tax Capital Gains." *Forbes*, August 17: 67–68.

Middlebrook, Kevin. 1995. *The Paradox of Revolution: Labor, the State and Authoritarianism in Mexico*. Baltimore: The Johns Hopkins University Press.

Miller, Morris. 1986. *Coping is Not Enough! The International Debt Crisis and the Roles of the World Bank and the International Monetary Fund*. Homewood, Ill.: Dow-Jones-Irwin.

Moffett, Matt. 1989. "Mexico Loosens Investment Rules for Foreigners." *Wall Street Journal*, May 16: A11.

Montecinos, Verónica. 1988. Economics and Power: Chilean Economists in Government, 1958–1985. Ph.D. dissertation Department of Sociology, University of Pittsburgh.

———. 1993. "Economic Policy Elites and Democratization." *Studies in Comparative International Development* 28 (1): 25–53.

———. 1998. "Economists in Party Politics: Chilean Democracy in the Era of the Markets." In Centeno and Silva, eds., 1998: 126–41.

Mora, Gonzalo. 1935. "El aspecto económico del problema agrario." Undergraduate thesis, School of Economics, UNAM.

Morgan, Mary S., and Malcolm Rutherford, eds. 1998. *From Interwar Pluralism to Postwar Neoclassicism*. Durham, N.C.: Duke University Press.

Mosk, Sanford A. 1954. *Industrial Revolution in Mexico*. Berkeley: University of California Press.

Moulton, Brent R. 1996. "Bias in the Consumer Price Index: What Is the Evidence?" *Journal of Economic Perspectives* 10 (4): 159–77.

Nacional Financiera and Sociedad de Ex-alumnos de la Facultad de Economía de la UNAM. 1994. Videoteca de testimonios para la historia económica de México, testimonio del Lic. Victor Urquidi, November. México, D.F.: Nacional Financiera.

Nadal Egea, Alejandro. 1996. "Balance-of-Payments Provisions in the GATT and NAFTA." *Journal of World Trade* 30 (4): 5–24.

Negrete, Sergio. 1988. "Entrevista a Aníbal de Iturbide, fundador de la Asociación Mexicana de Cultura." *Opción* 8 (40): 9–11.

Nelson, Joan M., ed. 1990. *Economic Crisis and Policy Choice: The Politics of Adjustment in the Third World*. Princeton, NJ: Princeton University Press.

"The New Hero." 1981. *The Economist*, October 3: 68–69.

N'haux, Enrique. 1993. *Menem/Cavalo: El poder Mediterráneo*. Buenos Aires: Ediciones Corregidor.

Nieto L., J. de Jesús. 1986. *Diccionario histórico del México contemporáneo (1900–1982)*. México: Alhambra Mexicana.

Noriega, Margarita. 1985. *La política educativa a través de la política de financiamiento*. México: Universidad Autónoma de Sinaloa.

North, Douglass C. 1990. *Institutions, Institutional Change and Economic Performance*. New York: Cambridge University Press.

Nuñez, Eric. 1998. "New Costa Rican President Assumes Office Promising Better Economy." Associated Press, May 8.

O'Donnell, Guillermo A. 1973. *Modernization and Bureaucratic-Authoritarianism: Studies in South American Politics*. Berkeley: Institute of International Studies.

Ormerod, Paul. 1994. *The Death of Economics*. New York: St. Martin's Press.

Orrú, Marco, Nicole Woolsey Biggart, and Gary G. Hamilton. 1997. *The Economic Organization of East Asian Capitalism*. Thousand Oaks: Sage Publications.

Ortega Mata, Rolfo. 1939. "Problems económicos de la industria eléctrica." Undergraduate thesis, School of Economics, UNAM.

Ortega Salazar, Sylvia. 1999. "La evolución del Programa de Becas-Crédito del Conacyt en los años noventa: Características y acciones futuras." *Confluencia*. Organo informativo de la Asociación nacional de Universidades e Instituciones de Educación Superior, June 1999: 19–24.

Padua, Jorge N. 1988. "Presiones y resistencias al cambio en la educación superior de México." *Estudios Sociológicos* 6 (16): 129–203.

Pallares Ramírez, Manuel. 1952. *La Escuela Nacional de Economía: Esbozo histórico 1929–52*. México: UNAM.

Pánuco-Laguette, Humberto, and Miguel Székely. 1996. "Income Distribution and Poverty in Mexico." In Bulmer-Thomas, Victor, ed., *The New Economic Model in Latin America and its Impact on Income Distribution and Poverty*. London: Macmillan: 185–222.

Pérez López, Enrique. 1991. "El desarrollo estabilizador: Lecciones del pasado." In Banco de México, ed., *Rodrigo Gómez: Vida y obra*. México, D.F.: Fondo de Cultura Económica: 137–68.

Peterson, Thane, and Karen Lowry Miller. 1999. "Enter the New Economy." *Business Week*, February 15: 22.

Petras, James F., and Robert LaPorte, Jr. 1971. *Cultivating Revolution: The United States and Agrarian Reform in Latin American*. New York: Random House.

Petricioli, Blanca M., and Clark Winton Reynolds. 1967. *The Teaching of Economics in Mexico*. New York: Education and World Affairs.

Pfeffer, Jeffrey, and Gerald R. Salancik. 1977. *The External Control of Organizations*. New York: Harper and Row.

Piore, Michael, and Charles Sabel. 1984. *The Second Industrial Divide: Possibilities for Prosperity*. Boston, Mass.: Basic Books.

Porta, Pier Luigi. 1996. "Italian Economics through the Postwar Years." In Coats, ed., 1996: 165–83.

Porter, Theodore. 1995. *Trust in Numbers: The Pursuit of Objectivity in Science and Public Life*. Princeton, N.J.: Princeton University Press.

Problemas agrícolas e industriales de México. 1949. 1:1.

Puryear, Jeffrey M. 1994. *Thinking Politics: Intellectuals and Democracy in Chile, 1973–1988.* Baltimore: The Johns Hopkins University Press.

Ramírez Hernández, Guillermo. 1978. "Problemática de la enseñanza y la investigación económica en México. *El economista mexicano* 12 (3): 9–17.

"Raúl Bailléres, fundador de la Asociación Mexicana de Cultura." 1988. *Opción* 8 (40): 6.

"La reforma académica en la Escuela Nacional de Economía." 1969. *Investigación económica* 24 (116): 657–64.

"Respect Restored." 1993. *The Economist*, February 13: 3–4.

Reynolds, Clark W. 1977a. *The Mexican Economy: Twentieth-Century Structure and Growth.* New Haven, Conn.: Yale University Press.

———. 1977b. "Por qué el desarrollo estabilizador de México fue en realidad desestabilizador." *Trimestre económico* 44 (176): 997–1022.

Rico Galán, Víctor. 1972. "Ellos sí saben lo que quieren." *Siempre* 985: 12, 69.

Rico Samaniego, José Uriel Humberto. 1971. "La demanda de servicios del economista y sus funciones en el sector financiero privado de Nuevo León." Undergraduate thesis, School of Economics, Monterrey Tech.

Rosen, George. 1985. *Western Economists and Eastern Societies: Agents of Change in South Asia, 1950–1970.* Baltimore: The Johns Hopkins University Press.

Rosenberg, Emily S., and Norman L. Rosenberg. 1994. "From Colonialism to Professionalism: The Public-Private Dynamic in United States Foreign Financial Advising, 1898–1929." In Drake 1994: 110–32.

Rueschemeyer, Dietrich, and Theda Skocpol, eds. 1996. *States, Social Knowledge and the Origins of Modern Social Policies.* Princeton, N.J.: Princeton University Press.

Rueschemeyer, Dietrich, and Ronan Van Roseem. 1996. "The Verein für Sozialpolitik and the Fabian Society: A Study in the Sociology of Policy-Relevant Knowledge." In Rueschemeyer and Skocpol, eds., 1996: 117–62.

Saavedra, Mario M. 1941. "Aspectos económicos de la industria azucarera en México." Undergraduate thesis, School of Economics, UNAM.

Salinas Lozano, Raúl. 1944. "La intervención del estado y la cuestión de los precios." Undergraduate thesis, School of Economics, UNAM.

Sandelin, Bo, and Ann Veiderpass. 1996. "The Dissolution of the Swedish Tradition." In Coats, ed., 1996: 142–64.

Santiso, Javier. 1999. "Wall Street and the Mexican Crisis: A Temporal Analysis of Emerging Markets." *International Political Science Review* 20 (1): 49–71.

Sarmiento, Sergio. 2000. "En el ITAM." *La Reforma*, January 13.

Schneider, Benjamin. 1998. "The Material Basis of Technocracy: Investor Confidence and Neoliberalism in Latin America." In Centeno and Silva, eds., 1998: 77–95.

Schweber, Libby. 1996. "Progressive Reformers, Unemployment, and the Transformation of Social Inquiry in Britain and the United States, 1880s–1920s." In Rueschemeyer and Skocpol, eds., 1996: 163–200.

Scott, Richard. 1995. *Institutions and Organizations.* Thousand Oaks: Sage Publications.

Scott, Richard, and John Meyer, eds. 1994. *Institutional Environments and Organizations: Structural Complexity and Individualism*. Thousand Oaks: Sage Publications.

Seabury, Paul. 1979. "The Advent of the Academic Bureaucrats." In Seabury, Paul, ed., *Bureaucrats and Brainpower: Government Regulation of Universities*. San Francisco: Institute for Contemporary Studies: 7–47.

"Sección de la Escuela de Economía." 1967. *Tribuna*, July 1967: 6.

Secretaría de Hacienda y Crédito Público. 1999. Official Website.

Shadlen, Kenneth. 1999. "Neoliberalism, Corporatism, and Small Business Political Activism in Contemporary Mexico." *Latin American Research Review* 35 (2): 73–101.

Shafer, Robert Jones. 1973. *Mexican Business Organizations*. Syracuse, N.Y.: Syracuse University Press.

Shambayati, Hootan. 1994. "The Rentier State, Interest Groups, and the Paradox of Autonomy." *Comparative Politics* 26 (3): 307–31.

Sheahan, John. 1997. "Effects of Liberalization Programs on Poverty and Inequality: Chile, Mexico, and Peru." *Latin American Research Review* 32 (3): 7–37.

Shelton, David H. 1964. "The Banking System: Money and the Goal of Growth." In Vernon, Raymond, ed., *Public Policy and Private Enterprise in Mexico*. Cambridge, Mass.: Harvard University Press: 111–89.

Shils, Edward. 1982. "Great Britain and the United States: Legislators, Bureaucrats and the Universities." In Daalder and Shils, eds., *Universities, Politicians and Bureaucrats: Europe and the United States*. New York: Cambridge University Press: 437–88.

Sikkink, Kathryn. 1991. *Ideas and Institutions: Developmentalism in Brazil and Argentina*. Ithaca, N.Y.: Cornell University Press.

Silva, Patricio. 1991. "Technocrats and Politics in Chile: From the Chicago Boys to the CIEPLAN Monks." *Journal of Latin American Studies* 23: 385–410.

———. 1999. "The New Political Order in Latin America." In Gwynne, Robert N., and Cristóbal Kay, eds., *Latin America Transformed: Globalization and Modernity*. London and New York: Arnold: 57–84

Silva Herzog, Jesús. 1954. "Resumen histórico del desarrollo de la enseñanza de las ciencias económicas en México." *Investigación económica* 14 (1): 17–23.

———. 1967. *A un joven economista mexicano*. México: Empresas Editoriales.

———. 1970. *Mis trabajos y los años*. Vol. I. México: Author's edition of 300 copies.

"Silva Lining." 1986. *The Economist*, March 22: 80–81.

Simmons, Beth. 1999. "The Internationalization of Capital." In Kitschelt et al., eds., 1999: 36–69.

Singer, H. W. 1997. "Editorial: The Golden Age of the Keynesian Consensus—the Pendulum Swings Back." *World Development* 25 (3): 293–95.

Skidelsky, Robert. 1977. "The Political Meaning of the Keynesian Revolution." In Skidelsky, Robert, ed., *The End of the Keynesian Era*. London: MacMillan: 33–40.

Skocpol, Theda, and Dietrich Rueschemeyer. 1996. Introduction. In Rueschemeyer and Skcopol, eds., 1996: 3–14.

Smith, Geri. 1999. "Mexico: Could This Scandal Sink the PRI?" *Business Week*, August 2: 59.

Smith, Peter. 1979. *Labyrinths of Power: Political Recruitment in Twentieth-Century Mexico*. Princeton, N.J.: Princeton University Press.

Solís, Leopoldo. 1973. *La economía mexicana: Análisis por sectores y distribución*. Mexico: Fondo de Cultura Económica.

———. 1981. *Economic Policy Reform in Mexico: A Case Study for Developing Countries*. New York: Pergamon Press.

———. 1988. *La vida y obra de Raúl Prebisch*. México: El Colegio de México.

Soskice, David. 1999. "Divergent Production Regimes: Coordinated and Uncoordinated Market Economies in the 1980s and 1990s." In Kitschelt et al., eds., 1999: 101–34.

Sousa, Mario, and E. González Aparicio. 1938. *Dos conferencias sobre el problema petrolero*. México: Imprenta Universitaria.

Stallings, Barbara. 1992. "International Influence on Economic Policy: Debt, Stabilization, and Structural Reform." In Haggard and Kaufman, eds., 1992: 41–88.

Steinmo, Sven, Kathleen Thelen, and Frank Longstreth. 1992. *Structuring Politics: Historical Institutionalism in Comparative Analysis*. New York: Cambridge University Press.

Stinchcombe, Arthur. 1997. "On the Virtues of the Old Institutionalism." *Annual Review of Sociology* 23: 1–18.

Strachey, John. 1939. *Naturaleza de la crisis*. México: Fondo de Cultura Económica.

Stryker, Robin. 1990. "Science, Class, and the Welfare State: A Class-Centered Functional Account." *American Journal of Sociology* 96 (3): 684–726.

Teichman, Judith A. 1988. *Policymaking in Mexico: From Boom to Crisis*. Boston: Allen & Unwin.

Tello, Carlos. 1979. *La política económica en México, 1970–1976*. México: Siglo XXI.

Thacker, Strom. 1999. "NAFTA Coalitions and the Political Viability of Neoliberalism in Mexico." *Journal of Interamerican Studies and World Affairs* 41 (2): 57–58.

Thompson, John K. 1979. *Inflation, Financial Markets, and Economic Development: The Experience of Mexico*. Greenwich, Conn.: JAI Press.

Tilly, Charles. 1978. *From Mobilization to Revolution*. Reading, Mass.: Addison-Wesley.

Torres Gaytán, Ricardo, and Gonzalo Mora Ortíz. 1978. *Memoria conmemorativa de la facultad de economía*. México: UNAM.

Torstendahl, Rolf, and Michael Burrage. 1990. *The Formation of Professions: Knowledge, State and Strategy*. London: Sage Publications.

UNAM, Secretaría General de Administración, Dirección General de Servicios Auxiliares, Departamento de Estadística. 1981. *Cuadros estadísticos, 1929–1979*. México, D.F.

Unidad de la Crónica Presidencial. 1994. *La crónica del gobierno 1988–94*. México, D.F.: Unidad de la Crónica Presidencial.

Universidad de Nuevo León. 1978. *Boletín de la Dirección de Planeación Universitaria.* July.

Urquidi, Víctor. 1987. "Nicolas Kaldor (1908–1986)." *Trimestre económico* 54 (216):. 919–25.

Urrutia, Miguel. 1994. "Colombia." In Williamson, ed., 1994: 285–315.

Valdés, Juan Gabriel. 1995. *Pinochet's Economists: The Chicago School in Chile.* Cambridge: Cambridge University Press.

Van Dijk, Pitou. 1998. "The World Bank and the Transformation of Latin American Society." In Centeno and Silva, eds., 1998: 96–125.

Varela, Fernando. 1999. "Students Search for Unity, World Bank Documents Stir Up UNAM." *The News*, August 11.

Vázquez, Rodolfo E. 1936. "La reforma agraria." Undergraduate thesis, School of Economics, UNAM.

Vernon, Raymond. 1963. *The Dilemma of Mexico's Development: The Roles of the Private and Public Sectors.* Cambridge, Mass.: Harvard University Press.

"Vicente Fox of Center-Right Partido Acción Nacional (P.A.N.) Wins Presidential Election." 2000. *SourceMex*, July 5.

Villarreal, René. 1984. *La contrarrevolución monetarista: Teoría, política económica e ideología del neoliberalismo.* México: Océano.

Villaseñor, Eduardo. 1974. *Memorias—testimonio.* México: Fondo de Cultura Económica.

Villegas, Abelardo. 1993. *El pensamiento mexicano en el siglo XX.* México: Fondo de Cultura Económica.

Visser, Jelle, and Anton Hemerijck. 1997. *A Dutch Miracle: Job Growth, Welfare Reform and Corporatism in the Netherlands.* Amsterdam: Amsterdam University Press.

Wade, Robert. 1990. *Governing the Market: Economic Theory and the Role of Government in East Asian Industrialization.* Princeton, N.J.: Princeton University Press.

Weber, Max. 1946. "Politics as a Vocation." In Gerth, H. H., and C. Wright Mills, eds., *From Max Weber: Essays in Sociology.* New York: Oxford University Press: 77–128.

Weiner, Elizabeth, Stephen Baker, Geri Smith, Ann Charters, and Ken Dermota. 1992. "Latin America: The Big Move to Free Markets." *Business Week*, June 15: 50–62.

Weir, Margaret. 1989. "Ideas and Politics: The Acceptance of Keynesianism in Britain and the United States." In Hall, ed., 1989: 53–86.

Weir, Margaret, and Theda Skocpol. 1985. "State Structures and the Possibilities for 'Keynesian' Responses to the Great Depression in Sweden, Britain, and the United States." In Evans, Rueschemeyer, and Skocpol, eds., 1985: 107–63.

Weisbrot, Mark Alan. 1993. *Ideology and Method in the History of Development Economics.* Ph.D. dissertation, Department of Economics, University of Michigan.

Westney, D. Eleanor. 1987. *Imitation and Innovation: The Transfer of Western Organizational Patterns to Meiji Japan.* Cambridge, Mass.: Harvard University Press.

Wilensky, Harold L. 1964. "The Professionalization of Everyone?" *American Journal of Sociology* 70 (2): 137–58.

"Will Mexico Make It?" 1984. *Business Week*, October 1: 74–76.

Williamson, John. 1994. "In Search of a Manual for Technopols." In Williamson, ed., 1994: 11–28.

———. 1996. "Comments." In Coats, ed., 1996: 364–68.

———, ed. 1990. *Latin American Adjustment: How Much Has Happened?* Washington, D.C.: Institute for International Economics.

———. 1994. *The Political Economy of Reform.* Washington, D.C.: Institute for International Economics.

Williamson, John, and Stephan Haggard. 1994. "The Political Conditions for Economic Reform." In Williamson, ed., 1994: 527–96.

Wittrock, Björn, and Peter Wagner. 1996. "Social Science and the Building of the Early Welfare State: Toward a Comparison of Statist and Non-statist Western Societies." In Rueschemeyer and Skocpol, eds., 1996: 90–113

World Bank. 1997. *World Development Report.* Washington, D.C.: IBRD/World Bank.

———. 2000. *Global Development Finance.* Washington, D.C.: World Bank.

Yarza, Alberto. 1973. "Consideraciones sobre la organización del postgraduado de economía en México." *Investigación Económica* 32 (25): 177–88.

Yergin, Daniel and Joseph Stanislaw. 1998. *The Commanding Heights: The Battle between Government and the Marketplace That Is Remaking the Modern World.* New York: Simon and Schuster.

Yonay, Yuval P. 1994. "When Black Boxes Clash: Competing Ideas of What Science Is in Economics, 1924–39." *Social Studies of Science* 24: 39–80.

———. 1998. *The Struggle over the Soul of Economics: Institutionalist and Neoclassical Economists in America between the Wars.* Princeton, N.J.: Princeton University Press.

Zapata, Francisco. 1990. *Ideología y política en América Latina.* México: Jornadas del Colegio de México, no. 115.

Zebadúa, Emilio. 1994. *Banqueros y revolucionarios: La soberanía financiera de México, 1914–1929.* México: Fondo de Cultura Económica.

Zermeño, Sergio. 1978. *México: Una democracia utópica, el movimiento estudiantil del 68.* México: Siglo XXI.

Zuckerman, Mortimer B. 1998. "A Second American Century." *Foreign Affairs*, May/June 1998: 18–31.

Zúñiga, Juan Antonio. 2000. "Propone Cárdenas terminar la política de *castigo* a los salarios." *La Jornada*, January 12.

PERSONAL INTERVIEWS

Aguirre, Carlos, 4/2/96
Alanís Patiño, Emilio, 8/21/95
Alanís Patiño, Emilio, 9/13/95
Alego, Javier, 2/13/97
Alvarez Bejar, Alejandro, 1/17/97
Bassols Zaleta, Lic. Antonio, 3/20/96
Beltrán, Lic. Mario, 6/20/96
Beristáin, Javier, 4/10/96
Bolaños Lozano, Ernesto, 11/8/95
Bolaños Lozano, Ernesto, 5/29/96
Cabral Bowling, Roberto, 10/3/96
Calderón, Francisco, 8/23/95
Clariond, Eugenio, 11/9/95
Confidential 3/27/96
Confidential 9/15/96
Confidential 10/15/96
Confidential 11/5/96
Confidential 6/7/98 (by telephone)
Durandeau, Leoncio, 11/8/95
Espíndola, Silvano, 9/15/96
Flores, Edmundo, 10/24/95
García Cisneros, Pablo, 8/29/95
Garza, Francisco, 11/9/95
Garza Valle, Max O., 5/22/96
Ghigliazza, Sergio, 7/19/94
Gollás, Manuel, 10/23/95
Gudiño, Alfredo, 9/5/95
Gudiño, Alfredo, 9/18/95

Harrison, John, 6/17/95 (by telephone)
Ibarra, Davíd, 11/5/95
Izquierdo, Rafael, 7/3/96
Katz, Isaac, 3/27/96
Katz, Isaac, 4/9/96
Maldonado, Guillermo, 11/8/95
Meyer L'Epée, Consuelo, 7/15/96
Moguel Viveros, Julio, 9/18/96
Moguel Viveros, Julio, 9/27/96
Partearroyo, Araceli, 4/23/96
Peralta Gómez, Carlos, 9/5/95
Pérez López, Enrique, 4/17/96
Petricioli, Gustavo, 2/3/97
Ramírez, Guillermo, 10/15/96
Sada González, Francisco J., 11/10/95
Sáenz, Josué 10/3/95
Sáenz, Josué 10/6/95
Sales, Carlos 8/2/99
Sánchez Navarro, Juan, 9/29/95
Schreiver, Teresa, 6/18/96
Solís, Leopoldo, 8/6/96
Turrent, Eduardo, 7/22/94
Turrent, Eduardo, 8/15/95
Urquidi, Víctor, 9/1/95
Urquidi, Víctor, 9/19/95
Urquidi, Víctor, 9/26/95
Valle, Alejandro, 2/14/97

INDEX

Abbott, Andrew, 15, 24, 33, 101, 188, 212
ABM (Mexican Bankers' Association), 72
academic standards, 97–98, 251n.4
accountants, 33, 34, 36, 73, 101
accounting, 41, 100
Africa, 214
Agricultural Credit Bank, 28, 30, 31, 39, 45
agriculture, 36, 62, 78, 79, 80, 81, 91
AIESEC (International Association of Students in Economics and Commercial Sciences), 161
Alejo, Javier, 157, 250n.5
Alemán, Lucas, 61, 78, 187 (table)
Alemán, Miguel, 37
Alienes Urosa, J., 95 (table)
Alliance for Production, 112
Alliance for Progress, 86, 114, 214
Alumni Society (Sociedad de Ex-Alumnos), 102, 236–43
Ambirajan, S., 214
American Economics Review, 139
Americanization: of CIDE, 203; of economics, 5–6; of economics professions, 5, 11, 215; of ITAM, 126–35, 137, 146, 170, 180–81, 189, 207; of ITM, 92; of Mexican economics, 21, 199–209
Anahuac, 159, 165, 202
Andrés Oteyza, José, 250n.5
Angel Gurría, José, 177
Antezana Paz, F., 64 (table)
anti-imperialism, 152
Argentina, 2, 11, 46, 74, 179, 214, 219
Armour Research Foundation, 31
Arrow, Kenneth, 147 (table), 148
Aspe Armella, Pedro, 1, 116, 133, 159, 166 (table), 168 (table), 180, 182, 252n.16
Association for Social Policy (Germany), 50
austerity measures, 197
authoritarian corporatism, 109
authoritarianism, 108, 111, 124, 144
Autonomous Metropolitan University (UAM), 154
Autonomous National University of Mexico (UNAM). *See* UNAM (Autonomous National University of Mexico)

Autonomous Technological Institute of Mexico (ITAM). *See* ITAM (Autonomous Technological Institute of Mexico)
Autonomous University of Nuevo León, 91–92, 100, 101, 142, 189, 249n.19, 249n.22, 251n.14
Autonomous University of Puebla, 141
Autonomous University of Sinaloa, 141
Autonomous University of Zacatecas, 141
Avila Camacho, Manuel, 37, 61, 62, 78, 187 (table)

Bach, Federico, 55
Bach, Fritz, 64 (table)
Backhouse, Roger E., 51, 139, 150
Bailleres, Alberto, 130
Bailleres, Raúl, 71, 130
Baker, James A., 173
balances of payments, 78, 82, 90, 107, 182, 215; import substitution and, 9; peripheral countries and, 76; underdeveloped countries and, 93
Banco Azucarero, 71
Banco Comercial Mexicano, 71
Banco Cremi, 71
Banco de Comercio e Industria, 71
Banco de México, 28, 31, 37–38, 71, 72, 78, 83, 118, 126–35, 181, 189, 206; autonomy of, 88, 127, 128, 129; Department of Economic Studies at, 43–44, 83, 88, 92, 117, 130, 132, 169; Department of Industrial Research at, 91; Department of Industrial Studies at, 44; employment at, 42, 88–89, 127; Fondo de Cultura Económica and, 58; foreign-trained economists and, 117, 180; fringe benefits at, 89; ITAM graduates and, 168–69; ITM graduates and, 102; modernization of, 59; in postwar period, 87–92; salaries at, 41; scholarships, 132, 189, 191; study abroad program, 89, 90, 92, 119, 130, 132; training program, 83, 248n.10; UNAM and, 42–43, 91, 92, 95, 96, 130
Bancomext, 88

experts, 15, 16, 18, 24, 86, 105, 183, 207, 209, 219; on developing nations, 253n.2; economic, 172, 185, 186; global, 12; nationally trained, 215

exports, 27, 54, 76, 77, 107, 172; Latin American, 7

external actors, 18, 19, 20, 174

external constituencies, 210; and coercive isomorphism, 212–15

external debt, 9, 10, 79, 86, 107, 117, 182, 190, 194, 196, 253n.7; and gross domestic product, 114, 115 (table); and gross national product, 193 (table); in Latin America, 214–15; postwar, 191

external financing, 114

external legitimation: and coercive isomorphism, 190–95

external pressures, 181, 183, 185, 190, 192–93

external resources, 83, 114, 118, 192, 193, 210

Eyzaguirre, Nicolás, 219

Faculty of Economics. See UNAM Faculty of Economics

Fajnzlyber, F., 143 (table)

FAO (United Nations Food and Agriculture Organization), 85

fascism, 37, 57, 65, 93

Federal Reserve. See U.S. Federal Reserve

Fernández Hurtado, Ernesto, 92, 248n.7

Finance Minster, 89

Finance Ministry, 17, 38, 39, 40, 82, 83, 86, 116, 180; Banco de México and, 44; budgeting decisions and, 28, 81; conservatism of, 126–27, 192; employment in, 42, 238; Fondo de Cultura Económica and, 58; Gil Díaz and, 165, 195, 205; Ministry of Commerce and Trade and, 45; modernization of, 47; World Bank and, 181

financial bureaucracy, 168, 169, 176

financial markets, 84; collapse of, 190; global, 3, 214; international, 6, 46, 56, 114, 201; reglobalization of, 114, 192

financial sector: economists in, 164; liberalization of, 165

Financiero, 207

Fisher, Irving, 59

flexible production, 3

Flores, Edmundo, 77, 83, 85

Flores de la Peña, Horacio, 93, 95 (table), 97, 250n.5

Fondo de Cultura Económica, 58–60, 73, 200, 206

Ford Foundation, 140, 213, 252n.14

Foreign Commerce Bank, 39

foreign creditors, 38–39, 190

foreign investors, 37, 165, 172, 174, 183, 194, 247n.1; confidence of, 190, 215; in Latin America, 7; lending by, 114; oil industry and, 115; policymakers and, 5; property rights and, 1, 17; resources of, 19, 20, 84, 184; Salinas and, 21

foreign property, 70

foreign-trained economists, 1, 2, 12, 82–87, 113, 114, 117, 154, 171, 175–76, 186, 188–94, 207; Banco de México and, 90, 117, 180; CIDE and, 252n.10; in developing countries, 199, 213; and economic policymaking, 117; in Europe, 216; financing of, 133; higher education support and, 204; ITAM and, 134 (table), 202 (table); in Latin America, 215–16; policymaking and, 118; in postwar period, 213; role of, 198; in Taiwan, 212; from U.S., 2, 11, 19–20, 165, 170, 182, 192, 200, 201, 202, 209, 214, 215

foreign-trained technocrats, 172, 174, 177, 183–84, 217–20; from U.S., 20–21, 185, 192, 203

Fox, Vicente, 165, 182, 194–95, 202, 205–6, 208

France, 2, 5, 48, 50, 218, 250n.10

free enterprise system, 140

free-market radicalism, 250n.5

free markets, 76, 144, 145, 182, 183–86, 194; theses and, 148, 149

free trade, 27, 144, 145, 173, 180, 181, 194, 197; theses and, 148, 149

French regulationist school, 4

Frieden, Jeffrey A., 114

Friedman, Milton, 143 (table), 145, 146, 147 (table), 148, 195, 223, 251n.16

Fulbright, 160, 213

Furner, Mary, 51

Furtado, Celso, 143 (table)

García Reynoso, Plácido, 89

Garza-Sada family, 70

GATT (General Agreement on Tariffs and Trade), 8, 181, 182

General Theory (Keynes), 57–58